Extinction in a Human World

Extinction in a Human World

The Environmental Cost of Human Progress

T. Thomas Rathe

Cover design by the author.
Cover art: *Ivory-billed Woodpecker,* Robert Havell after John James Audubon, courtesy of the National Gallery of Art.

Contents

Chart of Geologic Periods

EON	ERA	PERIOD	EPOCH		Ma
Phanerozoic	Cenozoic	Quaternary	Holocene		0.011 —
			Pleistocene	Late	0.8 —
				Early	2.4 —
		Tertiary (Neogene)	Pliocene	Late	3.6 —
				Early	5.3 —
			Miocene	Late	11.2 —
				Middle	16.4 —
				Early	23.0 —
		Tertiary (Paleogene)	Oligocene	Late	28.5 —
				Early	34.0 —
			Eocene	Late	41.3 —
				Middle	49.0 —
				Early	55.8 —
			Paleocene	Late	61.0 —
				Early	65.5 —
	Mesozoic	Cretaceous	Late		99.6 —
			Early		145 —
		Jurassic	Late		161 —
			Middle		176 —
			Early		200 —
		Triassic	Late		228 —
			Middle		245 —
			Early		251 —
	Paleozoic	Permian	Late		260 —
			Middle		271 —
			Early		299 —
		Carboniferous / Pennsylvanian	Late		306 —
			Middle		311 —
			Early		318 —
		Carboniferous / Mississippian	Late		326 —
			Middle		345 —
			Early		359 —
		Devonian	Late		385 —
			Middle		397 —
			Early		416 —
		Silurian	Late		419 —
			Early		423 —
		Ordovician	Late		428 —
			Middle		444 —
			Early		488 —
		Cambrian	Late		501 —
			Middle		513 —
			Early		542 —
Precambrian	Proterozoic	Late	Neoproterozoic (Z)		1000 —
		Middle	Mesoproterozoic (Y)		1600 —
		Early	Paleoproterozoic (X)		2500 —
	Archean	Late			3200 —
		Early			4000 —
	Hadean				

Image:USGS

Introduction & Acknowledgments

In 1907, Walter Rothschild wrote one of the first books on species extinction. Born into the wealthy and powerful Rothschild banking family, he inherited the title of Baron de Rothschild from his father. Despite his pedigree, his natural involvement in his family's banking enterprise, and serving as a member of the British Parliament, his real passion was for the natural world. Beginning with collecting insects at a young age, he became one of the preeminent naturalists of his day. By the time he was 21, he had his own museum, building one of the most impressive natural history collections in the world. He described more than 170 new species, established a new zoological journal, authored more than 760 publications, and helped establish the British Trust for Ornithology. Like many naturalists of his time and before, being from a wealthy family allowed him the freedom to delve into scientific study in a way that few could afford. He was eccentric, to be sure. He had a penchant for cassowaries and owned more than 60. He also had a private carriage pulled by a team of zebras, but his passion for the natural world was unquestionable.

While his *Extinct Birds* was not the first book dealing with extinct animals, it was rather revolutionary. By Rothschild's time, species extinction was an accepted scientific fact. What made Rothschild's book different, however, is that, unlike many preceding works, it was not about species long dead but species lost in modern history. Lavishly illustrated by some of the best wildlife artists of his day, Rothschild's book covered dozens of species of extinct birds. Some, like the great auk, the passenger pigeon, and the Cuban macaw, we will revisit. He also compiled a list of birds on the brink, like the Carolina parakeet, the ivory-billed woodpecker, and Maui Nui 'akialoa, all now lost, which you will also meet. Primarily a scientific work, it certainly does not make for gripping reading. In fact, there is barely any narrative in the book past the introduction, but simply facts about the species concerned. However formal the work, Rothschild makes very clear in the introduction exactly why most of these birds are extinct: "The cause of recent extinction among birds is in most cases due directly or indirectly to man." Even well over 100 years ago, Rothschild understood the impact humans were having on Earth's species. He cites hunting, habitat loss, and the most damaging of all for birds, the introduction of non-native species. Little did he know that in the coming decades, not only would these threats continue for birds and countless other species, but they would accelerate to unimaginable proportions.

Today, the situation has become increasingly dire. We are now in the midst of a biodiversity crisis, and many have suggested that we may be at the beginning of the world's sixth major mass extinction event. Despite humanity's relatively recent progress in the recovery of some groups of animals, most notably the majority of whale species and many species of migratory waterfowl, species loss has only continued to increase. The rate of species extinction on Earth is now believed to be 100 times to as much as 1000 times the normal background rate. This is higher than any time in the last 66 million years. In the last 500 years, the Earth has lost nearly 700 vertebrate animal species. Plants have not fared better, with a recent global survey estimating that 571 species of plants have disappeared since 1750, although researchers believe that this may be a dramatic underestimate. Overall, the rate of extinction for plant species may be 500 times normal, and 1 in 5 plants may be threatened with extinction. However, only 14% of all known plant species have been assessed. Not only is the Earth seeing species disappear at an alarming rate, but the species that remain are in severe decline. The World Wildlife Fund's Living Planet Index estimates that the populations of the world's mammals, birds, amphibians, reptiles, and fish have declined by 68% since 1970.

For many other species on the planet, we simply don't know enough. Only 1% of the Earth's 1.4 million known invertebrate species have been assessed for their risk of extinction. However, even among the 1% that have been assessed, 40% are threatened, including a third of all coral species worldwide and a shocking 72% of the freshwater mussels and 74% of the freshwater snails found in the U.S. and Canada. Extinction rates among gastropods (snails) are higher than any other known group, approaching 10,000 times normal. Even less is known about the world's fungi species. Out of the roughly 146,000 species we know of, only 600, or just 0.4%, have been assessed as to their vulnerability to extinction. As many as half a million terrestrial species now have insufficient habitat for long-term survival, and in total, as many as a million species across all life could be in danger of extinction. It is possible, even likely, that the true number could be far greater. Despite our lack of knowledge, it is apparent that many of the Earth's species are in trouble, and, to paraphrase Rothschild, most of this is our fault. As our world becomes an ever more human-dominated one, the negative impacts on Earth's ecosystems and species continue to grow at an alarming rate. In our quest to make human lives better, we have threatened the underpinnings of the Earth's systems we need for survival. As we plowed the earth, felled the forests, and increased our technological prowess, we deemed it "progress". While these things have certainly made human lives longer, healthier, and easier, we may come to find that "progress" may turn into an ironic label indeed. In our rise to world dominance, we may have forgotten that we are not alone on this planet. That, despite our seeming invincibility as a species, we, on many levels, need the other species the world contains.

I've always been fascinated by people like Walter Rothschild, Charles Darwin, Alfred Russel Wallace, Jane Goodall, E.O. Wilson, and others. I think it's because I feel a kinship with them. The life of a naturalist is full of exploration, the search for the unknown, and the thrill of scientific discovery. All of these are combined with an intense passion for Earth's life. I think most of us can relate to wanting to know more, to understand deeper, and to immerse ourselves in nature, and I think the attraction of these naturalists is their unbelievable dedication to discovering the secrets of the natural world and maybe the wish that we too could be like them. It is the lives and works of many of these naturalists that inspired me to attempt a work of my own, in particular the work of Darwin.

I also love old books, especially those that deal with science. There's just something wonderful about holding a piece of history in your hand, and I love reading about the history of science from the very people who were making it. I'm fascinated by what they got right, what they got wrong, and the process of discovery. I am also fascinated by how many things we now consider common knowledge were once revolutionary ideas. Because of this, I am always on the lookout for these little bits of history. A few years ago, I was lucky enough to come across a Victorian-era copy of Darwin's *The Descent of Man*. While reading through this lovely copy, I started thinking a lot about species. While *The Descent of Man* is famous for Darwin's brave declaration that humans, like all other animals, are subject to the processes of evolution, the majority of the book actually deals with another subject altogether. It was this part of the book that got me thinking. Darwin spends a large amount of time on a very detailed argument for the existence of sexual selection as a major evolutionary pressure. In making his case, Darwin introduces the reader to a fascinating collection of species with unique traits, and he details how these traits could have arisen. It was this that piqued my interest. Not sexual selection, but the species he detailed. It made me wonder about how those species were faring today, and I decided that might make a good basis for a book. It turns out my initial idea was a dead end. Thankfully, the species that Darwin talked about and their fascinating adaptations are still around. But the idea of a book on extinct species stuck. Initially, I was considering a book strictly about birds (this is what led me to Rothchild's book), but I decided it might be more beneficial, in light of our current situation, to talk about a broader selection of animals. I also liked the idea of presenting, much as Darwin did, some of the fascinating aspects of the Animal Kingdom. Since Rothschild's time, there have been many books dealing with species extinction, and in the future, there will likely be many more. This will not be the final word on species loss or our role in it, but my hope is that it can contribute to our understanding of how we are impacting the natural world. While much of the focus here is on animals lost over the last 500 years or so, it's ultimately about what's still here. My hope is that, through studying what we have lost, we can forge a better future. Beyond simply presenting examples of modern species extinctions, I wanted to give the reader an extended background on the situation. We are the primary cause of many, if not most, of the Earth's recent extinctions, but simply stating this fact does not give any insight into why that is. Therefore, to help further a deeper understanding, I've started this book with several chapters dealing with how species come about, past mass extinctions, the importance of biodiversity and its distribution, as well as a brief history of human impacts on the environment throughout time. Also included is a chapter covering the current state of our environmental impacts and the damage they continue to cause. Preferring to round out what is inarguably a depressing subject, the final chapter contains some of what we can do as a species to stem species loss and keep Earth a place where all life can thrive.

Most of us will never become famous naturalists. We won't travel the world in search of new species, nor will we likely make any news-worthy discoveries. But despite this, we can still learn all we can about this fascinating world we live on. We can find adventure in things as simple as the birds in our backyard or the wildflowers on the side of the road. Life is fascinating; it is all around us, and we have a part to play in furthering our understanding of it and its protection. This is my simple goal in writing this book. I hope that you can not only find knowledge but also a deeper appreciation for Earth's life and the inspiration to do whatever you can to be a better steward to the planet.

I would like to take this opportunity to thank the many scientists whose work has made this book possible. Without their tireless pursuit of knowledge, we could have little understanding of just how amazing our world really is. I encourage anyone wanting a more in-depth look at any of the subjects discussed to read some of the many works cited in the bibliography. I have made an effort to use as many freely available sources as possible. Nearly all of the research I have cited can be read online in its entirety. I would also like to thank the authors of the many books that have not only provided facts but also inspiration. A list of many of these can be found in the suggested reading, and all are fantastic reads on a variety of subjects. Just as essential is the contribution of so many organizations dedicated to providing and preserving information on our natural world, including the U.N. Intergovernmental Panel on Climate Change (IUCC), IPBES, IUCN, BirdLife International, the World Wildlife Fund, The Biodiversity Heritage Library, and many, many others. Without these many organizations and the passionate people who work for them, there would truly be no hope of saving Earth's biodiversity. Above all, I would like to thank my partner Jessica for her support, encouragement, and patience throughout this process. Without you this would have not been possible.

Part I

The Natural Order
and Human Progress

1
Evolution, Extinction, and Humans

Our planet has existed for somewhere around 4.5 billion years, forming around our star from trillions upon trillions of particles of dust and rock. At first, it was nothing more than a hot, barren rock, but sometime around 4 billion years ago, life sprang forth. Earth, for nearly its entire existence, has been synonymous with life, and life with it. It started out simple, beginning as nothing more than collections of organic molecules that were able to replicate, then on to simple single-celled organisms, multicellular life, and on and on until reaching the complex and fantastically varied life we see today. Millions upon millions of generations of life, adapting and changing to take up residence in every environment that exists from deepest of seas to boiling hot thermal pools to the coldest and driest parts of the planet, even miles underground. Earth, devoid of life, would be unrecognizable. Entire islands are built on top of once-living coral reefs, and forests and grasses fill our landscapes. Everywhere we look, we find traces of life. Even the make-up of our atmosphere is a result of life's existence. The very oxygen we breathe was thrown into the atmosphere by bacteria billions of years ago and is even now continually maintained by life.

Countless species have come into being and died out over this vast amount of time, and this process is what we have come to call evolution. While not the first to consider it, the idea of evolution by natural selection was brought into our collective consciousness by Charles Darwin in his pivotal 1853 publication *On the Origin of Species.* In it he lays out the idea that life's ability to modify and alter aspects of itself to better survive in its environment is at the heart of species creation. The idea, revolutionary at the time, seemingly obvious to the modern reader, states that species that are better suited to their environment will be more successful, outcompeting and replacing those that are less well suited. This, of course, is a bit of an oversimplification, but you get the general idea. This process, repeated countless times over billions of years, created the vast diversity of life that we are familiar with, allowing life to flourish and exploit every facet of our planet. Of course, this ability is not a conscious choice; it is driven by the natural pressures experienced by life competing to survive (hence "natural selection"). We now understand, in a way that Darwin could not have imagined, the molecular secrets of DNA, mutation, gene combination, and epigenetics that give rise to new aspects of life.

The natural process of species evolving into new forms, filling the ecologic voids, and their ability to exploit ever more specific resources, leads to a wealth of diverse, interesting, beautiful, and sometimes unbelievable creatures. This process, combined with the inevitable changes in our planetary home, however, leads to an inevitable outcome, for all species cannot survive: extinction. How many species have existed since the first life appeared on our rock is impossible to know. So many left little to no trace of their existence, slipping away into history millions, if not billions, of years before creatures that could contemplate their existence even evolved. The number is surely in the tens of millions, maybe hundreds of millions or more, all living, adapting, flourishing and dying long before us. In fact, as little as 2 to 4 percent of all the life that has ever evolved on our planet is alive today. This process continues; species adapt and change, appear and disappear, and in this first chapter we will explore some of the ways this happens.

There will be many mentions of species throughout this book, it being, of course, a book about lost species, so I think it's prudent to try to provide a definition of what exactly constitutes a species. Everyone, I think, has a good general idea of what the word means. It describes a distinct plant, animal, etc., apart from other distinct plants, animals, etc. Unfortunately the reality isn't as neat and tidy as this general concept, and although we have recognized the divisions of life for quite some time, there is still an ongoing debate as to what exactly makes any organism a distinct species. Early on among naturalists it was found necessary to have some sort of standard naming system. We call this naming of life "taxonomy." Life was then, and is still now, often known by numerous common names that described the same thing. To avoid confusion, the binomial system, first developed by Carl Linnaeus in 1735 for plants, became the basis of scientific naming. It consists of two Latinized names typically derived from Latin or Greek words. The first of these is a genus name which represents a larger group of organisms than the second name, the species. The species is a distinct unit, like a single atom, specifically different from other types of atoms, and constitutes the lowest division in the system. As this system evolved, species that were the most alike in characteristics were grouped together in the same genus; these are grouped together into families, those into orders, and those in turn into class, phylum, kingdom and finally, domain.

These levels of classification help to describe the evolutionary relationship of all life to all other life. Closely related species will be grouped together. For example, all cats are members of the family Felidae, showing their close association and common lineage. However, members of the genus *Panthera*, such as lions, tigers, and leopards, will have a closer relationship to each other than to the other members of Felidae (there are subgroups to most of these levels which I will omit for simplicity). While initially grouped primarily by outward appearance and anatomy, the use of genetic analysis has allowed us to more specifically define these groupings.

Let's look at a couple of examples. First of all, our Latinized name, *Homo sapiens* (the English translation of which is maybe ironically "wise person"; I'll leave it to the reader to decide if that's a fitting moniker), describes our genus *Homo* (of which we are the only members currently living) and our species *sapiens* to differentiate us from other members of the genus *Homo*. As we look up the taxonomic classification, as it is called, we come to the next grouping, family. Our family is Hominidae. Here we are grouped with our closest relatives, the great apes, which include gorillas, chimpanzees, bonobos, and orangutans. On the next level up, we come to our order, which is that of the Primates and includes apes, old- and new-world monkeys, and lemurs. In the next higher grouping, we find the class of which we are members, Mammalia, the mammals. This class includes all animals that produce milk for their young and is diverse enough to include not only us but an incredible variety of seemingly disparate animals such as mice, bats, kangaroos, and whales. Next, we find that we are members of the phylum Chordata, or the chordates, and in this grouping we find all life that possesses a spinal cord. Then we arrive the kingdom of which we are a part Animalia, the animals. This level includes all animals and signifies in our naming system the relationship that all members of the animal kingdom have with each other. The final and most inclusive grouping is domain. Humans are grouped into the domain Eukaryota (the eukaryotes), which contains all life whose cells contain a nucleus, differentiating us (and all other plants, animals, and fungi) from the other two domains that do not (the prokaryotes): Archaea and Bacteria. All life falls into one of these three domains.

Let's look at this all together and compare it with one of our closest relatives, the chimpanzee (*Pan troglodytes*), and another primate, the yellow-cheeked gibbon *(Nomascus gabriellae).*

	Humans	Chimpanzee	Gibbon
Domain	Eukaryota	Eukaryota	Eukaryota
Kingdom	Animalia	Animalia	Animalia
Phylum	Chordata	Chordata	Chordata
Class	Mammalia	Mammalia	Mammalia
	Primates	Primates	Primates
Family	Hominidae	Hominidae	Hylobatidae
Genus	*Homo*	*Pan*	*Nomascus*
Species	*H. sapiens*	*P. troglodytes*	*N. gabriellae*

It's easy to see when comparing taxonomies how closely related we are to chimpanzees, and we can easily derive that humans are at least as closely related to chimps as the members of the cat family are to each other. The yellow-cheeked gibbon still lies close to humans on the tree of life but is less closely related to us. The gibbons are, like us, members of the order Primates, but are members of a different primate family. This system of classification not only allows us to differentiate between different forms of life, but also shows how closely related they are by grouping species with similar anatomy, modes of life, and genetic make-up together. Let's look at one more example, but with an organism that is much less but still related to us: the gold-mouthed sea squirt *(Polycarpa aurata)*.

	Humans	GM Sea Squirt
Domain	Eukaryota	Eukaryota
Kingdom	Animalia	Animalia
Phylum	Chordata	Chordata
Class	Mammalia	Ascidiacea
Order	Primates	Stolidobracchia
Family	Hominidae	Styelidae
Genus	*Homo*	*Polycarpa*
Species	*H. sapiens*	*P. aurata*

When looking at a sea-squirt, there is little resemblance to the other members of the animal kingdom that we typically think of. These stationary and beautifully colored and patterned creatures of the ocean are little more than a hollow tube animal that filter-feeds on plankton by moving water through a pair of siphons, but they highlight the fantastic diversity of the animal kingdom. Although certainly different from us in appearance and mode of living, physiologically we are not that different from this simple creature. As you can see, we both share the same cell structure as members of the domain Eukaryota, we are both members of the animal kingdom, and are both chordates, showing that in the distant past humans and all other chordates share a common ancestor with this colorful sea creature.

A species being the most basic unit is generally true, but readers versed in both physics and biology will know that, indeed, there is a smaller division to the atom, and likewise to life, which we call a subspecies. Subspecies tend to be distinct enough from others of their kind to warrant an extra name after their species name (for example: *Ursus arctos horribilis* is the formal name for the grizzly bear, distinguishing it from other brown bears, *Ursus arctos*) but, like species themselves, there is considerable argument as to what constitutes a subspecies and when and under what circumstances these should be recognized. All of this is merely an attempt for scientists to be clear on what form of life they are talking about in specific terms. Yet after all of this explanation we still have not defined a species.

The actual definition, according to Webster's, is: *"a category of biological classification ranking immediately below the genus or subgenus, comprising related organisms or populations potentially capable of interbreeding..."* As you can see, this definition may not be extremely helpful, but there is one key part to it. It's about interbreeding, but this definition still falls short. I think a better definition would be: "a distinct population of organisms that freely interbreed in nature." Not just that they are capable of it, but they actually do. Tigers and lions are capable of interbreeding, but they have never been known to do so in the wild. Species that are closely related often can produce hybrids with other species, as in the case of closely related birds, but *typically* do not. Species that are less closely related often cannot produce offspring due to their differing genetics. Put another way, a species is: "a distinct group of organisms that typically only breed with their type of distinct organism in nature." This is life's attempt to conserve the genes that make a species unique, while also conserving the traits that have allowed them to survive and subsist, and the advantages they have over other species. Scientists refer to this as the "biological species concept," but it is not the only species concept that exists, and the debate over what constitutes a species and how they should be grouped will continue to evolve.

So how do species come about? Two things play a large part: competition and isolation. Competition makes it beneficial for species to adapt to new food sources, new habitats, or a move to a new location to reduce competition, or, in other words, to occupy their own particular "niche" (I'll discuss this more in the next chapter, but at its most simple, an organism's ecological niche is the specific habitat, food sources, and interactions that a species utilizes for its survival). The traits that allow them to do this give them an advantage. Isolation is when populations of the same species are in some way separated. This can be physical, such as populations being separated by a land mass, migration to an island, or a structural change in habitat. It can also be behavioral, such as a move to a novel food source or a change in breeding preferences. Isolation limits the interbreeding of populations and increases the likelihood that these populations will continue to diverge. Over time, these populations may diverge so much that little relationship can be seen between them. Multiplied over very long periods of time, species can diverge to amazing lengths. Certainly, we can see this in the taxonomic relationships previously discussed. Humans and chimpanzees are very closely related, but even so, they differ greatly in physical appearance, behavior, and abilities. Despite this, we are still much more similar to one another than we are to an elephant or a whale in spite of our common ancestry. Adaptation plus isolation, given time, can often result in speciation.

To explain how a species might come about, let's look at a hypothetical situation in a population of finches. This species of hypothetical finch is widespread, has a small, stout beak, and can use a range of food sources. A chick or group of chicks are born with a much finer and longer beak. These individuals can access a food source that is abundant but unavailable to the rest of their species owing to bill shape. Here begins the process of a new species coming into being. These now modified birds can breed with a typical member of their species, and several of their offspring possess this new modification. Over time, these modified finches become more numerous and flourish with their new access to food. As this population grows, it becomes more isolated from its parent population. Other attributes such as nesting style or plumage changes might make them more distinct than the finches they came from. At some point interbreeding with the old population and the new finch ceases. Once these populations cease to interbreed, they become two distinct but closely related species.

This is a hypothetical example, based on very real finches. In 1835, Darwin, on his trip on the *Beagle*, arrived in the Galápagos Islands. There he found his famous finches, 13 different species (now expanded to 18), all very similar but with varying sizes and shapes of bills. These finches were all the descendants of a single species of bird from the South American mainland that evolved to exploit differing food sources. The above example follows the well-established fact that a change in an individual or group of individuals can lead to new traits and behaviors and can work to form a new species. The process observed in Darwin's finches of a single species giving rise to multiple others is called radiation. It's not always how evolution progresses, but under the right conditions, a single species can give rise to dozens of others.

Evolution is a constant process on our planet, and the fascinating fact is that we can observe some of this process in time scales short enough for scientific study. One example we can observe is the case of the house finch *(Haemorhous mexicanus)*. Similar to Darwin's finches on the Galápagos but with the help of man, the house finch was introduced to the East Coast of the United States in the 1940s. Native to the West Coast, they once lived on open lands from California to the Rocky Mountains. The house finch now can be found throughout the United States in a wide variety of habitats, from the cold temperate regions of New England and the Midwest to the warm semitropical environs of the Southeast. Research conducted in the early 2000s showed that there are marked differences in wing length, leg length, beak size, and body size between these disparate populations of house finches. This same research found that populations separated by just a few decades were as different as populations separated by hundreds of thousands of years. Just as fascinating, these traits were not the result of any significant change in the genetics of the birds.

How can this be? How do new traits arise, and how do they get passed along without genetic change? Despite the differences in these house finch populations, it's not believed that any of them currently constitute a new species, but the changes that have been observed are likely the start of the process of speciation and maybe even the radiation of the house finch into a number of species. We know of many groups of animals that are prone to radiation. Some birds, particularly finches and tanagers (Darwin's finches are actually related to tanagers, not true finches) and fish, among other groups, show a great deal of what is called phenotypic plasticity. This means they have the ability to change their physical attributes on short time scales to fit their surroundings without the need for a change in their genetics. Rather, they change their gene expression. This is not genetic, but epigenetic change. Epigenetic change happens in all animals in response to our surroundings, but the extent of change varies with species. Where animals with high phenotypic plasticity may have noticeable differences in just a single generation, others with low plasticity could see little change over hundreds of generations, but these non-genetic changes can play an integral part in how traits come about and how they are passed from generation to generation.

It had been long believed that mutations or the rearrangement of genes in an animal's DNA (genetic change) were the only way adaptations could arise. This, of course, does play a role in the evolutionary process, especially in the long term. Populations of organisms breeding over time will always incur some sort of genetic change, either through mutation, errors in cell division, or the reshuffling of genes. Advantageous traits will typically be conserved and may lead to speciation, while detrimental traits typically disappear quickly as individuals with these traits struggle to compete. However, epigenetic change plays a much larger role in evolution than once thought. Researchers point out that even though there is an enormous variety of animals on the planet, many share numerous identical genes. The only explanation for this is that genes are typically highly conserved throughout time, but although animals share many of the same genes, we obviously use them to varying degrees. So how do phenotypic plasticity and epigenetic change work in evolution?

Once again, phenotypic plasticity is the ability of an organism to change some physical attribute to better suit its environment. The underlying mechanisms for this plasticity are due to epigenetics. This term is a bit confusing because it has been used in different ways throughout the last several decades, but in this case, it refers to an inheritable change in gene expression that does not require a change in the organism's DNA. This is a relatively new and extremely interesting field of study and demonstrates that there are other mechanisms of inheritance than the purely genetic one that we have long known about. Epigenetic change does not require a mutation in the ATCG code of DNA. Nor does it require a reshuffling of genes or the DNA that regulates them. The genome and its order stay unchanged, but the regulation of genes (turning them on, off, up, or down) is affected. This change in gene regulation is then expressed as a physical or physiological change in the organism. The expression or suppression of certain genes is accomplished in several different ways.

One of these ways is the methylation of key parts of the DNA strand. Here, what chemists refer to as a "methyl group" (CH_3) is added to the strand. Environmental factors can cause a specific sequence in DNA to be methylated. This methylation and its position within an organism's DNA can change how DNA is read and expressed, leading to phenotypic changes (the physical manifestation of the genes), physiological changes, or both, and is caused by specific enzymes in response to environmental factors. Methylation, however, is not the only way epigenetic change can happen. Several other pathways have also been identified, including the role of histone proteins and small segment RNA. It is likely that there are others yet to be identified. Also still shrouded in mystery is how the environment influences epigenetic changes, and the mechanism for this has yet to be identified. Technical specifics aside, this means that gene expression in an organism can be changed in response to a change in the environment, allowing organisms to quickly adapt to changing conditions and is a part of the survival strategy of all organisms, including humans.

Epigenetic change has profound effects with regard to speciation and evolution as a whole. Certainly, changes in gene expression happen all the time in response to a number of factors. That's how our bodies adapt to all kinds of situations. The key to affecting an organism's evolutionary path is that some of these changes can be passed down to our offspring and become permanent. In the natural world, if a particular change confers enough of an advantage, then normal natural selection pathways could eventually lead to a new species. But epigenetic change doesn't just affect specific traits; it can also have farther-reaching consequences that could drive species evolution. Epigenetic changes have been shown to alter behavior in animals. Rats, when exposed to a DNA methylating toxin, showed changes in their mating preferences, and this change in the sexual selection of an organism could have profound effects on the direction a species goes in regard to evolution. Methylation has also been seen to promote a base change from C(ytosine) to a T(hiamine) nucleotide in DNA. These changes, called "point mutations," depending on where they occur, could have significant effects on gene function and expression. Here, epigenetic change (the methylation of a certain gene segment) actually causes a genetic change within the organism, with potential implications for the evolutionary path of the organism.

Understanding the role of epigenetics as a much more rapid way for organisms to adapt, based directly on environmental factors, is a huge step forward in understanding how species evolve in response to their environment. These epigenetic changes could have been what allowed Darwin's famous finches to survive long enough to radiate into the species we find now, and there is evidence that this process is still ongoing. Researchers investigating two species of Darwin's finches, *Geospiza fortis* and *Geospiza fuliginosa,* wanted to look at epigenetic differences between populations living in urban areas and ones in more wild habitats on the island of Santa Cruz. They did in fact find "dramatic" differences in the methylation patterns in the DNA of the two populations. This suggests that the difference in the birds' environments is driving change within these finches and perhaps also driving their evolution.

Of course, a relatively quick radiation of species from a single progenitor explains how many species have come about, especially in isolated environments like islands, but what about the emergence of entire new groups of animals or the emergence of highly specialized traits? The process is the same, but drastic changes often come in gradual form. Genetic and epigenetic change allows traits to arise, change, and disappear. Natural selection then presses the refinement of these traits. This, over a long period of time, can produce highly specialized groups of animals far different from their ancestors. We have many examples of this. Processes such as these allowed fish to eventually occupy the land as amphibians. This led to the development of reptiles, dinosaurs, and eventually modern mammals, some of which returned to the sea. An excellent fossil record of whales shows how, over time, the refinement of traits can dramatically alter a group of animals.

Whale origins were once steeped in mystery. It was eventually accepted that they were in fact mammals, but it was difficult to imagine which group of mammals they belonged to. Whales are actually members of the order Artiodactyla, the even-toed, hoofed animals. Yep, as unbelievable as that seems, whales are related to cattle, pigs, and deer. Over time, new traits arising and being improved upon turned a whale ancestor from a raccoon sized, dog faced, deer-like animal with an affinity for water, into the enormous and highly specialized aquatic mammals we know of today. As time went on, the ancestors of whales became ever more adapted to life in the water, changing their body shapes, the shape of their limbs, and developing powerful tails to drive them through the water. Eventually, front limbs became flippers, and back limbs disappeared nearly all together. Modern whales still have vestiges of the pelvis that once carried these limbs. The emergence of a distinct group of animals, unlike the relatively quick emergence of species, can take millions of years, and even then, they will continue to change.

One of the more fascinating things observed in evolution that I will quickly mention here is the case of convergent evolution. Confusing scientists for centuries and now largely clarified by modern genetics, convergent evolution is the appearance of a similar trait or behavior in unrelated species. This has happened countless times throughout history, and selective pressures often select for surprising similar traits even in species that have little relationship. For example, sharks and dolphins have very similar body structures despite being separated evolutionarily by hundreds of millions of years. The now extinct marsupial thylacine (that you'll meet later) looked remarkably canine, though nowhere near dogs on the mammal family tree; the still extant fossa of Madagascar looks very much like a cat despite being in an entirely different family; and both whales and bats have highly developed echolocation abilities that evolved completely separately. Of course, before we understood molecular genetics, animals were often grouped together based on shared traits, and convergent traits often led to misidentification. I bring this up to point out the fascinating fact that nature seems to often come up with the same solutions over and over again, despite species origins or relationships, showing us the importance of how the environment shapes species and just how difficult it has been to determine the origins of many species. Because of this, our understanding of the relationships between Earth's life is also still evolving. It is common for species to be reclassified and renamed as we find new information, all in an attempt to understand their origins.

Evolutionary change and the emergence of new species can be difficult processes to understand. Change over time in response to natural pressures is the hallmark of the evolution of a species. Whatever form that change takes depends on a myriad of factors, and the time scales involved range from decades to billions of years. While we can see species adapt and change right before our eyes, we still may struggle with the concept of incremental change over millions of years. Adding to the difficulty may be the fact that evolution is a chaotic process. Sometimes fossils show us the slow development of a trait over time, but other times traits and species seem to rapidly appear. Some species continue on for hundreds of millions of years, while in the same span of time entire groups of organisms have come and gone. There is no single evolutionary path. Species diverge, converge, appear, and disappear based upon the environment they are exposed to. A species' survival is sometimes secured by the development of a novel trait, sometimes by just plain luck, but we understand more than ever what controls this chaos. While the long-held idea of genetic change giving rise to new traits is still at work, we now know that gene mutations may not play as large a role in evolution as once thought, and that gene regulation may be the most important factor. Again, it is observed in many species that major genes are highly conserved and, therefore, have not significantly changed over time. According to researcher Philip Hunter, "it is the regulation, rather than the modification or creation, of genes that has driven macroscopic events throughout evolution." Genetic and epigenetic change, combined with natural pressures and time, all work to mold species.

Given enough time, the inevitable outcome for all species is, once again, extinction, and throughout the history of life on our planet there has been a fairly steady rate of extinction, roughly 0.1 to 1 extinctions per million species per year. Reasons for the disappearance of species vary. Changes in the local environment, competition from other species, loss of a primary food source, or other factors can all lead to a species' decline and eventual disappearance. The natural pace of extinction is punctuated by what scientists call "mass extinction" events. They are exactly as they sound, events that cause a large number of species to disappear rapidly. There have been five of these extinction events in the history of the world, of varying intensities, interspersed with smaller extinction events. In each one of these events, the face of the world has changed. As the majority of species disappear, new ones arise to take their place. Groups that were once dominant may entirely disappear, and groups that may have been minor may rise to prominence. Entire new ecosystems may arise, while others disappear, but in all of these major extinction events, dramatic and lasting change always occurs.

Around 540 million years ago, quite the opposite of an extinction happened. It's called the Cambrian Explosion. Until this time, life on earth consisted of simple life forms. Bacterial mats and simple multicellular organisms dominated the world. It is in this period that nearly all major phyla of animals emerged, and the diversity of life in the oceans (anything on land was still millions of years into the future) grew immensely. The reasons for this rapid expansion of life are debated. Higher oxygen levels, the development of certain genes, just generally favorable conditions, or a combination of all of these have been put forward. Whatever the reasons, the increase in the variety of life on Earth was dramatic.

During this explosion, a creature evolved that would become one of the most successful animals in history. There may have been as many as 25,000 species of trilobites in the years that they existed. Ranging from the deep ocean to shallow tidal flats, they dominated the landscape for millions of years and became some of the most successful of the early animals of the Paleozoic. Because of this, they came to dominate the fossil record of the era. One of the richest sites for these fossils is the Burgess Shale in the Canadian Rockies. The ancient sea floor, now raised into high mountains, shows us just how plentiful these creatures once were. Entire scree slopes of ancient shale, now above tree-line, are littered with the fossilized remains of thousands upon thousands of trilobites. Similar in appearance to a modern horseshoe crab, these hard-shelled creatures with compound eyes and an array of different types of antenna were true survivors, so much so that they survived two major mass extinction events.

The first of these mass extinction events took place in the period following the Cambrian at the end of the Ordovician period. During the Ordovician period, starting 485 million years ago, life in the ocean was flourishing. At the start of the period, there were more than 60 families of trilobites, attesting to their abundance. However, sometime around 445 million years ago, drastic changes in the Earth led to the extinction of as much as 85% of all marine life in just the span of 1.4 million years. Marine life was the most affected, for the simple fact that nearly all of Earth's life was still contained in the seas. What precisely caused this rash of extinctions is still being debated, and finding answers is not easy after more than 400 million years. What we do know is that Earth experienced a dramatic cooling at the end of the Ordovician. This caused mass glaciation in the oceans and on the world's southern supercontinent of Gondwana. It is likely that this glaciation disrupted ocean currents, resulting in a diminished flow of nutrients through the oceans. This, coupled with the colder temperatures, may have severely disrupted plankton growth, leading to a wide collapse of the ocean ecosystem. There is also evidence of widespread anoxia (lack of oxygen) in the oceans at the time, possibly caused by a rapid warming period after glaciation. This warming may have increased algal growth through the release of nutrients from the land as a result of rapidly melting glaciers. The eventual death of these huge blooms subsequently stripped the oceans of available oxygen. The timing of all of this is still in question, with some studies suggesting that anoxia was already occurring during the peak of glaciation. Whatever the combination of factors or their causes, the rapidly shifting climate at the end of this period clearly took its toll. While the majority of life was wiped out, members of all of the major groups of animal life made it through the event, including our friends the trilobites. However, they declined from more than 40 families at the end of the Ordovician to just 19 in the early days of the following Silurian period.

After the Silurian period came the Devonian period, starting some 420 million years ago, and it is at the end of this period where we find Earth's second mass extinction event. Beginning around 380 million years ago and lasting on and off for as much as 25 million years, the Devonian extinctions claimed as much as 75% of the world's species. A range of causes have been proposed, from volcanism, to a nearby supernova explosion or an asteroid impact, but the most significant trigger may have actually come from life itself. During the Devonian, there was an explosion of terrestrial plants. It is possible that this caused a drawdown of atmospheric CO_2 as these new plants pulled carbon dioxide out of the atmosphere, resulting in a period of global cooling. Maybe a combination of all of these ultimately led to the extinctions. What we do know is that the world's oceans were the most impacted and once again suffered severe anoxic events, while life on land was much less affected. Despite these severe challenges, the plucky trilobites persisted, though they were reduced to just a single order and only four families as they entered the following Carboniferous period.

During the Carboniferous period, life exploded on land. Amphibians became the dominant group of land animals, but we also see the emergence of reptiles and the group of animals that would eventually give rise to mammals. We also see an explosion of insect diversity with increased oxygen levels, allowing them to grow to immense proportions. Huge dragonflies, some with wingspans of more than half a meter (2 feet), hovered through the Carboniferous forests. Cooling and drying of the climate then allowed reptiles to become the dominant land animals into the following Permian period, but at the end of this period life would be challenged like never before. This has been called "The Great Dying," an event so severe that the world would never be the same biologically. Not even the trilobites would survive it. The exact number of species lost is, of course, hard to pin down after 251 million years, but more than 90% of all the species on the planet may have been lost. Here was the end of the 270 million-year run of the trilobites, and based on the fossil record, almost everything else.

The cause of The Great Dying is also debated, but what is certain is that the globe warmed rapidly from the influx of huge amounts of CO_2 in the atmosphere. As a result, global average temperatures skyrocketed by as much as 8°C (14°F). The influx of heat into the oceans raised surface temperatures by more than 10°C (18°F) causing severe heat induced anoxia of the ocean (the oceans lost as much as 80% of their oxygen). This, combined with the change in water chemistry due to acidification from the influx of CO_2, collapsed marine ecosystems. There is evidence of widespread fires all across the globe and mass deforestation. The die-off was incredibly fast in geologic terms, taking place in as little as 20,000 years and likely no more than 200,000 years. Current research puts the blame on the massive volcanic eruptions of the Siberian Traps. Although these eruptions may have occurred for hundreds of thousands of years prior to the extinction, there is evidence that magma from these eruptions may have pushed into volatile rock features, and that reaction was ultimately responsible for the massive release of CO_2. Whatever the case it is clear that the period surrounding the end of the Permian was volatile. Recently published evidence shows massive volcanic eruptions from Eastern Australia preceding the eruption of the Siberian Traps, suggesting the Siberian Traps may have been the final blow to already stressed ecosystems.

Note that while the 270 million years trilobites survived on Earth may be impressive, their extinction highlights that even the most successful animals can disappear in the geologic blink of an eye. No matter how wide-spread or long lived a group of animals is, there is always the possibility of extinction.

Considering our own species and our recent ancestors' lineage, which reaches back only a couple of million years, it would appear that humans have been little tested in the crucible of time. Surely we have outcompeted our fair share of other species in our rise to global prominence, but there is little evidence of our resilience in the face of another global extinction event. We would do well to keep this in the forefront of our minds, especially as we add huge amounts of CO_2 into our atmosphere with entirely predictable results.

Despite an event as severe as the Great Dying, life is amazingly resilient, and it eventually rebounded from nearly being extinguished all together. However, life was to be tested again in the period following the Permian, the Triassic period. At the end of this period 201 million years ago, it is believed that, once again, massive volcanism, this time caused by the breakup of the Pangea supercontinent (creating the Atlantic Ocean), might be the culprit in this set of extinctions. Just like in the Permian extinctions, the influx of CO_2 into the atmosphere raised global temperatures and acidified the oceans. Global average temperatures increased by 3-4°C (the exact same amount predicted if our current warming continues unabated). This resulted in the extinction of 40-70% of Earth's species and more than 90% of shallow water corals, but the void left by these species allowed others to thrive. The following Jurassic period not only gave rise to some of the most memorable of the dinosaurs, like the huge *Brachiosaurus* and the plated *Stegosaurus*, but also our mammal ancestors and the birds that still grace our skies.

The most famous and most recent of the Earth's mass extinction events is, of course, the end-Cretaceous extinction 66 million years ago that led to the extinction of the dinosaurs. We now know through geological exploration that a huge space object hit the Earth just off the coast of what is now the Yucatán Peninsula. Research recently published shows evidence that this object was a possibly long-period comet that was disrupted by Jupiter's gravity. After Jupiter's gravity broke this object apart, one of the resulting cometary fragments was sent on a path toward Earth. The fragment is believed to be somewhere around 7-10 km (4-6 mi) wide and hit the earth at a velocity of roughly 20 km/s (44,000 mph). Whatever the impactor was, asteroid or comet, the geology of the impact site, unfortunately for the dinosaurs and millions of other species alive at the time, was such that huge amounts of sulfur were released, making the situation far worse than if the impact had hit another part of the planet. This vaporized sulfur mixed into the atmosphere and created huge amounts of sulfur dioxide. This light blocking substance, combined with dust and ash, blotted out the sun. Evidence suggests that reduced sunlight caused photosynthesis to cease on a global scale. Organisms that were not killed by the initial massive impact explosion or the subsequent global fires were slowly killed by the destruction of the world's food webs and the tumultuous climate shifts of the post-impact Earth, defined initially by a severe cooling period as particulates and SO_2 blocked out the sun. This was followed by a period rapid warming as the effect the huge amount of greenhouse gases released by the impact took over. In all, 60–70% of all life on earth perished.

Scientists' first clue that an impact from an extraplanetary body occurred was the discovery of the K-Pg boundary, or Cretaceous-Paleogene (formally the K-T boundary) by geologist Walter Alvarez and his Nobel prize winning father Luis. This thin layer of iridium-rich material geologically separates the age of the dinosaurs found below it and their absence above. As it turns out, comets and meteorites are much richer in iridium than earth rocks, and an enormous impact of something not of our world was the only way to explain the K-Pg boundary showing up in the rock strata, at the same level, all around the world. Alvarez and father postulated that this impactor must have been responsible for for the fate of the dinosaurs. Like many new ideas, the idea of a mass extinction caused by an asteroid impact was met with skepticism. However in 1978, the crater that was made by this impact, dubbed the Chicxulub crater after the nearest town, was found hiding in decades old oil survey data. This confirmed the idea that Earth was indeed impacted by a huge object from the cosmos, but the conclusive connection to the extinction of the dinosaurs wasn't made until the 1990s. The impact paved the way for many of the animals we see today and is likely the reason that mammals became the dominant large life forms on the planet. In geologic terms, the recovery was rapid, taking as little as 10 million years for the Earth's biodiversity to reach the level it was before the disaster. However, in human terms, it took five times the length of all of human history.

Clearly, mass die-offs naturally happen, but unlike the dramatic end to the dinosaurs, the causes of these events are not always so clear. In all cases, huge climatic shifts are always associated with the events. Whether through the arrangement of land masses creating mass glaciation as in the Ordovician, or an increase in volcanism and atmospheric CO_2 that results in global warming, ocean acidification, and anoxia, or other unknown climate factors, it's clear that shifts in climate have a dramatic impact on the makeup of life on earth. Stability is key for maintaining biodiversity, and the destabilization of global climatic norms even over millions of years can have a significant impact. It's interesting to point out that even the huge object from space that wiped out the dinosaurs ultimately did it through the climatic changes that it caused. It's clear that whether a dramatic shift or something more subtle, climate is the key.

All of these mass extinction events are extreme examples, but while significant, they are not the way in which extinction normally happens. How then does extinction happen in the periods between these severe events? There are many reasons a species can go extinct. As species adapt, they may outcompete and replace less well-adapted species (leading to their extinction), but this isn't as common as one might think. A major part of evolution is that species try to avoid competition, and becoming more specific in the habitats or food sources they utilize helps them avoid competing. It is far more common throughout history for species loss to be caused by changes in environment. Climatic changes for various reasons (less severe than in mass extinction events), loss or restructuring of habitat, natural disasters, predation, and disease all play a part in the natural cycle. Old species are replaced by new, not necessarily because they were able to outcompete old species directly, but were simply better adapted to the *new* environment.

For example, it is certainly possible that, say, a certain species of grazer is more efficient at processing grass than an existing species. This new species could displace the old, but if the old species was already thriving in the existing conditions, given enough habitat, it's likely they would simply coexist. However, let's say that the conditions in the grassland change, and a climatic shift has brought less rain, creating less nutritious grass. In this scenario, the new species would have the upper hand. Their higher efficiency allows them to extract more nutrients out of the environment, allowing them to reproduce in greater numbers than the old species. As time goes on, they eventually displace the old species all together. Other factors will come into play to determine whether the old species will cease to exist. Can they move to a better habitat, or are there other populations in other locations that are not declining? If the answer to these is "no," then the species will probably not survive. Of course, this example is just one of a near-infinite number of situations that could lead to a species replacing another, but it serves to highlight how an extinction could progress. It is also certainly possible that a species could disappear for a particular reason and be replaced by another at a much later date, but whatever the case, we will probably never know what specifically caused the extinction of most of the species throughout Earth's history. I am speaking, of course, of the natural cycle of extinction, one that humans are increasingly disrupting.

There are several different types of extinction, or, maybe to put it better, categories of extinction, that you'll see discussed. Types may graduate into each other as a species' population dwindles, and then, if doomed by multiple factors, eventually disappears. Many of these will be referenced throughout the book, so let's look at them and some of the factors that are associated with extinction. First, there is local extinction. In this type of extinction, a species does not cease to exist in its entirety, but as the name suggests, ceases to exist from a particular location. This is the most common type of extinction event. There are many reasons a particular species can become locally extinct. Changes in the size or makeup of its habitat, invasion by a competing species, not enough influx of breeding individuals from other populations, among others. The local population numbers are an important factor. A general biological rule is that species with a larger population will tend to survive in a locality, whether on a small plot of land or in an entire country, for a longer period of time. This seems like an obvious conclusion, but it is important for the functioning of a species. Once the population of an area drops too low, issues begin to arise. A small population may have a majority of females or males, may have primarily older members that are past breeding age, or the population might be too closely related and suffer from a lack of genetic diversity. It is worth noting that local extinctions can be quite common. Species appear and disappear from habitats all the time, and this does not necessarily mean that a particular plant's or animal's total population is dwindling overall. Species that have been extinct in a certain area for years can migrate back and reestablish themselves if a nearby population exists, and it is possible that even if a population is diminishing in one particular area, it can be growing in another.

However, with enough local extinctions, the total population might fall to unsustainable levels. This loss of multiple populations can become what is called "functional extinction." This is the beginning of the extinction of an entire species rather than a single population. In this case, members of the species still exist in the wild but are too old, the wrong sex (i.e., all females/males), and/or have too small a population or too little genetic diversity to keep the population intact. This is a species in its last death throes. It really exists only in a technical sense in that some of its members remain, but they are doomed to eventually disappear.

Total extinction is exactly that, the entire loss of a particular species. At this point, there are no living biological remnants. As more and more populations of a species dwindle and progress toward functional extinction, populations become either too small or too isolated from one another to survive and eventually disappear. Habitat loss and fragmentation can play a large role. One biological rule we find is that the larger a given area, the more species it contains. So universal is this rule that we can actually quantify the relationship between area and species diversity. We find that a 10-fold reduction in habitat roughly halves the number of species that it can support. This is particularly relevant to what we see today as natural landscapes are divided into smaller and smaller pieces (I'll talk about this in more detail in the next chapter). If a species' population, even if robust on the whole, is divided into too many smaller populations, more local extinctions can occur and result in the eventual loss of all of the populations. Apart from the actions of humans, there are natural causes of habitat loss. Natural disasters, shifts in climate, and fire all play a role in habitat change.

A species' vulnerability increases as it becomes more specialized to a specific environment. For instance, if a butterfly's caterpillar state only feeds on one specific type of plant, as monarch butterflies do, a disease that could significantly reduce or eliminate these plants would inevitably spell disaster for the butterfly. Likewise, a species that has an extremely limited range, say a species of salamander that's found in a single creek, could easily be wiped out by disease or a change in water flow. Animals that migrate, such as birds or butterflies, are particularly sensitive to habitat loss owing to their need to have two or more intact habitats to exist. The removal or severe degradation of any of these habitats, either in a species' wintering grounds, breeding areas, or even the habitat they need for rest and feeding along their migration path, could seriously affect their survival. The introduction of non-native species is also a significant factor in species loss. Often plants and animals that evolved in much different living conditions, when suddenly introduced to a new habitat, free of predators or disease, can take over and out-compete native species. This rapid species introduction rarely happens in nature, but is now extremely common due to human activity.

Species themselves can possess particular factors that make them more or less prone to extinction. Through evolution, species have obtained advantages over others or can exploit aspects of nature others can't, allowing them to succeed. When conditions change, these adaptations can become a liability. Take an animal's size, for instance. A black rhino in Africa can weigh several tons. While this size largely keeps them safe from predators, it comes at a cost. It is yet another general rule in biology that the larger the mass of an animal, the smaller the population size. Much of this has to do with the resources required to obtain a larger size, but this size can work against the rhino in several ways. Large animals have long gestation periods, have few young, and require large tracts of land. The low inherent population combined with the slow reproductive rates means that any significant loss in population, especially among breeding age adults, could seriously impact the species as a whole. Bacteria, on the other hand, being quite small and having rapid reproductive rates, are much more resilient to significant losses. Even an isolated species of bacteria, if taken down to one individual, could rapidly rebound to millions in the right conditions. It is of note that humans, unlike all other species, do not follow the rules concerning size. We are vastly more plentiful than nature should allow and, in fact, does allow. Humans consume resources at an unnatural level, and this will inevitably work against us to our peril if not brought back to a natural balance.

The last type of extinction is much of man's creation. This is extinction in the wild. Formally, if an animal, plant, etc., were to no longer have the population required to sustain itself, it would cease to exist in totality. Many cases exist today where humans have intervened in order to try to save a particular species through captive breeding programs in zoos and research institutions. These species are functionally or totally extinct in nature, but members do still exist outside of natural conditions. Many species will not make it back to the wild, but there have been some successes. Unfortunately, the small population problem comes into play heavily in this situation, with typically not enough members left to perpetuate the species.

Several species of frog currently live in this evolutionary limbo. They include the Panamanian golden frog *(Atelopus zeteki)*, the Wyoming toad *(Anaxyrus baxteri)*, and the Kihansi spray toad *(Nectophrynoides asperginis)* of Tanzania. In all 3 of these species, an invasive chytrid fungus called *Batrachochytrium dendrobatidis* or Bd is at least partially to blame. We'll talk about how this fungus is decimating frog populations all over the world when we look at the pressure facing frogs and other amphibians. Amphibians are not the only animals in this precarious position, and other species include the northern white rhino *(Ceratotherium simum cottoni)*, Spix's macaw *(Cyanopsitta spixii)*, the Hawaiian crow *(Corvus hawaiiensis)*, and the Père David's deer *(Elaphurus davidianus)*.

For billions of years, natural processes have solely controlled the evolution and extinction of species. While nature still certainly plays an important role, humans, through their direct impact on nature and climate, are now a greater and greater driver of everything that happens on the blue planet. As we change land use, water flows, introduce species into new environments, pollute the air and water, and change the global climate, we force Earth's life to adapt to these new pressures, and those who can't are disappearing at an ever-increasing rate. We will delve deeper into humans' impact throughout history and today and see species lost to these impacts, but let me quickly address in this chapter of evolution and extinction just a bit how humans are changing Earth's species.

The human impact on the environment is so broad that I suppose it should not be surprising that humans are changing the evolution of the species around us. It is ever more of a human world, so of course species must adapt or die. Scientists have documented some of these human-induced changes, and there are many such examples, but I'll mention just a few. Of course, the case of Darwin's finches mentioned earlier is a prime example of how urban environments push species to adapt to human landscapes, bringing about changes in their behavior and physical attributes. Doubtless, many other species we come across in our daily lives are affected in the same way. The species we introduce around the world are also forcing adaptation. One well-documented example is the snail kite *(Rostrhamus sociabilis plumbeus)*, a small raptor that feeds, as its name suggests, almost exclusively on snails. Endangered in the United States, in the state of Florida, they traditionally fed largely on the native Florida apple snail *(Pomacea paludosa)*. However, the introduction of several invasive apple snail species from South America, the most common being the island apple snail *(Pomacea canaliculata)*, are displacing the native snail throughout their range becoming twice to 100 times more prevalent.

The island apple snail is a significantly larger species than their Florida relatives, and in response to this new food source, the snail kites have not only dramatically increased their beak size but also their body masses in to deal with the larger prey. Studies show that the first year survival of chicks with larger beaks and body mass is higher than those without and this is leading to a population-wide change in the snail kite's morphology. This change in body structure has happened in the span of just a decade, and the change is only seen in areas where non-native snails have invaded. This strongly suggests that it is, in fact, the kites adapting to a new and larger food. In areas where the non-native snails have not invaded, the kites retain their standard attributes. In this case, we cannot only see the change of a species due to a human introduction, but if these populations continue to be isolated based on their food source, (if the non-native apple snails stop expanding), the possible beginnings of ultimately human-caused speciation.

Human-caused climate change is, of course, acting as an evolutionary pressure. Changes in the distribution of plant species and changes in plant communities affect feeding behaviors, migration, and the distribution of animals. However, there is evidence that rising temperatures themselves may also be a direct driver of physical change in animals as well. Many animals, especially birds and mammals, use their appendages to regulate body temperature. Recent research has suggested that in multiple animal groups, increasing temperatures are beginning to physically change the shape of species as they gain larger appendages to help release heat in a warmer world. Among the examples are the Australian parrots. Using measurements from museum specimens, scientists have shown that bill sizes among these birds have increased between 4 and 10 percent since 1871. Similar changes have been observed in other birds, particularly the dark-eyed junco *(Junco hyemalis)*. A number of small mammals have also experienced changes, including several species of shrews and bats that have seen their relative ear, tail, leg, and wing sizes increase in response to warming global temperatures. Support for these findings comes from laboratory experiments and observations in nature confirming that mice, for instance, reared in warmer temperatures have longer tails and that invasive bird species, like the house sparrow *(Passer domesticus)* and the starling *(Sturnus vulgaris)*, show larger beaks after settling in warmer climes.

No matter what we do, the very fact that we exist as a part of the Earth's living system will influence other species. This is simply a fact of nature, but the disturbing result of human dominance is the outsized effect of our existence. Nowhere is this more evident than in the impact we are having on the extinction of Earth's species. It is becoming increasingly clear that humans are likely now precipitating the world's sixth mass extinction. Humans have now escaped the restrictions of the natural world, and we have evolved to be able to modify our environment for our own survival to such an extent that it is modifying the entire planet. Because of this, the current rate of extinction has accelerated to rates only seen in previous mass extinction events. The danger now is not from a huge chunk of rock and ice from outer space, or an outbreak of extreme volcanism, humans have become the destructive force. Unlike a threat from the cosmos or some geologic catastrophe, this seemingly unstoppable force is self-made. It is estimated that species are becoming extinct at a rate tens to hundreds, and in some cases thousands, of times faster than the normal background rate. Human actions have resulted in the extinction of at least 680 vertebrate species and over 860 species overall in the last 500 years, with an estimated 200-400 vertebrate species going extinct in just the last 100 years. As many as 1,000,000 species across all life may currently be at risk of extinction. More than any other factor, humans are increasingly the reason for current extinctions.

These numbers above are just estimates, and the situation in regards to extinction is most likely worse than known, masking the true impact of human actions. It is impossible to know for sure how many species we are losing. The primary reason for this is that we have little knowledge of how many species actually exist on the planet. We'll look at the best current estimates in the next chapter, but the low-end estimate for a biologically rich area like the rainforest could be as many as 10 million species. Famed Harvard biologist E.O. Wilson estimated more than 20 years ago that the rate of species loss was potentially as high as 27,000 species across all life every year. He based this number upon conservative estimates of population distributions and habitat loss, but the true number of human-caused extinctions is as hard to know as the true number of species. We do know, however, that there have been dramatic population losses across most of the world over just the last several decades. The World Wildlife

Fund's Living Planet Index estimates that wildlife abundance worldwide decreased by a staggering 68% between 1970 and 2016, and the loss of species abundance has only accelerated since then. This acceleration has been so rapid that it is actually hard for science to keep up. Lack of funding and the extreme difficulty of locating rare species limit population counts. Surveys done decades ago, even just a few years ago, may no longer reflect the reality of current population pressures or population counts. As the world rapidly changes and human pressures continue to intensify, entire species can disappear between assessments. While conservation focus has been on endangered species, there are clear signals that without action, today's common species may rapidly join the list of species that are endangered or even extinct.

We should be deeply concerned by species loss. Not only because it's the moral thing to do but, at least, in the selfish desire to see humanity survive. Despite the unparalleled success of *Homo sapiens,* we still ultimately rely on the Earth and the complex interplay of species on it for our own survival. In at least four of the previous major extinction events, 70% or more of all species on the planet were lost. It is very unlikely that at the end of a sixth mass extinction, even if human-caused, humanity will remain. We will take a closer look at the importance of life and its interactions on our planet in the next chapter, but it should be clear that if we are to have any hope of saving humanity, we need to save every species we can and quickly restore the Earth's natural balance.

Humans, through the adaptations that we have acquired naturally over millions of years, mostly in the realm of intelligence, can now operate outside of the normal natural processes. Our amazing ability to change our environment, exploit natural resources on a mass scale, and our use of increasingly advanced technologies separates and insulates us from many of the challenges of nature. This has allowed us to succeed as a species far beyond what should be possible. No species of our body size has ever been so successful. Members of our group of animals, the primates, are usually scarce and the larger the scarcer, but our domination has allowed us to be 100 times more numerous than any other mammal the same size, *ever*. Natural laws largely no longer apply to us, and that fact has created an immense biological imbalance in our favor, at least for the time being.

Beyond this, there is a difference to humanity that sets us apart from any species before us. Our intelligence does not just allow us to adapt and change our environment. We are one of the few species on the planet that recognizes what we are. We are cognizant of our own existence, but more specifically, beyond the ability of all other creatures, we are able to understand concepts far beyond ourselves. Our fellow animals survive largely by instinct, and even a surprising amount of intelligence, but none can understand their place in the natural world, or the impact, or the importance of their existence. Humans can comprehend all of this. We understand the gross workings of the biosphere, we understand how we are affecting it, and we have the capacity to understand our role in it. This understanding, this ability of the human mind to grasp concepts much larger than ourselves, gives us a perspective that no other creature possesses. With that understanding must come responsibility. We, as a species, are now largely responsible for what happens to the Earth and all of the other life on it. Humans more than ever control the levers of evolution and extinction. We have worked hard to put ourselves in this position and now, like it or not, the fate of the world's species and our own could be in our hands.

2
Biodiversity

Now that we have talked a bit about how species evolve, let's talk about the result of that evolution. Evolution is the engine that drives what we have come to call biodiversity. As more life came into being, yet more life evolved to exploit it or the effects of that evolution. New environments were created by emerging life, and yet newer life evolved to interact with those new environments. Throughout time, as life continued to diversify, it changed the planet even more, creating yet more environments for more life to fill, until, recently in geologic history, life reached the maximum level of diversity that has ever existed on Earth. It fills every ecological niche that the planet offers, and we are still finding these niches.

Nearly everywhere we look on the planet, life persists, even in the most unlikely of places. From the single-celled Archaea *Pyrococcus furiosus* that lives in geologically heated marine sediments (not only can it live in scalding hot water, but actually thrives best in water that is 100°C and would be perfectly at home in a pot of boiling water), to a variety of life found living 550 meters (1,800 feet) under the ice of Antarctica, more than 150 miles from the nearest open ocean. We have even found life in deep drilling cores thousands of feet below the surface of the Earth. Some of them, like those found in Sweden, are species of bacteria that live at a depth of more than 3 miles. Maybe most surprising is a species of worm *(Hesiocaeca methanicola)* whose environment may be unlike any other on Earth. It was found inhabiting methane ice at the bottom of the Gulf of Mexico, where it's believed to feed on bacteria that live off of the methane itself. All of this is in addition to the more familiar life that makes up our forests and grasslands, fills our oceans, enriches our soils, and even lives within us.

All of these are examples of Earth's fantastic and sometimes surprising biodiversity. So what is biodiversity, and what is the nature of Earth's bio-diversity? Definitionally, biodiversity is quite simple; it refers to the variety of life that exists, whether we are talking about a local park, a country, or the entire planet. It encompasses the larger creatures we are familiar with — the trees that shade us, the flowers we admire, and the bees that visit them — but it also includes things we often take little notice of or simply are too small to see, like the tiny insects that abound, or the soil microbes and fungi that are so essential to those flowers and trees. Biodiversity can mean many things on many different levels, and one can talk about biodiversity in terms of genes, species, communities, and entire ecosystems, but at every level, it speaks to the level of diversity within.

Numerous things play a part in the level of biodiversity that exists in any environment, and the number of species can vary widely based upon the conditions of life in the areas in which they live. Temperature, availability of water and nutrients, amount of annual sunlight, and, of more recent concern, the availability of natural habitats, all play a role in the amount of life that exists in a given landscape. These also play a role in determining niche availability. The more niches available for life, the more life that will come to occupy them. I briefly mentioned niches in the last chapter, but let me expand on that a bit. A species' ecological niche is simply where it fits in the grand scheme of the ecosystem. It encompasses the specific habitat and food sources that a species utilizes in the environment, as well as its interactions with other species. Is it predator or prey? Does it burrow, fly, or swim? What does it require, and what does it provide? Many species can inhabit similar niches. For example, all large grazers, in general, utilize similar habitats, have similar behaviors, and are food for large predators, but no two species will occupy the same niche simply because they will never interact with their environment in identical ways.

Because there are many factors that determine the level of biodiversity, life's abundance is not distributed equally across the planet, but it does follow some general rules. One overarching rule is that Earth's biodiversity increases as one moves from the poles to the equator. This is referred to as the latitudinal gradient of biodiversity or species richness. For example, in the Northern Hemisphere, Greenland has fewer breeding bird species than Newfoundland, which has fewer than New York State, and so on as you move south. No one knows precisely why, but most likely it has to do with the stability of the environment as the climate warms and becomes less variable closer to the equator. Seasonal temperature changes at lower latitudes are less variable, and ecological productivity is higher with longer or even year-round growing seasons. This stability allows for a greater abundance of ecological niches and a greater number of species to fill them. This is most pronounced in the tropics. Because there is little seasonal variation, the equatorial regions have a constant amount of light year-round and much more stable temperatures than climates to the north and south. These regions of the planet can be thought of as the Earth's "greenhouse," where conditions are nearly always favorable for life. Harsher environments have fewer niches available, and this is seen in the Arctic, Antarctic, and the world's deserts. In these environments, resource availability is limited largely by a lack of available water, but other factors such as short growing seasons, very hot or very cold conditions, or the combination of these factors, limit life and lead to less variation overall, but often produce unique species to meet these challenges.

This varying niche availability may explain why temperate Europe has only around 124 tree species compared to thousands in the Tropics. Worldwide, tropical regions of our planet may contain 40,000 or more tree species. In the rich rainforests of South America, just a few acres of land may contain 1,000 species of tree, as many as all of North America. This same pattern is seen in other organisms as well. All of North America north of Mexico has around 700 species of butterflies, compared to over 3,300 in Brazil alone. While the latitudinal gradient holds true across the world, there is still variation among comparable latitudes. Even within the tropics, biodiversity is highly variable, and the tropical forests of South America hold nearly twice as many species of plants as the forests of tropical Africa. The latitudinal gradient exists not only on land, but also in the ocean, with diversity in shallow water environments increasing from the Arctic to the Tropics.

The ultimate example of richness in biodiversity is the equatorial rainforests, where the abundance of life creates the conditions for more life, with biodiversity begetting more biodiversity. Because of the unique conditions here, plants can grow upon plants, which grow upon yet other plants. With the abundance of moisture and sunlight, fully mature trees can grow upon other, yet larger trees. A mature tree in the rainforest can support as many as a thousand epiphytes. These are plants that grow on other plants by using soil trapped high up in large trees or open root systems. Multiplying the surface area of the forest, these plants support an immense amount of animal life, providing them with food and habitat. The forest canopies support primates and other mammals that feed on their fruit, as well as an unbelievable number of insects, reptiles, and even tree-dwelling amphibians high above the forest floor. Yet more life exists below in the shade of the immense canopy, with more ground-dwelling insects and species as diverse as big cat predators and ant colonies with members millions strong. These forests, while only occupying around 6 percent of the Earth, may account for more than 50 percent of all terrestrial species.

Paralleling the latitudinal gradient, we also see an altitudinal gradient for species richness. Here, less biodiversity is found at higher elevations than those at lower elevations, likely for many of the same reasons as seen in the latitudinal gradient. An increase in elevation mimics the climate and seasonality of a higher latitude, and a corresponding decrease in species diversity is seen. This effect is very pronounced in high mountain ranges that have lower tropical elevations, such as the Andes. In these landscapes, as elevation increases, the environment changes from tropical rainforest, to a temperate zone to an arctic-like high alpine zone, with a corresponding change in species types and diversity that one might see moving north from the Equator to high Arctic latitudes. Species typically found in much higher latitudes are also often found far north or south of their normal ranges at high altitudes. For example, the white-tailed ptarmigan (*Lagopus leucura*) is found in the high alpine environs of the Rocky Mountains as far south as New Mexico in the United States, despite the bulk of its range being north of the Canadian-U.S. border and into Alaska.

What we know of species distributions highlights just how important protecting rainforests are to protecting species. We know where most of the life on our planet occurs, and it happens, unfortunately, to be in the areas that are most threatened. In fact, the tropics are seeing some of the largest numbers of species extinctions. Protecting these forests is crucial to keeping biodiversity loss to a minimum, but it's important to remember that all species have value and, as we will see, are valuable components in a complex biological system. While rainforests have greater biodiversity, less biodiversity does not equate to less importance. Protection of the rainforests should be of paramount concern for the species they contain and for the crucial role they play in the regulation of the global climate. However, less species-rich environments still play important roles, and these species-poor systems may be more susceptible to major disturbance. Despite its high latitude, the Arctic Ocean, while being less diverse than the coral environs of the Tropics, still contains a huge abundance of life and provides plentiful feeding grounds for a multitude of fish, whales, seals, and polar bears.

Many other factors can affect biodiversity. For instance, size plays a role in the diversity of animals. Larger animals tend to be much less diverse than smaller and this is easily observed. There are about 6,000 species of mammals known, but potentially several million species of insects. Isolation, niche availability, and resource availability play a large part. The small size of insects makes isolation of populations much more likely than with much larger animals. A group of insects immigrating to a new tree in the rainforest mirrors the effects of a bird or mammal migrating to an ocean island. Hundreds of generations of insects could live out their lives in the life span of a tree and may end up greatly diverging from the population they came from. Also, the smaller an organism is, the more niches are available to them and the less resources they need for success. For something as small as bacteria, an entire microscopic ecosystem can exist in a handful of soil or a liter of water, and just a single gram of soil can contain thousands of species of bacteria.

Biodiversity, like the species that make it up, is constantly changing in the environment. Species immigrate, emigrate, or become locally extinct, and new ones come into being. All of this can change the local biodiversity of the landscape. Areas of the Earth that support species diversification will ultimately add to global biodiversity. Isolation of populations promotes speciation, and naturally, island habitats are very effective in this. Islands often contain many species unique to themselves and dramatically increase global biodiversity. However, the same isolation and limited resources also make island species vulnerable to extinction, especially on smaller islands.

The availability of habitat naturally affects species diversity. That is why islands have less diversity overall than large landmasses. As I mentioned in the last chapter, there is a quantifiable relationship between the amount of available land and the number of species it can support. In any given habitat, a tenfold smaller land area will contain 50 percent fewer species. For example, say an island in the tropics has 500 species in total. A nearby island that is one-tenth the size would be expected to contain 250. This idea is a major component of island biogeography. The discipline, developed in the 1960s by Robert MacArthur and Edward O. Wilson seeks to explain the physical constraints on species diversity. Attempting to expand biogeography from simply the "what and where"of species distributions to include the "why and how", they set out to explain how species diversity works on islands. What they discovered were insights into how species establish themselves, how communities change over time, and the constraints on species diversity. Using islands as a model, they were able to apply these to any size landscape (essentially because anywhere can act as an island on a big enough scale). The research, in light of today's issues, takes on new meaning. Most of the world's natural habitats now increasingly exist as smaller and smaller islands, not surrounded by water but by human-made environments. Whether it's our extensive agricultural land or the cities we live in, humans have divided up the world's landscapes into ever smaller chunks, and island biogeography can help to explain the effect that has on diversity. Habitat loss and fragmentation are some of the largest threats to the world's species, and as the islands we create continue to shrink, we have a really good idea of the outcome of the fragmentation of Earth's ecosystems.

One of the most important things to be realized from the study of island biogeography is that the total land area of a lost natural habitat is not representative of the true impact on diversity. To illustrate, let's take a 100,000-acre landscape that's being developed for agriculture. 10,000 acres will be converted to crops. While it seems like it shouldn't matter how that land is developed, we now understand that it does. If 10 farmers each develop 1,000-acre fields, distributed throughout our 100,000 acre landscape, there are still 90,000 acres of natural habitat left. This would be the same if all 10,000 acres were taken in one continuous piece, but spreading out where the land is developed has a different effect. Instead of one island with 90,000 acres, we have fragmented the landscape into 9 islands of 10,000 acres each. Because of this, we would expect to see a species reduction of roughly half in each island, far more than we would predict for a continuous 90,000-acre parcel. Of course, how many species would actually be lost would depend on the connections between the remaining islands, but this illustrates the increased damage that fragmentation has over just the loss of land. Like the latitudinal or altitudinal gradient, the area/diversity relationship of island biogeography emerges as one of the biological rules that control Earth's diversity, but unlike the formers, it is one that human actions can greatly influence, and understanding this will be essential for helping to save diversity in the future.

Although we have a good general understanding of how species are distributed throughout the planet, it may come as a shock that we don't even know within an order of magnitude how many species there are. It could be as little as 10 million, or as many as 100 million, 100 billion, or even a trillion. In the 1950s, Curtis Sabrosky of the United States Department of Agriculture (USDA) gave an estimation of 10 million insects based on the number of new species he was seeing each year. In the 1980s, entomologist Terry Erwin proposed an even larger number of 30 million based on his studies of tropical beetles. He extrapolated this number after finding an amazing 163 species of beetles living on just one species of rainforest tree. Various other scientists have weighed in over the years, but the consensus from the scientific community seems to range somewhere between 5 and 20 million total species. However, most of these estimates are unfortunately little more than educated guesses.

In 2011, using taxonomic patterns, a group of researchers gave us one of the better estimations to date of just how many species could exist, at least for some life. They estimated that there are about 8.7 million eukaryotic species. 7.7 million of these in the animal kingdom alone. This seems like a reasonable estimate, but it does exclude the prokaryotes (such as bacteria and archaea) which could account for a large part of the life on the planet. A potential issue with this estimate is that it is based on known taxonomic groups, and any discovery of one or more major unknown groups could change the number significantly. Truly, if we are still finding where life lives on the planet, there is the potential to be overlooking large numbers of species. Maybe more convincing that this estimate may still be off, is the currently known number of plant species. This stands at just over 370,000; however, the conclusions of the 2011 research estimated that there should only be about 290,000 species of plants, plus or minus 8,200. Regardless of the potential inaccuracies, this estimation is probably still our best guess based on the knowledge of the best-described taxonomic groups.

While we may have a relatively good idea of the number of larger eukaryotes on the planet, the same is not true for the majority of the world's microbial life, and researchers from the University of Indiana may have insights into just how limited our knowledge really is. It has been long thought that microbial life may be vastly more abundant than we understand, and most of what we know about biological life comes from the cataloging of species that we can easily see and study. Using large sets of molecular data and scaling laws, researchers were able to mathematically predict how many microbial species might exist, and while, once again the estimate varies by an order of magnitude, the number is larger than many would have believed possible. If this is correct, we might not know of 99.999% of the 100 billion to 1 trillion microbial species that exist, a staggering number that may be hard to comprehend, but for some perspective, take how little we know of the ocean. According to the National Oceanic and Atmospheric Administration (NOAA) in the U.S., "more than eighty percent of this vast, underwater realm remains unmapped, unobserved, and unexplored." When taking into account that the ocean makes up 70% of the globe's surface and has a volume of 300 million cubic miles, we are unfortunately ignorant of most of the Earth's biosphere. This constitutes an unbelievable amount of habitat for life that we know so little about. The sheer size of the ocean, combined with the fact that explorations into its depths almost always discover new species, and that each of these species has its own unique microflora, makes the figure of a trillion seem less fantastic. With the vastness of the ocean and the enormity of the seafloor, it seems reasonable that an enormous amount of life is being missed. Take, for example, the most abundant organism in the world's tropical oceans, the bacteria *Prochlorococcus*. This photosynthetic organism makes up 20 to 40 percent of all photosynthetic biomass in tropical waters, but despite its abundance and enormous importance to the ecosystem, it remained unknown until 1988.

Whatever the true number of species actually is, it is clear that we may have a severe lack of knowledge when it comes to Earth's biodiversity. Sadly without this knowledge we also cannot know the true number of species lost due to our activities, and there will be many species lost that we never discover nor their place in the ecosystem. Without a better understanding of the species that exist on the planet, we also risk missing an essential piece of the puzzle that may help us to prevent species loss and ecological degradation or miss a species that could be amazingly beneficial to humans. We really don't know what we could be missing. It's estimated that it could take humanity 1200 years or more to catalog all of the Earth's life. Unfortunately, at the current rate of extinction, we cannot wait for this knowledge to stem biodiversity loss. We must find a way despite what we do not know while pushing to learn as much as we can.

We have only guesses on how many total species there are, but what do we know? The Catalog of Life lists nearly 1.9 million known and described species, but the Catalog acknowledges that this is probably only 80 percent of the total and that the true total of described species is somewhere around 2.2 million. Even among the species that science has described, we have little certainty about the precise number. This highlights the enormous task of finding, describing, and compiling data on Earth's life. What we do know includes more than 6,000 mammals, 11,000 birds, over 30,000 species of fish, 146,000 species of fungi, nearly 400,000 species of plants, and an astonishing 1 million described species of insects. Despite the numerous difficulties of finding new species, we are making progress, and scientists describe somewhere around 18,000 new species every year.

Even more important than the diversity of life, are the interactions between that life. Even though we look at Earth's organisms as distinct species as we name and categorize them to further understand what our world contains, species do not exist in isolation. They are all part of a rich tapestry of interwoven life, threaded together as a single system that blankets the world. Life is dependent on other life, and that life is dependent on still more in a never-ending web of interactions.

All organisms inherently depend on others. These relationships are easiest to see when they intimately depend on another organism for survival. These close relationships in nature we call symbiosis, and the closest of these symbiotic relationships is called mutualism. This is where one species is highly reliant on the existence of another, to the benefit of each. These species have typically evolved together over a long period of time, each benefiting from the other in a way that makes both more successful. One of the more common examples of this relationship, and one most of us have experienced, is lichen. Lichen is a fungus that has, living within its filament structure, photosynthetic algae or cyanobacteria (also called blue-green algae, although they are not algae). In this relationship, the fungus receives nourishment from the algae or cyanobacteria made from the sun, and in return, it receives protection and a better living environment. There are thousands of species of lichens attesting to the success of this arrangement, and lichens are found throughout the world in a wide range of environments.

Another striking example of mutualism is a particular species of South American flower that is nearly solely dependent on a single species of hummingbird, not only an example of a mutualistic relationship, but also a fantastic example of coevolution. The flower is *Passiflora mixta,* a member of the passion flower family, and its companion is called the sword-billed hummingbird (*Ensifera ensifera*). Upon seeing this fantastic little bird, the reason for its name is immediately apparent. These hummingbirds have one of the longest bills of any bird relative to their size. With an overall length from head to tail of just 14-15 cm (5.5-6 in), they can have a bill as long as an amazing 10 cm (4 in). The reason for this supremely extended sword-face is the flower in which it likes to feed. The *Passiflora* has a long tube-like flower, and the swordbill is the only hummingbird with an appendage long enough to reach the back of this flower where the nectar is found. As the swordbill feeds, its feathers pick up pollen from the interior of the flower, carrying it to the next flower it feeds on. This arrangement gives benefit to both species. The swordbill has evolved alongside this flower and gained an exclusive food source, a highly valued asset to any animal, especially one with the caloric demand of a hummingbird. The *Passiflora*, in turn, gains an especially effective mode of pollination.

One of the most important symbiotic relationships found in nature is common to nearly every terrestrial plant. Thought to have originated when plants first began to inhabit the land, the intimate relationship between soil fungus and plants has been going on for hundreds of millions of years. More than 90% of plant species form these symbiotic relationships, called mycorrhiza. Filaments of soil fungi intersect and sometimes even infiltrate the roots of living plants. The fungi provide several services to plants. They help protect from disease and predation by insects, provide the main source of phosphorus for plants by extracting it from the soil, and provide structure to house beneficial soil bacteria, especially ones that fix nitrogen. In exchange for their services, the fungi and bacteria receive carbon-rich exudates from the plants. These relationships underlie the productivity of all of the terrestrial ecosystems on Earth, and without them, the existence of terrestrial plant life would not be possible.

There are numerous other types of symbiotic relationships. In commensalism, a species is directly dependent on another species without harming or benefiting the species it depends on. These commensal species are highly diverse and, many times, highly specific to the species they depend on. Almost every animal on the planet has one or more species of mites that live on it, humans included. We actually have two *Demodex folliculorum* and *Demodex brevis.* These tiny, nearly microscopic, creatures feed in our sweat glands and hair follicles; we are their habitat, but are entirely unaffected by their existence. Another example of this style of symbiosis is the cattle egret *(Bubulcus ibis)*, which, as its name suggests, follows cattle and other large grazers. As the grazers move through the environment, the egrets collect insects and other small prey disturbed by their movements, thus getting an easy meal without bothering the grazers themselves.

There exists a third major type of symbiosis among life: parasitism. In this relationship, one species benefits, while the other is in some way harmed. In these cases, one species lives off another by consuming blood, tissue, or robbing nutrients from its host species. Common examples include intestinal worms, flukes, and certain types of insects. Large parasites are typically rare, but two notable examples are the vampire bat, of which there are three parasitic species, and two species of oxpecker bird. These animals both survive through hematophagy, or the drinking of blood.

While close symbiotic relationships are clearly representative of the dependence of life on other life, the connection between species is rarely so clear. A multitude of species may rely on the interactions of a few, or even a single species in surprising ways, and these relationships can impact entire landscapes. Species that occupy these important roles are often called "keystone" species. Their existence can help hold together an entire ecosystem by promoting biodiversity through their interactions with the environment and other species. The sea otter (*Enhydra lutris*) is one such species. Native to the Northern Pacific coasts, these adorable mats of fur spend their days floating and swimming about in the cool waters from Northern California to Alaska, extending across the Arctic Sea to Russia. They are excellent divers, and this is the mode by which they procure their food, which typically consists of small crustaceans, clams, mussels, and snails, but one of their particular favorites is the most important. Sea otters eat sea urchins. Where they live off the coast of the United States, the undersea environment is dominated by kelp forests, and just like a forest on land, these forests support countless other organisms. This rich and diverse environment supports numerous species of rockfish and shelters the young of many offshore species of fish, providing them with a critical habitat in their early growth. It also provides habitat for the prey of dozens of species of birds, sea lions, and even helps support gray whales and their young. Sea urchins prey on kelp. Left unchecked, they can turn a thriving kelp forest into a sea urchin barren. Sea otters help keep down the population of sea urchins by eating them, thus allowing the kelp beds to thrive. Without the sea otter, the kelp forests could disappear, and with them, the rest of the biodiversity they support.

Some species may seem unlikely promoters of biodiversity. Many people who live in the western United States are probably familiar with prairie dogs, but many may not realize the important role they play in the diversity of America's Great Plains. Prairie dogs, consisting of five different species, are members of the squirrel family, and like their relative, the ground squirrel, they are a burrowing species but live in large groups called towns. Over 100 different species are aided by these colonies, and measurably higher biodiversity is observed in landscapes that contain prairie dog colonies. Not only are they an important prey species for many plains hunters, such as the endangered and once thought extinct black footed ferret *(Mustela nigripes)*, ferruginous hawks, red tailed hawks, harriers, prairie falcons, coyotes, and swift foxes, but they also change the environment around them. Their burrows provide shelter and nesting for a variety of prairie species, including burrowing owls, several species of rabbit and hare, foxes, the Great Plains toad, and the prairie rattlesnake. Not only this, but their burrowing integrates organic matter into the soil, breaks up compaction, and allows water to better penetrate the soil, storing vital subsoil moisture in the often parched plains. Their constant pruning of the vegetation surrounding their towns also changes the makeup of the vegetation. The short cropped grass attracts the threatened mountain plover *(Charadrius montanus),* and prairie dog towns are among their favorite nesting sites. Some prairie plants only grow in the presence of the colonies, and both the native grazers and domestic cattle prefer grazing on the results of the prairie dogs' work.

In some cases, the actions of multiple species boost biodiversity, and an unlikely pairing between one of Africa's smallest creatures and its largest is vital to maintaining the life of its storied plains. Waterholes are essential features in the African landscape. Without them, many of the species found on the plains of the continent would struggle to survive the dry seasons, or be restricted to habitat within reach of rivers. These vital oases allow Africa's wildlife to spread across the landscape and utilize greater resources, increasing the wealth of life in the African grasslands. The creation of these waterholes starts with a termite. Termite mounds dot the landscape of the plains. A key component of these mounds is a special clay manufactured by worker termites. Besides being an excellent building material, this clay is rich in nutrients and salts. Inevitably, these mounds will be abandoned, and after some time, wind and water will degrade them to a clay patch, scarring the grassland. Elephants are attracted to these clay patches. They seek them out for the salt and minerals they contain, and here begins the building of a waterhole. Elephants excavate some of this clay, leading to a depression. At the first heavy rain, these depressions collect water and turn the clay to mud. Elephants love mud. They use it to keep cool and to protect themselves from the sun and insects. The depression quickly becomes a mud wallow. As the elephants remove mud from the wallow (as much as a ton per visit), the hole widens and deepens, and after a few years it becomes a full-fledged pool. Elephants even serve to channel water into these new pools. The tracks they make to and from wallows and waterholes act as conduits that channel rainwater into the depressions. They further increase the richness of the oasis by helping to transport seeds, fish eggs, and nutrients in the form of dung. Dozens of species benefit from the watering holes, from the large mammals of the plains and their predators to fish, amphibians, and birds. Without the elephants, these oases would not exist, and without the termites, the mineral-rich clay would not exist. A loss of either species in this unlikely pairing could have a profound effect on the entire plains ecosystem.

One of the most important ways life interacts is through the transfer of energy and the recycling of nutrients and organic matter. All ecosystems have two main types of organisms, producers and consumers. Producers are typically photo-synthesizers (primarily phytoplankton and algae in the oceans and plants on land), and consumers either directly eat these organisms or eat organisms that eat producers. So a simple illustration of how this works and how important even a small, single-celled producer can be goes like this: We start with a phytoplankton bloom. This impressive natural event happens when the conditions are right for an explosion in the population. Dust blown from the deserts of Africa, for example, can fertilize huge swaths of ocean. The phytoplankton takes advantage of this opportunity to multiply on a massive scale by combining rich nutrients with solar energy. In weeks, the blooms explode into trillions of individual plankton, so large they are visible from space. Within these blooms, the minute organisms take sunlight and convert it into a usable form for other ocean life. These phytoplankton are then consumed by larger zooplankton. These are small, unicellular or multicellular animals that abound all throughout the ocean. These zooplankton are consumed by larger animals like small fish, which are consumed by larger fish, who are consumed by a yet larger consumer such as a dolphin. Energy is flowing up the food chain, starting ultimately with the sun and ending at a large consumer. These large consumers and the smaller ones below them on the chain give back to the system in the form of nutrients they excrete through waste. This in turn feeds more types of plankton in the water column, and as it descends to the ocean floor, it feeds a host of creatures that have adapted to this "marine snow" (the ever-falling detritus from the shallower parts of the ocean that includes shed fish scales, the carcasses of all kinds of sea life, and of course a huge amount of fish and mammal poop) as a food source.

The reality, of course, of the flow of energy and nutrients throughout the environment is much more complex than this linear example. Steps are sometimes much shorter. For example, baleen whales subsist on small fish and krill, which both feed directly on phytoplankton, but the basis for food webs in both marine systems and on land are nearly always the same. Producers largely use photosynthesis to produce energy as the starting point, and consumers utilize this energy from there by either eating producers directly or eating things that do. I say largely because there is a system that operates outside the normal sun-driven cycle. Deep in the ocean, where no light exists, most organisms still rely ultimately on energy from the sun, but thanks to the geology of the Earth, there are species that have adapted to live independent of the sun. This life surrounds boiling hot, nutrient rich water from volcanic under-sea vents. Instead of energy from the sun, bacteria living near these vents can produce energy from hydrogen sulfide and other chemicals contained in this scalding environment. Here, these bacteria comprise the basis for a diverse ecosystem of creatures that once again surprise us with their existence.

We've briefly seen how energy flows from the bottom up, so to speak, but as organisms integrate nutrients from growth, what completes the cycle as these organisms eventually die? The organisms responsible for recycling nutrients are broadly called decomposers, and these consumers play a vital role in the system. Without them, nutrients that are integrated into the structures of plants, animals, and us would be locked away with no way to return the resources for others to use. Without their action, the earth's land would quickly be stripped of available nutrients, and with nothing decaying, life as we know it would soon cease. Most have seen mushrooms growing on dead logs, and they are one of the most visible of this group. Fungi, along with types of bacteria, molds, and insects, all do the work to break down organic matter, providing nourishment for themselves while releasing nutrients back into the environment. In the oceans, many of the nutrients from waste and expired creatures end up on the seafloor and are lost to producers until they are brought near the surface by ocean currents. Nutrients originating on land also play important roles in the ocean ecosystem, and, in part, the ocean relies on the same organisms to recycle nutrients as terrestrial ecosystems. Nutrient transfer between the ocean and land can occur in both directions, with land-based nutrients being released into the ocean by wind and freshwater sources. Nutrients from the ocean make their way to land via fish consumed by land-based animals such as sea birds, bears, and, of course, humans.

In any of these cases, the extinction of a key species could have far-reaching consequences for others or even ensure the extinction of another. However, it is worth noting how crucial certain groups of organisms are to life on Earth. Without fungi on land to support plant life and recycle nutrients and phytoplankton in the ocean to feed a wealth of organisms, life on Earth would be dramatically different. Anything threatening the functioning of either of these groups of organisms could be catastrophic to the way life functions on Earth. Biodiversity helps protect against such an occurrence. There are 140,000 or more species of fungus and more than 25,000 known species of phytoplankton, many of which play the same roles in the environment. Even in the event of the loss of some, the vital functions they provide will continue. This is seen throughout life, and just like the web of an orb weaver spider, the links in the web of life are largely redundant. Even if a few elements are lost, the structure remains sound. As the loss increases, the structure begins to break down and eventually fails. Some parts of the structure are more important than others. Key attachment points of the web, just like keystone species in nature, are essential for the structure of the web, and loss of these elements severely affects its form. The web might still exist without one of these elements, but in a deteriorated and less functional state. As the natural processes of Earth continue, environments eventually change, species die out, new ones emerge, and populations shift. All of this has an effect on the environment and other organisms. The more links there are in the web, the less any one event will cause major disruption, but as we've seen with mass extinction events, species loss can create a domino effect. As more and more species in the web are lost, the system begins to break down. Other species relying on them suffer, and the entire system becomes weaker. As this process continues, the system becomes more fragile, and this will inevitably lead to collapse.

The Earth is now rapidly losing species. It's easy to believe that the resilience of life will prevent the collapse of our planet's ecosystems, but the reality is that we do not have an understanding of how much loss can be tolerated before the system begins to fail. It appears more and more likely that with some systems, we may already be approaching critical turning points. The key to preserving the structure of the web of life is keeping as many species as possible in the system. It is true that the system would most likely recover, but in the case of a mass extinction event, one we may currently be causing, recovery will take millions of years, a long time for future humans to wait for a functional ecosystem, if they still exist at all. Thus, biodiversity is just as essential for humans as it is for all the other life on the planet. Even though humans have been able to largely free ourselves of many of the biological constraints that all other species must live by, we are still entirely reliant on our home planet for our survival. Despite our intelligence and technology, we are simply not able to replace the vital functions that are provided to us by the Earth's ecosystems and are, like it or not, inextricably linked to human well-being. These systems, kept in balance by a combination of geologic processes and the rich biota of the Earth, work together to regulate the atmosphere, provide nutrients, clean and regulate water, and function to keep Earth's climate stable.

The Earth's biodiversity is important, and humans need to make it a priority. If not for the sake of the non-human life on our world, then at the very least for our own. 70 percent of the world's oxygen comes from the oceans, from phytoplankton, algae, and kelp, with the remaining largely from tropical rainforests. We are completely dependent on these photosynthetic organisms, like nearly all life, not just as a basis for our food but also for the very necessary component of air we breathe. A major disruption in one of these ecosystems would not only severely impact the species that use them for food or habitat, but could affect all aerobic species on the planet. Both aquatic and terrestrial ecosystems also function to remove 5.6 gigatons of carbon from the atmosphere annually. These carbon sinks are not only necessary for maintaining atmospheric gas balance; they are also becoming increasingly important in combating climate change. Here again, disruption could be catastrophic in terms of climate. These biological carbon sinks sequester up to 60% of human carbon emissions, and increasing losses and degradation to these ecosystems could result in billions of tons more CO_2 remaining in the atmosphere, leading to even faster global warming.

Biodiversity is essential for our production and procurement of food. 75 percent of all food crops rely on animal pollination, and losses of these pollinators could collapse global food supplies. As important, are the health and productivity of our soils, which depend on the aforementioned fungi and soil microbes that fix nitrogen, break down organic matter, and are essential for nutrient and phosphorus availability. Disruptions in these crucial soil systems are already restricting the availability of arable land. 3.3 billion people rely on seafood for their primary source of protein, and fish make up 17 percent of the animal protein consumed worldwide. Stocks of fish and other seafood are obviously highly reliant on a healthy ocean ecosystem. Coral reefs are essential to the health of many of the ocean's fish stocks and serve as breeding grounds and shelter for young fish. These same reefs also protect 200 million people in coastal communities from storm surges and wave action.

Water movement across the globe is largely regulated by the life contained on the planet's landscapes, and the most important of these are the tropical rain forests. The size and location of these forests affect the weather patterns of the entire planet. Deforestation of the rainforests converts them from dense canopied forests that absorb water and then release it, as much as 20 billion tons per day, to dry open savanna. As a result, normal weather patterns are disrupted, and this can severely affect populations that rely on the moisture and regulation these forests provide. São Paulo, Brazil, is a key example. The 20 million residents of this South American city rely on the water that the forest supplies. Forest loss has decreased the amount of water the city sees, and as a result, in 2014, São Paulo nearly ran out of water in the worst drought seen in over 80 years. Forest loss is expected to reduce annual rainfall here by as much as 20 percent, meaning the water crisis will continue. The effects of this drying of the rainforest are not just local, and continued reduction of this valuable resource will affect rainfall patterns globally. There is significant concern among scientists that rainforest loss in the Amazon may already have approached a point where an irreversible conversion to savanna might occur.

According to the USDA, 40 percent of the prescription drugs in use today are derived from natural sources, and the top 20 best-selling medications are all plant derived. Fully 70 percent of cancer fighting drugs used today are naturally derived or are synthetic compounds based on naturally occurring substances. Additionally, nearly 4 billion people rely on natural medicines for their health-care. These facts, combined with the large gap in our knowledge of species, suggest that there could be any number of useful medicinal compounds produced in nature, almost none of which we know of or can exploit at this time. Bio-diversity loss could, especially in highly biologically rich environments, easily wipe out a cure for any number of human diseases. For example, scientists in Brazil have come across a component in the venom of the Brazilian jararacussu pit viper (*Bothrops jararacussu*) that can help combat COVID-19. A peptide isolated from the venom can disrupt the action of an enzyme in the coronavirus that is essential to its reproduction. Laboratory tests using monkey cells have shown that this peptide inhibits the reproduction of the COVID-19 virus by 75%. Not only could this finding be helpful in our fight against viruses like COVID-19 and other emerging diseases, but it reinforces the fact that extremely beneficial novel compounds could come from anywhere in nature.

While monetizing the value of nature and its biodiversity should not be the primary reason to protect it, there are legitimate economic reasons to retain biodiversity. It's estimated that more than 50% of the world's GDP, more than $44 trillion USD, is moderately or highly dependent on the services provided by nature. For example, birds provide many important services of great value. Estimates in Sweden's Stockholm Urban National Park put the value of the seed distribution and planting of seeds from just the park's Eurasian jays (*Garrulus glandarius*) at between $210,000 and $950,000. In the United States for humans to perform the dispersal of white pine seeds in the absence of the Clark's nutcracker (*Nucifraga columbiana*) would cost between 11.4 and 13.9 billion dollars across the tree's range. In the state of Washington, the value of the evening grosbeak's (*Hesperiphona vespertina*) consumption of the spruce budworm each year is placed at $1820 per square kilometer. These are just a handful of examples among thousands. It's impossible to put a true dollar value on all of the services that nature provides, but it's clear that biodiversity loss comes at a huge economic price. It is prohibitively expensive to replace the functions of lost biodiversity if, indeed, we could replace them at all.

Besides the ecosystem services that species provide, there are the adaptations that allow them to perform these functions, and within each species are the stores of genetic information that allow them to do it. The potential loss of genes through extinction and population collapse puts biodiversity at risk and can lead to yet more extinctions. It's known that the more genetically diverse a population of organisms is, the more likely it is that some members will have a natural immunity to, say, an emerging disease, or will have the genes necessary to adapt to a changing environment, or an introduced species. Small populations, with little diversity, could easily succumb to a new disease or other stressor. Rich genomes also have a greater chance of giving rise to new species, and the loss of this genetic biodiversity could hamper speciation. This loss of diversity over time may result in a much less diverse world as a whole, putting ecosystem productivity and resilience at risk. The loss of biodiversity will be felt now and likely far into the future. Of course, the impact on humanity is evident. Less robust ecosystems will threaten us as much as any other species, providing yet another valid reason to preserve the life around us.

The multifaceted benefit of biodiversity to humans runs deeper than many imagine, and it is becoming more evident that we rely on nature for more than what it physically provides for us. There is mounting evidence that suggests that biodiversity plays a part directly in humans' psychological well-being. It has been well documented that natural surroundings are of great benefit to humans. Studies have shown that patients in hospitals with natural views recover faster, and that natural environments are beneficial in the reduction of stress, high blood pressure, are beneficial in pain management, and that access to natural environments promotes overall well-being. What we didn't realize was that the nature of this nature may also play a role. Researchers in the UK have found that the benefits of natural landscapes increase with increased biodiversity. This unexpected revelation means that the species richness of an environment seems to have an effect on how we benefit psychologically from that environment. They found that areas perceived to have a greater biological diversity had a more positive effect on human test subjects than less diverse surroundings. Humans seem to be more at ease when surrounded by more life. This suggests that not only is the loss of natural places harmful to humans' mental health, but that a reduction in diversity in those natural spaces may be to our detriment at even a physiological level.

Lastly, nature has always played an important role in human culture and society, going back as far into history as we can find. Throughout human history, we have looked at nature with reverence. Our ancestors saw nature and its majesty and integrated the natural world into their most sacred beliefs and institutions. From the ancient Norse "tree of life" to the status of cats in ancient

Egypt to the lion that has represented the strength of the British monarchs for a thousand years, nature has played a crucial part in so many human cultures. We often saw animals as spirits or gods, and the Earth as our life-giving mother. We even see these traditions continue in our sports teams, so often named to invoke the cunning spirit of the tiger or the strength of the bear. The loss of nature and the life we share this planet with degrades this common heritage. It's important to remember that there are sound scientific and moral reasons for preserving Earth's biodiversity, but these are not the only reasons. The natural world has played a pivotal role in human culture, and the extinction of something that someone finds sacred should be abhorrent to all of us.

By far the two greatest factors that cause a loss of biodiversity are habitat loss and the introduction of species around the world. Certainly, the main driver of habitat loss is agriculture, which now takes up more than one third of the entire planet in land area. The majority of this land is used as pasture for cattle or for the production of animal feed, thus highlighting the huge environmental cost of human consumption of animals and the way in which we raise them. Agriculture's impact has already led to the near extinction of entire habitats, including the vast majority of global wetlands and the tallgrass prairies of the American Midwest. In fact, even places we see as wild, untouched landscapes have usually seen significant human impacts at some point in the past. Deforestation is largely driven by the expansion of agricultural lands, and the ever-growing human population increases the urbanization that is ever-encroaching on wildlands. Research predicts that if current rates of urban expansion continue, by 2030 urban areas will expand by 1.2 million sq km, or three times the total global urban area in 2000. More concerning for the effect on biodiversity is that much of this growth is expected to take place in the highly biodiverse tropics.

Nearly as devastating as the loss of habitat, and in some cases more, is the introduction non-native species. Organisms can be moved by stowing away in ships, planes, and even people. The result is the worldwide spread of species to new environments. When native species meet these newcomers, they can struggle to cope with organisms that evolved in different parts of the world. Examples of the havoc caused by these invasive species abound. Most likely, humans helped to spread the deadly species of chytrid fungus that is now devastating the world's frog populations and has already led to numerous extinctions. On the island of Guam, 60 percent of its native bird species are now extinct, largely due to invasive species introductions, particularly of the brown tree snake *(Boiga irregularis)*. Native to Southeast Asia, they were inadvertently brought to Guam, likely stowed away on planes or cargo ships arriving from their native range. Their presence on an island with no native snakes has led to the extinction or extirpation of 9 out of the 12 species of forest birds and is considered an enormous ecological threat to the entire region. Zebra mussels, accidentally introduced into the Great Lakes in the 1980s, are now spreading throughout the U.S., threatening waterways and native species by outcompeting native mussels and filtering out plankton that they rely on for food. These tiny mussels multiply extremely rapidly and are easily transported, unseen, to new waterways. Once established, they can initially reduce phytoplankton biomass by 80-90%, collapsing local aquatic ecosystems and pushing already stressed species to extinction.

Plants are also susceptible to invaders with potentially devastating effects, a case in point is the story of the American chestnut tree *(Castanea dentata)*. The chestnut once dominated the eastern forests of the United States, making up one quarter of all the trees found in its range. This majestic tree, with a combination of a straight long trunk, durable rot resistant wood, prolific nutritious nut production, and rapid growth rate, led many to call it the perfect tree. Growing to 30 meters (100 ft) tall and up to 4 meters (14 ft) in circumference, they produced thousands of nuts each season and constituted an impressive and significant presence in the forest. Once numbering in the billions of individuals, they are now functionally extinct, unable to reproduce as chestnut blight kills back the new growth from still living roots. The few remaining trees still living in the wild struggle on in isolation. The blight is caused by a fungus from Asia *(Cryphonectria parasitica)*, introduced in the early 1900s on Asian chestnut trees imported into the U.S. By the 1950s, the rapidly spreading fungus had nearly wiped out the entire population of the American chestnut, and with it, an entire forest ecosystem.

As disappointing as the cases above are, they are at least accidental, but humans have an unfortunate history of intentionally introducing species to the peril of native flora and fauna. For example, in the 1930s, Australian farmers having issues with cane beetles in their sugar cane fields imported the cane toad from South America. These highly toxic toads not only did not eat the cane beetles but left the fields and started feeding on the native wildlife. Having no natural predators in its new environment and being fatally toxic to Australia's native predators such as birds, lizards, and even crocodiles, populations quickly exploded, and today they are found throughout the entirety of northeastern Australia. Particularly threatened by the toad's existence is the northern quoll. This predatory marsupial's population has been in decline, with many having been poisoned by eating the toads. This species may be particularly vulnerable due to an oddity in its breeding behavior. Male quolls die after breeding, making additional losses from a toxic non-native invader much more impactful. It's also been shown that up to a third of the nests of native rainbow bee-eater bird fail due to destruction by the extremely numerous cane toads. According to the WWF, there are now an estimated 200 million of these toads, and little can now be done to stem their spread.

One of the worst cases of intentional species introduction gone wrong is in Africa. In the late 1950s, British colonists introduced the Nile perch into the waters of Lake Victoria, which is famous for its 500 species of cichlid fish that are all likely descended from a single ancestor. The colonists thought that the huge predatory fish would make for good sport fishing; what they didn't take into consideration was the toll on the native fish that had never encountered such a predator. The result was an ecological disaster, with entire communities of species lost and a complete reorganization of the Lake Victoria ecosystem. After 20 years, the perch populations hit critical mass and exploded. Surveys in 1978 found that native cichlids constituted 80% of the biomass of the lake. By 1984, some parts of the lake were showing that 80% of the fish biomass were now Nile perch, and that only a few small populations of native fish remained. In all, 200 species of cichlids in Lake Victoria have either gone extinct or are threatened with extinction.

The human-caused transfer of species across the globe also leads to a phenomenon called "species homogenization." As non-natives replace local species, biodiversity decreases. As a result, fewer species are found globally, leading to a planet that is less diverse and thus homogenized in respect to species. Instead of a rich and diverse world, invasive species make communities of plants or animals more similar over time. This not only leads to a less interesting world but can have severe consequences for the functioning of healthy ecosystems by removing key species and the services they provide. The loss of genetic diversity as a result of homogenization also risks life's ability to adapt in an ever changing world. In the U.S. alone, there are over 6,500 species identified as harmful invasive species, with an estimated economic cost of 100 billion dollars per year. The environmental cost is even higher. 40% of all species extinctions that have a known cause are due to invasive species.

While habitat loss and species introductions are historically the largest factors in biodiversity loss, there are other direct human-driven pressures that are issues of concern. For example, legal and illegal hunting can have devastating impacts on particular species. The loss of a huge number of Africa's most iconic animals is a good example. The two species of African elephant, the endangered bush elephant *(Loxodonta africana)* and the critically endangered African forest elephant *(L. cyclotis)*, have been hunted for their ivory for centuries. In an attempt to save these animals, a ban on the sale of Ivory was put in place in 1990. However, illegal poaching for ivory continues to be a lucrative endeavor. There were as many as 26 million elephants at the onset of European exploration, the ivory trade and sport hunting had reduced the elephant population to just 600,000 by 1989. Since the ban, some populations have seen recovery, but unfortunately, populations overall are still decreasing. Between 2007 and 2014, the Great Elephant Census observed a 30% drop in total elephant populations. Due to poaching, elephant populations are estimated to be dropping by 8% per year. Even more alarming is the decline of some specific populations of elephants. The forest elephant populations in central Africa declined by 66% from 2002 to 2011; likewise, the savanna elephant populations of Selous Wildlife Reserve in Tanzania dropped by the same amount in just five years from 2009 to 2013. There are now probably less than 400,000 elephants total left in the wild. African rhinos share the elephants' unfortunate circumstance. Now critically endangered, the black rhino's (Diceros bicornis) population was once as high as 100,000 as late as the 1960s. Poaching had reduced that number to fewer than 2,500 animals 20 years ago. Fortunately, through protections, this number had at one time doubled.

Unfortunately, poaching is once again on the rise and is expected to continue to increase. Research suggests that there will be a continued decline in rhino populations. Poaching has already resulted in the extinction of two African rhino subspecies in the wild, with current estimates indicating that fewer than 4,000 black rhinos remain. Sadly, as you will see later, the loss of species through direct killing by humans is not as uncommon as one would think and continues to threaten numerous animals around the world.

Certainly the greatest emerging threat to Earth's life is human-caused climate change and the myriad of associated threats that come with it. It is likely that the effects of a hotter Earth will soon become the primary driver of species loss. Already, the warming of the climate has begun to change ecological communities as species shift in response to the warming temperatures. Climate-caused range shifts have been recorded in more than 30,000 species of plants and animals. To escape their ever-warming environments, terrestrial species are now moving towards the poles at a rate of 15 km (9 mi) every decade, and marine animals are moving as much as 75 km (46 mi). Mountain species move to higher elevations (if they can) and aquatic species to deeper waters. As these species move, the makeup of ecosystems, and the species interactions within them change. Mobile species seek out better conditions, and less mobile species are left behind. As a result, the rapid restructuring of ecological communities disrupts their stability, with species dealing not only with rising temperatures and less stable weather patterns but also with a new set of unfamiliar species. Disrupted ecosystems are much less resilient to stress, and this comes just as they need that resilience the most. In the foreseeable future, many of the world's ecosystems and the species they contain will be in constant flux as temperatures continue to rise. This will seriously risk the world's biodiversity and many species will not be able to survive this instability. The emergence of climate change, coupled with the already severe pressures humans are placing on nature, may prove to be a devastating combination for Earth's living systems.

All of Earth's life works in concert to maintain the ecosystems of the planet, even while often competing with one another. It's one of the beauties of nature. Disparate organisms, connected in remarkable ways, are all a part of a wildly complex system that maintains life as we know it. Unfortunately, this life is now under serious threat. Generations of human impacts have damaged key parts of Earth's systems, and preserving the Earth's biodiversity is now more important than ever. With the recent surge in species extinctions and the specter of climate change in mind, the importance of strong interconnectedness in the web of life is critical and necessary to offset the instability to which the planet's environments could be increasingly subjected. The only way we can meet the challenges that are now before us is to help nature continue to thrive so it can, in turn, help us thrive. There is no way forward without this relationship. If the observed rate of biodiversity loss continues, by the middle of this century, Earth could reach a point where species loss is great enough that permanent, irreversible damage could be done to Earth's ecosystems, ushering in a new era on the planet. We could be in danger of creating a world we do not recognize, with little ability to predict what that world may look like and equally little ability to predict which species losses might precipitate such a change. We have flourished in the world the way it is, and we will only continue to flourish if we can prevent, or at least limit that damage. It needs to be done, if not because it's the right thing to do, then for ourselves. It, paradoxically, can be a pursuit that is both selfish and selfless at the same time.

3
The Beginnings

Since humans first evolved on the plains of Africa, we have been, like any animal, impacting the environment around us. This is in no way extraordinary, but what is extraordinary is the unprecedented growth of humans into a global powerhouse. Rapidly multiplying from a small band of upright apes, we and our human cousins changed the world. Our novel use of fire, complex tools, and coordinated hunting was a paradigm shift in the effect of one species on another. As our population grew, our use of ever more complex technology increased our ability to mold the world around us like no other species before. Here we explore the beginnings of this human impact and look at how the development of human societies began creating very modern problems much earlier than most would expect. From the very onset of humans through the "Great Acceleration" beginning in the 1950s, our impact has always been there.

It's hard to imagine what the world was really like before humans, or even in the early days of human history. We fall into the trap of adjusting to the world in which we are born, and each generation in general experiences less abundance in the natural world than the one before it. It skews our ideas of what a rich natural world looks like. Today, one might visit African or American national parks and marvel at the abundance of wildlife, but the reality is that what we see today is often a shadow of what once existed. Nevertheless, there are glimpses into the past. Accounts from explorers and naturalists from even the relatively recent past can give us an idea of what a more natural world looked like. In the western half of the United States, not long after the Revolutionary War, parts of the landscape still looked much like they had for the last several thousand years. Just 200 years ago, parts of North America teemed with an abundance of life scarcely imaginable today.

In 1803, Thomas Jefferson tasked two military men, one his secretary at the time, Meriwether Lewis, and the other, William Clark, to survey the soon-to-be acquired Louisiana Purchase. Their job was to ascend the Missouri River and attempt to find a water linkage to the Pacific coast. During the trip to the Pacific and back, they were to record everything they saw, including the lay of the land, rivers, minerals, indigenous peoples and their habits, plant life, and, most importantly for our purposes here, the animals that they encountered. They began in St. Louis in May of 1804 and, as they began to ascend the river, they were almost immediately taken aback by the richness of the environment around them. Clark describes a virtual Midwestern Eden, covered with rich green grass, wildflowers, bushes of "the most delicious fruit," and crystal clear brooks and streams shaded by copses of stately trees. The rivers teemed with fish, the shores with elk, deer, and bear. At night they camped in verdant prairies with grass 8 feet tall interspersed with wild plums, raspberries, currents, and grapes. As the journey continued north into the shortgrass prairie of the upper Midwest, the sheer quantity of wildlife astounded them. In September of 1804, Lewis is moved by the sight of a herd of bison, writing, "I do not think I exaggerate when I estimate the number of Buffaloe which could be compreed at one view to amount to 3000." Little did he know at the time that this sight would pale in comparison to what was to come.

Everywhere the party looked, there was abundance, and on top of every prominence, a view of a vast and seemingly endless wilderness full of life. Upon ascending a high prairie hilltop, Clark writes that he can see 50 miles, the entire way scattered with bison to the horizon. As they reached (now) South Dakota, they began to see signs of grizzly bears far beyond their current range and were witness to a huge migration of pronghorn antelope, now long forgotten. They often use the word "immense" to describe herds of bison, elk, antelope, and deer. Lewis relates that they can look in any direction at any time and see one or more of these animals. Almost as common were wolves, with Lewis writing that gangs of buffalo are rarely seen without being trailed by the bison's "scarcely less numerous shepards." Wolves were not the only abundant predators, and by the time they reached what is now Montana, they were encountering grizzly bears almost daily. Beaver and river otters flourished in the streams and rivers, and only increased in numbers as they moved west. The Pacific Coast held treasures of its own. Great quantities of salmon were to be found far up the Columbia River, as well as seals, and (once again) "immense" flocks of waterfowl. Even more of an example of the intact natural environment was the sighting on multiple occasions of several California condors *(Gymnogyps californianus)*. These, North America's largest bird, now only number a little over 300 wild individuals *after* an extensive recovery program.

After wintering on the Pacific Coast, the expedition returned the way they had come, but the wonders of this vast wilderness only seemed to increase. Once again reaching buffalo country, the size of the bison herds they observed was truly mind-boggling. Lewis estimates one herd at 10,000 individuals, and Clark estimates another at 20,000. Lewis recounts his party having to wait as much as an hour to let a single herd cross in front of them. As unimaginable as the vastness of these herds is, they only seemed to get larger. While traveling on horseback, Lewis and his group passed what he believed to be one single herd of bison for a distance of 12 miles. The number of animals, surely in the tens of thousands. Clark, at one point, even writes, "for me to mention or give an estimate of the different species of wild animals on this river particularly buffalo, elk, antelopes and wolves would be incredatable." Lewis and Clark encountered an American West that we today can scarcely imagine, and certainly one that no living person has seen. Their journey describes an enormous, thriving grassland ecosystem rivaled only by the great grasslands of Africa. Others would follow to see and describe these same wonders.

In 1843, the famous American naturalist, John James Audubon, repeated the first segment of Lewis and Clark's journey on the Missouri River, traveling as far north as its confluence with the Yellowstone River in what is now North Dakota. The reason for the trip was to collect and draw specimens for his book on the quadrupeds of North America. Being a naturalist, Audubon gives a detailed account of the birds and animals he encountered on his journey, and the abundance and variety that he observed are no less impressive than what Lewis and Clark encountered. His journals reveal that 40 years later the Midwestern U.S. still teamed with an amount of life unheard of today. In a journal entry for May 4th, 1843, he gives an account of the wildlife encountered on just that single day while traveling the river some miles south of St. Joseph, Mo. Besides recording and collecting numerous small mammals, his list includes more than 50 species of birds, including bald eagles, peregrine falcons, numerous species of woodpeckers, warblers, thrushes, waterbirds, and finches including a new and undescribed species of finch, and dozens of the the now extinct Carolina parakeet. Audubon does not relate how many miles they traveled that day, but they were traveling upstream at the time. Progress on the river was slow, and it's likely that all of these species were found within just a few miles of each other. Any naturalist today would be thrilled at seeing such diversity in such a small area in what is now the farmlands of Kansas and Missouri.

As they move north along the river, his party begins to see more of the wildlife of the Great Prairie. Of the bison herds, Audubon remarks, "In fact it is impossible to describe, or even conceive the vast multitudes of these animals that exist even now, and feed on these ocean-like prairies." Like Lewis and Clark, he too encountered grizzly bears, elk, antelope, and bighorn sheep. Wolves and coyotes were so numerous and the encounters so frequent that he stopped mentioning them in his journal entries. Upon his return trip down the river, he describes encountering a flock of more than 200 meadowlarks on their migration south, and on the lower stretches of the Missouri on the 1st of October, he describes the geese as "innumerable," and two days later "the Geese and Ducks are abundant beyond description."

Even with all the abundance that he did observe, Audubon noticed that some things had changed since Lewis and Clark. The modern world was seeping into the prairie. No longer did beavers and river otters swim this stretch of the Missouri, trapped to near oblivion since Lewis and Clark. He observes that even though the bison herds are still vast, they are noticeably smaller than they once were, stating, "Even now there is a perceptible difference in the size of the herds, and before many years the Buffalo, like the great auk, will have disappeared." Audubon's concern for the bison and wildlife in general was well founded. By the early 1900s, bison were on the brink of extinction. Hunters relentlessly pursued them, killing them by the millions, until, in 1889, the entire population of North America was somewhere around 1,000. Only 85 of these were free-ranging individuals in the United States, and 200 were in the federal herd of the U.S. in Yellowstone National Park. By 1902, this was down to just 23 animals. Audubon was no stranger to seeing the changes coming to North America, and had seen before the human capacity for destruction. On his trip to Labrador in 1833, he saw this destruction firsthand. In his account, he speaks of the tens of thousands of seabird eggs collected by "eggers." He was informed by two of these men that they expected to collect 2,000 dozen eggs in one season. This was multiplied over and over again all throughout the North. Of this rampant exploitation of animal and fowl he laments,

> Nature herself seems perishing. Labrador must shortly be depeopled, not only of aboriginal man, but of all else having life, owing to man's cupidity. When no more fish, no more game, no more birds exist in her hills, along her coasts, and in her rivers, then she will be abandoned and deserted like a worn out field.

While some of North America's pre-European splendor still existed during Audubon's time, it is clear that its rapid destruction was already underway.

These writings give us just a glimpse of the abundance of life that once existed in North America, and certainly a view of a North America that no living person has seen. One that, not too long ago, housed a species abundance and diversity we could scarcely imagine today. However, the Great Plains, while a rich ecosystem, were not as much of an untouched wilderness as it may have appeared to Lewis and Clark. Even here, there was the influence of humans, long before the arrival of European settlers. To be sure, the abundance of plants and wildlife benefited greatly from having millions of acres at their disposal, but the nature of that habitat was considerably influenced by the native peoples living there. For example, humans had been setting fires on the plains for hundreds, maybe even thousands, of years by the time Lewis and Clark arrived. Fires were not only used to signal each other from long distances, they were intentionally set to keep the grasslands healthy and free from trees, and most of all, to attract the animals the Plains peoples used for food. Early on, humans must have learned the connection that fire has with grasslands. Fire is a natural part of the plains and is usually started by lightning. It helps maintain the grassland by releasing nutrients back into the soil. New shoots springing up from a burned area attract grazers, and these grazers are what native peoples used to survive. Setting these fires probably expanded the great grasslands of North America, and humans may have helped to create the awe-inspiring landscape that Lewis, Clark, and Audubon witnessed.

Fires were not the only impact that humans had on this landscape, and there is evidence that humans may be responsible, at least in part, for something that Lewis and Clark did not find. In 1804, the idea of animals going extinct in prehistory was still a relatively new and controversial idea. It wasn't really known if any ever had, or if that was even possible (in fact, Linnaeus himself believed that the number of species was fixed and unchanging). Thomas Jefferson was in the camp that believed that animals did not naturally go extinct (of course, humans had wiped out several species by then and were rapidly killing others). In 1739, a group of 400 French soldiers led by Charles le Moyne (whose snooty sounding official title was the Second Baron de Longueuil) found something no one expected in the Ohio River valley. His men found a marsh with hundreds of huge bones sticking out of it. Longueuil, sensing they had found something important, ordered his men to lug several of the huge bones, including an enormous tusk, through the wilderness. Traveling west towards the Mississippi, they eventually reached New Orleans and arranged to have the bones shipped back to France. The bones perplexed scientists for decades, but Jefferson was convinced that they belonged to a huge living creature that was, as of yet, undiscovered. In his instructions to Lewis, he makes particular mention of observing "the animals of the country generally, & especially those not known in the U.S.; the remains & accounts of any which may be deemed rare or extinct." In 1796, after seeing the bones Longueuil had sent back to France and several other examples from the Ohio Valley and elsewhere, a young scientist in France named Georges Cuvier posited the theory that the bones might be from several animals now extinct. Jefferson's instructions to Lewis were in response to this theory; essentially, he was telling Lewis and Clark to go find this huge animal and prove Cuvier wrong.

The bones that Longueuil found back in 1739 were those of a mastodon that Cuvier later determined was an extinct relative of modern-day elephants. Lewis and Clark didn't find Jefferson's mastodon (much to Jefferson's and my disappointment) or mammoths, giant ground sloths, or cave bears either. By 1804 nearly all of North America's Pleistocene-age megafauna (those weighing more than 55 kg) had vanished. But why? Lewis and Clark report a huge and thriving ecosystem with wildlife in amazing abundance. Similar habitats in Africa still had elephants, multiple species of big cats, and numerous other large mammals. Why were they missing here? The answer may be the evidence of humans' contribution to widespread extinctions and some of the first global scale changes humans would initiate.

It's true that in Lewis and Clark's time Africa was, and still is, home to many large animals, but it turns out even Africa lost multiple species of megafauna long ago. All around the world, there is evidence of the extinction of large mammal species during the Pleistocene. Certainly, climate shifts played a part, but interestingly, these extinctions happened at different times in different parts of the world. The one factor consistent with almost all of these extinctions is that the arrival of humans preceded them. The Pleistocene epoch started 2.5 million years ago. Around this same time, animals of the genus *Homo* came into being on the continent of Africa, and here began the human relationship with the world. While it is hard to know the impact humans had at the early stage of our evolution, there is evidence that even early on, the human relationship with the world was going to be like no animal that had ever come before. Around 1 million years ago, one of our human relatives in Africa, *Homo erectus,* is implicated in the die-off of several species of elephant relatives and a decline in the diversity of carnivores on that continent. This included saber-toothed cats, which continued to thrive on other continents such as North America, still at the time, devoid of humans. This suggests that it is possible that even our early human ancestors could have started the string of extinctions we have seen up until today. Much of the megafauna of Africa, of course, still survives, and when looking at patterns of extinction and human migration in the late Quaternary Period (which includes the Pleistocene and the current Holocene epochs), an interesting thing emerges. Africa, our point of origin, has seen the least amount of large species loss, but as one follows the path of our ancient human relatives and later modern humans, one sees that the farther humans traveled from Africa, the more pronounced these extinctions become. In fact, the places where megafauna loss is most pronounced are the ones where modern humans were the first to arrive, and species losses are more severe with later human arrival.

While this is not fully understood, theories suggest that the long co-evolution of humans and the species of Africa likely reduced, but obviously did not eliminate, the impact that humans had. Likewise, on the continent of Asia, a similar long history of early human habitation may have blunted the impact of later arrivals (at least for a time). Species on these continents had time to adapt to our presence and better tolerate pressures from humans, whereas on other continents such as Australia, North America, and South America, the sudden appearance of modern humans brought an entirely new type of animal to the landscape with extant species ill adapted to their presence. This is not at all surprising given what we know about species introductions today. Humans, in this case, act much like the brown snake introduced to Guam. As human cultures became more adept at hunting through increased cooperation and technology, their impact continued to increase.

As our human ancestors pushed out of Africa and into Eurasia, they began to impact the environment there. Like on the continent of Africa, by the time modern humans arrived to stay 40,000–50,000 years ago, several groups of hominids had already occupied parts of Europe for hundreds of thousands of years, and this may have blunted some of the effects of their arrival. Despite this, losses of megafauna in Eurasia were greater than in Africa during the Pleistocene, but less pronounced than on other continents. The climate, particularly in Europe, appeared to be a significant factor in limiting the reach of ancient and later modern humans. Due to these constraints, animals like the mammoth were able to survive until as recently as 10,500 years ago, although an isolated population of mammoths in Russia lived as recently as 4000 years ago. In this region of the world, it seems that while humans certainly had an impact, and Pleistocene humans certainly were hunting the native fauna, climate seems to be the primary cause of megafauna extinctions. Here, humans may have only had a bit part in these extinctions. Interestingly, the extinction most closely related to the arrival of modern humans is that of *Homo neanderthalensis,* and it's possible that we may be responsible for the extinction of one of our own human relatives.

The somewhat modest effect of humans on native wildlife in Eurasia was not to be seen elsewhere in the world. On the continent of Australia, it has long been believed that humans arrived sometime around 50,000 years ago. This is the first time in history we see modern humans first on the scene. Within 4,000 years of their presumed arrival date, a marked collapse of megafauna species is observed, and fossil evidence suggests that as much as 85% of the large fauna of Australia disappeared. To date this decline, researchers used cores taken from the ocean off the southwest coast of the continent. In these sediment cores, they looked for the spores of a specific dung fungus called *Sporormiella.* The presence of this fungus suggests widespread large land animals. Lots of spores equals lots of poop, which in turn equates to lots of animals making this poop. The dates of the cores spanned from 150 to 43 thousand years ago (kya), and even though there were several known significant climatic shifts during this period, the presence of *Sporormiella* remained high throughout the period until about 45 thousand years ago. After this date, "*Sporormiella* underwent a marked and irreversible decline from 45 to 43.1 kya," indicating a rapid collapse in megafaunal populations. While not definitive proof, it seems highly likely, given the correlation between this collapse and the recent arrival of humans, especially since climatic changes seemed to have little impact, that humans were the main driver of change. Other researchers place climate as an added factor causing long-term stress on populations, while human impacts precipitated the final collapse. New findings may place the date of human arrival as far back as 65,000 years ago, but since no human remains of this age have been found, and this evidence is based on a single site, it's difficult to know how widespread the human population was at the time. It is possible that humans began impacting the continent much earlier than originally believed, but it's clear that many of Australia's megafauna disappeared rapidly, without an identifiable climactic cause, leaving humans as a prime suspect.

Around 20,000 years ago, humans found their way to North America, but it's believed that they didn't become widespread until about 14 kya. Within 2000 years, 37 genera of mammals would be gone, along with 70% of all North American megafauna. While once again, correlation with the arrival of humans does not prove causation, it's hard to deny the coincidence. Further evidence supports that not only did the arrival of humans in general coincide with megafaunal extinctions, but the extinctions themselves parallel the north-south pattern of human migration. Meaning, megafauna extinctions started earlier in the northern part of North America and progressed, in time, southward to South America. Climatic changes certainly played a part, and there is evidence to suggest that some megafaunal extinctions, such as those of mastodons and sloths, were more likely climate-related. That same research suggests, however, that the demise of the mammoth, North America's horses, and its saber-toothed cats were likely due to humans. The primary culture at the time, the Clovis people (named for their very distinctive spear points), were known mammoth hunters. So much so that when Clovis points are found associated with animal remains, 80% of those are from mammoths. While some research suggests that humans may not have been the primary cause of the extinction of North America's giant ground sloths, there is good evidence that at least some of the ancient people of North America were tracking and hunting them. This evidence comes from the deserts of New Mexico in the U.S., where preserved tracks from sloths and humans were found on the edge of an ancient lake. Study of the tracks showed no separation between the sloth tracks and the human tracks laid on top, suggesting that this fascinating bit of geology preserved humans in the act of tracking ground sloths. Of course, this may just be a case of idle curiosity, but is more likely physical evidence of sloth hunting in North America. Supporting the theory is a much more definite find from South America. Here, the 12,600-year-old remains of a giant ground sloth were found, most certainly butchered by humans. Clearly, the early cultures of the Americas were hunting sloths and other large animals and climactic changes or not, humans were likely a significant factor in the disappearance of many North American species.

Finding a butchered sloth in South America should not be surprising. There is little evidence that climate played any major role in megafauna extinctions there. In North America, some megafaunal extinctions do precede when we believe humans first arrived, suggesting climate factors were at work ahead of human arrival. However, South America shows little sign of this, with populations of megafauna considered low, but stable prior to human arrival. South America's megafauna collapse rivaled even North America's, with 40 genera of mammals disappearing and 82 percent of megafaunal species going extinct during the Pleistocene. Sometime about 13,000 years ago, spear points similar to those of the Clovis people appear in the archeological record of the continent. These fishtail projectile points appear at nearly the exact same time as the beginning of South American megafaunal declines. Even more, as the density of these fishtail points increases in the archeological record, the loss of megafauna also increases. This was the case for about 600 years, until around 12,500 years ago, when the number of fishtail points began to decline sharply. This coincides with a drop in the continents' megafauna, and by around 11,000 years ago, these fishtail projectile points and South America's megafauna had almost completely disappeared. The simultaneous rise and fall of hunting points and megafauna populations is clear evidence of a culture hunting large animals at an increased rate until population losses limit the resource. Eventually, as the prey disappears, so does the tool to hunt them. Interestingly, the sloth found butchered by ancient humans and mentioned above coincides almost exactly with the peak of the use of fishtail projectile points.

Humans' role in these extinctions and the timing of their arrival on continents outside of Africa are still hotly debated in the scientific community. We may never know the full extent of the impact of early humans on the environments that they inhabited. However, it is clear that in many cases, early humans played a significant role in shaping the fauna where they lived. Lack of data in the fossil and archeological record prevents a definitive answer. New discoveries will give us insight, but ultimately human behavior may answer this question. We've clearly seen the impact that humans have had over the last 200 years with the near extermination of the bison in just a few decades, not to mention many species that you will meet later. What do we know that would suggest that our ancient ancestors were any different? Certainly, technology increased our ability to destroy, but less technologically advanced humans, given much more time, seem perfectly capable of the same destruction.

One of the last major land masses to be settled by modern humans were the islands of New Zealand, and here we see the last of the major Late Quaternary megafaunal extinctions. Before the arrival of Polynesians in New Zealand at the beginning of the 14th century, there were around nine separate species of large flightless birds living there. Collectively known as moa birds, the largest of these could reach an impressive 3.5 m (12 ft) tall and weigh as much as 230 kg (500 lbs). Following the pattern of later human arrival having an increasingly severe impact, it is believed that all of the species of moa were extinct within 100–200 years of human arrival. There is no doubt here that humans are the primary and likely sole cause of the extinction of these birds. The early New Zealanders wasted no time in exploiting this new and plentiful food source, and moa hunts quickly became a part of Māori culture. The archeological evidence for this is overwhelming, from moa bones found as a part of ritual burials, to the immense number of moa bones found in kitchen middens, and huge arrays of ovens used to cook the birds. The early Māori essentially barbecued the moa into extinction. Supporting evidence also comes from genetic studies performed on the moa. Researchers were able to determine that populations of moa were stable and even increasing for the 4,000 years prior to the arrival of humans. There is no indication that the moa were doing anything other than thriving before humans. While devastating to the moa, the relatively recent arrival of humans to New Zealand can provide valuable information that can shed light on the impact of earlier human arrivals. Always a question in earlier Pleistocene extinctions is what population density of humans would be required to cause a large number of species to disappear? The excellent archeological record of humans in New Zealand allowed researchers to estimate how many people would have been required to cause the disappearance of the moa. The number is surprisingly small. Researchers found that as few as 2,000 humans could have been responsible for wiping out the moa in the entirety of New Zealand. Such a small population of people on New Zealand suggests that earlier extinctions on other continents may not have required large populations of humans to have significant impacts.

Long before the modern era, and even before we spread to the entire globe, we were having a global impact on the Earth's environments. Species extinctions, especially those of large herbivores and predators, not only removed the animals themselves but also caused lasting changes to the environments in which they lived. Entire landscapes changed as humans spread around the world, and while our numbers were still relatively small for thousands of years (as few as 2 million 10,000 years ago), we were still having a consequential impact. As humans moved from strictly hunter-gatherer societies to agricultural ones as far back as 8000 years ago, we began to change soil regimes, clear and burn land, domesticate wild grains, and herd cattle. All of this increased our impact on the environment. Some scientists even suspect that, even at this early date, these activities were changing the world's atmosphere. The trend in prehistoric concentrations of CO_2 and methane in the atmosphere was downward in all of the interglacial periods. However, around 7,000 years ago, CO_2 concentrations abruptly stopped declining and began to rise. The same was seen in methane concentrations about 5,000 years ago. Evidence suggests that the rise of agriculture could be the cause of these observations. The case for the rise in CO_2 is speculative, but climate simulations confirm the possibility, and the rise of methane is almost certainly due to the intensification of rice production at this early time. Surprisingly, even our influence on the atmosphere may go back much farther than ever thought.

Of course, the impact of humans continued. As our populations expanded and our technology increased, we had an ever greater impact on the natural environment. Historians point to around 1500 as the onset of the modern age, and this date is often used as the beginning point for modern species extinction. Although trade had been established in ancient times between many cultures, it is at this point that trade is globalized to include the New World, and driven by ever-increasing maritime technology, the movement of goods between all of the continents increases dramatically. Over the next three centuries, the human population would more than double from 450 million people in 1500 to 1 billion in 1800. Throughout the early modern period, roughly 1500–1800, human impacts on the environment would continue to increase, and the rise of problems we are still dealing with, such as the spread of invasive species, deforestation, and air and water pollution, were already becoming serious issues.

As early as the middle 1500s, international trade and exploration had already distributed new food crops and various other plants around the world. Wheat came to the New World with Columbus, followed by African yams and cashews brought by African slaves, and bananas and citrus fruits introduced by the Spanish. Maize and potatoes had already found their way to Europe and then to Asia, and maize found its way to Africa along with cassava shortly after. For example, the American naturalist William Beebe, on his expeditions to Guyana in the early 20th century, found stands of bamboo from Asia already hundreds of years old, planted by early Dutch settlers in the 17th century. Likewise, the famous Dr. Livingstone, while traveling through Africa in the 1850s, found long abandoned plantations containing South American plants such as pineapple and guava that he presumed were planted by the Portuguese sometime in the 1600s. This rapid spread of new foods around the globe was so pervasive that naturalists were often unsure of where they originated. Not only plants but other organisms were being transported across the world, including viruses, bacteria, insects, and rodents. This is, of course, in addition to the intentional introduction of livestock.

Not only plants and animals were moving but also people. Between 1500 and 1800, over 800,000 Spanish alone migrated to the New World, not to mention thousands more Portuguese, Dutch, and British to North, Central, South America, and the Caribbean.

Like today, the challenge of feeding the human population was present and ever-growing. Already at the start of the 17th century, agricultural demands were changing landscapes around the world. While the data is sparse, it's clear that land conversion was accelerating rapidly during the period. Long before the conversion of America's grasslands to crops, a similar conversion occurred in the steppe landscapes of the southern Russian empire. In the richest parts of the region, tillage nearly doubled between 1719 and 1796, increasing from around 25% to 47%, paralleling expansions in Europe. Japan saw its land tillage double between 1600 and 1720 to almost 3 million hectares, or more than 11,500 square miles, and with it an increase in the manipulation of waterways to irrigate rice fields. Thousands of hectares of wetlands were drained and put into agricultural production. The same was happening in Europe, but on a much larger scale. With limited dry land, the Dutch drained 250,000 hectares (600,000 acres) of land between 1500 and 1815, but this pales in comparison to England's efforts. In 1600, the British parliament passed the General Draining Act, which began the destruction of Britain's fenlands. Over the next several hundred years, thousands of square miles of wetlands would be drained for agricultural use, leading to what some call the single greatest environmental disaster ever to occur in England. Overall modeling of pre-industrial land use estimates that globally between the years 800 and 1700, humans had already converted some 5 million square kilometers (2 million square miles) of natural habitats to agricultural land, greater than the total land area of all of today's European Union.

Deforestation was already becoming a major issue in the Old World even at the outset of the modern era. Japan already had a national timber industry by the start of the 16th century, and high demand for wood products had stripped many of Japan's mountainous areas of lumber by the middle of the century. England was already unable at this time to meet the demand for wood internally to maintain their enormous naval fleet, and the demand for wood in the British Isles created a global demand for wood, pitch, and tar. Particularly in demand was oak due to its superior strength, and the loss of the oak forests of England was rapid. Surveys of England's royal forests at the time show this loss. For example, Duffel Forest went from a population of 92,232 oaks in 1560 to just 5,896 oaks by 1587. A nearly 94% drop in just 27 years. The demand for lumber products also drove the British to exploit the forests of their Irish colony. In 1600, woodlands covered around 12% of Ireland. Intensive logging reduced this to just 2% a century later. The lack of timber remaining on the British Isles also forced an increase in the use of coal as an energy source. In the 1560s, British mines were supplying the nation with around 227,000 metric tons of coal per year. By 1700, this number had grown to 2.64 million tons.

As Europe's forests dwindled, demand shifted to the newly discovered New World. In 1500, the Portuguese, having found Brazil and its vast woodlands, began trading and shipping its native brazilwood almost immediately. Used for dying textiles and popular for making furniture, the Portuguese and French traded with the native coastal people for the desirable lumber. Estimates of brazilwood shipped to Europe in the 1500s amounted to around 8,000 metric tons per year. As many as 2 million trees were felled during the century, leading to the depletion of much of the country's coastal forests. As a result of the intensive harvesting, brazilwood *(Paubrasilia echinata)*, the national tree of Brazil, is now missing from most of its native range and is classified as endangered.

The seemingly endless trees of South America were matched by the vast expanses of trees in North America, and settlers to the new world wasted no time in exploiting this valuable resource. Sawmills began appearing as early as the 1620s in Dutch New Amsterdam (now New York) and the 1630s in the British colonies of the New World. Throughout the 17th century, the industry grew, and by the middle of the 1700s, environmental impacts were being felt despite restrictions placed by the British Crown. In an account from around 1750, already denuded landscapes in New England were seriously affecting water flows, ironically drying up the very streams that were being used to run the sawmills. Even though this should have come as a warning, the felling of trees only increased after the Revolutionary War, with the young United States looking to cash in on its forest wealth. For example, from October 1791 to September of the following year, the combined lumber exports from just New Hampshire, Massachusetts, Rhode Island, and Connecticut amounted to over 36 million board feet of pine, 700,000 board feet of oak, and over 16 million shingles.

Sheep and cattle grazing exploded around the planet as millions of animals were raised on natural grasslands, dramatically altering landscapes. Cattle being raised for hides, just on the island of Hispaniola show the rapid increase. Just 40 years after Columbus landed, 200,000 hides a year were being exported to Spain. By 1620, the Spanish were raising 7 to 10 million animals, mostly cattle and sheep, in Mexico alone. The Portuguese in Brazil brought cattle to the country in the 1530s, and ranching became a popular and lucrative way of life. Accounts estimate that by the early 1700s, 1.3 million head of cattle were already being raised in Brazil, and the country was exporting over 100,000 hides to Europe every year.

To protect these herds, bounties were offered to exterminate predators. Reaching back into the Middle Ages, multiple monarchs across Europe set bounties and even employed state-sponsored wolf catchers to eliminate wolves throughout their lands as part of a broader effort to eliminate predators from the bulk of Europe. These long-held traditions were carried on to the New World, with one of the first bounties for wolves enacted in Massachusetts all the way back in 1630. In New Hampshire, they wanted to rid the colony of wolves so badly that in 1778 they offered the huge sum of 10 pounds for the killing of a wolf, equivalent at the time to the yearly salary of a sergeant in the British army. The persecution of predators was not just limited to Europe and North America, and as early as 1656, the Cape Colony in South Africa was offering 6 Spanish reales for the killing of a lion and 4 for a leopard or hyena in an effort to reduce predators there. It seems that nearly everywhere in the world, sums of money were being offered up to eliminate the predator threat to humans and their assets, with many of these programs persisting into the 19th and 20th centuries.

The increasing demand for sugar in Europe also significantly impacted landscapes. Huge amounts of land in the New World were put into sugar production. By the 1580s, the Portuguese in Brazil were already exporting around 6,000 tons of sugar per year, and by 1650, this number had risen to 28,500 tons. By 1700, an estimated 1,000 square kilometers of primary forest had been cleared for sugar production, with another 1,200 square kilometers of secondary and mangrove forest also cleared to fuel the sugar mills. The huge growth of sugar operations in the early 1800s demanded yet more land, and between 1700 and 1850, an additional 7,400 sq km (2800 sq mi) of forests were cleared, with sugar exports from the nation peaking in 1823 at 99,000 tons.

As large as the Portuguese operations in Brazil were, they were already surpassed by the islands of the Caribbean as early as 1680, and by the late 1700s, they were completely eclipsed. Between 1770 and 1774, the islands of the West Indies were exporting over 180,000 tons of sugar every year,. By 1815, this had grown to over 270,000 tons. To supply the growing demand, large sugar plantations began to dominate the landscape of many Caribbean islands, with predictable ecological results. Much of the lush tropical forests native to the islands were felled to make way for sugar plantations, fuel for the mills, and pasture and farmland for the plantation owners and their slaves. Lost along with the forests were the habitats for numerous species of wildlife, including birds and even primates, many of which are now extinct. So complete was the destruction that even several species of trees were lost to extinction.

Many islands underwent a complete ecological shift with a much different makeup of flora and fauna. Environmental impacts varied greatly between the islands, but even islands with less intensive sugar operations like Jamaica still added to the overall environmental destruction of the Caribbean. Jamaica had the unfortunate distinction of being the "turtle hunting capital of the West Indies." Sea turtles were a valuable resource for meat and eggs, and hunters based in Jamaica made a profitable business of raiding nesting grounds in the Cayman Islands. Tens of thousands of turtles and their eggs, of all four species of sea turtle, succumbed to hunters. Green turtles were the most desirable, and by the late 1600s, 13,000 green sea turtles were being brought into Port Royale every year. By the 1800s, the entire nesting population of the Cayman Islands was exhausted, with only small remnant populations left—populations that are still working to recover today.

Pollution was becoming an increasing problem even before the onset of the Industrial Revolution. The increase in the use of coal in England was becoming problematic as open pits and water pollution began to endanger the public and livestock. In 1620, a complaint was brought to the British courts, amounting to what we would call a lawsuit today, on behalf of the owners of a manor whose lands and waters were affected by the coal mining. The complaint outlined that the mines had dried up the manor's springs and wells; coal dust was ruining crops and hay; the meadows were flooded with polluted water; and no less than five people had fallen and drowned in open pits. The ruling from the courts amounted to a split decision, sounding much like that of today. The ruling attempted to placate those affected while reaffirming the importance of industry. The mines were told to fill and fence open pits and increase compensation to the manor, but also that the mines were essential to the state and that the mines had the right to continue on any of the lands laid out in their lease agreement. Sadly, environmental policy in regards to industry seems not to have progressed all that much in 400 years.

If the mining of coal in Britain was problematic, the burning of coal was more so, with air pollution also becoming a problem. London's ever-increasing air quality issues prompted one of the world's first writings on the subject of air pollution. In 1661, John Evelyn published a pamphlet entitled *Fumifugium*. Addressed specifically to King Charles II, Evelyn decried the state of London's air, describing how the acrid smoke from burning coal pervaded all of London:

> It is this horrid Smoake which obfcures our Churches, and makes our Palaces look old, which fouls our Clothes, and corrupts the Waters, fo as the very Rain, and refrefhing Dews which fall in the feveral Seafons which, with its black and tenacious quality, fpots and contaminates whatforver is expos'd to it.

He goes on to lament that the smoke and coal ash are killing bees and preventing the flowering and fruiting of plants stating, "the City of London refembles the face rather of Mount Aetna, the Court of Vulcan, Stromboli, or the Suburbs of Hell then an Affembly of Rational Creatures, and the Imperial feat of our incomparable Monarch." Even as early as Evelyn's account is, people were complaining about air pollution as far back as the Roman Era, and complaints of burning coal in London go back at least to the 1200s. Clean water was also becoming more of a concern. This time period saw the beginning of widespread use of natural fertilizers, usually manure from livestock, increasing yields. However, this also introduced excess nutrients into waterways and fouled drinking water. This, along with the growing problem of human waste in the ever growing cities, threatened humans and the ecosystem at large.

Europe was not the only place struggling with pollution in this early age. Extensive gold mining in Mexico and Peru using mercury led to serious environmental contamination in both nations. Mercury pollution, according to historian John Richards, was "the single largest source of industrial pollution in the entire early modern world." Between 1558 and 1816, imports of mercury into the Mexican colonies alone amounted to a shocking 64,470 metric tons. Little thought was given to the responsible handling of the toxic mercury, and as a result, nearly all of it ended up in the environment. Pollution was not the only ill effect of the search for gold. In Brazil, the extraction of gold and diamonds from rivers and the surrounding banks was responsible for the clearing and destruction of vast amounts of land. Miners overturned some 4,000 sq km (1,500 sq mi) of Brazilian forest in the quest for these valuable materials.

This was also the age of exploration, especially by Western Europeans, and there was an enormous drive to exploit the natural riches of newly discovered lands. This exploration was followed by colonial expansion into much of the world, which nearly always followed the same pattern. As European settlers displace native peoples, these new settlers often have a much greater environmental impact than the people they displace. European agriculture replaced many societies that were still largely hunter-gatherers or had very basic forms of agriculture. This, combined with intensive resource extraction for European markets and the extraction of wealth from the lands conquered, took an immense environmental and human toll. Little regard was given to the impact on people or nature in these foreign lands, and expansion and profit took priority. It is during this early colonial expansion that we see the modern models of stockholder- and government-owned mega companies such as the Dutch East India Company, founded in 1602 (still thought to be the largest company ever to exist), Britain's competing East India Company in 1670, and the Hudson's Bay Company the same year to support the fur trade in North America. The efficiency and scale of these companies and their ability to move huge amounts of goods at the time drove demand around the world for global goods. Trapping, hunting, and fishing all became commercialized. Large capital investments improved efficiency and technology to meet the ever-increasing demands.

One of the most stark examples of how this early colonization could affect wildlife is in the Cape of South Africa, where the Dutch East India Company set up a trading settlement in 1653. As this new colony and its capital city, Cape Town, grew, an increasing amount of land was needed for farming and livestock grazing. Wildlife was a valuable source of meat and relatively easy to hunt with the firearms the Dutch possessed, and the areas around the Cape were awash with wildlife. Due to relentless hunting for food and sport and the elimination of predators, the start of the 18th century saw the Cape's wildlife nearly completely eliminated in the lands farmed by colonists. By the end of the Dutch era in the late 1790s, nearly all of the large wildlife species native to the Cape region were gone. These include savanna elephants (now endangered), hippos, black rhinos (now critically endangered), giraffes, water buffaloes, two species of wild pigs, several subspecies of zebra (one now extinct), nearly 30 species of antelope (one now extinct), spotted leopards (now critically endangered), cheetahs, lions, two species of hyena, African wild dogs (now critically endangered), striped and black-backed jackals, and the Cape fox. To put the loss into a modern perspective, imagine the wildlife of the Serengeti today being completely wiped out.

South Africa is but one example. All across the Old and New World, native fauna and flora were hunted, collected, and traded by these new European colonists. Much of this was a continuation of the similar utilization by the peoples that came before, but driven by the profits of trade rather than their own personal needs. As a result, the colonial impact on the environment, in many cases, quickly outstripped that of the peoples the Europeans replaced. Nature was increasingly commoditized, and with money to be made and now an entire world to sell to, many were eager to cash in.

By the early 16th century, fur-bearing animals in Europe were becoming increasingly rare. The Eurasian beaver was already extinct on the British Isles and rare elsewhere, and other animals were so depleted that even rabbit skins were becoming increasingly rare and expensive. Because of this, the price and demand for furs in Europe were extremely high. Attention of course turned to the still rich and wild resources of North America. Beaver was in the highest demand and used widely for the manufacture of hats, but furs from many of North America's animals were sought after, including: raccoon, martin, fisher, mink, otter, muskrat, fox, lynx, bobcat, wolf, black and brown bears, and even polar bears.

Fur trading with the native peoples of North America began nearly immediately upon European arrival in the 1500s. These first trades were of a casual nature, but they became increasingly organized with the first French fur expeditions in the 1580s. Demand among the native populations for European goods changed these peoples from subsistence hunters to commercial hunters. This, along with the introduction of firearms from Europe, placed never-before-seen demands on North America's wildlife. In the early 1600s, French trade with just the Huron people was bringing in 12,000–15,000 beaver pelts per year. In 1627, total exports of pelts to France reached more than 30,000. Reports from the time show some beaver populations in Canada were already depleted as early as 1634. The fur trade, in combination with the increased effectiveness of European weapons, also led to a depletion of the region's moose, bear, and game birds. The French were not the only European country trading in furs. The Dutch and the English were both trading furs farther east in New England. English trade never amounted to huge numbers in these early years but still had a significant impact on local wildlife. The Dutch, however, were more successful, shipping as many as 46,000 beaver pelts to Europe in 1657 before being taken over by the English in 1664.

French explorations in the 1670s and 80s increased their reach south and west, eventually encompassing the entire Mississippi River valley. This expanded trade area paid off, and the French saw their exports explode. In the 1680s, the French were now shipping 73,000 pelts every year. Between 1700 and 1763, this grew to an average of 122,000 beaver pelts per year. As already mentioned, beavers were not the only wildlife being hunted and shipped to Europe. While beavers were the single most plentiful species trapped, they made up just 40% of the total furs and skins shipped. Between 1728 and 1755, exports from just the French ports in Quebec amounted to more than 286,000 animals. As the fur trade expanded, the number of animals killed continued to climb into the 19th century, when beaver harvests dropped dramatically as populations became exhausted. From an initial estimated population of 60–100 million, the beaver population of North America fell to just 100,000 by 1900. The total known take for all species is astounding. In just the period from 1700 to 1763, over 400,000 skins per year from the French and the British were being sent abroad, amounting to more than 25 million animals.

Fur was not the only valuable animal resource found in the new world. With small numbers of quality fur-bearing animals in the southeastern parts of the yet-to-be United States, traders tapped the vast amounts of deer held within these lands. Employing native tribes, much like the early fur traders, a prolific deerskin trade was set up. The supple and soft hides of deer were in high demand in Europe after declines in their own managed deer herds. By 1700, 50,000 deer skins were leaving the South. 30 years later, this number had grown threefold. By the time trade peaked in the 1760s, between 250 and 300 thousand deer hides per year were being shipped abroad

The demand for animal goods was by no means contained on land in this period, and the most lucrative pursuits were cod fishing and whaling. While cod fishing on the European side of the North Atlantic had been going on for hundreds of years, cod stocks in the New World were almost completely untapped. Fishermen working their way across the North Atlantic discovered the rich fisheries off Newfoundland and began exploiting them as early as the 1490s. The seemingly inexhaustible shoals of fish were a boon to European fish markets. By the late 1500s, hundreds of European ships from numerous countries were fishing the New World from the Arctic to Newfoundland. In 1602, this expanded south into New England as far south as the newly named Cape Cod. By the late 1600s, French and British ships were bringing around 47,000 metric tons of dried codfish back to Europe from the North Atlantic seas. Estimates of the total fish caught are huge, especially considering the technology of the time. The total live catch per year from roughly 1600 to 1750 was between 200,000 and 250,000 tons per year. By the late 1700s, the total catch had jumped to nearly 400,000 tons per year. Even with this fishing pressure, cod stocks were resilient, although average catches did diminish over time. This suggests the fishery was already stressing cod populations at this early date. Total catches however, continued to increase in the coming centuries with the ever-growing fishing fleets.

By the time that Europeans began whaling, whale hunting by the native peoples of the North had been going on for thousands of years. Unlike European whaling, the impacts to whale populations of native hunting were likely not significant, maybe only 130–150 whales per year for the entire Arctic region. The Basques were the first Europeans to widely practice whaling as far back as the 11th century, and they were the ones that introduced European whaling into the northern seas in 1500. Basque sailors were also the first to venture into the waters east of Greenland, and by 1530, they were crossing the Atlantic and killing whales off the coast of Newfoundland. Their target was primarily bowhead whales, but they also caught right whales as these species were slow and easier to catch than some of the other species. Between 1530 and 1607, the Basque whalers killed some 25,000 whales. By the start of the 17th century, the Basques were joined by Dutch, French, German, and English sailors hunting the same prey. The Dutch and Germans became by far the most prolific whale hunters. Between 1661 and 1719, they combined to pull in over 49,000 whales and another 40,000 between 1720 and 1800. In total, in just the northern seas, as many as 200,000 whales were killed in a 300 year period. As a result, the eastern Arctic bowhead population was driven to near zero. Unlike the cod stocks that could keep up with the increasingly intensive take, whales, like most large-bodied animals, are long-lived, slow to mature, and have extremely low reproductive rates. For example, a female bowhead whale will not reach sexual maturity until she is 15 years old, and after that, she will only calf once every 3 to 4 years. Whaling was not limited to the northern seas, and by the 18th and 19th centuries, it had spread around the world, with the United States eventually becoming the center of the world's whaling industry. From the early 1700s to the late 1800s, 300,000 sperm whales were taken out of the southern seas, and thousands more right whales were taken from the east and west coasts of the United States and Canada. As technology improved, the hunt expanded to all species of whales.

As potent as the influence of Western European expansion was and the environmental damage it brought, they were not always moving into sparsely populated wildlands. In several cases, Europeans were confronted with intensely modified agricultural and urban landscapes equivalent to those seen in Europe. In 1519, the Spanish, led by Hernando Cortez, moved from the West Indies to the mainland of what is now Mexico. There they were first confronted with an advanced agrarian society on the coast. As they moved inland, they were stunned to find the Aztec culture, which at this time numbered around 5 million people, and their capital city of Tenochtitlan (now Mexico City), home to between 100 and 200 thousand inhabitants (more than London at the time). When their numbers are added to the 10 million Incas who still lived in South America, the once-vast Mayan empire, and the millions of other native peoples in South and Central America, it is clear that the environments of this part of the New World had seen significant human disruption prior to European arrival. Beyond the impacts of cultivation and urbanization, the peoples of Central and South America also had a significant impact on wildlife, especially birds. Many cultures valued the bright, colorful feathers of many tropical birds, and a thriving trade in these birds existed long before European arrival. This trade was so large that it is believed that the distribution of species throughout Latin America was changed by it.

In total, around 250,000 square kilometers (96,500 square miles) of Mexico were already intensively cultivated when the Spanish arrived. Ironically, due to the depopulation of the native peoples from mass disease brought by Europeans, land use in Mexico actually decreased after the Spanish conquest, as the total population of Mexico dropped from at least 10 million in 1519 to around 1.5 million by around 1600. This was repeated in many parts of the New World as newly introduced diseases spread through the native populations, but it is clear that prior to European arrival, many parts of the New World had already been significantly impacted by human development.

By 1800, the industrial revolution was well underway, and the speed of technological progress would only increase in the coming decades. Between the beginning of the nineteenth century and 1950, our global impact increased steadily. However, in this period, we see a fundamental change in humans' use of energy. Beginning with the advent and spread of steam power, then electrification, and finally the internal combustion engine, we see human contributions to atmospheric CO_2 begin in earnest. As each one of these new technologies demanded more and more fossil fuel use, we see the emergence of today's fossil fuel based economy. Dramatic growth in human populations also drove increasing demands on the natural world. Technology allowed us to meet a growing demand for food and finished goods, but these brought new challenges of their own.

From around 1 billion people in the world in 1800, the human population added another 600 million in just 100 years and doubled to 2 billion by the 1920s. By the time World War II broke out, it had increased to somewhere around 2.3 billion people. Agriculture obviously needed to greatly expand to meet the demand for food, and the 19th century saw the great prairies of America plowed under to make way for crops. According to U.S. census data from 1850, there were over 293 million acres of land occupied by farms. By 1900, this had grown to 838 million acres, and by the 1930s, it had grown to over a billion. The invention of synthetic fertilizers in the early 1900s increased yields but also pollution of waterways.

Livestock numbers also saw dramatic growth during this period. In 1840, there were around 15 million head of cattle being raised in the U.S. By 1880, this had grown to 40 million and reached 70 million by 1900. This, in addition to 20 million sheep and 25 million hogs in 1840, growing to just over 60 million for both by 1900. As these herds expanded, so did the fences crisscrossing the plains. Thousands of miles of barbed wire fencing, invented in the 1860s, were erected to keep livestock contained. This split up the remaining prairie that was not lost to the plow, cutting off millennia old migration paths. Agricultural expansion was not just for food production but also to support the thriving textile industry with cotton and wool. According to a U.S. Federal Reserve bulletin from 1923, the United States produced roughly 73,000 bales of cotton in 1800; by 1850, it was over 2 million; and by 1900, it was over 10 million bales.

In the heart of this period was the Victorian Era, roughly 1820–1914, called as such by the reign of England's Queen Victoria (1837–1901). The British Empire was at its height and was a leader in the ongoing industrial revolution. Culturally and scientifically, the English were setting the tone for much of the Western world. This was a new age of communication, transportation, and scientific inquiry. During this period, we see the invention of the telegraph in 1837, the first modern railroad line in 1838, the publication of *On the Origin of Species* in 1859, Mendeleev's periodic table in 1869, the invention of the telephone in 1876, Edison's lightbulb in 1878, and the discovery of the electron in 1897. This era could also be called the "golden age of natural history," and it was marked by an intense interest in the natural world and a rapid increase in our knowledge of Earth's life. The study of plants, animals, insects, and geology were all popular pastimes during the era. Passionate amateur scientists spent countless hours collecting and classifying specimens. Taxidermy and natural history collections were wildly popular, and Victorians were eager to show off their private collections to guests. Museums and their collections were all the rage, with several prominent natural history museums opening, including the American Museum of Natural History in 1869, the British Natural History Museum in 1881, the Museum of Natural History in Vienna in 1889, and Chicago's Field Museum in 1894.

Unfortunately, this era was also marked by an equally intense exploitation of nature. As Muir and Thoreau were exalting the wonders of what they saw around them and Darwin and Wallace explored the depths of life's relationships, much of the natural world was under siege. Although the Victorians had a desire to learn about nature, their attitude toward it seemed to be one of dominance over it. The categorization, classification, and collection of nature became a symbol of human dominance over nature, both physically and intellectually. Even with nature and wildlife being a primary theme in Victorian art, literature, and architecture, they had few qualms about destroying it. In this era, we see the near extermination of bison, the extinction of the great auk, the passenger pigeon, and the Carolina parakeet, among others. In all of these cases, overhunting for food, hides, or the obsession with collecting took its toll. In fact, some of the last of the Carolina parakeets were probably killed by ornithologist Frank Chapman in 1889, when he killed 15 of the increasingly rare birds. During this time period, studying wildlife often meant killing the very thing being studied, and naturalists frequently killed animals to make detailed drawings or add them to their specimen collections. Often, it seems that there was competition to see who could build the largest collection, even if their collections already contained a particular species *ad nauseam*. As some species became more rare, this seemed to only drive naturalists to hurry and add them to their own collections or the collections of the museums they worked for.

While thousands of birds and other animals were being killed for study, many more were being killed for an unfortunate trend in women's fashion. In keeping with the Victorian aesthetic, it was wildly popular for women to wear hats with feathers, even entire stuffed birds. Other popular accessories included iridescent insects, butterflies, and even small rodents. The detriment to birds was so great that it led the same Frank Chapman, who may have helped assure the extinction of the Carolina parakeet, to ironically give a talk entitled "Woman as Bird Enemy." Shooting what was, by all accounts, an endangered species for science was apparently acceptable, but killing birds for fashion was not. Hypocrisy aside, Chapman and other observers at the time recognized the negative impact fashion was having on birds and other species. By late in the 19th century, an estimated 5 million North American birds were being killed each year to supply the industry. Chapman, observing women's hats in New York in 1886, found that out of the 700 women's hats he observed, 542 were decorated with the feathers of more than 40 different bird species. A young William Beebe, sent to investigate the feather markets of London in 1912, found that just four firms had sold over 500,000 birds. As the popularity of putting once-living things on hats and clothing expanded, there was an increasing pushback. The sentiment among many naturalists of the time was much the same as that exhibited by a section in *Entomological News* from 1890.

> Not content with her slaughter of the innocents in the matter of birds, Dame Fashion has extended her murderous designs to moths and butterflies... Fanciful, it is granted, but never appropriate...it is easy to estimate in what enormous quantities these creatures must be taken to satisfy even a small demand...Truly a fashionable toilet is becoming a composite thing, with dead birds and butterflies, hair from Indian beggars, and Mexican bugs as jewelry, held by golden chains.

Fashion did not just take its toll on birds and butterflies but continued to support a thriving fur trade. Muskrat overtook beaver as the most trapped animal by the 1850s, and by the late 1800s, 2 million a year were being killed. Total numbers of fur-bearers killed each year in the 19th century hit their peaks in the 1870s at 4.3 million animals and in the 1880s at 4.9 million animals.

Beyond fur and fashion, millions more animals were killed to fill the markets, so much so that game in New England was becoming increasingly scarce. This is despite game laws to limit the killing, some even dating as far back as the 1600s. Little to no enforcement of these laws made them of little use. As early as the 1820s, increasing scarcity made shipments of game into the markets of New England an event, often making the news. The shortage was alleviated by the improvement of shipping via steamboat and rail. This allowed hunters to exploit the abundant wildlife further west in order to satisfy the demand of the East's hungry populace. Wild game was a common item in the markets of Victorian America and included almost every animal imaginable. Besides waterfowl, deer were the most common, but one could find any number of different animals, including bison, elk, moose, caribou, bighorn sheep, mountain goats, pronghorn, rabbits and hares, and various species of squirrel. Less common but still occasionally consumed were raccoons, beavers, otters, skunks, groundhogs, opossums, porcupines, and even black bears and lynx.

Despite the impact, fashion was not the greatest threat for birds at the time. Millions upon millions of birds were killed for the market as a result of commercial hunting. Advances in firearms helped commercial hunters take down dozens of ducks or geese with a single shot using huge double-barreled shotguns, called punt guns, which looked more like something from a battleship than a hunting tool. Many commercial waterfowl hunters of the time reported shooting as many as 200 ducks each day. The rise of the railroad and telegraph allowed hunters to track the migratory passenger pigeon flocks and allowed millions of passenger pigeons to be killed in short order. For example, 1.8 million pigeons were sent to market from a single New York nesting site in 1851. Even as the birds were becoming increasingly rare, the hunt continued. In 1878, at one of the last large nesting sites in the state of Michigan, hunters killed 50,000 pigeons a day for five straight months. The railroads were also used to transport the spoils of other bird hunts. Tons of grouse and quail from the Great Plains, as well as many other prairie species, were shipped to eager eastern markets. As many as 30,000 prairie chickens and 15,000 bobwhite quail were shipped out of the state of Nebraska alone in 1874.

Many would be surprised to learn that an enormous trade of songbirds also once existed in the U.S., but this trade was not for science or for fashion, but for food. Millions of songbirds every year ended up in the markets of the United States, including robins (one of the most popular and classified by some states at the time as a game bird), bobolinks, northern flickers, meadowlarks, horned larks, pipits, red-headed woodpeckers, cedar waxwings, catbirds, towhees, juncos, pine grosbeaks, cuckoos, purple finches, hermit thrushes, and orioles. To give an example of the scale of these songbird takes, the number of bobolinks killed and shipped to market during their annual migration in 1912 from just the town of Georgetown, South Carolina, amounted to 60,000 dozen, or three-quarters of a million birds.

The Victorian Era also saw the rise of the sport of big-game trophy hunting, popularized by men like Roualeyn Gordon-Cumming, the so-called "lion hunter of South Africa." The Victorian penchant for collecting animals saw wealthy Europeans and Americans eager to claim the prize of shooting an exotic animal such as an elephant or lion from Africa, a tiger from India, or a jaguar from South America. Exotic trophies became a status symbol of wealth and the European ideal of colonial dominance. Often, large tracts of British colonial lands became little more than hunting preserves reserved for European elites. Accounts of these hunters' exploits were common in a wide variety of publications in the middle to late 1800s, and most of them are highly glorified accounts of adventure and bravery. The toll of this hunting was immense. In India alone, an estimated 80,000 tigers were killed between 1875 and 1925. The titles of hunter and naturalist often blurred the lines between trophy hunting and science. One of the more famous of the late Victorian hunters was naturalist and friend of Theodore Roosevelt, Frederick Selous. Selous alone in his exploits in Africa killed a reported 106 elephants, 177 buffalos, 31 lions, 51 rhinos, 67 giraffes, and some 600 antelope, not to mention numbers of 60 other species of African wildlife, many of these for major museums around the world. Selous was not blind to the toll that was being exacted on wildlife, however, and ended up a serious conservationist. Because of his contributions to the conservation of African wildlife, the 50,000 square kilometers (19,000 sq mi) Selous Game Reserve in southern Tanzania was named in his honor.

Throughout the period, technology advanced in the world's oceans and the whaling and fishing industries only continued to increase their catches into the 20th century. Whaling now covered the globe from pole to pole. Whalers could use faster steam powered and later diesel-powered boats rather than hand-rowed boats. This was combined with explosive harpoon guns, allowing them to go after even the fastest and largest whales. From 1900–1909, 52,000 whales were taken from the world's oceans, including 5,500 of the world's largest whales, the blue. The takes only increased from there. The decade before WWII saw just over 400,000 whales caught, with nearly 165,000 of those being blue whales. To put that into perspective, the current total global population of blue whales stands at only around 15,000 individuals

The commercial fishing industry also continued to grow. Reported numbers from the United States show that the products of the U.S. fishing industry amounted to a little over 6 million dollars in 1860, excluding whaling. By 1880, this had grown to over 22 million dollars. Even in the 19th century, there were clear indications that the rich cod fisheries of Europe and New England were diminishing. The use of steam powered trawlers considerably expanded the industry's abilities and dramatically increased catches. Research from Britain showed that steam trawlers were almost five times more efficient than their sail counterparts when fishing for cod. Landings of bottom fish in the UK more than doubled from around 300,000 tons in 1889 to 800,000 tons in 1940, and the impact on fish abundance is still being felt. UK ships in 1910 were landing four times as many fish as today's vastly technologically superior fleet. This is repeated on many waters around the world, with historical catches far outweighing current catches despite dramatically more fishing effort. The reason is simple: there are just a lot fewer fish in the sea.

Logging also continued at a breakneck pace. According to the U.S. Forest Service, the latter half of the 1800s saw more than 13 square miles of forest cleared every day for a period of 50 years for agriculture, fuel, and wood products. In 1850, the United States produced about 5.4 billion board feet of lumber each year. By 1910, this had increased to 44.5 billion. While the overall area of forested land in the U.S. has stayed stable since the 1920s, this fact hides the massive loss of old-growth forests, and their unique ecosystems. In California, redwoods, some two millennia old, were nearly logged into extinction. Resistant to rot, the wood was highly prized for numerous applications, including railroad ties. At the start of logging, there were nearly 2 million acres of old-growth redwoods. Today, only 5% of this original forest remains. The old-growth forests of the Eastern United States were likewise devastated. As early as 1897, only 9 million acres of the original 30 million acres of Pennsylvania's forests still remained, of which only a few hundred acres of true old-growth forests were still standing. Losses such as these were common throughout the eastern U.S.

As the industrialization of the world progressed, energy use skyrocketed. Steam power, the making of iron and steel, and eventually electricity, as well as the internal combustion engine, all demanded an energy source. The world turned to fossil fuels to meet this demand. Coal production in England went from 15 million tons in 1800 to over 64 million tons in 1854, peaking at 292 million tons by 1913. A similar rise was seen throughout the industrialized world. The United States lagged behind England, producing just 8.4 million tons of coal in 1850, but rapidly increased production to 270 million tons by 1900 and far surpassed England's peak, producing 680 million tons each year by 1918. Oil, discovered in the 1850s in the United States, rapidly became the energy of choice. In 1870, U.S. oil fields were producing 14 thousand barrels of crude oil per day. This had increased to 174,000 barrels by 1900 and to over 3.4 million barrels every day by 1939. Driving the demand for oil was the rise of the automobile. In 1900, there were just 0.11 cars per 1,000 people in the United States; 40 years later, this had grown to 245 cars per 1,000.

The result of the burning of these and other fossil fuels was that humans began to change the composition of the Earth's atmosphere dramatically by adding huge amounts of CO_2. It is estimated that humans released around 29 million tons of CO_2 into the atmosphere in 1800. By 1850, this had grown to 198 million tons; by 1900, just under 2 billion tons; and by the start of WWII, 4.7 billion tons. In the same time period, atmospheric CO_2 concentrations rose from 280 ppm to 310 ppm.

Pollution of the environment also increased with the Industrial Revolution. Little to no regulation on industry meant that human and industrial waste were free to pollute anywhere and everywhere. Air pollution was increasingly bad, especially in the cities, leading to most being covered in perpetual smoke. Britain's air quality certainly had not improved since Evelyn. Accounts from the time describe a London full of smoke and grime. The effect was not merely one of aesthetics, and research has shown that the highly polluted industrial areas of Britain also came with a significant increase in mortality by the latter half of the 19th century. Estimates suggest that London air particulate concentrations likely often exceeded 600 µg/m^3 (micrograms per cubic meter) and probably exceeded this by multiple times on bad days. To compare, concentrations in modern Delhi, India, which is notorious for its air pollution, are typically around 400 µg/m^3.

A similar issue could be found in the U.S. The industrial center of Pittsburgh was long known for its dirty air. With plentiful coal nearby and a thriving steel industry, Pittsburgh became synonymous with smoke and dinge. Coal was the primary fuel here going back to the city's founding in the 1750s. By 1804, the air quality was already so bad that it prompted calls for action, but these were largely ignored. By 1860, 50% of U.S. glass and 40% of U.S. iron were being produced in Pittsburgh. Estimates of total particulate matter (TPM) show concentrations probably exceeded 700 µg/m^3 and could have been as high as 7000 µg/m^3 in the 1800s. The problem worsened until the 1940s, with a brief respite in the late 1800s when much of the city used natural gas for a time. Pittsburgh was not the only city dealing with poor air, and maybe not even the worst. Actual measurements from Chicago in 1913 yielded total particulate matter concentrations of between 300 and 2,000 µg/m^3 reaching a high of 9,000 µg/m^3. Cleveland averaged an unbelievable 14,000 µg/m^3 in data prior to 1915, with a high reading of nearly 40,000 µg/m^3. Comparing these numbers to modern concentrations is difficult. Total particulate matter concentrations are an outdated method of air quality measurement, and air quality monitoring now distinguishes between particle sizes and focuses on smaller and more damaging particles, but these readings clearly show the horrible state of the air at the time. If seeing is believing, one can still find pre-war buildings in cities throughout the world that still are marred by the coal soot clinging to their facades.

Of course, the appalling air quality affected not just humans but all life in these industrial centers and beyond. One of the effects was acid rain. The coal burned in this era was particularly high in sulfur. When the coal was burned, it released sulfur dioxide (SO_2), and this, mixed with water in the air, makes sulfuric acid. During rain, this acidified water leached nutrients and metals from the soil, harming plant life, and transported those nutrients into waterways, harming aquatic life. Adding to the problem was the later addition of the burning of diesel fuel, which also contained sulfur. Soot and sulfur were not the only things coming from the unregulated smokestacks of industry, and emissions often included toxic by-products of materials being made and heavy metals such as lead and mercury.

The threat to freshwater continued to grow as the cities of Europe and the United States became ever larger. Human waste and the increasing effluent from industry turned rivers and lakes from bodies of freshwater to serious environmental hazards. London was the world's largest city in the 19th century, with its population more than doubling between 1800 and 1850 to two and a half million people. With most of the waste from this city going directly into the river Thames, it is not surprising that the river was polluted. Human, animal, and industrial waste all flowed into the river, and the result was nothing short of horrific. By the 1850s, the stench had gotten so bad that the parliament was treating the window curtains with chloride of lime to cut down on the smell. In 1855, scientist Michael Faraday wrote a letter to the London Times about the condition of the river and described it as truly a "sewer." In fact, by that time, it was. A hot summer in 1858 exacerbated the stench and led to what Londoners called "The Great Stink." Things got so bad that it kept parliament from meeting, effectively shutting down England's government. The Thames wasn't London's only problem. Human waste from sewers often contaminated London's aging freshwater system, leading to several severe outbreaks of cholera. Obviously, the levels of pollution destroyed most of the Thames ecosystem, and its once valuable salmon fishery was gone by the late 1840s. Pollution also wreaked havoc in the Thames tidal estuary. Even with a major overhaul of the London sewer system in the late 1800s, the pollution persisted for decades, with the river being declared biologically dead in 1957.

Waterways in the U.S. did not fare better in the 19th and early 20th centuries. Some of the worst problems were in the Eastern United States, which contained the bulk of the thriving textile industry, with Massachusetts at its very heart. Dyes and other chemicals from the industry, among other pollutants from various other industries, flowed untreated into rivers. So bad was the pollution that by the 1880s, the Concord River was considered a sewage basin. Records from the time show some of what was being dumped into a tributary near the city of Lowell, Mass. This included a daily release of some 60,000 gallons of oil-laden wash from a local cartridge factory; 300,000 gallons of wastewater containing wash and dye from a woolery; and millions of gallons of water from a local bleachery that was used in washing, bleaching, and dyeing cloth. All of this flowed into the Concord, where another million gallons of wastewater was being dumped every day from various industries on the river itself. Paralleling what London saw in the Thames, the citizens of the area were confronted with a stinking river, often covered with dead and dying fish. In fact, many, if not most, of the rivers in the eastern United States near urban centers were then little more than open sewers.

Throughout most of history, humans' impact on our world grew at a fairly steady pace. There were leaps and bounds along the way as our technology improved, but starting around 1950, something changed. It was at this time that human development went into overdrive and the environmental impacts of humanity went from a steady rise to growing at an exponential rate. Thus began a meteoric rise in atmospheric CO_2, N_2O, and CH_4 concentrations, ozone depletion, percentage of fisheries exploited, loss of woodlands, motor vehicle transport, water use, fertilizer consumption, damming of rivers, and species extinctions, just to name a few. This has come to be called the "Great Acceleration." In just the last 70 years, humans have done more to change the Earth than all of human history preceding it, and our impact on the world only continues to increase.

In 1950, the human population reached 2.5 billion people. In the coming years population growth would accelerate to a rate never before seen in human history. To give an idea of just how much, take into account that for the population to double from 1 billion in 1800 to 2 billion in 1928, took nearly 130 years. Before 1800, it took nearly 300 years. In contrast, the time required to double 1950's 2.5 billion people, was just 37 years! Currently, our population stands at around 8 billion people and grows by roughly 200,000 people every day. Obviously, this rapid increase in population has created a rapid increase in demand for resources. Advances in agricultural fertilizers and pesticides ushered in a "Green Revolution," allowing the growing of more food to support the population. These advances thankfully reduced the amount of land needed to grow crops, but agricultural land use continued to grow and remains one of the largest environmental impacts of humans and the largest reason for the loss of wildlands around the world. In 1954, roughly 64% of the globe was still what we would call "wilderness." By 1989, this had dropped below 50%, and by 2020, it had been reduced to just 35%; much of this loss was in the world's forests.

While consumption of all of the Earth's resources increased dramatically after WWII, the hallmark of the Great Acceleration was and is the consumption of fossil fuels. Coal, the fuel of choice for the 19th century, continued to grow, primarily for the production of electricity. Shockingly, a fuel source that we often associate with the Industrial Revolution and a dirtier, less technologically advanced time, remains a huge part of our fossil fuel use. For example, one would think that coal production in the U.S. would have peaked by early in the 20th century, but surprisingly it did not peak until the early 21st. Not until 2008 at 1.1

billion tons. Worldwide coal production continued to grow throughout the remainder of the 20th century and into the 21st. In 1970, the world produced 5.5 billion tons of coal. Since 2011, the world has been producing and consuming nearly 8 billion metric tons every year. Coal still accounts for the most common fuel used for electrical generation at 36% worldwide.

Paralleling the massive increase in coal production was an even more enormous increase in oil production, largely driven by the transportation sector. By 1950, global crude oil production had increased to just over 10 million barrels per day. 10 years later, this had more than doubled. By 1980, production had jumped sixfold to over 60 million barrels per day, and 80 by 2008. The current consumption of oil sits at just under 100 million barrels per day. 2019 total production for oil was over 36 billion barrels, or, in units that are more familiar, 1.5 trillion gallons or 5.7 trillion liters. Currently, 66% of all oil produced is used for transportation. Despite a short-lived reduction in demand and production due to the COVID-19 pandemic and the desperate need to reduce reliance on fossil fuels, both oil production and demand are forecast to grow in the next several years.

Impacts on wildlife early in the acceleration brought many species to the brink of extinction, not just through loss of habitat but also through the continued exploitation of them as resources. Fisheries around the world were exploited like never before. The world cod fishery is a prime example. In the 1950s, the cod catch in Europe peaked at over 1.3 million tons per year. By the 1960s, the U.S. cod fishery peaked, with annual catches in the order of 800,000 tons. Within decades, both populations had collapsed, and the coming decades would see the collapse of yet more species. Whaling continued at an unbelievable pace. Even in the midst of the Second World War, some 256,000 of the world's largest animals were taken out of the oceans. With the war over, whalers ramped up the hunt over the next decade. Between 1950 and 1959, over 613,000 whales were killed by the global whaling industry. The decade that followed saw the largest take of whales in history. Over a hundred years had passed since the days of Melville's *Moby Dick* and the period most would assume was the heyday of the whaling industry. No, whaling's peak was not in the 1860s but in the 1960s, when whalers hauled in a staggering 703,235 whales. Whale populations plummeted species after species as whalers depleted one and moved on to the next, prompting some species to be banned from whaling as early as 1931. Even with bans in place, the damage from still-legal whaling and the continuance of illegal whaling led to the near extinction of both the North Pacific and North Atlantic right whale populations. These species have yet to recover, and it is feared they may never do so. The total number of whales killed in the 20th century stands at over 2.8 million, most of which were killed before the eventual global moratorium on whaling in 1982. Fin whales suffered the greatest loss at 874,000, followed by over 761,000 sperm whales and 379,000 blue whales.

Wildlife losses on land also accelerated, and nowhere was this more apparent than on the continent of Africa. Human conflict, habitat loss, the bushmeat trade, and the demand for elephant ivory and rhino horn took their toll. Africa lost fully half of its elephant population in just the 10 years between 1979 and 1989. Demand from ivory was the primary cause. Species like the black rhino fared even worse, with the population dropping from around 65,000 in 1970 to 15,000 in 1979 as the U.S. considered them for Endangered Species Act protection. Just 10 years later, the population was just 2,500. Even with an extensive network of protected areas throughout Africa, overall species declines continued. Research shows that even within protected areas, the abundance of Africa's wildlife decreased by 59% between 1970 and 2005.

Even though cities like London had been experiencing pollution problems for centuries by the start of this period, and despite laws passed to combat such issues, pollution in the industrialized West continued to plague their populations. Several notable events happened that would bring the West's continued pollution problems to the forefront. In 1952, the city of London was mired in a relentless fog, but consistent with hundreds of years of London's fogs, this wasn't just water vapor but smog, a dangerous concoction of pollutants from the continued burning of coal. The difference in this event was the duration. Londoners were used to these fogs, and they usually cleared out after a couple of days, but in the winter of 1952, the weather pattern that trapped the pollutants within the city persisted for 5 days. This more than doubled the time the population was exposed to extremely high levels of air pollution. So bad was the pollution that it blocked out the sun and reduced visibility within the city to as little as 3 feet. Sulfur dioxide combined with nitrogen oxide from coal burning turned London's fog into a deadly cloud of sulfuric acid vapor. A modern analysis of the event determined that as many as 12,000 people died as a result of the fog, with more than 150,000 people hospitalized. The impact of the event was not fully realized at the time but did become the catalyst for Britain's Clean Air Act in 1956. This legislation became one of the first nationwide pollution acts ever passed and a model for similar legislation around the world.

The United States continued its legacy of pollution dating back to the Industrial Revolution, with nearly all of its major cities having serious pollution problems early in the period. It is during this time that many new and extremely toxic pesticides came into wide use. Most are familiar with the story of DDT, but dozens of other extremely toxic compounds were also in common use. As a result of widespread and indiscriminate spraying, millions of birds, fish, and countless other animals were killed. Humans too lost their lives to these poisons. Entire local ecosystems of animals were nearly wiped out. In just one of thousands of examples, runoff from pesticide plants into the Colorado River near Austin, Texas, resulted in one of the worst fish kills in U.S. history. Dead and dying fish began turning up in Town Lake on January 15, 1961. By the end of the month, fish were dying along a 200-mile length of the Colorado. For as much as 140 miles downstream from Austin, fish losses were near total. Unfortunately, this was not an isolated incident. According to a U.S. EPA report published in 1978, between 1961 and 1975, pollution-caused fish kills were responsible for the deaths of more than 465 million fish in the U.S. However, the report also clearly states that this number is "probably only a fraction of the kills that actually occurred."

One particular event brought America's continued pollution problems into the spotlight. In 1969, the Cuyahoga River outside Cleveland, Ohio, was little more than an industrial sewer full of effluent from steel mills and numerous other industries. The condition of waterways in these industrial areas of the U.S. had changed little in the past 100 years. Around noon on the 22nd of June, 1969, sparks from a passing train ignited oil-soaked debris, lighting the river on fire. As shocking as an American river near a major city actually being ablaze sounds, locals thought little of it. This was not the first, or even worst fire that had happened in the river. So polluted was the Cuyahoga that at least a dozen fires dating back to the 1860s had occurred. The difference this time was a heightened awareness of pollution issues brought about in part by Rachel Carson's influential 1962 book *Silent Spring*, and President Richard Nixon's focus on air and water pollution during his presidential campaign. However, few would have noticed yet another, and in this case fairly minor, fire on the river without an article in *Time* magazine highlighting the fire and the pollution that caused it. Given national attention by an already receptive public, the 1969 Cuyahoga Fire helped push change, eventually leading to the formation of the U.S. Environmental Protection Agency (EPA) and the Clean Water Act of 1972.

Pollution in the West certainly has not ended, but events like the above helped to galvanize public opinion and force change. Water and air pollution in the UK, mainland Europe, and the U.S. are much better than in decades past, largely due to regulation, but on a global scale pollution overall has not diminished. Due to stricter pollution controls in the West in the 20th century, industries began to clean up their operations but also increasingly moved manufacturing to countries with less regulation. Seeing the profits to be made abroad, industries and their pollution simply shifted, in most cases, to Asia. As a result, pollution dropped in the West while dramatic increases were seen in the East. China is a prime example. China has become one of the world's leading industrial centers and has seen enormous growth. The country's total exports in the 1960s amounted to around 2 billion USD per year. By the 1980s, this had increased to $11 billion. By 2000 China's exports had exploded to to $250 billion and by 2020 had grown to more than $2 trillion. This economic expansion has resulted in serious environmental concerns. Much of the industry is fueled by coal. China consumes more coal than any other country on the planet—some 4 billion tons every year—and while the West's air has improved, China's has deteriorated. As a result, many cities in China have struggled with poor air quality similar to what London once experienced. According to a recent report in the *New York Times,* a recent audit in Northern China found that over 14,000 Chinese businesses, a full 70% of the businesses examined, did not comply with air pollution laws. The Chinese government is promising similar audits all over the country, and preliminary results show that 75% of the nation's industry does not meet environmental standards. Much like the issues the United States once struggled with (and often still does), pollution plagues China's water. 70% of China's waterways are so polluted they are not safe for human use, and 80% of

China's groundwater is too contaminated for consumption. Pollution in one of the largest rivers in China, the Yangtze, is so severe that it has already contributed to multiple extinctions. China's pollution problems are not unique, and are found repeated all over the continent of Asia and much of the continent struggles with the same issues that once plagued Western nations going back to the Industrial Revolution.

It's clear humans have had significant impacts on the Earth's environments for nearly our entire existence and this chapter is just few facts from humans' long and often turbulent relationship with the natural world. While our impact has grown over the centuries, we have experienced a fundamental change in the last 70 years. The rapid acceleration of our influence has propelled us into a unique position among all life on the planet. Humans are now the single most influential species on Earth. Our impact is now so large that it affects, not only all other life on Earth, but the very processes of the planet that make that life possible. Many of the issues that we continue to struggle with today are merely extensions of issues from the past, some centuries old. While progress has led to significantly better lives for humans in some regards, the ultimate price for this progress may be much too great in the end. Despite centuries of working against nature for the betterment of people, we have still not found a way to secure humanity's needs in a way that both humans and nature can thrive. In many ways, we have failed to learn from the lessons of the past. We have depleted, toxified, and changed the world in so many ways, and we continue at an ever-increasing rate. The situation has now become increasingly dire. We can ill afford to be who we were, but despite this, we continue on very much the same path we have followed for millennia. Because of this, today's world is more than ever a human world. Next, we explore this world.

4
Where We are Now

The time we are living in now is the Anthropocene, the human age. The term, derived from the Greek word for human, *Anthropos,* was first popularized by Nobel Prize recipient Paul Crutzen. Crutzen and others recognized that the impact humans were having on the planet was playing a major role in the fate of the Earth, and that it would certainly show up in the geologic record. Although still not recognized as an official geological period, the term still seems irrefutably accurate. When exactly it started is hard to pin down. It seems that once established, human beings, from their outset, started impacting the environment around them, changing the landscapes in which they lived within a few thousand or even a few hundred years. This impact, as we have seen, exploded in the 1950s with increasing industrial expansion, deforestation, expansion of agriculture, and massive fossil fuel use, and it has continued to intensify to this day.

The start of the era is maybe less important than the fact that we are clearly in the midst of it. Our ability to impact, on a global scale, every aspect of life is proof enough. The entire planet's biosphere and its subsequent evolution are now driven by our actions. Humans, broken free from the constraints of nature, are now in charge, and humanity, at best, has been a poor steward of Mother Earth. Change is, of course, inevitable. Humans will always have an impact on the world, just as any species does; it is part of how the natural world works. However, the world without humans would be a vastly different place, and we have failed to establish the equilibrium to which all species must inevitably adhere. Humans' migrations to nearly every corner of the planet, our enormous reproductive success, and our unprecedented resource consumption have led to potentially catastrophic global changes that threaten not only other species, but also our own. What follows is a breakdown, but by no means a comprehensive look, at the current state of our relationship to the planet and some of the major issues that humanity needs to quickly find solutions to if we are to preserve the Earth's biodiversity and ourselves.

It is hard to overstate the seriousness of the situation. Among the litany of serious environmental threats, the stability of our global climate is now potentially spiraling out of control, and we can see it daily on the news. Fires, floods, droughts, hurricanes, heat, and cold of record proportions have become all too commonplace. In 2020, the U.S. saw a record number (22) of weather events costing more than a billion dollars each. The Atlantic had one of the worst hurricane seasons in history, with a record number of named storms at 30, the second highest recorded number of major hurricanes (category 3 or higher), and the highest number of U.S. landfalls. This marks five consecutive years of above average hurricane activity in the Atlantic. Data from the United Nations Office for Disaster Risk Reduction shows that in the 20 years between 2000 and 2019, there were 7,348 major weather-related disasters with an estimated economic cost of 2.79 trillion dollars. These numbers eclipse the prior two decades that saw just 4,212 major disasters with losses of 1.63 trillion dollars.

Data also shows that major floods have more than doubled around the world, and severe storms have increased by 40%. Devastating floods hit Europe in July of 2021, and the northeastern United States was hit with three all-time record rainfall events from August to September of the same year. The same region was hit again in July of 2023 with some parts of the Hudson River Valley receiving as much as 7.5 inches of rain in just a six hour period. Tornados, once limited to the summer months, now occur throughout the year in the southeastern U.S., and outbreaks of dozens at a time are becoming more common. All of this is a result of the planet getting hotter. As of 2022, globally, 8 of the hottest years on record have occurred since 2015 (for those counting, yes, the last 8 years have been the 8 hottest years on record). In 2021, the western United States and Canada experienced a heat wave with the highest temperatures ever seen in those regions. All-time high temperatures were set in June for Portland, Oregon, at 46.7 °C (116°F), and all-time highs for Oregon and Washington were set at 47.8°C (118°F) near the borders of both states. Even more frightening, the all-time record for Canada was set at a blistering 49.5°C (121°F) in Lytton, British Columbia, after the previous 5 days matching or exceeding Canada's old record of 45°C (113°F). This temperature may not only be a record for Canada but is likely the hottest temperature ever recorded globally above the 45th parallel, coming after the highest temperature ever recorded above the Arctic Circle. In June 2020, in Russia's Siberian region, a high of 38°C (100.4°F) was seen more than 70 miles north of the Arctic Circle. 2023 is shaping up tp be the hottest year ever recorded as the unofficial global average temperature reached an all time record 3 days in a row in July.

The increasing heat doesn't just bring floods, but drought as well. The Western United States is now in the middle of the worst drought seen in the last 1200 years. Record fire seasons are now happening almost yearly somewhere in the west, but even these pale in comparison to the fires that hit Australia in 2019-2020 that quickly became the worst fire event in recorded history. Fires burned throughout the eastern coast of Australia, even into areas of rainforest. In total, 60-80 million acres were consumed. To put this in perspective, the entire amount of land protected by the U.S. National Park Service, including national parks, monuments, battlefields, military parks, historical parks, etc., encompasses just over 85 million acres.

Unfortunately, the list goes on and on, and so rapidly do new record-breaking events happen in the world that it's almost impossible to keep up. Already by July of 2022 the U.S. Southwest had seen record-breaking heat, the giant sequoias of

California had again been threatened with fire, and the Great Salt Lake in Utah had hit its lowest level ever recorded. Europe was in the midst of the worst drought it has seen in at least 70 years. At the same time, it was baking under record heat, with the UK even declaring a national emergency as temperatures in London soared to an all time record of 40.2°C (104.4°F). Spurred on by the heat and drought, wildfires plagued numerous European nations. As the year progressed, Europe's drought reached levels not seen in a thousand years. Highlighting the extremes of the Earth's new fickle climate, just 2 years after the worst fires ever recorded, parts of Australia saw record flooding, with Sydney experiencing its wettest year ever. Elsewhere, Pakistan struggled with devastating floods that inundated fully a third of the entire country.

These are the warning signs of a system that is beginning to destabilize. The amazing climate stability that the world has seen over the last 10,000 years (the global average temperature has only varied by + or - 1°C over that entire period), the stability that has allowed humans to flourish, the stability that allowed agriculture and civilization to develop, is beginning to break down. Biodiversity is in serious decline, and the Earth's ability to offset the impact of humanity is waning. While Earth has numerous mechanisms that allow it to be resilient in times of stress, working much like one enormous organism to keep things in balance, humans are now stressing these systems to the breaking point. This balancing act is complex and involves factors across the globe. Life was crucial to helping establish this balance, and life largely maintains it, especially on time scales useful for humans. However, we know from looking into the history of Earth that change does happen, and when the balance of Earth's systems is upset, a new equilibrium must be established. These changes can happen rapidly, and the nature of this new equilibrium cannot easily be predicted. We are now, on multiple fronts, upsetting Earth's balance, and if we continue, change will come— abrupt and potentially catastrophic change. This change may be so severe that we and many species on Earth might not be able to adapt.

For much of human history, we have seen the planet as an infinite resource, and many have thought that our actions could not possibly change the entire globe. There are some that still believe this, but unfortunately, the evidence of our impact is overwhelming. Our inability in the past to see the Earth as one single interconnected system probably led to this misconception. It is hard for humans to see the "big picture." We evolved to respond to the problems we can see in front of us, that affect us directly, and the global consequences of our daily actions are hard to internalize. Humans, though, are smart. We can grasp these abstract concepts if we are taught to think in those terms. Our fantastic ability to think in this way—to explore, build, and create—has allowed us to do things no other creature on this planet has ever done. Unfortunately, these same qualities have led us to the serious environmental challenges we have today. With these same abilities, we can meet these challenges. Rather than merely exploiting what the earth has to offer, we can be stewards of the global environment for our benefit and that of the species with whom we share this amazing place.

The greatest of these challenges, but by no means the only, is climate change. I'll begin with this because so many of our other challenges add to or are affected by climate change, and going forward, its effects will more and more dominate our actions. Let's first try to answer a few basic questions regarding climate. First, why is the climate changing, and what is causing it to change? Second, and this is the more difficult question, what is and will be the outcome of this change?

The first question has a simple, short answer: an increase in atmospheric CO_2, and humans. The details are more complicated. Since the start of the Industrial Revolution, humans have been adding enormous amounts of carbon dioxide into the atmosphere—billions of tons of it. The nature of CO_2 is such that, in the atmosphere, it traps heat; the more CO_2, the more heat trapped, and the result is a warming of the planet. This fact is not at all a recent discovery, and science has known of the properties of CO_2 and other "greenhouse gases" for generations. Work was done on the properties of these gasses early as 1820. Their impacts on the atmosphere were reported in the journal *Nature* as early as 1882 and Swedish scientist and Nobel laureate Svante Arrhenius had published an extensive paper on the warming effect of CO_2 in the atmosphere by 1896. This publication was based on work done by John Tyndall nearly 40 years earlier. Even though some of this early work did not expressly link the burning of fossil fuels to atmospheric warming, the connection was still made early on. Arrhenius thought the burning of coal could potentially warm the Earth, and even the media was reporting as such. For example, a famously circulated article from a New Zealand newspaper in 1912 stated quite clearly that the current burning of coal and the CO_2 it released would eventually warm the planet.

The scientific community, as well as others, have been seriously concerned for many decades about CO_2 emissions and have been continually warning about the consequences. U.S. President Lyndon B. Johnson was warned of growing concerns in a report from his own science advisory committee in 1965. The climate issues raised in this same report were presented to the American Petroleum Institute's annual meeting that same year by its president, Frank Ikard. What he found in the report concerned him enough to speak out seeing the obvious implications for the future of his industry. Ten years later, the first climate models began predicting how much the Earth could warm, with the first coming from Wetherald and Manabe in 1975. By 1988 NASA was alerting the U.S. Senate about the ever growing climate problem with NASA scientist James Hansen testifying that planet-wide warming had already been detected. Again, the oil industry was never in the dark about the risks of our use of fossil fuels. Exxon released an internal memo in 1982 based on research from its own scientists that read like a report released by the IPCC, predicting many of the same climate consequences that scientists were then publicly talking about. By 1986, Shell had its own, even more extensive, internal report that highlighted the very real dangers of climate change.

Despite decades of warnings, there are still some that maintain (some rather disingenuously) that the problem either is not as severe as scientists are reporting, or humans are not the cause, or amazingly denying the whole concept of human caused climate change all together. Unfortunately, some of these people are in our own governments, but the science is not new, and the facts are what they are. More unfortunate is that we have known about this threat for so long and have yet to do much at all about it.

There is no debate, humans are releasing immense amounts of carbon into the atmosphere, and that leads to warming. We know this because we understand the properties of CO_2 and other "greenhouse gasses," and we know from ice cores and the geologic record that the Earth is warmer when its atmosphere contains more CO_2. Prior to the industrial revolution, the CO_2 content of the atmosphere was around 280 parts per million (ppm), and this had been the norm for at least 100,000 years prior. Now, within the last several decades, that concentration has risen to almost 415 ppm, higher than at any point in the last 3.6 million years. Also concerning is the large increase in methane in the atmosphere. Methane (CH_4), like CO_2, traps heat in the atmosphere, but methane is nearly 30 times more effective at it. Already, the atmospheric concentration of methane has risen from 800 parts per billion (ppb) to over 1800 ppb, and human actions, especially in the agricultural sector, are the main contributors. Unfortunately, with respect to these emissions, the situation continues to deteriorate. Despite a global shutdown in 2020 due to the COVID-19 virus, CO_2 and methane emissions continue to grow. The U.S. National Oceanic and Atmospheric Administration (NOAA) measured an increase in global CO_2 of 2.6 ppm in 2020, despite a 7% reduction in emissions due to the economic slowdown caused by COVID-19. This makes the 2020 increase the fifth highest in the 63 years NOAA has been recording such data. In the absence of a global pandemic and its resulting economic recession, 2020 would have topped the list for the greatest increase in a single year. The global average of methane in the atmosphere also rose by 14.7 ppb, making this the largest increase since records began in 1983. Unfortunately, 2021 fared little better, with another 2.6 ppm increase in average atmospheric CO_2 concentrations and another record rise in the amount of methane released. Certainly, these are disturbing statistics in a world where we desperately need to see a decrease in emissions.

Global CO_2 emissions are now approximately 40 gigatons (40 billion tons) per year, and for every 1,000 GT released, we would expect to see about 0.5°C increase in global temperatures. Since 1850, humans have put around 2,400 GT of CO_2 into the atmosphere. So where does all of this CO_2 come from? According to the EPA, globally, 25% of total carbon emissions come from heating and electrical production. 24% comes from agriculture and land use, including deforestation. 21% comes from industrial sources, 14% from transportation, 10% from the energy sector (not included in the direct production of electricity), and 6% from buildings. In the United States, however, transportation is the leading source of carbon at 29%, followed by electrical generation at 25%. It is important when talking about emissions to realize that while humanity at large is to blame for CO_2 emissions, some are certainly more to blame than others. 40% of the world's emissions come from only the wealthiest 16% of the population. China, the U.S., and India are the 3 largest emitters of greenhouse gases, respectively, but looking at emissions per person, the citizenry of the U.S. has a much greater impact at the individual level. Even though China is by far the largest total emitter, China's emissions per capita are less than half of those in the U.S. The average Chinese citizen is responsible for around 7.6 tons of carbon each year, compared to 16.7 tons for the average American. In total, India's 1.3 billion people produce half the greenhouse gases as the U.S. and only about one-tenth the emissions per person. The wealthy nations of the United States, Australia, and Canada all have per capita emissions more than twice that of China and more than three times the global average.

Now that we've seen why the climate is changing and where this change is coming from, what is the result of the huge amounts of CO_2 we are putting into the atmosphere? In respect to humanity, we have created an atmosphere that humans have never before experienced. The last time atmospheric CO_2 was this high, the genus *Homo* would not arise for another million years. Already, the planet has warmed by 1°C on average, which seems like an insignificant change, but without action we could see a 4°C increase in the next 100 to 200 years. To put it into perspective, the last time the Earth was just 2°C warmer, sea levels were 13 to 21 ft higher, which would put many coastal cities under feet of water. Simply put we are already nearly halfway to catastrophe. The real danger of climate change is not just the rise in temperature, but the associated effects that rise can have.

The Earth's systems are stabilized by negative feedback loops. In these systems, a rise in a factor, such as temperature or CO_2, causes a change in the system that reduces that factor and eventually brings it back into balance. For example, there are a couple different mechanisms to remove CO_2 from the atmosphere. One is biotic. Increases in CO_2 and temperatures can increase plant growth, which results in more CO_2 being taken up from the atmosphere. Some of this CO_2 is stored within the tissues of the plants for various amounts of time, depending on the plant and conditions. As a result, CO_2 in the atmosphere lowers. The other is abiotic. The natural weathering of silicate rich rock along with rainwater pulls CO_2 out of the atmosphere by creating carbonate rock that binds the CO_2 semi-permanently. This mechanism can also be influenced by life, with increased plant growth also increasing weathering. Much of the CO_2 we are putting into the atmosphere will eventually meet this fate but tempering this happy fact are the timescales in which this feedback operates. We know through ice cores that a quick warming period called the The Paleocene–Eocene Thermal Maximum (PETM), precipitated by yet another major volcanic event, happened about 55 million years ago. Global average temperatures soared 5-7 degrees C in as little as 20,000 years (much slower than they are currently rising for perspective). This obviously caused a major disruption in the earth's ecosystems, but it may still be mild in comparison to our current state. Research suggests that we are today adding CO_2 to the atmosphere at 9–10 times the rate as in the PETM. Eventually, CO_2 levels fell and the planet cooled, with silicate weathering doing its job. Unfortunately, this mechanism will likely not be of much use to us in our current situation. Only after 150 to 200 thousand years were the high levels of CO_2 of the PETM mitigated.

There also exist positive feedback loops, and these are a cause for great concern with regards to climate change. These loops operate opposite of their negative counterparts, and instead of having a dampening effect, changes in these loops further a greater change in the system. A major player in historical climate shifts is the feedback loop of the ice cover on Earth. Particularly of concern in our current warming state, this loop can act on relatively rapid time scales and have wide-ranging effects. Ice cover, whether on land or in the sea, modulates global temperatures by reflecting sunlight back into space. In a warming loop, as we see today, an increase in temperature reduces ice cover, which reflects less sunlight. In the absence of ice, the darker surfaces of open water and exposed earth absorb sunlight and, as a result, heat up. This heat is then transferred to the atmosphere, resulting in higher temperatures and more ice loss. Even the ice itself has a built-in loop. Melting, slushy ice is darker than frozen ice. As a result, even in still ice-covered areas, more heat is absorbed by this melting ice, which further increases melting. This loop can also work in reverse, with a decrease in global temperatures increasing ice, resulting in more reflected light and thus more heat loss, which reinforces more ice formation. These positive feedback loops can reach "tipping points," where the system can progress to a point where rapid change to an alternate state occurs. In our current state, this would mean rapidly moving from a world with large ice sheets and seasonal sea ice to one that is relatively ice-free.

It is clear that we are in a warming cycle, not only due to the observed increase in atmospheric temperature but also due to the changes that have been observed in global ice. For example, in 2012, data showed that over a 4-day period, the Greenland ice sheet was melting. The *entire* Greenland ice sheet was melting for the first time in recorded history. Summer temperatures on the ice sheet have hit nearly 27.7°C (80°F) at least twice in recent years, and in 2019, melting began a full month earlier than normal. In 2021, in another first for the Greenland ice sheet, rain was recorded for the first time ever at its highest point. The summit of the ice sheet sits at over 10,000 feet in altitude and has only reached above freezing three times in the last decade. Ice cores suggest that even this is abnormal, and the last time melting occurred on the summit was sometime in the late 1800s. Modeling shows that ice loss in the 21st century will exceed anything seen in the last 12,000 years. Greenland is now losing an average of 268 billion metric tons of ice per year and has had a net loss of ice every year since 1998.

The Arctic's sea ice now covers an average of 30% less area than it once did, and its extent continues to shrink on average, opening up nearly 40,000 sq km (15,000 sq mi) of more heat absorbing open water every year. This dramatic reduction is having significant effects on arctic species such as the polar bear *(Ursus maritimus)*, which rely on sea ice for hunting habitat. As a result, researchers following polar bear populations have noticed a sharp increase in starving bears and dramatic behavior changes as the bears attempt to adapt to a new, warmer, Arctic. Severe population declines are also being observed, and one population in the southern Beaufort Sea declined by 25–50% in just the two years between 2004 and 2006. Antarctic ice has fortunately not seen the rapid loss that the Arctic has, but there is evidence that this trend will likely not hold. Around the world, nearly every glacier on the planet is in severe retreat, not only diminishing their cooling effects but also risking the water security of billions of people and countless natural habitats from the Himalayas to the Andes.

Glacial advances and retreats have happened several times in the last 2.6 million years, in roughly 100,000-year cycles, creating the "ice ages" that most are familiar with. These are a normal circumstance of Earth's recent climatic norms. These periods are controlled by variations in Earth's orbit, which change the amount of solar energy Earth receives; however, our addition of historically significant amounts of CO_2 into the atmosphere seriously risks upsetting the recent norm of glacial cycles. This creates a real danger that we will pass a point where we enter a "Hothouse Earth" scenario where the glacial cycles stop and Earth settles into a new state with a much warmer climate and a vastly different global biosphere.

One of the obvious results of this mass loss of ice is, of course, sea level rise. We know from the geologic record that, again, a global 2°C increase over current norms can drive sea levels up 13-21 feet. Already, low-lying areas of the globe are seeing the impacts of a higher sea, and thus far, according to NASA, we have observed around a 90 mm (3.5 in) rise in sea level since 1900. Even with aggressive emission-cutting measures, we are likely already locked into a significant sea-level rise. If the Earth warms enough and a tipping point is reached, pushing Earth towards being ice free, an unrecognizable map of the Earth emerges. The loss of the Greenland ice sheet alone, which evidence shows has happened in the last 150,000 years, would raise sea levels by as much as 8 meters (26 feet) and a total loss of the Antarctic ice sheet would raise sea levels by a staggering 70 meters (230 ft). Melting ice is not the only factor in sea level rise. Like nearly everything else, water expands when it is heated, and the ocean is no different. It has absorbed as much as 90% of the heat that has been added to the atmosphere. This thermal expansion alone accounts for one-third of the sea level rise already measured.

The influx of anthropogenic CO_2 into the atmosphere affects the ocean in more ways than just sea level. The ocean is one of the largest carbon sinks on the planet, and it absorbs 30% to 40% of the carbon dioxide we release. On the surface, this sounds like a benefit for us, but as concentrations continue to rise, more CO_2 is forced into the ocean. This has a couple of effects. One is that as the ocean absorbs more CO_2, it can absorb less, increasing the amount of CO_2 in the atmosphere. Second, and potentially devastating to sea life and the ocean ecosystem, is acidification. As seawater absorbs carbon dioxide from the atmosphere, it reacts with it and creates carbonic acid (H_2CO_3), which in solution increases the amount of free protons (H^+). pH is measured on a scale of 0 to 14. A pH above 7 is alkaline, or dominated by hydroxyl ions (OH^-), and a pH below 7 is acidic, dominated by protons (H^+). A pH of 7 is neutral and has an even concentration of both. Essential members of the ocean ecosystem, including corals, types of plankton, sea stars, urchins, clams, mussels, countless other ocean invertebrates, and even numerous types of seaweed, utilize calcium carbonate ($CaCO_3$) for essential parts of their structures. Anyone who remembers dropping acid on a limestone rock in school (made from the ancient calcium carbonate rich corpses of these organisms) will immediately understand the problem with this scenario. These calcifying organisms struggle in a lower pH environment due to the increased energy demands of combining calcium (Ca^{2+}) and carbonate (CO_3^{2-}) ions. At lower pH levels, this is made altogether impossible.

Mean ocean pH has already dropped from a pH of 8.2 to 8.1 since 1900. This seems like a small change, but the pH scale is logarithmic, so the 0.1 drop in pH constitutes a 30% increase in acidity. If CO_2 emissions continue as they are, by mid-century, the mean pH in the ocean could drop to 8.0 and to 7.8 by the end of the century. Studies of CO_2-releasing volcanic vents in the seas off Ischia, Italy, show that with increasing acidity, a marked decrease in ocean biodiversity is observed. At a pH of 7.9–7.8, a 30% reduction in species is seen. At a mean pH of 7.6, shelled organisms such as snails begin to dissolve, and as pH decreases closer to the vents, all calcium carbonate-dependent life disappears.

The effect of this lowered pH on ocean ecosystems is apparent and could certainly affect the ocean food web in a catastrophic way. The impact on coral reefs, already under severe stress from warming seas, could push them rapidly toward extinction. Globally, many coral reefs have suffered extensive bleaching events as they release their symbiotic algae in response to heat stress. While corals can recover from these events, they all too often result in the death of the corals and the rich biodiverse habitat that they create. According to NOAA, 75% of all the coral reefs on Earth experienced bleaching events between 2014 and 2017, of which 30% died as a result. In the world's largest coral reef, the Great Barrier Reef of Australia, the losses have been staggering. Fully half of the reef was lost between 1985 and 2012, and 42% of that was directly from bleaching events. Of the remaining reefs, the severe bleaching event of 2016 caused an observed 51% reduction in live coral cover and, as a result, caused significant restructuring of the local ocean ecosystem. New research shows that since the first major bleaching event on the Great Barrier Reef in 1998, only 2% of the reef has escaped bleaching. To put how significant that is into perspective, the Great Barrier Reef is 2300 km (1429 mi) in length, or roughly the distance from Paris to Casablanca, Morocco.

Studies suggest that we may have already lost as much as 50% of the world's corals already, and although predictions vary, we could very well see the remainder disappear within 50 years or less. As warming continues, bleaching events will increase in shallow, warmer reef systems, but even in deeper reefs less affected by warming, ocean acidification may eventually prevent their existence altogether. The loss of these complex "rainforests of the seas" would be devastating to ocean biodiversity and the over 4,000 species of fish that rely on the world's coral reefs. Their loss would not only affect these species, but would also be a detriment to the entire global ecosystem.

If there is any question about the potential devastating effects of huge releases of CO_2 into the atmosphere, let me now remind you of the fate of trilobites and the worst extinction event ever seen on our planet during the end-Permian extinction. Let me also state that we humans are certainly not as hardy as the trilobites. I will let the reader draw their own conclusions about our potential for survival if human actions may be initiating something like that again.

Climate change is of course one of our greatest challenges, and many other issues not only affect climate change but are in themselves difficult issues that need to be addressed. Two of the most influential and closely related issues are deforestation and agriculture, and both not only influence climate and each other but also have severe impacts on the Earth's biodiversity, both directly and indirectly. Deforestation is the second largest source of human CO_2 emissions, and the loss of forests not only exacerbates our CO_2 problem but also obviously severely affects species that depend on them. Forests help to mitigate the carbon dioxide that we are putting into the atmosphere by absorbing vast amounts of carbon and storing it within the tree's tissues. Deforestation is doubly damaging with regard to carbon emissions. Not only does the loss of our forests release carbon directly, but it also reduces the uptake of carbon out of the atmosphere.

The majority of the world's deforestation comes from clearing of forests for agricultural use, and the most land-intensive of these are cattle grazing, soybean production, and palm oil production, all of which are severely encroaching on vital rainforest habitats. For example, Brazil alone devotes a total of 170 million hectares (650,000 sq mi) to cattle grazing, much of it in former rainforest, and throughout South America, 120 million hectares (463,000 sq mi) are used just for the production of soy, 70% of which is used for animal feed. 21 million hectares (81,000 sq mi) are taken up worldwide for palm oil production, most of which is in Southeast Asia.

Humans cut down an estimated 15 billion trees a year worldwide. Between 1970 and 2017, the harvest of raw timber worldwide increased by 45% and forest loss, especially the the tropics, has been astonishing. The largest and most biodiverse of all the rainforests, the Amazon, has lost an estimated 17% of its historic cover. In Brazil alone, 65 million hectares (250,000 square miles) of rainforest have been lost to agriculture just since 1985, and this number includes only legally cleared forest area. The total, according to Brazil's own estimation, is more than 700,000 sq km (270,000 sq mi) since the 1970s, or an area larger than the countries of France and England combined.

Driven by oil palm plantations, the legal and illegal lumber trade, and fires exacerbated by the opening up of forests, the immensely biodiverse island of Borneo in Indonesia has lost more than 50% of its native forest cover. From 1973 to 2015, 18.7 million hectares (72,000 sq mi) of Borneo's old-growth forests were cleared to make room for oil palm and wood pulp operations. The old-growth forests of Borneo and the nearby island of Sumatra are not only important for our global fight against climate change; they are also home to one of humans' closest animal relatives, the orangutan. In Borneo, half of the population of these intelligent arboreal apes has already been lost, and an estimated 2,000-3,000 orangutans are lost each year. The critical habitat they rely on continues to be cleared and fragmented. Once ranging widely throughout Indonesia and the surrounding island nations, they are now isolated in small patches of what remains of their once vast forest home. Today, all three remaining species are critically endangered.

On the island nation of Madagascar, 90% of the species found there are endemic, including over 100 species of lemur. These ancient and unique primates are now under severe threat due to habitat loss, and one third of them are now critically endangered. 98% of all lemurs are threatened, according to the International Union for the Conservation of Nature (IUCN). Madagascar has lost 44% of its forests since the 1950s, and the loss continues at a rate of nearly 100,000 hectares (24,000 acres) per year. Once again, agriculture and logging are largely to blame, putting lemurs and thousands of other species that are unique to Madagascar in extreme peril.

Unfortunately, deforestation in rainforests can lead to more deforestation. The loss of tree cover can create feedback loops that can result in an even greater loss of forest cover resulting in dramatic shifts in the makeup of the forest, accelerating habitat and species loss. As I mentioned earlier, the clearing of rainforest opens up the edges of the forest to drier air. This causes a loss of vital moisture, drying out the landscape and transforming rich, dense rainforest into dry, open savanna. The result is an obvious and dramatic loss of biodiversity and the essential water-holding abilities of these forests. The immense loss of biomass sequesters less carbon and leads to higher atmospheric CO_2 levels.

Rainforests are not the only forests under threat, and in temperate climates, climate change is beginning to affect forests with increased droughts and insect infestations. Both of these factors drive wildfires, and in 2020, the western United States saw one of the worst fire seasons ever. Over 10 million acres burned throughout the West, and the states of California and Colorado both saw their largest fires in history. Forest fires, while a natural process, are unfortunately doubly concerning for climate change. Like deforestation, the fires release vast amounts of CO_2, and the reduction of forest sequesters less.

Protection of remaining forests, and especially mature old-growth forests, will be essential in preventing future biodiversity loss. Primary rainforests or old-growth temperate forests cannot simply be replanted. Once lost, they can take a generation or more to regrow to their former splendor. While we can and should replant forests, these young trees will do little good for struggling species that require mature forests. Overall, we may have 3 trillion fewer trees today than when human civilization began, and we still continue to lose mature forests. Losses in the Amazon are now the highest they have been in the last 15 years, with the region losing 13,235 square kilometers (5110 square miles) of forest between 2020 and 2021. Worldwide, the loss of forest cover was equivalent to an area the size of the UK, or 253,000 sq km (97,000 sq mi).

Agriculture constitutes one of the largest impacts that humans have on the Earth. Not only is it the primary driver of habitat loss globally, which has severe impacts on biodiversity, but it also directly impacts climate change and atmospheric CO_2. Just the practice of plowing fields for crops has released one-quarter to one-third of the total atmospheric CO_2 added to our atmosphere since the beginning of the Industrial Revolution. To make matters worse, modern agricultural practices have normalized the use of huge amounts of pesticides and fertilizers, resulting in profound environmental impacts worldwide while diminishing the health of our soils.

Globally, agricultural land now occupies 5 billion hectares (19 million sq mi) of land. This is a land area equivalent to the entire continents of North America, South America, and Australia combined and constitutes 38% of the Earth's entire land surface. Two-thirds of this is used primarily for cattle grazing, with the remainder used for crop production. Without significant changes in agricultural practices or diet, agricultural land use could increase 10% to 25% by 2050. Of the habitats most severely affected by agriculture, wetland environments have taken the most severe hit. These rich ecosystems, which are home to fish, amphibians, insects, and a huge abundance of bird life, have been reduced by 85% worldwide. Not only are wetlands essential habitats, but coastal wetlands act as buffers against increasing storm surges. Here and elsewhere, wetlands help to control the impacts of flooding and promote clean water. The world's grasslands have suffered as well, and nowhere is the conversion of wild land to farmland more visible than parts of the Midwestern United States. Here, where a huge amount of the world's grain is produced, up to 85% of the total land area is used for crop production. Much of this was formerly tall-grass prairie. This rich ecosystem may be the most endangered on the planet, and all that remains of this once vast landscape are isolated patches. Of the original 170 million acres of North American tall-grass prairie, just 4% remains. Once again, much of the tilled land in the world is used to produce food for the livestock we raise, and it's an unbelievable amount. Worldwide, we raise around a billion head of cattle, and nearly 70% of all the birds on the planet are domestic chickens.

Among the many negative impacts of our agricultural practices is the enormous use of fertilizers. These synthetic chemicals applied to croplands add huge amounts of nitrogen and phosphorus to the environment and are usually applied in great excess of what the plants can actually use. For example, fully half of the nitrogen applied to U.S. crops is not taken up by the plants it is meant to fertilize. While increasing our short-term productivity and saving yet more land from the plow, runoff of these nutrients into our waterways has severe negative impacts. The result of this high nutrient runoff is the promotion of huge algal blooms in freshwater and saltwater ecosystems, primarily due to the influx of phosphorus into the environment. This excess of nutrients is called eutrophication. This seems as though it would be a benefit, as many species feed on algae, but in these cases the growth is so rapid and widespread that the ecosystem cannot deal with the overabundance. As the algae dies, it sinks in the water column, and the decomposition of this huge amount of algae creates anoxia, or the depletion of oxygen. This leads to fish die-offs and, ultimately, a large decrease in local biodiversity. Many have seen this in their local communities as the runoff of fertilizers from lawns results in nearby ponds going rapidly from clear to thickly scum-covered with the onset of early summer heat.

The same is seen on a massive scale with agricultural runoff of excess fertilizer and waste from large animal productions entering the world's major waterways. This nutrient-rich runoff creates enormous dead zones as the water is stripped of oxygen. In the Gulf of Mexico, runoff from the Mississippi watershed, which drains the farmland of the central United States, creates a dead zone that is over 13,000 square kilometers (5,000 square miles) in extent on average. In 2017, a record for the size of this dead zone reached nearly 9,000 square miles. In Europe, the Baltic Sea was once thought to have the world's largest dead zone. It covers nearly a sixth of the entire extent of the sea, or nearly 70,000 sq km (27,000 sq mi). Agricultural waste is a major factor, but human waste is also a contributor. Shockingly, one of the largest polluters into the Baltic, St. Petersburg, did not have a single modern wastewater plant until 2013. As massive as the Baltic Sea's dead zone is, it is still small when compared to the extent of the dead zone in the Arabian Sea. Here, nearly the entirety of the Gulf of Oman, some 63,000 sq mi, is anoxic. In this case, however, agriculture seems less to blame, but the culprit is likely increased warming due to climate change.

The mass use of pesticides is also a severe consequence of our agricultural practices and has far-reaching effects on a multitude of organisms. The overall amount of pesticides (chemicals used to control insects, animals, micro-organisms, and plants in total) used every year is staggering. Annually, 5.6 billion pounds of pesticides are applied worldwide, with the United States alone using more than a billion pounds. With this comes a myriad of negative environmental effects. These pesticides, while useful to control organisms attacking crops, are harmful or deadly to non-target species. The enormous amounts used mean that these chemicals can easily spread far beyond their intended area of use through wind and water. This results in the contamination of wildlands and waterways near and far from the point of origin. Pesticides easily enter waterways and have been shown to have dramatic effects on aquatic species, causing mass fish die-offs, reproductive disruptions, and disruptions of aquatic food chains. Amphibians can be acutely affected by absorbing these chemicals through their skin. One study observed a 96–100 percent die-off of tadpoles exposed to glyphosate through spraying adjacent to their habitat. As many as 90% of fish in the U.S. can be found to have traces of at least one or more pesticides in their tissues, and pesticides have been specifically implicated in the decline of numerous species in and out of water.

Pesticide use in combination with lands displaced by agriculture are also contributing to the loss of key insect species that serve to pollinate not only wild plants but the majority of our crops. The decline of these pollinator species is of dire concern. Particularly concerning is the effect of neonicotinoid insecticides on numerous species of bees. Exposure to this class of insecticides has been shown to reduce queen production in the buff-tailed bumblebee *(Bombus terrestris)* by as much as 85%. Other studies have seen a halving of the reproductive output of the mason bee, *Osmia bicornis,* when exposed to neonicotinoids. In an 18-year study completed in 2016, researchers in the UK were able to link the long-term decline in wild bee populations there to the use of neonicotinoids. They were able to show that bee species that fed on oil rapeseed treated with this class of insecticides were 3 times more negatively affected than species that did not. Research from the United States paints an even more bleak picture, with researchers finding that in the U.S. "The toxicity loading of insecticides on agricultural land and surrounding areas has increased by approximately 50-fold over the last two decades, producing both direct and indirect effects on associated ecosystems." They go on to state that 99% (via oral toxicity) of this toxicity loading is due to neonicotinoids. For example, the neonicotinoid imidacloprid has a half-life (the time it takes for half of the initial amount to be degraded) in the environment of 174 days. This means that it will take as much as 2.4 years for 97% of it to degrade. Yearly applications could mean huge amounts persisting in the environment. This is potentially disastrous for bees considering the reported LD_{50} (dose lethal to 50% of those exposed) for imidacloprid in the honeybee *(Apis mellifera)* is just 0.0035 µg when ingested or 3.5 billionths of a gram. Even worse, research suggests that bumblebees may be even more sensitive.

Due to the concerns raised by the use of this class of chemicals, the European Food Safety Commission was asked to assess their use and concluded that they posed an unacceptably high risk to bees. In 2018, the EU banned the use of most neonicotinoids outside of greenhouses, but unfortunately, they are still in wide-spread use around the world, including in the United States. Neonicotinoids have been indicated to be harmful to birds as well. Studies in the U.S. on the white-crowned sparrow *(Zonotrichia leucophrys)* during its migration showed that exposure to neonicotinoid pesticides caused these birds to lose a quarter of their body mass and fat stores, a potentially devastating outcome for a migrating bird. Neurotoxic effects were also observed with exposure to neonicotinoids, which impaired the birds' migratory orientation.

Use of these pesticides in the United States has exploded in recent decades, going from almost zero in 1992 to nearly 8 million pounds by 2014. According to a 2015 USGS study, 50% of the water tested in the U.S. and Puerto Rico contained neonicotinoid pesticides, the most common being the imidacloprid mentioned above. In an effort to convince the U.S. Congress to pass the Saving America's Pollinators Act of 2015, the American Bird Conservancy tested food from the congressional dining halls. They found that, out of the 66 samples they took, 91% contained traces of neonicotinoid pesticides. Despite their findings, the act still died in committee.

Unfortunately, it seems that neonicotinoid pesticides may not be the only type affecting bees. A study published in June of 2022 found that the world's most popular weed killer, glyphosate, commonly sold under the brand name Roundup®, was also negatively affecting bees. Studies with bumblebees, once again *Bombus terrestris,* showed that exposure to glyphosate inhibited their ability to thermoregulate their hives, a dangerous outcome for bees that may already be stressed by a lack of food. Researchers have also found that exposure to glyphosate also impairs the memory and navigation abilities of honeybees, and leads to the disruption of the bees gut bacteria as well. While maybe not as toxic to bees as neonicotinoid pesticides, the use of glyphosate is even larger and more widespread. Worldwide, more than 826 million kg (1.8 billion pounds) of glyphosate are applied to crops and lawns every year. Since 1974, almost 19 billion pounds of glyphosate have entered the environment.

Like bees, other pollinators such as butterflies have seen measured decreases as well. In Europe, there have been dramatic declines. Butterfly populations in the UK have seen a 50% reduction since the 1970s, and 8% of native species have already gone extinct. On the mainland of Europe, the number of grassland butterflies has decreased by as much as 39%. In Belgium alone, 20 species of butterfly have gone extinct, accompanied by severe declines in overall butterfly populations in just the 15 years between 1992 and 2007. Much of this decline has been attributed to agricultural intensification. Few systematic studies exist outside of Europe, but one such study in the United States mirrors the losses seen in Europe. Population counts over the past 20 years in the state of Ohio show a 33% decline in butterfly abundance there between 1996 and 2016.

There is evidence that insects may be in severe decline overall, and this may drive further losses in biodiversity across the world's ecosystems. Studies of insect populations, covering all major groups, show that globally, populations have declined by 45% in the last 40 years, and research from the German Krefeld Entomological Society showed that the biomass of flying insects throughout Germany has decreased by as much as 76%. Studies of bumblebees in the United States show dramatic declines and range contractions across the U.S., with one study finding a 96% reduction in species abundance in four common bumblebee species. Recent studies suggest that the world may be losing insects as quickly as 1% of the population per year. It has become increasingly clear that all over the world, insects are under threat, but to what extent this is true is still difficult to establish. Scientists are hampered by the absence of long-term research to establish trends, and once again, our severe lack of knowledge of the number and characteristics of many insect species limits accurate predictions. Despite this, it is very likely that our mass use of pesticides is a major contributor to insect losses.

Ironically, the application of these chemicals to agricultural land, while beneficial to agricultural yields, can undermine long-term productivity. The complex fauna of healthy soils is severely impacted by pesticide overuse and the constant disruption of tillage. These practices lead to sterile, depleted soils. Without the essential microorganisms and fungal networks to provide services like the breakdown of organic matter, the fixing of nitrogen, and the uptake of nutrients by crops, soils can be diminished to the extent where they are no longer viable to support growth. These diminished soils rely even more on human-applied nutrients to grow anything. Soil sterilization, whether unintentional or intentional (entire fields are sometimes intentionally sterilized to kill potentially harmful organisms or competing plant seeds), increases reliance on human-produced fertilizers while amplifying their negative environmental effect of degrading the world's soils.

Of course, the effects of pesticides on pollinators, insects, and soils are of great concern, but the broader effect of pesticides in the environment may be vastly more harmful than once thought. This threatens not only living systems but humans as well. Take, for instance, the glyphosate mentioned above. Multiple studies confirm that glyphosate can cause liver damage in numerous species. It has also been shown to cause immune suppression, oxidative stress, mineral deficiencies, birth defects, DNA damage, epigenetic methylation, and is a known endocrine disruptor (I'll talk more about these EDCs later). Glyphosate is also a known cancer promoter. In fact, a meta-analysis of a large body of research concluded that people exposed to high levels of glyphosate-based herbicides have a 41% greater risk of developing non-Hodgkin lymphoma. However, the effect of glyphosate may be even broader. Glyphosate is structurally very similar to the amino acid glycine. Glycine is widely found in the proteins essential for life, and it is theorized that glyphosate may actually be able to replace glycine within the proteins of plants and animals. The result of this change could disrupt a myriad of metabolic and hormonal pathways that all forms of life utilize. This is a controversial theory, but if true, this replacement could explain the huge rise in recent decades of gut-related issues, autoimmune diseases, autism, Alzheimer's, reproductive declines, diabetes, and obesity found in humans. In fact, the increase in many of these conditions is closely correlated to the rise in glyphosate use. (For more on this, please see MIT researcher Stephanie Seneff's book *Toxic Legacy.*)

The prevalence of pesticides in the environment is shocking. We and much of the rest of the world's life are almost constantly exposed to them. Pesticides are found in nearly every waterway in the United States. It's estimated that at least 50 million people in the U.S. get their drinking water from groundwater that could be contaminated. Most conventionally grown grain products contain measurable levels of glyphosate, which is commonly used in their production, but it is so prevalent in the environment that trace amounts can even be found on organically produced foods. The U.S. Centers for Disease Control and Prevention found the presence of glyphosate in the urine of more than 80% of people tested, and despite most types of organochlorine pesticides (like DTT) being banned for decades in the U.S., their presence is still detectable in recent blood serum samples of Americans. It is estimated that as many as 25 million agricultural workers per year suffer from some type of pesticide poisoning, and numerous studies have shown increased cancer rates among agricultural workers exposed to pesticides. Many of these chemicals, particularly glyphosate, are used on our lawns and in our neighborhoods, making this a widespread problem for pollinators, wild plants and animals, and us.

Gone are the old days of pesticides and the mass spraying of highly toxic chemicals like DDT, dieldrin, or heptachlor, and the resulting mass losses of birds, wildlife, and even livestock that plagued the mid-20th century. Despite our past experience with the devastating effects of pesticides, the less acute toxicity of today's pesticides has lulled us into a false sense of security. While spilling a pesticide like glyphosate on your arm may not kill you, the long-term exposure to it through multiple avenues and the hundreds of other commonly used pesticides are doubtless doing significant harm to the Earth's biological systems and us.

Agriculture's far-reaching impact not only uses land and contributes to climate change but is also a huge driver of the use of freshwater around the globe. With climate change severely impacting the global distribution of rain, the future of the world's water resources is of increasing concern. According to the World Bank, around 70% of the world's freshwater is used for agriculture, stressing water resources around the planet. Ironically, agriculture itself may be largely to blame for limiting the water it relies on. Not only are its contributions to warming the globe a factor, but the mass loss of forests and wetlands directly change water flows, reducing the amount of water that is captured and stored on the surface and underground by increasing runoff and evaporation. Decades of intensive agriculture have depleted soils, decreasing their ability to absorb and retain water, leading to worse flooding, decreased drought tolerance, and the fouling of water resources by increased erosion.

Often overlooked, groundwater is a particularly important source of freshwater. Due to over-extraction and the reduction of habitats that encourage water transfer to subsurface aquifers, 30% of the world's aquifers are in distress, and groundwater levels globally are falling. This affects wildlife and aquatic systems that rely on groundwater to supply lakes, rivers, and wetlands. On average, 30–40% of the water in U.S. rivers and streams is supplied by groundwater sources. This influx of water maintains stream and river flows, keeping them flowing throughout the year and preserving the life they contain. This is especially important in drier parts of the world where aquatic systems may be largely maintained by groundwater sources. Groundwater pumping, primarily for agricultural irrigation, has already reduced streamflows by as much as 50% in the U.S. As a result of these losses, several species of brook salamander in Texas are now threatened or endangered, and at least one species of fish is now extinct in Arizona. In the 20th century alone, the U.S. has pumped 800 cubic kilometers of groundwater, almost twice the volume of Lake Erie. Globally, between 1993 and 2010, as much as 2 trillion tons of groundwater were lost from the world's aquifers. In fact, recent research has discovered that humanity is pumping such a large volume of groundwater that it is actually changing the Earth's axis of rotation, causing the North Pole to drift some 4.36 cm each year!

Surface water sources are also under stress as climate change reduces the amount of precipitation in certain regions and droughts intensify. The Colorado River in the United States supplies water to 40 million people, but a prolonged 20- year drought has reduced the flow of this crucial river by 20%. This drought, the worst seen in nearly 1,250 years, and the overuse of the river's water are now threatening the water security of a large swath of the American Southwest. One of the largest reservoirs on the Colorado River, Lake Mead, has not been full since 1983 and now hovers around 30% full. Here again, agriculture plays a dramatic role. 80% of the river's water is extracted to irrigate crops, the majority of which is alfalfa grown to feed cattle. 10% is utilized by cities, and what little is left over sustains what is left of the river's natural systems. As a result of the intensive demands, the Colorado River rarely reaches the Gulf of California, where a lush and diverse river delta ecosystem once existed. Here, the lack of freshwater and nutrients brought down by the river has reduced the productivity in the Gulf by 95%. Gone is the rich wetland ecosystem that naturalist Aldo Leopold observed in 1922 and that once covered 8500 sq km (3300 sq mi). His eloquent description of this now-lost environment speaks to its richness.

> A verdant wall of mesquite and willow separated the channel from the thorny desert beyond. At each bend we saw egrets standing in the pools ahead, each white statue matched by its white reflection. Fleets of cormorants drove their black prows in quest of skittering mullets; avocets, willets, and yellow-legs dozed one-legged on the bars; mallards, widgeons, and teal sprang skyward in alarm.

Also gone is the once-thriving fishery that allowed as much as 4 million pounds of fish every year to be caught early in the 20th century.

The threat of water insecurity is not unique to the Colorado Basin and is played out around the world. As climate change alters rain patterns, snowfall rates, and global temperatures, more and more of the globe and its ecosystems are dealing with a lack of water. Between 2015 and 2017, a reduction in annual rains created a severe drought in South Africa, and as a result, the city of Cape Town, South Africa, came perilously close to running out of water. Reservoir levels have since recovered, but scientists believe the chances of this happening again will rise from just 0.7% to 25% by 2100. Severe droughts have been seen throughout the world in recent years, and globally, the number of people experiencing extreme droughts could double by the end of this century.

Not only does agriculture utilize a huge percentage of the world's fresh water, but dams used to control and store water have changed the globe's movement of water. Worldwide, there are approximately 50,000 large dams and 17 million reservoirs. There are around 90,000 dams of all sizes in the United States alone; many, if not most, of these dams may no longer be needed. Free-flowing rivers from their source to the ocean are becoming increasingly rare, and dams have fragmented more than 60% of the world's rivers. While dams can mitigate the impacts of severe floods, store water for times of drought, and provide a source of clean hydropower, they can have devastating impacts on ecosystems by locking up nutrients from sediments, changing water temperature regimes, preventing fish migrations, and flooding thousands of acres of habitat upstream.

The deterioration of the Colorado Delta seen above is just one example of how the interruption of the natural flow of a river can have severe impacts on the biodiversity and ecological health of a river. In the Pacific Northwest of the United States, dams prevent salmon from accessing or have flooded critical spawning habitats. This, combined with vast overfishing in the 19th century, further loss of river habitat, pressures from pollution, and a litany of other sources, the salmon of the U.S. Northwest are now in dire trouble. Once numbering in the millions in the Pacific Northwest, salmon and their close cousin, the steelhead trout, are now in danger of extinction in many watersheds. A clear example of the impact dams can have is the Elwha River. Thanks to the removal of two dams, the Elwha is once again flowing freely for the first time in 100 years. Salmon populations are beginning to increase, and the once-missing delta is coming back, along with the species that use this habitat. The salmon, instead of 5 miles of river habitat, now have 45. Unfortunately, even here there is evidence that it might be too late for some species, like the pink salmon *(Oncorhynchus gorbuscha)*, whose numbers continue to be low. At one time, as many as 100,000 pink salmon would return to the Elwha River to breed. This number now stands at just 100-200 individuals, but there is hope the pink could have a turn around in the Elwha and eventually recover.

While land-based efforts to supply humanity with calories are one of the largest drivers of biodiversity loss and climate change, the over-utilization of the world's oceans is also a serious consequence of the need to feed our expanding populations. As of 2015 data, 33% of fish stocks are overfished, with another 60% being fished at maximum capacity. Exacerbating the problem, as many as a third of all fish caught are caught illegally. Overfishing leads to the collapse (defined as a 90% reduction in historical populations) of commonly fished species, and many populations of fish humans routinely consume have collapsed, including: bluefin tuna, Pacific salmon, orange roughy, local populations of anchovies and sardines, and maybe the most notable, the collapse of the North Atlantic cod populations of North America in the 1990s. Overexploited for decades and fished intensively for hundreds of years, the population of North Atlantic cod dropped to just one percent of their historic populations. Despite 30 years of intensive controls on the fishery, populations are nowhere near historical levels, and there is fear that the cod may never recover completely. Research published in 2006 alarmingly predicts that every species of wild-caught seafood could collapse by 2050, and how we manage the world's fisheries will become increasingly important to preserve ocean biodiversity on a wide scale. Fortunately, this trend is improving with better regulation and protection, but little of the ocean escapes human pressures, and only 13% of the ocean could be considered wilderness. Not only are the fish intended for catch affected by fishing activities, but other organisms such as whales, dolphins, sea turtles, and sea lions are inadvertently caught, killed, or injured. Deep-water organisms are also affected by certain types of deep-ocean fishing using nets that dredge the seafloor. This can destroy delicate and critical deep-water coral habitats, turning these areas from surprising islands of deep-water biodiversity into lifeless wastelands. Some of the world's deep coral communities have already been nearly completely destroyed through these practices. The pressures of commercial fishing combined with the stress of ocean warming, acidification, and loss of habitat to shelter young fish, threaten to undermine entire aquatic food chains, imperiling countless species. By the end of the 20th century, it is believed that industrial fishing had already removed 90% of the large fish in the ocean.

Even as some ocean species are seeing positive population trends, the future for sharks and rays seems increasingly grim. According to a recently published paper in the journal *Nature,* the abundance of these species in the world's oceans has declined by 70% since 1970. Fully half of all shark species are considered endangered or critically endangered. Here again, overfishing and unintentional catches are the main culprits. Driving the overfishing is the demand for shark fins used in shark fin soup, a status symbol in China. Rather than using the entire shark, in shark finning the dorsal fin is removed and the remainder of the shark discarded. The high value of shark fin, often as much as $500 per pound, also drives a huge illegal trade in shark fin. Overall, 100 million sharks are taken out of the oceans annually.

Potentially adding insult to injury, the enormous impact of feeding humanity is only made worse by the embarrassing amount of food that humans waste. According to the UNEP, one-third of all the food produced globally for human consumption is wasted, some 1.3 billion tons. As much as half of all the fruits and vegetables produced worldwide go to waste, as does as much as 30% of cereal grains. The United States alone throws away $48.3 billion dollars' worth of food per year, with an extended cost of between $90 and $100 billion dollars. Wealthy nations produce nearly twice as much food as poorer nations, but their consumers waste nearly 10 times as much as their poorer counterparts. If just 25% of the food wasted globally were saved, it would feed a staggering 870 million people. The environmental cost of this waste is obvious, especially when considering the vast amounts of land displaced by agriculture, not to mention the carbon-intensive aspects of agriculture production. A land area of roughly 1.4 billion hectares, or fully 28% of our agricultural land, is used to produce food that is wasted—an area larger than Canada. Put another way, we are encroaching on rainforests and other critical wildlands for agricultural land we don't even need because we simply waste too much. The carbon cost of this waste is the equivalent of a large nation, at 3.3 billion tons or more than the annual output of the entire nation of India.

Often overshadowed by other environmental concerns, pollution is still an ongoing issue around the world that affects wildlife and the resources they rely on. Certainly anthropogenic CO_2 is a type of pollution and gets the bulk of attention, but it's important to remember that other types of pollutants can have devastating short-term effects as well as chronically affect ecosystems. Already mentioned, overuse of pesticides and fertilizers continues to be a global problem, especially when they find their way into aquatic environments. 80% of global wastewater is untreated before being released into the environment. Even in countries that do treat their wastewater, pollutants can still make it through the treatment process. Of concern are the various types of pharmaceuticals that humans consume. Research in Germany found 156 different pharmaceuticals in the environment, most of which occur in surface water. In the United States, the effluent of 50 large wastewater plants was tested for 56 different pharmaceuticals. At all 50 sites, the diuretic drug hydrochlorothiazide was found. The beta-blockers metoprolol and atenolol and the anti-seizure drug carbamazepine were found in 90% of samples. Antibiotics, hormones, analgesics, and antidepressants are also routinely found in the discharge of wastewater plants. Effects of exposure to these substances (especially on aquatic life) vary, but beta-blockers, such as those listed above, have been linked to endocrine disruption in aquatic life. Antibiotics pose an obvious risk to microbial life, and hormones such as ethinylestradiol (a synthetic estrogen) have been linked to the feminization of male fish and frogs. In addition, the presence of antidepressants has been found to affect the behavior of certain fish species. In total, 600 different types of pharmaceuticals have been discovered in the environment around the world.

According to the 2019 IPBES report, "300-400 million tons of heavy metals, solvents, toxic sludge, and other wastes from industrial facilities are dumped into the world's waters each year." Industrial waste is still a significant problem around the world. Often, these wastes can persist in the environment, leading to prolonged impacts. In the U.S. alone, there are 1327 sites on the National Priorities List, representing the worst of the most polluted sites in the country identified by the EPA. The pollution at many of these sites goes back decades. The irresponsible disposal of toxic materials throughout the world, sometimes going as far back as the Industrial Revolution, is still impacting the environment as we continue to add to the problem. Even toxins banned decades ago can still cause problems today. Highlighting this ongoing battle to identify and mitigate past transgressions is the recent discovery of thousands of barrels of toxic waste, a byproduct of the production of the long-banned pesticide DDT, off the coast of California.

In operation from 1942 to 1982, the Montrose Chemical Company was once the country's largest manufacturer of DDT. Over its four decades of operation, thousands of barrels of waste and thousands of gallons of contaminated water were dumped into the ocean. One of these dump sites was known and is now a U.S. Superfund site slated for cleanup. Over the years of operation, an estimated 132 tons of waste were deposited on the Palos Verdes Shelf, just off the coast of Los Angeles. Large concentrations of DDT and PCBs are found in ocean sediments here, and as a result, these chemicals have made their way into the food chain. Sea lions in the area have been found to have high levels of both of these chemicals in their blubber, and the effect of DDT and PCB exposure has been suggested as one of the causes of the astonishing 25% cancer rate among California sea lions.

Despite the tons of waste deposited at the Palos Verdes Shelf, tons more were apparently deposited in the ocean between the California Coast and Catalina Island. During the accidental discovery of this second, previously unknown site by researchers at the University of California, Santa Barbara, 60 barrels of disposed waste were detected. In an analysis of the discovery in 2019, researchers found levels of DDT in ocean sediments 40 times higher than those at the site mentioned above. They also characterized the disposal as "sloppy," finding many of the barrels had ruptured upon reaching the ocean floor. A follow-up study by the Scripps Institution of Oceanography found approximately 27,000 barrels of waste using advanced sonar technology and as many as 100,000 total objects, many of which were believed to be more barrels of the highly toxic chemicals. An extensive search of old records from MCC associated with the decades of dumplings suggests that in total there may be as many as half a million barrels lying on the seafloor. Unfortunately, this discovery represents only a small portion of the toxic waste that has been (and continues to be) dumped in locations all over the world.

Even with recent strides in air quality in the last several decades in the United States and Europe, air pollution is still a worldwide issue. Pollution from industry, transportation, and power generation, coupled with increasing wildfire activity, all combine to foul the world's air. Over half the world's population has seen an increase in air pollution. The regions most impacted are primarily in sub-Saharan Africa and Central and East Asia. Besides fine particulates, which according to the WHO are responsible for 4.2 million deaths annually, ground-level ozone (O_3) is an increasing issue. While ozone is beneficial high in the atmosphere for blocking UV light, at ground level it becomes the primary component of smog. Ozone is created when nitrous oxide compounds combine with volatile organic compounds in the air. Sunlight catalyzes reactions between these compounds, resulting in the formation of ozone. Sources are primarily from cars, industry, and oil and gas production. Ground-level ozone can irritate the lungs, cause shortness of breath, aggravate pre-existing lung conditions, and is a major contributor to asthma. Multiple studies have also linked higher ozone concentrations to an increased risk of death from cardiopulmonary diseases. Ozone also has a significant effect on plant life by reducing the efficiency of photosynthesis, thus slowing a plant's growth rate. It can also make plants more susceptible to disease and insect infestations. This is particularly worrisome given the increasing fragility of the world's forest ecosystems. Ozone can travel long distances from the cities where it originates, and many U.S. national parks experience as many days of high ozone levels as do the 20 largest U.S. cities.

Climate change-driven wildfires have been a major contributor to poorer air quality around the world, particularly in the western United States, where record fires occurred in 2020 and 2021. Fully half of the particulate pollution in the U.S. can now be attributed to wildfires. Unfortunately, pollution is not limited to the west and can account for up to 25% of particulates in the rest of the country. Of course, this issue is not restricted to America. The record fires in Australia in 2019–2020 pushed an estimated 1 million metric tons of smoke into the atmosphere. Smoke from these fires covered the entire Southern Hemisphere and reached as high as 22 kilometers (14 miles) into the upper atmosphere. This warmed the stratosphere and most likely contributed to a large and persistent ozone hole above Antarctica in 2020. This clearly demonstrates that not only are there health impacts to these large wildfires, but potentially harmful global impacts in atmospheric chemistry.

Pollution can come in many forms, and it's not always in the form of a toxic chemical. Probably one of the most under-recognized pollutants that we release is the enormous amount of light we produce. Although not a pollutant in the traditional sense, humans' use and overuse of artificial light can have serious consequences for wildlife, and its impact on migrating birds and sea turtles is well documented. Both are disoriented by the lights we use to illuminate our homes and cities, leading to the deaths of countless animals, but the ill effects are not limited to birds and turtles. Many species can be harmed by our lights, from migrants like monarch butterflies to other insects attracted to artificial light and the species that feed on them. The ever-increasing brightness that we have created also impacts the behavior of numerous nocturnal species that rely on the dark. The decreasing darkness affects us as well, and our near constant exposure to light disrupts our sleep cycle, reduces melatonin production, and can lead to sleep disorders, anxiety, and other health issues. Much of this light pollution stems from our inefficient or unnecessary use of lighting. This not only spreads light into the sky and into our neighbors' windows, away from where we want it, like on our roads, but also wastes a huge amount of energy to light things other than what's intended.

Many of the pollutants humans introduce into the environment have an apparent and straightforward effect. The release of toxic wastes into the environment has often had obvious and expected results. However, many pollutants and their effects go unnoticed or are hard to pin down. They may be an obscure component of another material or may affect a certain species but not others. This is the case with a recently identified pollutant affecting the already imperiled salmon of the U.S. Pacific Northwest. The culprit is the tires we use on our cars, but this is not a case of tires illegally disposed of in the salmon's waters, it's much more subtle than that, and it's something I'm sure few of us have ever considered. The culprit endangering salmon is the rubber worn off tires under their normal use. In this case, the simple act of driving and the unique physiology of coho salmon *(Oncorhynchus kisutch)* add to an unexpected result. Scientists had long observed that spawning coho salmon were for decades experiencing mass die-offs in urban streams following periods of heavy rain, as many as 60-90%. The suspected issue was something contained within the stormwater runoff, but what specifically was causing the die-off was a mystery. Researchers from the University of Washington set out to identify the mysterious cause.

They hit upon a likely candidate when they exposed fish to a solution containing tire wear particles and found it had a toxic effect. They were eventually able to narrow it down, out of the thousands of potential toxins contained in tires, to one. It turns out that these salmon are particularly sensitive to an antioxidant additive in tires called 6PPD. 6PPD is added to tires to keep ground level ozone from degrading the tires. When exposed to ozone, 6PPD converts into several chemicals, including one called 6PPD-quinone. This is the chemical that has been devastating the coho. Even small amounts of 6PPD-quinone are extremely toxic to these salmon. Other fish appear to be less sensitive to the chemical, but unfortunately for coho, 6PPD is almost universally used in all car tires. Tests in urban streams in San Francisco and Los Angeles also show the presence of 6PPD-quinone, and it is assumed that it will be found in any waterway where runoff from roads would be common. Almost nothing is known about the wider effects of 6PPD-quinone, but it has the potential to be a serious and widespread toxin in aquatic systems. If the amount of particles coming off our tires may seem insignificant, you may be surprised to learn that over 1.1 million metric tons of tire wear particles are released every year onto U.S. roads.

While some of the pollutants that we release have a temporary effect, the most concerning pollutants that humanity produces are ones that do not go away. These are synthetically produced materials that do not chemically breakdown in the environment and are also extremely difficult or impossible to remove from it. The most common of these is, of course, plastic (which we'll discuss next), but less widely known substances can also persist almost indefinitely. Of increasing concern are PFAS, or per- and polyfluoroalkyl substances, also known as "forever chemicals" due to their extreme persistence. They are used widely in both industry and everyday applications, largely to prevent one thing from sticking to another, and are commonly found in food packaging, non-stick cookware, cosmetics, and waterproofing and stain-proofing for textiles. The most familiar are PFOA, or perfluorooctanoic acid, widely known for being used in Teflon™, and PFOS, or perfluorooctanesulfonic acid, the functional ingredient in Scotchgard™. The use of both of these chemicals has now been limited due to the numerous adverse health effects associated with them, including endocrine disruption, liver damage, reproductive and developmental disruption, and cancer. For example, it was recently shown that those with high levels of PFOS in their blood were 4.5 times more likely to develop liver cancer. Newer alternatives in the same class of materials are now in use, but unfortunately, it is likely that these substances have many of the same deleterious effects as the old ones.

The real issue with this class of chemicals is not just that they have clear negative effects on living systems but the fact that, once in the environment, they persist almost indefinitely. This allows them to become widespread throughout the environment, and they are now found virtually everywhere. Because of this, detection of PFAS is almost universal in the blood of Americans. Disturbingly, a recent study has even found that *all* of the world's rainwater contains detectable levels of PFAS. Even more disturbing is that the concentrations of PFAS in rainwater often exceed the newly revised U.S. EPA advisory levels. In June of 2022, the EPA lowered what it considered to be a safe exposure for PFOA and PFOS after finding, among other effects, that these substances suppressed vaccine response in children. They revised the level from 70 ng/L (nanograms per liter) for a combination of both to just 4 pg/L (picograms per liter) for PFOA and 20 pg/L for PFOS (note that these are extremely small concentrations and the strictest recommendation of any country, but suggest that the U.S. EPA believes them to be highly toxic). Unfortunately, studies show that even rainwater from the remote Tibetan Plateau exceeds the recommended level for PFOA at 55 pg/L, or 14 times greater, and concentrations for both are exceeded in rainwater from both rural and urban environments around the world.

Even countries with much lower standards are violated by rainwater concentrations. Researchers found the concentration of 4 common PFAS (PFOA, PFOS, (PFHxS) perfluorohexanesulfonic acid, and (PFNA) perfluorononanoic acid) in rainwater often exceeds the Danish EPA's standard of 2 ng/L for drinking water for the combination of the 4. To put this another way, the Danish EPA would not consider much of the world's rainwater safe to drink. Of course, the environmental implications are clear. While we may be able to treat rainwater to remove these PFAS and make it safe to drink, this does nothing for the water falling onto our soils and crops and flowing into our lakes, rivers, streams, and the rest of the world's environments. With adverse effects on us and presumably all other life as well, there is a good chance that we are creating a significant environmental problem that we can do little to fix. With thousands of different PFAS being produced in the millions of tons per year, the concentrations of these chemicals found throughout the environment will continue to climb unless quick action is taken to curtail their use.

Of all the pollutants that humans are introducing into the environment, there is one in particular that may be more harmful than all the rest, not simply because of its effects on the environment but because of the unbelievable enormity of the problem. I believe it may very well be one of the largest threats to the Earth's biosphere, next to climate change. This threat is plastic. Every single person, no matter where they live on the planet, and every other organism, save maybe those that live deep underground, is right now, this very second being exposed to plastics large and small. Plastic is now ubiquitous in the environment, and it has been found everywhere on the planet. Plastics are in our oceans, our rivers, our drinking water, our food, and the air we breathe. They have been found from the deepest part of the ocean to the snows of Mt. Everest, and they are most certainly inside of us. The same plastics that make modern life so convenient and that we use every day in so many different ways have invaded our environment, and we are just now discovering how seriously damaging they can be. Immediate threats to wildlife from large and visible plastic pollution are apparent and easily observed. Marine plastic pollution has increased tenfold since 1980, and in the last decade, ingestion of plastic particles by marine animals and deaths by entanglement have risen by 40%. At least half of all seabird and marine mammal species and 85% of all sea turtles encounter plastic in their environments, and the situation is only getting worse. Plastic trash from land and leftovers from the fishing industry threaten marine species across the board, from whales, dolphins, seals, sea lions, sea birds, and, of course, fish and sea turtles. The massive amount of plastic that enters our waterways is carried around the world by ocean currents, fouling the once-pristine beaches of even the most remote of islands and coalescing in the ocean's gyres into massive patches of floating waste. In the Pacific, this patch is now *twice* the size of the state of Texas. Carelessly discarded plastics also litter our land, and land animals, likewise, can suffer from debilitating or deadly entanglements and are severely impacted by ingesting plastic waste.

Aside from the unsightliness of carelessly discarded waste and the very real danger that animals face when coming into contact with it, what harm can they cause? First, let's look at some of the properties of plastics that make them such an issue, then move on to just how big the problem is. You might have heard that plastics don't go away, and this is largely true. Traditional plastics are made of polymers of hydrocarbons, usually made from oil. These polymers are extremely durable, and the bonds between them are very difficult to break. This strength makes them great for all kinds of uses. They are light, durable, easy to mold into all kinds of shapes, and, most importantly, cheap to make. Once in a landfill, something like a plastic soda bottle could be buried intact for hundreds of years. While seriously adding to the problem of where humans put all of the trash we produce and the leaching of chemicals contained within the plastic, this is actually the best case scenario for plastic in our environment. Of even greater concern is the plastic that ends up on the land or in our waterways. Here, exposed to sun, wind, and wave action or the force of a moving river, the plastic begins to break down as the sun breaks the polymer bonds and waves and water turn larger plastics into smaller plastics. At first blush, this seems like a good thing, but plastics are an unnatural substance, and they don't break down like, say, a tree. The bonds that make up wood are eventually broken down (by organisms, providing them with energy), and the molecules that make up a tree are returned to nature and reused. Plastics break down into smaller plastics, and yet even smaller plastics, and still smaller still as they become microplastics and even smaller nanoplastics. As these plastic particles get ever smaller, they begin to enter the food web as they are consumed by fish and other primary consumers who mistake them for plankton. Plastics are now part of the food chain, and the smaller these particles become, the easier it is for them to pass from an external problem to an internal one. It is at this point where they become a potential biosphere-destroying problem.

Microplastics (< 5mm in size) and nanoplastics (< 0.1 μm) through being ingested, or even inhaled, put their hydrocarbon makeup and various other compounds such as stabilizers, fire retardants, and dyes within living organic tissue. Added to the potential harm native to the plastic materials themselves, these microplastics have been shown to absorb toxic chemicals, various pharmaceuticals, and heavy metals, thus becoming effective vectors for concentrating and delivering toxins. In fact, numerous pesticides have been shown to be able to be absorbed and transported via microplastics, as well as the PFAS discussed above (some plastics already come with PFAS associated with them or are themselves types of plastic). Unfortunately, this has the potential to increase the exposure and damage from many environmental pollutants. As the particles become smaller and smaller, their ability to pass into the body through the gut or the lungs increases. Research has shown infiltration of living tissues by plastics in numerous species, both aquatic and land-based, from invertebrates to humans. A metadata analysis from researchers in British Columbia estimates the average American adult may be taking in between 98,000 and 121,000 microplastic particles annually through ingestion of food, drinking, and inhalation. The most common sources cited of microplastics were the consumption of seafood (highlighting the above concerns with aquatic food chains), the consumption of bottled water, and inhalation. Although these numbers seem significant enough to be of concern, the authors admit that their estimates are "likely drastic underestimates overall." They note, for example, that while data on microplastics in seafood is available, this is not the case for widely consumed protein sources such as beef and poultry, not to mention a plethora of other consumables for which little to no data is available. They go on to state that the actual per-annum consumption could exceed several hundred thousand particles. In fact, another study with drinking water estimated that the average adult worldwide may consume up to 485,000 microplastic particles per year from tap water alone and an astounding 3.5 million from bottled water.

Multiple studies have confirmed that not only can microplastic and nanoplastic particles enter the body by inhalation and affect the viability of lung tissues, but these nanoplastics can continue through the lungs to the rest of the body. The presence of microplastics in the human bloodstream has long been suspected, but only recently confirmed. Researchers in the Netherlands were able to confirm the presence of microplastics in nearly 80% of the people they tested. It has also been demonstrated in mice and humans that these microplastic and nanoplastic particles can find their way into the placental tissues of pregnant females. These plastic particles can then be transferred to developing young. Pregnant mice exposed to polystyrene nanoparticles through the lungs of the adult resulted in polystyrene nanoparticles being found in numerous fetal tissues, including the liver, heart, lungs, kidney, and even the brain. These results would likely be repeated in any placental mammal, including humans, with the biological impacts potentially severe in regards to the production of viable young. The most worrying result of this exposure is possibly the introduction of endocrine disrupting agents contained in plastics or, associated with them, being introduced directly into a developing fetus.

The long-term effects of these compounds as a result of microplastic and nanoplastic exposure are still being researched, and unfortunately there is not a large body of data to give any definitive answers, but the research that has been done is not good news. Studies show that in many vertebrate species, ingestion of microplastics causes clear signs of oxidative stress, disruptions of gut microbiota, changes in gut permeability and gut mucus production, inflammation, and immune toxicity. Neurotoxicity has also been observed in several studies, with disruption of acetylcholinesterase activity leading to disturbance of nerve impulse transmission.

Many of the chemicals associated with plastics are endocrine-disrupting chemicals (EDCs). These chemicals affect hormone production and the effectiveness of an organism's endocrine system by mimicking natural hormones, antagonizing hormone action, changing the production or degradation of hormones, or changing the expression of hormone receptors. These chemicals are additives to plastics, and many are known to be unstable within the plastics they are a part of. Leaching of these compounds is of serious concern. These EDCs include bisphenol A (BPA), which is widely used in food packaging, including heat-resistant trays and linings for cans and lids. Phthalates, found in many types of plastics, are used as plasticizers to give base plastics their desired flexibility and elasticity, as well as brominated flame retardants, which are used to impart flame resistance in many household items such as pillows, carpet, upholstery, and appliances. These EDCs have been linked to a wide array of conditions, including hormonal cancers, reproductive harm, metabolic disorders, asthma, and neurodevelopmental conditions. BPA specifically has been linked in various studies to obesity, cardiovascular disease, reproductive disorders, and breast cancer. Studies in Europe concluded that exposure to BPA was likely the cause of over 42,000 cases of obesity among 4-year-olds. In a study by the U.S. Geological Survey to identify possible organic compounds in groundwater, BPA was the second most common chemical found, highlighting its ability to leach from its native plastic. Of the 47 sites tested, spanning 18 U.S. states, BPA was found in 30% of the samples.

Six million tons of phthalates are produced globally each year, making them extremely prevalent in the environment and in the plastics that wildlife and humans come into contact with. Phthalates are often found in higher concentrations in the environment than any other EDC. In addition to the above listed effects of EDCs, certain phthalates have been specifically identified as reproductive toxins and have been shown to cause prenatal and postnatal developmental disorders in animals. This fact, linked with the certainty that microplastics can invade a developing fetus, demonstrates the potential devastating consequences of plastic exposure to wildlife and humans alike. Certain EDCs have been banned for use by the EU due to the risk to human health and the environment, but many of those same chemicals are still widely used around the world, including in the United States.

Many are surprised to find that plastics also contain a wide variety of heavy metals, including antimony, aluminum, zinc, bromine, cadmium, copper, mercury, arsenic, tin, lead, titanium, cobalt, chromium, barium, and manganese. These metals are used for various purposes, such as the aforementioned fire retardants but also as stabilizers, pigments, and biocides. Most of these metals are known toxins in humans, with a variety of effects. The most familiar, of course, are lead, mercury, and arsenic, but the others on the list are often associated with the same toxic effects as their more well-known counterparts, including neurological damage, DNA damage, and cancer promotion.

It is interesting to note that it is very likely that the most severe impacts from microplastics are likely due to a combination of factors contained within or carried by the plastics. For example, microplastic exposure is very often associated with oxidative stress, which creates an increase in reactive oxygen species (many people consume antioxidants for this very reason) and can damage vital molecules such as lipids, proteins, and DNA. This, combined with a heavy metal that also damages DNA or a compound absorbed by the plastic that is also carcinogenic, could make plastics a much more effective cancer promoter. Likewise, a microplastic that has inherent to it an endocrine disrupting agent, that also has bound with other EDC's from the environment, could increase the effect of both. Multiple studies have shown that the presence of microplastics increases the toxic effects of various compounds. Here again, the complex combination of multiple factors contained within plastics and their ability to attract and concentrate other environmental pollutants work in combination to increase the effect of the individual components. To put it in the most simple terms possible, microplastics are everywhere, have toxic components within them, *and* are likely picking up environmental pollutants of various types and transporting them deep into the bodies of us and all the other organisms on the planet.

Let me quickly take an aside here. While it's easier to talk about pollutants in isolation from each other, the reality is that their action on us and all other life does not happen in isolation. Most of the environmental pollutants that we have discussed do have clear detrimental effects by themselves, but there is a large body of evidence that shows that the detrimental effects of many pollutants, whether it be exposure to multiple types of pesticides, a microplastic associated with a PFAS, or endless other combinations, are increased by their association with other pollutants. This compounding effect is exactly why the pervasiveness of so many toxic human-made chemicals in the environment is so damaging.

Since the 1950s, over 8.3 billion metric tons of plastic have been produced, with the vast majority, approximately 6.3 billion tons, being disposed of as waste, and of this, 79% has accumulated in landfills or the natural environment. If current trends continue, there could be as much as 12 billion metric tons of plastic waste contained in our landfills and in the environment by 2050. It is nearly impossible to calculate how much of this waste ends up in our water, air, and bodies. There could be as much as 12 million tons of plastic entering the oceans every year, and plastics are widespread in freshwater systems that transport urban plastic waste to the ocean. This leads some to the stunning conclusion that by 2050 there could be more plastic in the ocean than fish by weight. Plastics are not just found in surface waters, and a study of tap water from around the world found microplastics in every country where water was collected, including in 94% of the tap water samples from the United States.

The growth of plastic production worldwide over the last 65 years has outpaced any other manufactured material, increasing 20-fold since 1964 and could double again in the next 20 years. Its cheap and durable properties make it ideal for an unbelievable number of uses. Unfortunately, in humanity's rush to exploit this novel invention, little thought was given to what to do with the waste produced or the impact on the environment. Despite the common misconception that much consumer plastic is recycled, only about 9% of plastics are recycled globally; many of the plastics we use on a daily basis are either not recyclable or are typically too expensive to be recycled. It is also important to note that while the act of recycling is certainly better than not recycling, recycling merely delays disposal. Plastic cannot yet be indefinitely recycled like glass or aluminum, and ultimately, will end up in the environment, a landfill, or be incinerated.

Plastic may be the longest-lasting legacy that humans leave behind. The pervasiveness and quantities of plastics are now such that we are leaving plastics in the geologic record, in the very strata of the earth. This is the clear physical evidence of the Anthropocene. There is a real possibility that a future geologist (if in the distant future there still are geologists) might find this plastic layer and use it, much like the K-Pg boundary from 66 million years ago, as the geologic separation between a thriving and diverse world below and the mass extinction event above. Humans are assuredly leaving their mark on the world, but unquestionably not in the way we have always aspired.

At the root of most of our environmental issues are the ever-growing human population and our increasing consumption. Biodiversity worldwide is diminishing, and all of the causes of these declines can be traced back to humanity's direct impact, much of which you just read about. Regardless of the details, we are simply using so many of the planet's resources that there is little left for anything else. For instance, 96% of the mass of *all* mammals on the planet are humans and the cattle we eat. Every other mammal we know of comprises the other 4%. Let that sink in for a bit, and the enormous impact we have is apparent. The current global estimate of the human population is now 8 billion. By 2030, that number is expected to grow to 8.5 billion, and by 2050, it will top 9.7 billion. These billions more people will only increase the demands on the earth's fragile systems. Even more incentive for us to figure out, as soon as possible, how humans can live a biologically sustainable existence before we perpetuate the extinction of much of the planet's life and likely our own. There is not a single issue mentioned above that is not improved by fewer people being on the planet. The survival of our species hinges on living within our biological means, and as with every other species, we must not exceed the carrying capacity of our environment. Our ingenuity has allowed us to operate at populations and consumption levels far exceeding this capacity, but we are on borrowed time.

Humanity is now using 1.7 times the resources that the earth can regenerate every year, or, put another way, humanity needs more than 1.7 Earths to supply its needs. We are cutting into our biological capital, and this will only get worse as our population and resource consumption grow. According to the Untied Nations, humanity's material footprint (the amount of natural resources extracted to meet consumption demands) grew from 43 billion metric tons in 1990 to 92 billion in 2017, an increase of 113%. At the same time, the population grew by just 43%. Simply put, we are using more and more resources for each of us, and there continue to be more and more of us. Here again, some nations are more to blame than others, with wealthy nations being the worst offenders. If the entire world consumed at the rate of the United States, we would consume more than 4 Earth's worth of resources every year. As a byproduct of this enormous amount of consumption, an unbelievable amount of goods are shipped around the world, acting as a global conveyor of countless species that can have devastating effects, all while contributing to the huge amount of CO_2 our consumption produces. Surely we have little hope of reducing biodiversity loss and fighting climate change without addressing our consumption and how humans use the world's resources.

It is apparent that humans' impact on the natural world is enormous and, in most cases, detrimental to the rest of Earth's life. I realize, though, that all of this can seem very abstract. Statistics and figures, while important, sometimes fail to get the point across; they fail to "move" us. Even with all of our intelligence, the huge amounts of data and the enormity and complexity of the problems we face can be overwhelming. Humans are social creatures, and because of this, we are emotional creatures. While we can understand intellectually the desperateness of the global situation, we may not be able to connect with it on an emotional level. Even with a full understanding of the harm we are doing, we will not change unless we care. There will be more statistics and figures about the plight of so many creatures, but what follows will not just be numbers and projections but a picture of our losses. These organisms are a visible and quantifiable manifestation of the impact humans are having as the world's species attempt to survive in the Anthropocene.

Part II

The Face of Progress
and
a Way Forward

5
Birds (Aves)

Birds' evolution dates back more than 150 million years, as their small feathered dinosaur ancestors learned to glide. The appearance of modern birds, ones that we would recognize as such, dates back at least 100 million years. The earliest fossil relative of today's living birds is that of *Asteriornis maastrichtensis,* which lived some 66.7 million years ago, but many modern bird features arose much earlier. While not a direct ancestor of today's birds, *Archaeornithura meemannae* dates back 130 million years and had many of the recognizable features of modern birds, showing these traits developed very early on. The most famous of the prehistoric bird relatives, *Archaeopteryx,* dates back at least 150 million years. Recent in-depth analysis of *Archaeopteryx* now suggests that these animals could in fact achieve powered flight, possibly making them the first birds to truly take to the skies. This long evolutionary history has allowed birds to diversify into a fantastic range of shapes, sizes, and modes of life.

Birds range in size from the minuscule bee hummingbird *(Mellisuga helenae)* of Cuba, measuring just 5.7 cm (2.25 inches) and weighing in at less than 2 grams (.07 oz), to the ostrich *(Struthio camelus),* which can be 2 meters (6.5 feet) tall and weigh 136 kg (300 lbs). Their abilities are as diverse as their sizes. All hummingbirds can hover in place and even fly backwards. Peregrine falcons *(Falco peregrinus)* can dive at speeds approaching 320 kph, or nearly 200 mph, while the ostrich cannot fly at all but can run at a top speed of over 64 kph (40 mph). The Australian wedge-tailed eagle *(Aquila audax)* has eyesight eight times better than that of a human, and the amazing ability of the barn owl *(Tyto alba)* to see at night is only surpassed by its ability to hunt in complete darkness by sound alone.

Of all the abilities that birds possess, the most amazing might be those of the migratory birds. The extreme adaptations that allow these birds to fly thousands of miles are extraordinary, bordering on physiologically impossible. To have enough energy for these continent-crossing flights, birds have to put on a huge amount of fat. Godwits, which migrate nonstop for 11,400 km (7200 miles) from Alaska to New Zealand each fall, gain as much as 10 ounces of fat, doubling their weight before their migration. Fully 40% of their body mass is fat as they begin their trip, but for unknown reasons, this huge amount of fat doesn't seem to adversely affect their health, despite their blood chemistry mirroring that of an obese human. Migratory birds, unlike humans, have no trouble utilizing this fat and are ten times more efficient at burning fat than mammals. Not only do they gain mass amounts of fat and bulk up on muscle before their migration, but these migrants can also change the size of their organs, allowing systems unused during the flight, such as their digestive organs, to shrink away to near nothing, saving weight and the energy to maintain them. Upon arrival at the other end of their migration, they quickly reverse this process, slimming down on the muscle used for flight and regrowing their digestive organs. Adaptations like these allow the tiny 3.5-gram rufous hummingbird to fly as much as 6,200 km (3,900 miles) from Alaska to Mexico, with some even flying 24 straight hours across the open waters of the Gulf of Mexico, and the Arctic tern *(Sterna paradisaea)* to travel as much as an astonishing 91,700 km (57,000 miles) in a single year. More astonishing yet is how birds find their way during their migrations. A unique molecule found in their retina called cryptochrome 1a may allow them to actually visualize Earth's magnetic field!

With their fantastic diversity and vast range of abilities and behaviors, it's no wonder that humans have found birds so fascinating throughout our history. Birds have been used as symbols of strength, beauty, wisdom, and freedom for thousands of years, but even with this apparent reverence, birds face serious challenges in the modern world. It's estimated that North America alone has lost almost 3 billion birds since 1970. Birds of the grasslands are the most affected, losing 700 million individuals, or 53 percent of their population, the most of any single habitat. 74% of grassland birds are in decline and total of 1 billion birds have been lost from North America's forest habitats. Independent of habitat, migratory birds have suffered the most overall. Their populations have been reduced by 2.5 billion across the 419 native species of North America. The dramatic losses are not just restricted to rare or threatened species, either. Just 12 bird families make up 90% of the losses, and they include many common and widespread birds, like sparrows, warblers, finches, and blackbirds. Worldwide, at least 40% of all bird populations are in decline.

According to Birdlife International, the top five leading threats to birds worldwide are agriculture, logging, invasive species, hunting/trapping and finally climate change. Many of these threats are intertwined, with habitat loss as a result. For example, reclamation projects in the Yellow Sea tidal flats in China for agricultural and industrial use have severely diminished habitat in this critical stopover site for tens of millions of birds migrating through Asia. Of increasing international concern, these tidal flats once covered 2.7 million acres. Since the 1950s, two thirds of these tidal flats have disappeared, with 40% lost since just the 1980s. Compounding the threat to this critical habitat, the essential sediments that maintain these tidal wetlands are increasingly cut off by dams. The largest river in China, the Yangtze, now has more than 50,000 dams blocking its flow, including the world's largest hydroelectric dam, the nearly 1.5-mile-wide Three Gorges Dam. The "reclamation" of these wetlands and their degradation have caused a severe decline in the shorebird species that rely on them. In the last 15 years, population declines of 43% to 78% have been observed for species overall, with the population of the great knot *(Calidris tenuirostris)* falling by more than 80%.

Agriculture can have multiple deleterious effects on birds. Changes in land use are the most severe, but more and more evidence is building that pesticides, and in particular neonicotinoid pesticides, are increasingly threatening birds. The use of these pesticides may also explain the greater losses of grassland birds in North America compared to other biomes. A study of neonicotinoid pesticides in the U.S. showed that they were likely responsible for a 4% drop in grassland bird populations each year from 2008-2014. Also affected by these pesticides are insect-eating species. Their numbers dropped by 3% per year over the same period. Here, agriculture compounds losses through not only the loss of habitat but also the associated effects of crop production, dealing a one-two punch to the ever-decreasing populations of birds.

Overexploitation from legal and illegal hunting and trapping and the pet trade continues to be a major threat to birds, especially in the Mediterranean, Europe, Asia, and the Middle East. Worldwide, the illegal wildlife trade affects one quarter of all bird species. In many countries, the consumption of songbirds is still considered a delicacy. The capture of yellow-breasted buntings *(Emberiza aureola)* on their migratory route through China and in their wintering grounds in South East Asia is a prime example of the massive impact that hunting continues to have on song birds. Consumption of these birds has become a status symbol in recent decades with China's growing middle class, and many compare the rapid drop in population to that of the passenger pigeon in the 19th century. Populations throughout the bunting's range, which once ran from Eastern Europe as far east as Japan, dropped by as much as 89% in just the 10 years between 2003 and 2013. In Europe, the population of buntings went from as many as 300,000 birds to just 600. As a result, the species is now critically endangered. Protections are in place, but sadly, they are often ignored and poorly enforced. The yellow-breasted bunting may go from one of the most common land birds in the world to extinction within the next several years.

In Europe, legally allowed hunting is still responsible for the loss of 1.4 million birds every year, including nearly 300,000 thrushes, and until recently, hundreds of thousands of ortolan buntings *(Emberiza hortulana)* were killed each year for consumption in France, despite EU restrictions on hunting the birds. As many as half a million birds of all species are still illegally killed in France each year, but this number pales in comparison to other countries bordering the Mediterranean. The nation of Italy is the worst offender, with as many as 5.6 million birds illegally killed every year. This is closely followed by Egypt, where as many as 5.5 million birds are killed. All totaled, the loss of birds in the Mediterranean, North and Central Europe, and the Caucuses is somewhere between 11 and 38 million birds every year. The most heavily affected species are the Eurasian chaffinch *(Fringilla coelebs)* and the Eurasian blackcap *(Sylvia atricapilla)*, which see annual losses of 2.9 million and 1.8 million individuals, respectively.

Birds are often a wonder to behold with their fantastic array of colors, beautiful vocalizations, and charismatic personalities. Unfortunately, these same traits make them desirable pets, fueling a global demand for wild-caught birds. Nearly 600 species of birds have been caught in the pet trade, often with disastrous results for their survival. For example, once common in the western and central mountains of the island of Java in Indonesia, the rufous-fronted laughingthrush *(Garrulax rufifrons)* is now critically endangered. Intensive trapping for the songbird trade is largely to blame. Popular for its unique vocalizations, demand for the bird remains so high that even thefts from wildlife centers have occurred, a serious blow for those attempting to help the species recover. As a result, there may be only 250 of these birds left in the wild. These are not the only birds at risk in the country, and surveys of Indonesia's bird markets in 2015 found more than 19,000 individual birds for sale in just a 3-day period, with more than 200 different species being offered for sale. 98% of these birds were being sold illegally.

Long prized as pets, parrots are another example of heavily trafficked birds, and this popularity has made them the most traded bird of all, comprising 90% of the live birds traded worldwide. From 1975–2021, as many as 19 million parrots of 321 different species were traded internationally. While much of the global demand for these birds is filled by captive-bred birds, there is still a significant risk of wild populations being caught and laundered through the legal bird trade. Parrots as a group are one of the most threatened of any bird, with nearly 30% of all parrots considered threatened and nearly 60% experiencing population declines. Although numerous local and international laws exist to protect parrots and other birds from the pet trade, issues still abound. For example, Latin America still has a robust trade in illegal birds. Over 30 species of parrot are still traded in the pet markets of Santa Cruz, Bolivia, amounting to some 22,000 birds a year, 94% of which are illegal under Bolivian law. In Mexico, as many as 78,000 parrots are illegally trapped each year, with as much as 15% being smuggled into the United States. The capture of wild parrots has led to the decline of numerous threatened species, including the endangered African gray parrot *(Psittacus erithacus)*, the hyacinth macaw *(Anodorhynchus hyacinthinus)*, the now extinct in the wild Spix's macaw *(Cyanopsitta spixii)*, as well as more common and widespread species such as the scarlet macaw *(Ara macao)* that have suffered population declines and local extinctions as a result of the bird trade.

Birds are one of the most species-rich groups of any of the terrestrial animals, and there are around 11,000 species alive today known to science. Since the year 1500, approximately 187 bird species have gone extinct, many if not most due directly or indirectly to humans, including 3 species since the year 2000. Looking farther back in time, human occupation of the islands of Oceania may have been responsible for the extinction of more than 1800 bird species in the last two millennia. Historic reasons for extinctions parallel current threats to birds, including habitat loss from agriculture, urbanization, overexploitation, especially from hunting, and the introduction of invasive species. In fact, around 70% of the species that have gone extinct in the last 500 years are due wholly or partially to invasive species intentionally or accidentally introduced by humans. Currently, 14% of all birds are threatened with extinction, or 1 out of every 7.

Only a handful of species will be highlighted in detail in this chapter, all from the 19th and 20th centuries, but there are a few notable extinctions that I will briefly mention. Overall, the rail family has suffered the most extinctions of any group of birds, in particular the island-dwelling rails. There are currently around 144 species of these small, often flightless wetland birds, many of which are unique to the islands they inhabit. This single group makes up the bulk of the extinctions seen in island birds in the last 2000 years. At least 24 species have gone extinct in modern times, five of them in the last 100 years, and at least one since 1994. Almost all of the rail extinctions can be traced back to the same causes. As humans made their way to islands of the world, they brought with them predators. Rats, snakes, cats, and various other species arrived for which the rails had no defense. Humans also killed the birds, both young and adult, and robbed their nests of eggs. Under these pressures, the rails simply could not keep up. The threat continues today, with 35 species of rail currently considered threatened.

Another notable modern extinction includes yet another island-dwelling bird, the famous dodo *(Raphus cucullatus)* of the island of Mauritius. These plump and flightless, meter-tall (3 ft), turkey-sized members of the pigeon family were wiped out by sailors transporting food across the Indian Ocean as well as the introduced predators that accompanied them. Almost everything we know about them comes from a handful of bones, a few early descriptions, and some illustrations, many of which appear to be copies of other drawings. There is very little information at all about the habits of the living birds, and there are still debates on what precisely they looked like, but we do know they largely ate fruits and may have only laid a single egg. So scarce was the evidence that, for a time, it was thought that they might have simply been a legend. Fossil evidence eventually led to the dodo being formally described in the 1860s. The first European record of the birds is from 1598, when the Dutch arrived in Mauritius, and they were almost certainly extinct by the late 1600s. Reports of the birds became increasingly scarce after 1620, likely signaling that they were already in decline. The last sightings of the dodo are believed to have taken place in 1662, but they may have survived as late as the 1670s or 1680s. As you will see, this is just the first in a long list of extinctions from Mauritius and the surrounding islands.

The Passenger Pigeon (m)
April 14 1835
Columba Migratoria, Linn.

Passenger Pigeon
(Ectopistes migratorius)

Historically the most populous bird in North America, the passenger pigeon was once the source of great awe, not because of the brightness of its plumage or its melodic voice. No, the pigeon was a fairly plain bird with a rather unremarkable call. The awe that it inspired came from the birds' enormous congregations containing millions upon millions of birds. Accounts of their flocks, some going back hundreds of years, all tell of something nearly unimaginable. They describe immense flocks of pigeons reaching miles long and more than a mile wide so dense with birds that they blocked out the sun. This was accompanied by a thunderous roar of wings that drowned out all other sound. There could be so many birds, it would sometimes take days for them to pass. When these flocks came to roost, trees would be covered for miles, many so laden with birds that branches would snap from the load. Even entire trees gave out from the strain, toppling under the weight of thousands upon thousands of pigeons. When nesting, single colonies covered an area as much as 40 miles long and several miles wide. It truly must have been one of the most impressive sights in all of nature.

The passenger pigeon fed largely on acorns, beechnuts, and chestnuts provided by the deciduous forests of middle and eastern North America, but they also supplemented their diet with various insects. In the nesting season, they ranged from the Great Lakes to New England and as far north as Nova Scotia. In the winter, they resided in the Gulf states of the U.S. east to North Carolina. Passenger pigeons were often on the move; unsurprisingly, the enormous flocks would quickly deplete food resources and would need to shift to new areas. When they had exhausted seasonal sources of food, they likely dispersed more widely until the next food crop came into season, at which point they would again form their massive flocks. With their requirement of large amounts of food during the five weeks needed for raising their chicks, the timing of where and when a prodigious nut crop had occurred the previous fall (since they typically bred in spring, feeding off of the previous year's nut crop) was essential and determined nesting locations each season. How the pigeons determined where the maximum amount of food would be in any given year is still a mystery. However, many nut-bearing trees do follow a multi-year pattern in nut production. It is likely that these patterns and weather conditions throughout the year allowed the passenger pigeon to hone in on the best nesting sights. There appears to be some disagreement about how many times these birds could nest each season, with more modern sources claiming one, but others claiming two, one in the spring and one in the summer, or even three, one in the spring, summer, and winter. Given what we know of other birds, it is quite possible this could have changed year-to-year based on resources. This would also make sense in light of research suggesting that populations of the passenger pigeon probably varied quite wildly from several hundred million to several billion birds throughout time. Genetic analysis shows that historical populations of passenger pigeons exhibit many of the traits of a "breakout species." These species exhibit population behavior much like that of the locust, where in times of abundant food, the population can rapidly increase.

While there is always debate on the exact reason for what led to the downfall of a species, there is little doubt that humans were most likely the sole cause of the demise of the passenger pigeon. Either through gross and unrelenting overexploitation or the diminishment of essential habitats, there is no evidence to suggest that the loss of North America's most abundant bird was anything but our fault. By the 1850s, commercial hunting was killing millions of birds by whatever means could be devised. Birds were knocked out of the sky with poles, nettled, shot, poisoned, and burned out of trees. Competitions were held to see who could kill the most birds in a given time. No bird was safe, adult or young, and nesting colonies were frequently attacked. Originally difficult to find due to their migratory nature, the telegraph and train allowed them to be tracked down and quickly exploited. As a result, the market was flooded with pigeons. They became so cheap that they were even used as live shooting targets (a fact preserved by the "clay pigeons" that are now commonly used for target shooting). By the 1860s, populations were noticeably smaller. As the forests of the east were depleted, the population was increasingly restricted to the western part of its range, and by 1878, the last known large nesting colony was recorded in the state of Michigan. Here, a single hunter shipped a staggering 3 million birds to the markets, despite the birds being in severe decline. Laws were enacted to try to save the pigeon, but like many of the early wildlife laws, they were little enforced and largely ignored. Even as commercial hunting collapsed with the pigeon's reduced population, the birds were still widely hunted non-commercially. By the 1890s, there were few passenger pigeons left. For a species whose survival strategy depended on large flocks, not only for safety but also to find food sources, the few remaining birds were simply too few to keep the species alive. In desperation, the American Ornithologists' Union from 1909 to 1912 offered a $1,500 reward for any person finding a nesting colony of passenger pigeons. Unfortunately, by then, it was too late. From an initial population of between 3 and 5 billion birds, only one remained by 1914. Named Martha, she was housed in the Cincinnati Zoo. With her death on Sept. 1, 1914, the story of the passenger pigeon came to an end.

The demise of the passenger pigeon is an important reminder that even widespread and extremely plentiful species can rapidly go extinct. Our assumption that the huge populations of passenger pigeons were unassailable proved to be wrong. Protections came too late for the passenger pigeon, but there were still positive effects for other species that remained, with the plight of the passenger pigeon serving as a wakeup call for some. One of those moved by the loss was Iowa Congressman John F. Lacey. Seeing the damage that illegal hunting was doing to America's wildlife, he submitted an act to Congress that would make it a federal crime to move illegally obtained wildlife across state lines, stating in support of the act:

The wild pigeon, formerly in flocks of millions, has entirely disappeared from the face of the earth. We have given an awful exhibition of slaughter and destruction, which may serve as a warning to all mankind. Let us now give an example of wise conservation of what remains of the gifts of nature.

The Lacey Act was passed by Congress in April of 1900 and became the first of many federal wildlife laws in the United States.

The environmental impact of losing such an incredibly abundant species is likely to be as massive as the great flocks once were. Certainly, there is no situation where the loss of billions of individuals of any species would not have far-reaching impacts. The once huge and voracious flocks of pigeons could change entire landscapes, stripping them of food and damaging trees, but this damage also opened the forest canopy, allowing more light to reach the ground, spurring growth. The birds also fertilized dozens of square miles at a time, changing the chemical structure of the forest. There is also evidence that they had a significant impact on the distribution of species within the forests they inhabited, and the passenger pigeon was most likely responsible for the predominance of white oak in the eastern forests prior to its extinction. Unfortunately, the details of the ecological interactions of the passenger pigeon with its environment are little understood, and few studies of the pigeon's ecology were ever undertaken while they were alive. We probably will never know the ultimate environmental cost of the loss of the passenger pigeon, but it is certain that we have lost one of nature's great spectacles and, with it, a permanent change in the ecosystems of a large part of North America.

Great Auk
(Pinguinus impennis)

The great auk or garefowl was unique among the birds of the Northern Hemisphere. It was the only flightless bird to inhabit the North in modern times and made its living much like the more familiar penguin of the Southern Hemisphere. In fact, the great auk was actually the first bird to be called a penguin, before what we now call penguins received their name. Similar in mode of living and appearance, the great auk is not related to the penguins of the South but rather is a member of the Alcid family that includes the still living murres, guillemots, and puffins. Its closest living relative is the razorbill *(Alca torda)* with which it shares a similarly grooved beak. Large in size, nearly a meter (3 ft) tall, and weighing around 4.5 kg (10 lbs), it was awkward on land, but an excellent swimmer and spent the majority of its time at sea feeding on fish and small crustaceans. A native of the North Atlantic, these unique birds could be found from the northern Atlantic coasts of North America as far south as Cape Cod and east to Norway.

Being a seagoing bird, they rarely came ashore except to breed and then preferred only a handful of isolated rocky islands through their range. The largest of these was on Funk Island, off the coast of Newfoundland, which at one time held as many as 100,000 breeding pairs of great auks. Little detail is known about their breeding habits or biology in general. No naturalists recorded observing them in the wild, although several viewed captured birds. Records from sailors and explorers do give us some idea of the nature of these birds. The great auk had a low reproductive rate and only laid one large egg per year. Several observed if this egg was lost, they would not lay another. Being well developed at hatching, it's believed that the auk's chicks had a very short fledging period. The energy required to produce a large, nutrient-dense egg to accomplish this likely explains why they would not, or could not, lay another. Accounts also tell us they were very abundant, especially on the Newfoundland coast, so much so that sailors used them as indicators at sea of when they were approaching land. It's estimated that populations before intensive hunting were certainly in the millions of birds.

The hunting of the great auk was by no means a modern invention. There is archaeological evidence that many cultures utilized the auks for food going back thousands of years. As the modern world came about, the pressure on the auks greatly intensified, particularly in the western part of their range. As early as 1497, Europeans coming to Newfoundland began hunting the auk. Much of this centered around their main breeding colony on Funk Island. By the mid-1500s, hundreds of ships from European nations were coming to Newfoundland to exploit the rich cod fisheries, and the auk represented a valuable foodstuff to supply the ships. Many brought fewer provisions on the trip west, knowing that they would be able to obtain large quantities of the birds when they arrived, a task that was unfortunately all too easy. Their large size and cumbersome movements on land, combined with their inexperience with a land-based predator, made them particularly vulnerable. Sailors could easily round them up; some simply used spare sails to corral them. In an account from 1540, a single ship recorded capturing and salting 4 to 5 tons of the birds in addition to the 1,000 birds they used for fresh meat. It's likely that this was repeated among the several hundred ships that would arrive each season. The adult birds were not the only interest of the fishermen; auk eggs were also collected in huge quantities. The large egg of the auk, which was mostly yolk, was a rich source of nutrients and thus highly sought after.

By the late 1700s, the hunting of the auks had been commercialized, and the birds were slaughtered by the thousands at a time. Remnants of the stone corrals built on Funk Island can still be seen today. By this time, the auks were no longer sought for food but for their high-quality down. The auk's feathers had become valuable in Europe due to the decimation of their eider duck populations. Graphic descriptions of what occurred on Funk Island were recorded:

> If you come for their Feathers you do not give yourself the trouble of killing them, but lay hold of one and pluck the best of the Feathers. You then turn the poor Penguin adrift, with his skin half naked and torn off, to perish at his leasure. This is not a very humane method but it is the common practize. While you abide on this island you are in the constant practize of horrid cruelties for you not only skin them Alive, but you burn them Alive also to cook their Bodies with. You take a kettle with you into which you put a Penguin or two, you kindle a fire under it, and this fire is absolutely made of the unfortunate Penguins themselves. Their bodies being oily soon produce a Flame; there is no wood on the island.

Even after legal protections for Newfoundland auks were established in 1775, the slaughter continued. The auk's population suffered severely as a result of the near-constant hunting during their breeding season. In July of 1785, explorer and hunter George Cartwright records:

> But it has been customary of late years for several crews of men to live all summer on that island, for the sole purpose of killing birds for the sake of their feathers: the destruction which they have made is incredible. If a stop is not soon put to that practice the whole breed will be diminished to almost nothing,

Unfortunately, like many early wildlife laws, protections for the auk did little to stem mass exploitation. Even with the 1775 ban and others in place, the hunting of auks and the collection of their eggs continued. In fact, the grizzly account above is from the journal of sailor Aaron Thomas in 1794.

By 1800, nearly all of the auks of Newfoundland and the western North Atlantic were gone. Only one large breeding colony remained on an island off the southwest coast of Iceland called Geirfuglasker (which translates roughly to Garefowl Rock). In an unfortunate turn of events, this last refuge for the bird sank below the waves during a volcanic event in 1830, with the remaining population moving to a small island called Eldey. By this time, the auk was becoming increasingly rare, and a new demand was placed on them as naturalists around the world scrambled to collect specimens of birds and eggs for their collections. Trade in auk skins and eggs became profitable, with museums and individual collectors offering top dollar for them. The last two birds, and possibly the last breeding pair in the world, were killed for this very reason in 1844.

The cause of the great auk's extinction seems clear, although the disaster on Geirfuglasker certainly didn't help. However, without the mass exploitation of the bird's main breeding colony on Funk Island, the event should have been little more than an inconvenience. Explorations into the health of the great auk's population using genetic analysis show no signs of a decline before 1500. Unlike other animals, where it is likely that there are a combination of factors that lead to their demise, the auks have only one. Humans bludgeoned, boiled, plucked, ate, and collected these creatures into oblivion. They were easy prey, and with them came easy profit. Even as their numbers dropped, we persisted, and even at the very end, with full knowledge of the rarity of the great auk, humans were more concerned with collecting the birds that remained than saving them.

N°78   Ivory Bile Wood Pecker

Ivory-billed Woodpecker
(Campephilus principalis)

Once the largest species of woodpecker in North America and second only in size to Mexico's imperial woodpecker *(Campephilus imperialis)* (also presumed extinct), the ivory-billed woodpecker once graced the hardwood bottomlands of the American South. Its elegant flight and two and a half foot (.75 m) wingspan led to its nickname, the "Lord God Bird," attributed to the exclamations one would make when suddenly presented with its impressive characteristics. I believe I can personally attest to that response after witnessing two male pileated woodpeckers *(Dryocopus pileatus)* in a territorial dispute. These smaller, yet still majestic, birds are a remarkable sight. There is just something ancient and dinosaurian about these birds. In watching them, I felt as though I had been transported to some ancient forest of prehistory rather than a small tract of midwestern woodland. The sight of the ivory-billed must have been even more dramatically altering.

This awe-inspiring bird was once a common sight in the swamplands of the American South. Historically found throughout the Gulf states, from eastern Texas to Florida, and then north along the Atlantic coast as far north as North Carolina. On western border of the birds' range, the population penetrated north into the Midwest, following the Mississippi River and its tributaries as far north as Missouri, Illinois, and Indiana. A subspecies and possibly even a unique species in itself, *Campephilus principalis bairdii* was also once found on the island of Cuba. The ivory-billed utilized mature old-growth forest, with large trees being necessary for the construction of the sizable nesting cavities typical of large woodpeckers. In the Mississippi water-shed, they preferred bottomland forests, often feeding on sweet gum and red oak. In Florida, they utilized primarily cypress for nesting but often fed off surrounding pine forests. Wherever found, they seemed to prefer hardwood tracts in swamps and bottomlands. It's difficult to gauge how common the species originally was. Some suggest a low historical population density throughout its range, while others believe that these determinations were made when the species was already much in decline and the original populations were probably much more robust.

There is some controversy surrounding the bird's primary diet. With some seeing the ivory-billed as a specialist feeding primarily on beetle larvae from dead trees, others argue that it was a much more general feeder, eating primarily fruits, nuts, and seeds and utilizing beetle larvae only during nesting periods. Either way, deadwood was important for the ivory-billed, and they were quite adept at peeling large pieces of bark from dead trees. It's worth noting that the ivory-billed's utilization of dead trees highlights the importance of dead trees in the environment. Standing and fallen deadwood provides food, shelter, and nesting and denning space for a myriad of species. Often, forestry activities remove dead trees from the landscape and, as a result, could be removing as much as fifth of a forest's biodiversity.

It is likely that the cutting of old-growth bottomland hardwood forests and the resulting disruption of that ecosystem severely impacted the ivory-billed. Certainly, the declines in the birds' population closely followed the expansion of humans and the increase in logging that came with them. These woodpeckers began to disappear in some parts of their range as early as the 1860s and were entirely absent in the Midwest by the 1880s. By the 1890s, they were restricted solely to the Gulf Coast, Florida, and parts of the southern Atlantic coast. Hunting for food, sport, and collecting were certainly also factors in their decline. In fact, some argue that hunting may have been a primary cause of the birds' decline due to the fact that some populations seemed to have disappeared even with suitable habitat remain-ing. While the evidence is anecdotal (since no actual statistics were kept until well into the 20th century), interviews with people living in the ivory-billed's former territory suggest it was once quite common to hunt the bird for food. As the birds became rarer, as was the case with the great auk, the ivory-billed woodpecker's diminished numbers led to a rush by collectors to obtain birds before they went extinct. With no evidence of any other cause, loss of habitat, hunting, and collecting of birds are probably to blame for their demise.

There are many controversies in the scientific community about these birds, but none more so than when and if the ivory-billed woodpecker actually went extinct. The last universally accepted sighting of the bird in the U.S. was of a single female in 1944 in the Singer tract of Louisiana by Don Ekleberry on assignment from the National Audubon Society. Statistical analysis of known ivory-bill populations predicts that they became extinct in the United States around 1945, a likely date given that Ekleberry only found a single bird. The birds in Cuba were able to persist longer, but due to extensive habitat loss, they have not been seen since 1986, despite several searches. Now enter the controversy. In 2004, a video of what was believed to be an ivory-billed woodpecker came to light from the swamps of Arkansas. This obviously excited the ornithological community about the possible rediscovery of the species. The evidence was convincing enough that bird experts from Cornell University's prestigious bird lab mounted a full-scale search for the birds. However, despite promising sightings and reports of the bird's distinctive "kent" calls and double-bill strikes, no conclusive evidence was ever obtained. The evidence obtained was enough for the United States Fish and Wildlife Service to declare the bird rediscovered, but evidently, at some point, this was not enough, and in October of 2021, the ivory-billed woodpecker was declared extinct. The debate rages on today, with some maintaining that the 2004 video confirms the species may still exist, while others say the video likely shows the similar looking pileated woodpecker. While it is true that there are many examples of species thought lost turning up again, even after 100 years or more, the probability that there are still ivory-billed woodpeckers is extremely low, and they are almost certainly extinct. One can always hope that somehow they've been able to hold on in some remote southern swamp, and if they did, then maybe, just maybe, there is hope that other species on the brink might still have a chance.

Carolina Parakeet
(Conuropsis carolinensis)

The Carolina parakeet was unique among all the birds of the United States. Few today can imagine a species of colorful neotropical parrot living in the Midwestern state of Iowa or on the Atlantic coast of New Jersey, but this was once the case for the United States' only endemic species of parrot. These bright and gregarious birds once flocked together in the hundreds from southern Florida as far north as New York and as far west as the Missouri River basin and eastern Texas. These mid-sized parrots, about the size of a grackle, fed on a wide variety of foods, from nuts and seeds to fruits, berries, human grown crops, and even the toxic cocklebur. They were a common sight throughout the majority of their range, especially in the colonial era, but accounts of them go back as far as the 1500s with some of the first European explorers in the new world.

The species was made up of two distinct subspecies populations, each with its own range and behavior. The eastern population, *Conuropsis carolinensis carolinensis,* resided in the southeastern U.S. from all of Florida north, hugging the Eastern Seaboard, to North Carolina. *C. c. carolinensis* was smaller and brighter in color than its sister subspecies, *Conuropsis carolinensis ludovicianus,* which inhabited a more northwesterly range. These birds ranged from the Missouri River basin, east toward Pennsylvania, and north into New Jersey. They were larger-bodied, paler, and had more of a bluish hue. *C. c. ludovicianus* was probably migratory moving south and east each season as winter approached, but was quite cold hardy and occasionally seen in winter. *C. c. carolinensis* was likely not migratory and had a fairly stable range year-round. Both species preferred habitats near water, primarily swamps, and were often found near wetlands and rivers. Both subspecies ranges almost entirely overlapped that of the bald cypress, with the tree occurring throughout the entire range of *C. c. carolinensis* and all of the permanently inhabited range of *C. c. ludovicianus,* suggesting that cypress trees may have been an important aspect of their habitat. Even with shared habitat preferences, the ranges of the birds themselves had very little overlap and little to no population mixing. There is some debate as to how the species preferred to nest, with Audubon stating that they preferred to nest in tree hollows, while other accounts have them nesting in large groups in open nests. However, it could simply be that they would preferentially nest according to what was available, or there may have been differing nesting preferences between the two subspecies.

The extinction of the Carolina parakeet is really one of two separate extinctions of effectively two separate birds with much smaller ranges and populations compared to the whole. This certainly made the species more vulnerable, but both suffered from the same human pressures. Historical accounts place them as being very common throughout their range in the 18th century, but Audubon reports as early as 1832 that numbers were already significantly lower, with some local populations already extinct. The reduction in population closely coincides with the expansion of human development from the

Carolina Parrot

east to the west. Accounts are rarely specific to subspecies, but by the 1860s, they appeared to be all but extinct in the mid-Atlantic states and declining elsewhere. Just 30 years later, their extinction seemed imminent with ornithologists like Edwin Hasbrouck stating:

> For many years it has been a recognized fact that the Carolina Paroquet *(Conurus carolinzensis)* is fast approaching extermination, the last quarter of a century having witnessed such rapid diminution in its numbers and so great a restriction in its range that, "in the opinions of the best judges, twenty years hence it will be known only in history and from museum specimens."

What led to the rapid decline and eventual extinction of these lovely birds is still somewhat of a mystery. Many parakeets were killed, sometimes by the hundreds, for damaging crops and orchards, as they could be quite destructive. Here, the parakeets' close-knit social flocks were a detriment to their survival in an ever more human-influenced environment. When one or more of the birds was injured, the flock would noisily take flight, circle, and alight once again. Farmers looking to clear flocks could easily eliminate all of the members in a short period of time. This behavior made them particularly easy to hunt, and they were hunted for sport, food, collection, and to provide feathers for women's fashions. This, combined with logging and the draining of wetland habitats throughout their range, likely had very significant impacts on their populations. By the time Hasbrouck stated the above in 1891, the parakeets' range had contracted dramatically. They were now only found in a small area west of the Arkansas border (presumably the last remnants of *ludovicianus)* and remote areas of Florida (presumably *carolinensis*). As the birds became more rare, the race to obtain them for specimens increased. The population decline led Frank Chapman to head to Florida in 1889. Spending several months of the winter in remote swamps, Chapman was only able to find a total of 50 birds, of which he shot 15 for collections. These almost certainly would have been *C. c. carolinensis.*

By 1913, the *ludovicianus* subspecies was extinct in the wild, with the last captive of the species surviving until 1918, dying in the same zoo as the last passenger pigeon a few years before. Here is where the two subspecies' fates diverge for a time. By the time Hasbrouck reported on the populations of the Carolina parakeet in 1891, the populations of *C. c. ludovicianus* were likely very small and may have been too small to support the species. *C. c. carolinensis,* however, continued on in remote parts of Florida, and it is believed to have survived until the 1930s or '40s. Why these final members of the species eventually succumbed, even with ample habitat and limited human interaction, is not known. It has been theorized that exposure to an avian virus from domestic chickens might be to blame for the final collapse, but to date there is no direct evidence that this is the case. Research into the extinction of America's only parrot continues with implications for today's struggling species.

Huia
(Heteralocha acutirostris)

Species that inhabit islands are always more vulnerable to extinction, and this has certainly been true for birds. In fact, 90% of all known bird extinctions are species native to islands. The island nation of New Zealand has not avoided this trend and, since human arrival some 800 years ago, has lost more than a quarter of its bird species. One of the most fascinating of the recently lost bird species is the huia.

These striking birds were famous for a rather peculiar adaptation. While there are other birds that exhibit different beak shapes and sizes between the sexes, none are as dramatic as those found on the huia. So distinct was the difference that early naturalists often classified them as two different species. The male of these magpie-sized birds possessed a short, stout bill, which he would use to remove loose bark from trees, exposing grubs, in particular the large huhu grub, which was the bird's preferred food. The female possessed a long and delicately curving bill that allowed her to reach grubs that the male could not reach by probing bark he could not remove. This curious difference in the sexes likely developed to enhance cooperative foraging. The huia formed strong monogamous breeding pairs, and this unique beak adaptation likely allowed them to more effectively exploit their heavily forested habitat, increasing overall food availability. Although a specialist of the huhu, the huia could still exploit other food sources and consumed other grubs and even some fruits. The huia was a member of the wattlebird family (several species still survive in New Zealand), and in addition to their unique beaks, they could be recognized by their colorful fleshy wattles below each eye. In recent history, their range was restricted to the southern and eastern mountain ranges of the North Island of New Zealand, but likely were once common throughout both islands before human arrival.

The huia was considered a sacred bird to the Māori people and played a large part in Māori culture and spiritual life. A symbol of great honor, the wearing of Huia tail feathers was restricted to royalty alone, and even then, they were only worn in ceremony or battle. So valuable were the feathers that special, elaborately carved boxes were constructed to hold the feathers when not in use. The Māori became masters at catching the Huia and learned that mimicking their call would often bring a pair nearby. The birds could then be killed for their feathers or captured and kept alive in captivity. The impact of these practices on the birds' population before European arrival is not well known. It is more likely that logging by the Māori had a much greater impact, and it is believed that deforestation by the early Māori was likely responsible for the huia's range contraction seen historically. Between the 13th and 19th centuries, 40% of the forests of New Zealand's North Island were cleared. However, despite a large range contraction during this period, genetic studies show that they still maintained a healthy population.

With the arrival of Europeans in New Zealand in the middle of the 19th century, pressures on the huia began to rapidly increase. With European settlement came an increase in logging of the mature forests the huia inhabited. These new settlers were also responsible for bringing land mammals to New Zealand that natively had none. Among them were rats and stoats, both potentially devastating not only to the huia but much of New Zealand's wildlife. The unique characteristics of the huia also made them popular for natural history collections and museums, and naturalists raced to have them in their collections. Demand for the birds drove a market for them and led to a dramatic increase in the harvest of the birds. It's recorded that in a single month in 1882, a Māori hunting party was able to supply 646 skins to the market, and over a 10 year period, 212 of the birds were taken for the collections of the Vienna Museum of Natural History alone. The first European to study the birds extensively, W.L. Buller, had already recorded noticeable reductions in Huia populations by 1892.

Unfortunately, their sacred tail feathers would become popular with a new group of people. In 1901, the Duke of York was presented a huia tail feather by the Māori as an act of great respect, and the feather was placed in the band of his hat. Like many of the things the nobility of England did, Europeans rushed to make the huia feather a fashion, driving even more demand for the already diminished birds. Seeing the decline of their sacred birds, the Māori petitioned the New Zealand government to protect the birds, and protections under New Zealand's Wild Bird Protection Act were extended to the huia in 1892. These laws, however, did little to reduce the killing. For example, in 1896, the fine for killing a huia was just 5 pounds, far less than the value of a dead huia. After 1901, demand from Europe only increased their value, and a single tail feather was worth as much as a week's salary.

The increased demand on the population of already endangered birds rapidly depleted their numbers. From an original population of 30 to 90 thousand birds, by 1907 they were all but gone. The last known sighting of the huia is typically reported as 1907, though research into this sighting suggests that this particular report was potentially as far back as 1905. Researchers have also found a single bird that was said to have been collected in 1906. When exactly the huia disappeared is not known, but the bird collected in 1906 sadly highlights that even though by then the bird was extremely rare, they were still being taken for museum collections; an irony I will never be able to wrap my head around. There are reports of huia being spotted in the 1920s and even as late as the 1960s, but the last of the species probably died out sometime in the very early part of the 20th century.

It's likely that the huia's demise was the result of a combination of factors. Certainly, over hundreds of years, habitat loss dramatically reduced resources for the birds. This, combined with the introduction of predatory land mammals for which the huia would have no experience, and the ever-increasing pressure from the collection of the birds for traditional uses, museums, and fashion, all contributed to diminishing their numbers.

Hawaiian Honeycreepers
(Akialoa)

The Hawaiian honeycreepers are one of the most diverse groups of birds found anywhere in the world. At one time, there were as many as 55 different species of honeycreepers on the Hawaiian Islands prior to human settlement that all evolved from a single finch ancestor. Closely related to the Eurasian rose finch *(Carpodacus erythrinus)*, the honeycreeper's ancestors arrived from Asia sometime around 5.7 million years ago. Their fantastic diversification, rivaling even that of Darwin's finches, is a testament to what adaptive radiation can accomplish. Hawaii's single finch species evolved to fill many of the ecological niches occupied by a number of bird species on the mainland and evolved bill shapes that mimic what is seen in parrots, warblers, cardinals and grosbeaks, and a few unique to only them. Some specialized in seeds and nuts, while others developed large and powerful bills to tackle larger nuts and fruits. Others evolved into insectivores, similar to flycatchers and woodpeckers, while still others adapted to sip nectar. Of the more than 50 species presumed to exist before human arrival more than half are sadly now extinct.

Of all the species to originate from those ancient finches, none appeared more radically different from their ancestors than the honeycreepers of the genus *Akialoa.* Named for the common Hawaiian name for these birds, "'akialoa," there were four species out of as many as seven that survived into modern times. All closely related and similar in appearance, these 15-17 cm (6-7) inch long birds all possessed a distinctly long thin curved bill from 4-6 cm (1.5-2.5) inches (depending on species) which was used to probe trees for insects and their larvae. Also occasionally feeding on nectar, these birds lived in the dense, wet forests of many of the Hawaiian Islands. Little more is known about these unique birds. There is nothing reported of the nesting or breeding habits of any of the 4 species, and very little is reported of behavior at all. Early sightings and birds collected by early naturalists give the only insight to the distribution of the birds.

The lesser 'akialoa *(Akialoa obscura)* was once common throughout much of the Big Island of Hawai'i and was found both on the east and west coasts, but could be rare in specific regions. They were typically found in the island's dense forests at around 250–1200 m (900–4000 ft) in elevation. First observed by Europeans from the expedition of Captain Cook in 1779, they continued to be common through most of the 19th century. Severe declines in populations were observed by 1901, with some sources stating that the bird was absent on the west coast of Hawai'i as early as 1894, with the species disappearing entirely between 1907 and 1915. However, reports of the birds from later dates are unsubstantiated, and the last confirmed record of the lesser 'akialoa was in 1902.

The O'ahu 'akialoa *(Akialoa ellisiana)* was already uncommon by the time Europeans arrived. It was first recorded in 1837, when several individual birds were collected. The next report of them does not come until 1892, and after only a handful of reports from the 1930s. In modern times, O'ahu 'akialoa likely had a

Maui-nui ʻakialoa *(Akialoa lanaiensis)*

small population restricted to the southeastern forests of the island above 460 m (1500 ft). It is now extinct, with no confirmed sightings since the 1930s.

Much like the O'ahu 'akialoa, the Maui-nui 'akialoa *(Akialoa lanaiensis)* was rare in modern times. Found only on the island of Lana'i, they likely were once found throughout Maui Nui (which was comprised of the islands of Lana'i, Maui, Moloka'i, and Kaho'olawe prehistorically). When first observed in 1892, only six birds were positively identified. Subsequent searches found only one bird in 1894, and none have been observed since. It is probable that populations had already taken a severe hit by the time the Maui-nui was described, and this parallels what is seen in the populations of lesser 'akialoa and the O'ahu 'akialoa in the late 19th century.

Unlike the three other species of 'akialoa, the birds on the island of Kaua'i were able to persist for decades longer. The best known of all the species of 'akialoa, the Kaua'i 'akialoa *(Akialoa stejnegeri),* persisted well into the 1960s. Once probably quite common all throughout the forests of Kaua'i from sea level to above 900 meters (3000 ft) the population seemed to be more concentrated on the south central part of the island. Larger bodied than its Big Island cousins, the Kaua'i 'akialoa had a noticeably larger bill that could measure more than 6 cm (2.5 in) in the males. First described in 1888, the population appeared to be suffering from various diseases as early as 1900. There are few records of the birds from the early 20th century, but they were recorded in 1936, and a small flock was recorded in 1941. In 1957, two were observed near Alaka'i Swamp, with subsequent observations in 1965 and 1969. Extensive searches in the decades since have been unable to locate the bird. Added to the USFWS endangered species list in 1967, it was declared extinct in 2021.

The observations of many of the Kaua'i 'akialoa suffering from disease in the early 1900s may give some clue as to the rapid disappearance of the genus as a whole. Beginning in the early 1800s, species introduced into the islands, particularly the mosquito and a variety of non-native birds, likely carried diseases into the wild bird populations of the islands. Genetic studies of native Hawaiian birds from museum collections, found that the presence of the *Avipoxvirus* was already widespread by the late 1800s. Later, more than 100 species of birds intentionally released in the Hawaiian Islands in the twentieth century introduced avian malaria into the populations. It is highly likely that the introduction of new diseases early in the 19th century, habitat losses from growing agricultural operations throughout the 1800s, pressure from newly introduced land mammals such as rats and mongooses, and competition from introduced birds all conspired to devastate the 'akialoa.

Over 30 species of Hawaiian birds have shared the 'akialoa's fate since the arrival of Europeans, and many species continue to be threatened with extinction. The plight of the honeycreepers and other Hawaiian birds is shared with many birds endemic to islands and offers a prime example of the fragile balance of biodiversity found on them. Loss of these island species not only diminishes a valuable resource for understanding how evolution operates but also deprives the world of these often beautiful, unique, and fascinating creatures.

Hawaiian 'O'o (*Moho nobilis*)

ʻOʻo Birds of Hawaii
(Moho)

The ʻoʻos of the Hawaiian Islands have the hapless distinction of being members of the only family of birds known to have gone extinct since 1500, the Mohoidae. Once consisting of 5 species in total, 4 in the genus *Moho,* discussed here, and the kioea *(Chaetoptila angustipluma),* which was last seen in 1859. All members of the family were nectarivores, primarily feeding on the nectar of various flowering plants but also consuming insects and their larvae. Due to a fascinating case of convergent evolution, this family of birds was once grouped in the family Meliphagidae, or "honeyeaters," of Australasia due to their extreme similarities in appearance, behavior, and even song. Surprisingly, even though they were nearly indistinguishable from true honeyeaters, when the genetics of these five Hawaiian species were explored, it was found that they are not related at all to the birds of Meliphagidae, but are in fact most closely related to an entirely different group of birds from North America that include waxwings and their allies. Based on these findings, researchers concluded they should be placed in their own family and noted that without the genetic analysis, the true evolutionary history of the Hawaiian "honeyeaters" would probably never have been discovered.

These distinctive looking birds with patches of bright yellow feathers were highly sought after by Hawaiian royalty. All similar in appearance but with varying plumage, the ʻoʻo's yellow feathers were used to decorate the elaborate ceremonial dress of the native Hawaiians. These ceremonial pieces would often require the feathers of thousands of birds, and the birds were routinely trapped to remove some of the valuable yellow feathers. Traditionally, the birds would be released after capture with a few feathers missing to continue on. However, there is some debate as to how strictly this practice was followed. There are historical reports of fried ʻoʻo being a delicacy amongst Hawaiians. Even with the pressures from native Hawaiians over the centuries, it appears that, on at least two islands, the ʻoʻo was still quite common according to European accounts.

The Hawaiian ʻoʻo *(Moho nobilis)* was the most distinctive of the four species and was once quite common on the Big Island of Hawaiʻi. Europeans first became aware of the species and collected three specimens in 1779. These 30-33 cm (12-13 inch) birds inhabited many of the forests of the island of Hawaiʻi and had a range similar to that of the ʻakialoa. Most commonly found between 600-900 meters (2000 and 4000 feet) in elevation, they could be found as high as the tree line on Mauna Kea. During the winter, the ʻoʻo would often retreat downslope to the lower elevations to avoid the harsher weather higher up in Hawaiʻi's high volcanic mountains. Apparently still common through the majority of the 1800s, naturalists began to observe population declines in birds wintering at lower elevations as early as 1894. Just two years later, in 1896, marked decreases in the abundance of the Hawaiian ʻoʻo were being noticed, and the birds were becoming increasingly absent from areas where they were once common. In the next several years, the ʻoʻo population dropped precipitously. The last bird known to have been collected was in 1902, and only a handful of unsubstantiated reports of the bird's existence persisted into the 1930s. The Hawaiian 'o'o was considered extinct by the Hawaii State Division of Fish and Game by 1969. A statistical analysis of sighting records places the extinction of the Hawaiian 'o'o, sometime between 1906 and 1916, with the 'o'o declining from a fairly common bird to extinction in as little as two decades.

The Bishop's 'o'o *(Moho bishopi)* was native to the island of Moloka'i. At around an inch smaller than the Hawaiian, it was easily distinguished by the yellow tufts on the sides of its head. First seen by Europeans in 1892, the bird was already considered uncommon by naturalists, but could still be found primarily inhabiting the upper forested areas of the island. There is good evidence that like the Hawaiian 'o'o, the Bishop's 'o'o would change its distribution seasonally, moving from the windward to the leeward side of Moloka'i. According to Hawaiian accounts, the Bishop's 'o'o was once quite common all across Moloka'i, and subfossil evidence and a possible sighting on the island of Maui suggest that they likely could have once inhabited the majority of Maui Nui. By the turn of the century, the population of Bishop's 'o'o's had declined further, and the last substantiated observations were made sometime between 1902 and 1904. The Bishop's 'o'o was likely extinct by 1906.

The O'ahu 'o'o *(Moho apicalis)* is the least known of all the endemic birds of the Hawaiian Islands. Similar in size to the 'o'o's of Hawai'i, it was first collected in 1787, but there is nothing written about its prevalence at the time. By 1825, it was considered scarce, and the last bird known to have been collected was in 1837. It is quite possible that the O'ahu 'o'o was extinct by the time it was described in 1860. There is no information about its range, and the 10 individuals collected give no credible account of where they were found. Presumably it would have preferred mid-altitude forested areas as the other 'o'o, but this is not certain. Subfossil evidence suggests that the O'ahu 'o'o may have once been widespread, much like the 'o'o of other islands. Whatever the case, it is clear that these birds were already in severe decline by the time Europeans arrived.

The island of Kaua'i had its own species of 'o'o, the aptly named Kaua'i 'o'o *(Moho baraccatus).* Distinctly smaller than the 'o'o on the other islands, it was also the longest-surviving member of *Moho*. Likely first collected in 1836, it was found throughout the island of Kaua'i at all elevations of the forest. Unlike the 'o'o of other islands, the Kauai'i 'o'o was still common in the island's forests as late as 1894, but there were indications that the 'o'o was retreating to higher elevations. While faring better than the 'o'os on other islands, large population reductions were being noticed by 1915. Sparse sightings of the birds occurred through the 1930s and 1940s. By the mid-1940s, many were concluding that the birds were in danger of extinction. Then confined to higher elevations and increasingly rare, the Kaua'i 'o'o was listed by the USFWS as endangered in 1967. A population study in 1973 estimated only 36 birds remained in total. This dropped to only a dozen by 1978, residing in the same Alaka'i swamp that housed the last of the 'akialoa. In 1981, a single pair of birds was located nesting in a tree cavity within the swamp. The female of the pair was last sighted in May of 1981, with the male persisting alone until April of 1987. Extensive searches have since turned up no sign of the species.

The timing and distribution of the decline of the 'o'o's, with the exception of the O'hau 'o'o, closely parallel that of other Hawaiian birds such as the 'akialoa. This suggests that there is likely a common cause for the decline of many of these birds. It is fairly clear that introduced disease is indicated in the extinction of the 'akialoa, and while there is no direct evidence of the same in the 'o'o, the timing of its population declines and the rapid disappearance of its populations suggest that introduced avian disease from birds brought to the Hawaiian Islands was probably a major cause of their extinction. However, habitat loss, the introduction of non-native predators, and the historic pressures from native hunting all certainly would have been contributing factors. Whatever the ultimate cause for the 'o'o's disappearance, it is probable that multiple human-related factors are at the root of their decline and extinction.

Cuban Macaw
(Ara tricolor)

With the first landings of Europeans in the West Indies, starting with Columbus, there were numerous accounts of members of the parrot family on many of the islands. Historical accounts place as many as 15 species of macaw in the West Indies; how many of these were actually endemic or unique species is difficult to determine. Native cultures throughout South America, Central America, and Mexico actively traded in many parrot species, and the large and beautiful macaws were one of the most popular. Native tribes of the West Indies also traded in the birds and kept them as pets, and it is likely that many of the macaws first seen by Europeans were birds native to the mainland. However, there is evidence that at least some of these macaws were unique to the West Indies. Modern estimations conclude that the islands probably had 3–4 species of macaw native to them, including a species from the island of Guadeloupe that fossil evidence shows was present prior to human habitation. Among the possible native Caribbean macaws, the Cuban macaw is the best documented.

The case for the Cuban macaw being native to Cuba is quite good. Since it is the only species of West Indies macaw with any remaining specimens, it is possible to do genetic testing to glean its origins. Once thought to be a recent offshoot of the scarlet macaw *(Ara macao)* due to its similar appearance, genetic testing found that the Cuban macaw, rather than being a descendant of the scarlet macaw, is a sister species to it and the military macaw *(Ara militaris)*. The Cuban macaw's ancestors separated from this group some 4 million years ago, leaving little doubt that the Cuban macaw was a unique species unto itself that evolved on the island of Cuba.

The Cuban macaw was one of the smallest of the macaws, reaching a length of only about 50 cm (20 in), compared to the scarlet macaw at 81 cm (32 in) or the military macaw at around 76 cm (30 in). These diminutive macaws once ranged throughout the island of Cuba and the neighboring island of Isla de la Juventud, where, like most members of the parrot family, they fed on a variety of fruits, nuts, and seeds, especially those of the palm. They seemed to prefer the lush gallery forests that once covered Cuba but were also found in lowland savannas and low coastal forests. Almost nothing is known about the breeding habits of the birds, but evidence suggests that they nested in hollows typical of many parrot species. Likely widespread and common upon European arrival, they were becoming increasingly rare by the 1840s, and their range had contracted severely in the several hundred years of European occupation. By the 1850s, they were restricted to one region of western Cuba and Isla de la Juventud. By the 1860s, the population was confined to only a handful of locations and reported to be no more than a few pairs of birds. When exactly the Cuban macaw went extinct is difficult to determine, but the last recorded sightings were in 1867, with some believing that it may have still been present as late as 1885.

It is likely that the Cuban macaw suffered from multiple factors that led to its decline. It is well documented that hunting of all members of the parrot family was common throughout the West Indies, and descriptions of the period describe them as being particularly easy to catch. They were commonly used as a food source and highly valued for their feathers, which were used to adorn both ceremonial and everyday dress. As firearms introduced into the New World replaced snares and the bow and arrow, the take became even easier. The macaws' unfortunate lack of fear at the sound of gunfire made them even more vulnerable to this new threat. The centuries-old practice of trading parrots, which was a large part of the commerce of the Amerindians, particularly the prestigious macaw, also increased with the arrival of Europeans. These exotic birds and their magnificent plumage became as popular with the European aristocracy as they were with the upper echelons of native society. So many of the birds were shipped to Europe that only 34 years after Columbus, Spain already had a numerous and wide variety of species within its borders. By the 1730s, some parrots were being sold in Europe for as much as £1700 in today's money, making them a valuable and easy-to-acquire trade item. By the middle of the 1700s, the bird trade from the West Indies was making exotic birds a common sight in Europe, with their popularity peaking in the 1800s. Most desirable were young nestlings, and it was most common to simply cut down a tree containing the nest to retrieve the birds. This practice not only impacted populations by removing young birds, but also destroyed valuable nesting sites. Besides the direct pressures of hunting and trade, the macaws' habitat was increasingly under threat at the same time their numbers were rapidly decreasing. As of 1812, nearly 90% of all of the island of Cuba was covered with forest, but by 1900, this had decreased to just 54%. Nature may have also played a part in the destruction of the diminished macaws. In a turn of bad luck, a series of powerful hurricanes hit Cuba between 1844 and 1856. This possibly dealt a severe blow to the birds' populations, which were already severely affected by numerous human factors.

Hawaiian Crow
(Corvus hawaiiensis)

The last three birds we will look at all have the unfortunate distinction of having gone extinct since just the year 2000. Two of them continue the long-standing losses on the Hawaiian Islands, and the third is representative of the continued threat to the members of the parrot family. There is a glimmer of hope, however; two of the species, the Hawaiian crow highlighted here and the Spix's macaw, have members surviving in captivity. With luck and intensive conservation efforts, it is possible that these two species may one day return to the wild. We can only hope.

Many members of *Corvus* hold spiritual significance for numerous cultures around the world, and the Hawaiian crow, or 'alala, is no exception. It was once common to keep them as pets for the family's protection. Native Hawaiians considered the birds to be one of the favored animals to possess an "'aumakua," or personal spirit. This spirit originated from one of their ancestors, and the keeping of the birds could allow them to receive wisdom or good fortune from them in this way. Like other members of *Corvus,* they are quite vocal and highly intelligent. Research shows that the Hawaiian crow is one of a handful of birds that exhibit the ability to use tools. Amazingly, this same research shows that this ability is not learned but an innate skill. First observed by Europeans in the late 1700s and referred to as ravens, the Hawaiian crow wasn't formally described until the 1840s. They inhabited the mid-level forests of the southern and western areas of the island of Hawai'i and fed on a wide variety of foods in the wild. Around 30 to 40 percent of their diet consisted of fruits, but they also consumed the eggs of other birds, insects, various nuts and seeds, and even small mammals. They typically built nests high in trees, with a preference for the native 'ōhi'a lehua tree *(Metrosideros polymorpha)*. Fossil remains suggest these crows once ranged throughout the Hawaiian Islands.

The Hawaiian crow was reported as common in its Big Island range up until the late 1800s, but there were noticeable declines by 1896. By 1937, their numbers were reported as greatly reduced, and the last sighting of the birds around Hawai'i Volcanoes National Park came in 1940. By 1978, it was estimated that only 76 birds remained, and by 1986, the population had dropped to just 22 birds, restricted to the western part of their range. In the early 1990s, the population halved to only 10–12 birds, and by 2002, just two birds were left in the wild. Thankfully, capture and breeding efforts have kept the species alive. Several attempts at reintroducing the species have not fared well, with captive-bred birds struggling to deal with predation from the native Hawaiian hawk *(Buteo solitarius)*. There are currently no members of the species in the wild, and it is almost certain that without human intervention, the Hawaiian crow could soon be extinct.

The 'alala faced a litany of threats in the wild. Hunting by ranchers for decades into the 1970s took a toll. Unfortunately, even more recently, the birds

CORVUS TROPICUS

were intentionally killed to try to prevent conservation efforts. Predation of young by introduced species such as the mongoose is also implicated in their decline. Non-native animals are not the only invasive species of concern, and a grass accidentally introduced to Hawai'i from Africa in the 1920s, called fountain grass, has increased fires in the crows' habitat. The resulting habitat loss may have significantly impacted the nesting of the crows. Disease, as with many endemic Hawaiian bird species, is most likely the primary cause of the 'alala's extinction. Research has shown that the Hawaiian crow is highly susceptible to avian malaria and the avian pox virus. This may be the largest barrier to long-term reintroduction. Currently, there are around 110 Hawaiian crows in captivity, and they are actively being bred for future reintroduction. Large challenges remain in bringing the species back, including the threat of disease, a lack of genetic diversity, predation by their native enemy, the Hawaiian hawk, and a lack of high-quality habitat.

Po'ouli
(Melamprosops phaeosoma)

The po'ouli is yet another member of the Hawaiian honeycreepers to disappear from the world. Although not discovered until 1973, these birds were already rare at the time of their discovery and probably already critically endangered. At the time of discovery, the population was estimated at just 500–750 birds, occupying an extremely limited range of just 1,200 hectares (3,200 acres) on the eastern slopes of Mt. Haleakala on the island of Maui, and then only between 900–1800 m (3000–6000 ft) in altitude. Fossil evidence shows they once occupied the western slopes and lower, drier forests as well, but they were probably never very common. The petite 14 cm (5.5 inch) po'ouli was a snail specialist and fed on a variety of native ground snails, this trait was unique among the Hawaiian honeycreepers, demonstrating the groups fantastic variability. Only two nests were ever observed in the short time the species was studied, both found high up in native 'ōhi'a lehua trees.

Po'ouli populations were already in free fall when they were discovered, and they continued to decline. Estimates in 1980 saw the population fall to just 140 birds in less than a decade, despite being listed as endangered by the USFWS in 1975. Surveys in 1994-1995 were only able to locate six birds, and by the late 1990s, only three birds could be located. An attempt was made to capture the remaining birds; only one was captured and unfortunately died in captivity shortly after, likely due to its advanced age. The remaining 2 birds were last sighted in 2003 and 2004. Despite intensive searches, no remaining individuals have been located. Statistical analysis suggests the species' final members died sometime between 2005 and 2008. The USFWS recommended removing the po'ouli from ESA protections in 2021, citing its likely extinction, and the IUCN declared the species extinct in 2019.

There have been many theories put forward as to the causes of the po'ouli's extinction. Like most of the bird extinctions in the Hawaiian Islands, disease was probably a large contributor. In fact, the last member of the species caught was infected with avian malaria. The precipitous decline of the po'ouli's population is also consistent with disease affecting the population. Introduced species may have also contributed, with known predation from mongooses, cats, and rats, and habitat destruction from a 400% increase in feral pigs within the birds' range. The invasion of the non-native garlic snail, which displaced the bird's native prey, may also have had a significant impact by reducing available food resources. Unfortunately, it is clear that the pressures the po'ouli faced were not unique to the species, and it is likely not the last Hawaiian bird to become extinct. 33 of the 44 remaining birds endemic to Hawai'i are currently endangered.

Smit lith.　　　　　　　　　　　　　　　　Hanhart imp.

ARA SPIXI.

Spix's Macaw
(Cyanopsitta spixii)

The last bird on our list may have a fair chance of coming back from the brink. It was discovered by Western science in 1819, during the first expedition to Brazil of German scientist and namesake Johann Baptist von Spix. The Spix's macaw is one of the rarest members of the parrot family and has only been known historically in the wild from limited early specimens and infrequent sightings. It most recently occupied the gallery forests of the northern part of Bahia state in Brazil, but historical records seem to indicate that the species could have once wandered more widely. The rarity of these birds and lack of study in their natural habitat limit the amount of information about their behaviors in the wild. The last area known to have housed these birds is the seasonal rivers dominated by the trumpet tree *(Tabebuia aurea)*, and it is suspected as being an essential part of their habitat.

The Spix's macaw is the only member of its genus, and evolutionarily it is the oldest of the macaws, arising around 16 million years ago. It is smaller than other macaws at around 55 cm (22 in) in length, but is not as small as the Cuban macaw. In the wild, it fed on seeds and nuts, particularly those of the trumpet tree and other members of the Euphorbia family. Populations historically have never been reported as robust, with only several individuals typically being sighted at a time. It was clear by the 1980s that the population had collapsed, and it was believed that there might be as few as 3 remaining wild individuals by 1985. The last generally accepted sighting was that of a single individual in 2000, and they are believed to have gone extinct in the wild shortly thereafter. Although little is known about the birds in their native habitat, in captivity they are likely one of the most intensively studied of all the macaws. There is an extensive ongoing effort to breed these birds and reintroduce them to the wild, and their behavior and genetics have been closely studied. Currently, there are about 160 individuals in the captive breeding program, and a reintroduction program is in an advanced stage. In 2018, the Brazilian government protected 120,000 hectares (nearly 300,000 acres) of land to help with its reintroduction.

Even the rarity of these birds has not limited the threat from the wild bird trade, and in all probability, their rarity has actually increased the demand for the birds. In fact, it is believed that the three birds found in 1985 disappeared as a result of trapping and were sold to foreign buyers. This will likely continue to be a severe threat to the birds upon their reintroduction, with the extremely rare birds certainly fetching high prices on the black market. Deforestation of the macaw's habitat has likely also played a large role in the bird's decline, with much of the once high-quality gallery forest it depended on lost to grazing, crop production, and firewood. Only remnant patches of habitat housing trumpet trees remain in this area of Brazil. Even with the large area of protection, it is uncertain whether enough habitat exists for the long-term survival of the birds, and the specific habitat requirements of the Spix's macaw are slow to recover in the arid environs to which it is native.

6
Amphibians (Amphibia)

Amphibians are the oldest terrestrial vertebrates on Earth, originating from the lobe-finned fish that first took to the land some 370 million years ago. These land-going fish gave rise to the "true amphibians," the ancestors of all of today's amphibians, around 350 million years ago. However, the scarcity of amphibians in the fossil record obscures many of the details about the origins and evolution of today's amphibians. The class contains 3 orders, which are composed of the better known frogs and toads (Anura), salamanders (Caudata), and the lesser known snake-like caecilians (Gymnophiona). Common to nearly all amphibians is a unique life cycle that passes through a larval state. Undoubtedly, most of us are familiar with the amazing transformation of a legless, lungless fish-like tadpole, into a land-going, 4-legged, hopping frog. There are some exceptions, with a few amphibian species from all three orders having direct development, or having young that hatch fully formed from their eggs without having to go through metamorphosis. Some of these are viviparous. These species carry and develop their eggs internally and give "birth" to fully formed young. Some species can forgo metamorphosis all together if they so choose. Several species of salamander are paedomorphic, including the axolotl *(Ambystoma mexicanum)* and tiger salamander *(Ambystoma tigrinum)*. These species stay and grow larger in their larval state even as they become adults. As long as conditions are favorable, they retain the fully aquatic larval characteristics, but at any time, if conditions warrant, they can meta-morphose into a typical adult form, allowing the freedom of a truly amphibious lifestyle.

Also common to amphibians is the need for water. Nearly all amphibians require a source of freshwater or high humidity for reproduction. This is to prevent their eggs from drying out, but ties to streams and ponds vary with species. Some are entirely aquatic, and several species of giant salamander permanently retain their larval gills and stay this way throughout their lives. On the other extreme, some desert toad species rarely see any water at all. Most amphibians possess lungs for breathing air while on land, and all can obtain oxygen through direct gas exchange through the skin, whether in water or on dry land. Amphibians also have no need to drink, obtaining all the water they need through their skin from the surrounding environment. Amphibians are nearly entirely absent from saltwater habitats as their permeable skin gives them a low tolerance for high salt concentrations, but some species can tolerate seawater for short periods and brackish water indefinitely. As adults, all amphibians are carnivorous, with most species' diets consisting of worms, insects, and various other arthropods. However, some species of frogs will consume almost anything that will fit in their mouth, including small mammals and even birds.

There are nearly 8400 known species of amphibians, 90% of which are frogs, making them nearly as diverse as birds. They can be found nearly everywhere on the planet outside of the polar zones and live in a diverse array of habitats, from wetlands to forests and even dry grasslands and deserts, but are most abundant in the warm, moist tropics. While the tropics house the most species of amphibians overall, North America has the unique position of being home to the most species of salamanders, with one third of all species occurring there. 200 occur just in the United States, nearly double that of frog species. In contrast, Brazil only has 5 known species of salamander but over 1000 species of frog.

Amphibians are found in a vast range of sizes, with the smallest holding the distinction of being the smallest known vertebrate. This spectacularly diminutive frog, named *Paedophryne amauensis,* lives on the forest floor of the tropical rainforest of Papua New Guinea and measures an average of just 7.7 mm, or one-third of an inch! This is a far cry from the world's largest frog, the goliath frog *(Conraua goliath)* of central Africa. These behemoths can be a foot long, not counting their legs, and weigh as much as 3.3 kg, or more than 7 lbs. As large as these frogs are, they are not even close to the largest living amphibians, the Chinese giant salamanders. Once considered to be a single species, there may now be as many as three separate species, but they are all similarly sized, with the largest individuals being more than 1.5 meters (5 ft) long and weighing more than 45 kg (100 lbs).

Amphibians also display a fantastic array of specialized adaptations to the environments in which they inhabit. Tree frogs, for example, live most of their lives out of water, with most only coming out of the trees to lay their eggs and mate, although some species don't even leave the trees for this. Many of them have adapted to this life out of water by evolving waxy waterproof coatings produced by glands in their skin to reduce water loss, but this is not the most interesting of their adaptations. Several species have evolved to be able to take to the air using their oversized foot webbing. One such species is Wallace's flying frog *(Rhacophorus nigropalmatus),* from the tropical forests of Borneo and Malaysia. When threatened by a predator or needing to travel quickly, these frogs can simply leap into the air, spread their toes, and glide as much as 15 m (50 feet) through the forest.

How amphibians deal with harsh conditions has produced some of their most fascinating adaptations. For example, the wood frog *(Rana sylvatica),* which lives as far north as the Arctic Circle, has evolved a unique way of dealing with the harsh arctic winters. Rather than burying itself deep underground like most frogs in the winter, the wood frog stays near the surface. Hiding in leaf litter, these sturdy frogs simply allow themselves to freeze nearly solid. While the water around their cells becomes a block of ice (hibernating wood frogs are sometimes found nearly completely encased in ice), their cells are protected by large amounts of urea and glucose that act as antifreeze to prevent damage by ice crystals. As soon as temperatures rise above freezing in the spring, they thaw and go about their business. The wood frogs of Alaska have been found to be able to survive internal body temperatures as low as -16°C or 3°F.

While wood frogs only have to survive the winter, desert amphibians may have to wait much longer for better conditions. In Australia, one of its widespread amphibian residents has learned to deal with the harsh droughts that can impact much of this continent. The Australian water-holding frog *(Cyclorana platycephala)* has adapted to the lack of water by hibernating underground. As the name suggests, they have an amazing ability to store water. Before the seasonal sources of water dry up, these frogs fill their bodies with as much water as they can by storing it in their bladders and specialized pockets in their skin. They then bury themselves as much as 3 meters underground and secrete a protective layer that helps reduce water loss. Deep underground, with their body weight now 50% water, they wait for the next significant rain event to dig themselves out to feed and breed before the water again dries up. If these rains fail to come, the water holding frogs simply wait; they can survive in their underground cocoon for as long as 5 years.

For all of the amazing abilities that frogs possess, there is one group of amphibians whose abilities can rival those of nearly every animal on the planet, and it is one of the most fascinating things about the animals of Caudata. While re-generation does happen among several groups of vertebrates—for example, some fish can regrow their fins, many lizards can grow a lost tail, and geckos can even regenerate entire limbs—the abilities of salamanders are uniquely impressive in the vertebrate world. Not only can they regrow a lost limb or tail, salamanders have been shown to be able to regenerate numerous body structures, including the brain and parts of the central nervous system, including the spinal cord, the heart, and the retina and lens of the eye. The mechanism and extent of this regeneration varies depending on the species, but the ability to regenerate lost or damaged tissues is inherent to all salamanders. Unlocking the secrets to how salamanders are able to achieve this impressive feat gives scientists hope that it one day could be applied to humans, and there is no doubt that these delightful creatures have given us valuable insights into stem cell functioning and activation.

There are many threats to amphibians worldwide, and as with most species, habitat loss is a major factor. Centuries of draining wetlands for agriculture have had significant impacts on amphibian populations. This is coupled with deforestation which removes habitat for woodland species, changes water storage regimes, and decreases water quality. Clear-cutting of forests in the southern Appalachian region of the United States alone kills an estimated 14 million salamanders each year. Water quality and man-made pollution are also significant factors. Amphibians with their membranous skin, through which they can both breathe and drink, are particularly susceptible to pollutants and many are readily absorbed into their bodies. The beautiful and sometimes whimsical characteristics of many amphibians also make them popular for the pet trade. This is especially true for several species of tropical leaf frogs and the colorful dart frogs. Significant numbers of amphibians are wild caught, legally and illegally, for the pet trade every year. One study determined that between 1998-2002, imports into the U.S. alone amounted to 14.7 million wild-caught amphibians, with most destined for the pet trade. There are currently more than 1200 different species of amphibians traded internationally for a number of reasons (more than 800 for the pet trade). Of these, more than 1 in 5 are considered vulnerable, endangered, or critically endangered.

Among all the threats that amphibians face, disease has been the most devastating. The most deadly of these has been an introduced fungal pathogen, a type of chytrid fungus, called *Batrachochytrium dendrobatidis,* or *Bd* for short. After years of unexplained amphibian die-offs, *Bd* was eventually discovered by researchers in 1998. It has been responsible for many of the devastating declines in amphibian populations around the world, especially in South America, Central America, and Australia. This highly contagious fungus infects the keratinized portions of amphibian skin. The resulting disease, called chytridiomycosis, thickens and hardens the epidermis of the infected animal, shutting down the transport of oxygen and water through the skin ultimately leading to the animal's death.

Bd is thought to have originated in Asia and was likely spread to disease vulnerable groups of amphibians via introduced carriers. Not all amphibians are negatively affected by *Bd,* and several notable species are likely vectors for the spread of the disease into new environments. One significant species not affected is the American bullfrog *(Lithobates catesbeianus).* While this is good news for native populations of bullfrogs, the species is widely farmed around the world for food. Research has shown that these farming operations can harbor high amounts of *Bd* and, according to researchers, these "bullfrog farms constantly release substantial quantities of Bd zoospores into the surrounding natural environment." Other species indicated in the spread are African clawed frogs *(Xenopus laevis),* which were once widely transported across the world to be used in pregnancy tests, and the introduced cane toad *(Bufo marinus),* which is likely the reservoir for the disease in Australia. How and exactly when *Bd* first left Asia is unknown, but it is clear that the increase in the international trade of amphibians for the pet trade, food, and medical purposes has fueled the spread of the deadly pathogen.

While *Bd* is thought to potentially affect all orders of amphibians, a new threat has emerged for salamanders. A related fungus, *Batrachochytrium salamandrivorans,* was first identified in 2013 among wild and captive fire salamanders *(Salamandra salamandra)* in Belgium and the Netherlands. *Bsal,* like its cousin *Bd,* causes a similar disease and can have the same devastating effects. The once-thriving populations of fire salamanders in the Netherlands have now been reduced by 96%. Thought to also have originated in Asia, *Bsal* is believed to have been imported into Europe through the pet trade. Of great concern is the potential for *Bsal* to reach North America and the diverse population of salamanders there. To try to prevent the potentially devastating effects of an introduction, the United States has blocked the transfer of some 200 species of salamander that may harbor the fungus. Thankfully, there is still no evidence of *Bsal* in North America, but the risk of introduction remains extremely high, with dire consequences.

Amphibians are one of the most threatened groups of animals on the planet. Currently, 40%–50% of all amphibian species could be at risk of extinction. The IUCN Red List of Threatened Species lists over 1,400 species of frog, 279 species of salamander, and 11 species of caecilian as endangered or critically endangered. *Bd* alone has been implicated in the decline of at least 501 species and the likely extinction of 90 in the last 50 years. Unfortunately, these numbers are probably underestimates. With new species being discovered every year, it is likely, with the often devastating and rapid declines observed in *Bd* infected amphibian populations, that there are many species unknown to science that have already been lost. The majority of amphibian declines have been in the tropics of Australia, Mesoamerica, and South America, but declines in amphibian populations around the world have been recorded for decades. Thankfully, there have been some recorded recoveries in recent years, but these recoveries come nowhere close to the presumed initial populations. While cautiously optimistic, scientists still harbor serious concerns. Many species are still extremely vulnerable, and any significant disruption could end in their demise. As the threats to the world's biodiversity continue to increase, the pressures on these vulnerable species will continue to grow. Quick action to change the status quo is needed if humans are to avoid losing thousands of species of amphibians.

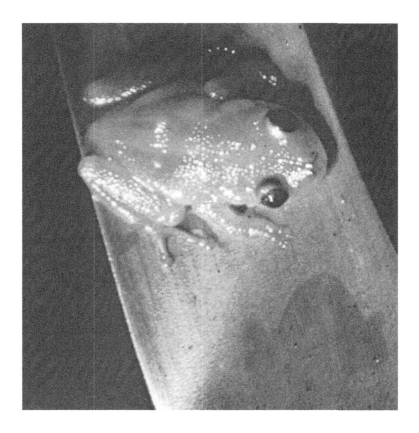

Golden Coqui Frog
(Eleutherodactylus jasperi)

The golden coqui was a rarity among frogs. There are only a handful of frogs around the world known to be viviparous, meaning they give birth to fully developed young. The golden coqui was the first viviparous frog found in the New World and the only known member of its genus to be so. Closely related to the common coqui *(Eleutherodactylus coqui)*, found throughout Puerto Rico, the 200 members of the genus are distinguished, as their scientific name suggests (Greek for free-toed), by the lack of webbing on their feet. There were once at least 16 members of the genus found on the island of Puerto Rico. The aptly named golden coqui was distinguished from the common coqui by its distinctive uniform golden coloring.

These small golden frogs, measuring 18–22 mm (0.7–0.8 in) in length, were unknown to science until they were first collected in 1973. They once inhabited a very small range, approximately 10 sq km (< 4 sq mi), in the Sierra de Cayey in the southern part of Puerto Rico at altitudes between 650-850 meters (2100

-2800 ft). In this range, the little golden frogs were found only in dense bromeliad clusters, suggesting that they were specialized for life on these plants. Being nocturnal, they hunted at night for various small arthropods. Females internally laid 3-6 small eggs that would then fully develop into froglets in about 30 days.

Unfortunately, little else is known about these unique little frogs, and scientists had little time to observe them. The last sighting of the golden coqui came less than a decade after their discovery, with the last record of the them coming in 1981. How prevalent the species was historically or its historical range is not known, but it's possible that it was never very common due to its specialization of habitat. The golden coqui is also not the only member of its genus to disappear from Puerto Rico. There are two others, the Puerto Rican stream frog *(Eleutherodactylus karlschmidti)*, last seen in 1976, and the Eneida's coqui *(Eleutherodactylus eneidae)*, last seen in 1990. Over 3,400 hours of searching between 1989 and 2001 failed to find any members of the 3 species, and all 3 are now presumed extinct.

What caused the extinction of the golden coqui or its two relatives is not definitively known. Many cite habitat loss and deforestation. Loss of forest cover on the island of Puerto Rico has been extreme, and Puerto Rico did not escape the severe land use changes common to the islands of the West Indies dating back to the late 1400s. Continuing the island's long history of habitat disruption, 94% of its remaining forests were lost between 1930 and 1950. It is possible that by the time the golden coqui was discovered, it was already well on its way to extinction. Research conducted on museum specimens to determine potential diseases failed to find the presence of *Bd* on any of the golden coqui specimens collected in 1973; however, it was detected on a specimen of *Eleutherodactylus karlschmidti* collected in 1976, confirming the presence of *Bd* in Puerto Rico. It is certainly possible that the golden coqui population may have been infected with *Bd* sometime after its discovery. This would explain the species' rapid disappearance, but there is no direct evidence to support the chytrid fungus as the cause of the coqui's decline. It is also possible that a yet unidentified disease could be the culprit, but it seems likely that the high level of habitat loss and the frog's restricted range played a large part in its eventual demise.

The case of the golden coqui is one of many likely human-associated extinctions from the Caribbean that we may never know the exact cause of, and sadly, there could be any number of species lost that are still unknown to science. The exploitation of the West Indies going back centuries has taken a massive toll on the species that once resided there. In the last 500 years, over 40 species of endemic mammals and birds have gone extinct from the islands of the Caribbean. In historically understudied and poorly fossilized groups of animals like amphibians, the toll could be far greater, and the true damage from our actions could be hidden by our lack of knowledge of many of the species that once resided there.

The Panamanian Golden Frog *(Atelopus zeteki).*

Harlequin Toads
(Atelopus)

It is often more useful to highlight the plight of an entire group of animals rather than a specific species and, like the birds of the Hawaiian Islands, there are many groups of amphibians imperiled. The members of the genus *Atelopus,* commonly referred to as the harlequin toads, are probably one of the most severely endangered groups of animals in the world. Out of the 113 described or proposed species that currently make up the genus, at least 52 are believed to be severely affected by chytrid fungus. Of these 52, 30 are now presumed to be extinct, and nearly all the rest have seen a greater than 90% drop in their populations. Only 2 members of *Atelopus* have been known to show any recent recovery: the clown frog of Costa Rica (*A. varius)* and *A. patazensis* of the Andes of northern Peru.

The species in *Atelopus* are members of the "true toads," of the family Bufonidae, although many are often referred to as frogs. In fact, there is little difference between the two names, and they are often interchangeable. The name toad often refers to an anurid that has bumpy skin and shorter legs compared to frogs that typically have smooth skin and longer legs. However, this is not always the case, and there are species that are called by either or both terms. The members of the family Bufonidae are called "true toads" because most of them fall into the typical description of a toad with shortened limbs, rough, dry skin, and more specifically, toxin-producing parotoid glands behind their eyes, but in general, there is little distinction scientifically between the two terms. The harlequin toads buck this trend by looking quite frog-like but still having the poison glands typical of toads.

The harlequin toads are endemic only to Central and South America and range from Costa Rica in the north to Bolivia in the south. Common among many species of the genus are distinctive bright and varied colorations, leading to the harlequin moniker. Also distinctive about these toads is that most are "earless," lacking a tympanum and middle ear column; however, they are not deaf and are quite adept at hearing high-frequency sounds. They prefer stream-side forested habitats and can be found from sea level to as high as the snow line, but the majority are found in the cooler, moist forests above 1,500 m (5,000 ft), with some species only found higher than 3,000 m (9,800 ft). Several of the genus' attributes compound threats to the group, especially from the chytrid fungus. The preference for higher altitudes may contribute to their exposure to the chytrid fungus, with many species living entirely inside the fungus' preferred climates. The survival of members of *Atelopus* may also be hindered by their population structure. Many of the species in the genus show a high degree of local endemism, meaning they are typically only found in small, distinct populations within their range. This makes them particularly vulnerable to extinction. Nearly a quarter of the known species are known from only one population at a restricted altitudinal range.

The most famous of these distinctive-looking anurids is the Panamanian golden frog *(Atelopus zeteki)*. It has become the poster child for amphibian extinction, for not only related species but amphibians worldwide. It is considered a national symbol of good luck in its native country of Panama. Once revered by the pre-Columbian inhabitants, the toads are still highly regarded among Panamanians, and they even have a national holiday in their honor. Once found in wet and dry montane forests in western central Panama at an altitude of 335–1315 meters (1,300–4,300 ft), the golden frog has a body shape typical of the genus, and it is easy to see why they are often called frogs with their quite un-toad-like look. These diurnal toads preferred to inhabit the banks of fast-flowing streams, where they fed on the small invertebrates of the forest floor. Measuring between 45 and 55mm (1.75-2in) in length, they are the most toxic of any of the members of *Atelopus,* and a single individual can produce enough toxin to kill as many as 1,200 mice.

Despite the belief that they confer good luck, the species has not itself been very lucky, and although once found in abundance, they are now believed to be extinct in the wild, with the last observations coming in 2009. It is the hope that captive bred frogs may someday be released back into the wild, and there is a large effort in and out of Panama to make this happen. However, like many other members of *Atelopus*, the Panamanian golden frog's populations were devastated by *Bd* and, as the fungus persists in the environment, the potential for reintroduction is unknown. Scientists are hopeful that a strategy can be found to make these and other remaining species immune to the effects of *Bd*. There have been encouraging results in studies using low-virulence versions of *Bd* as a vaccine against the fungus. When some species of frog are exposed to these hypovirulent strains, not only do they not develop an infection, but they also become as much as 55 times more resistant to virulent strains of *Bd.* Even better, these hypovirulent strains can be transmitted from frog to frog, making it a self-distributing vaccine. Besides a direct treatment for *Bd,* it may be possible with robust captive breeding to overwhelm the effects of the fungus. Some researchers believe that even if a small percentage of released frogs survive the fungus, with careful monitoring and more releases to bolster numbers, populations resistant to *Bd* may be established. Like other amphibians, chytrid is not the only threat to the golden frog, and there are a range of other issues that have exacerbated its decline. These include habitat loss, collection for local zoos and hotels, and the illegal pet trade.

While there is still hope for the golden frogs of Panama, for other members of *Atelopus* it is too late for human intervention, and many are almost certainly extinct. One of these members is the Chiriqui harlequin frog *(Atelopus chiriquiensis).* Once found in abundance throughout its range as recently as 1991 from the western cloud forests of Costa Rica to eastern Panama, these colorful frogs have not been seen since 1996 after a devastating population crash. The Chiriqui exhibited an interesting separation of the sexes, not only differing in size and color but even preferring different habitats. Females were around 1.5 times larger than the males, with a typical length of 36–49 mm (1.4–1.9 in) and the diminutive males around 28–34 mm (1.1–1.3 in). Females were typically orange with heavy black striping, while the males were often a solid color varying in a rainbow from yellow to chartreuse, lime green, red, orange, or even blue. Males preferred the banks of fast-flowing streams, while females typically preferred the shade of the forest floor.

Despite extensive searches in recent years in both Panama and Costa Rica, there has been no sign of the Chiriqui, leading the IUCN to list them as extinct. Causes for their collapse are the ever present habitat loss and possible predation by an introduced trout species, but chytrid is likely the largest factor. While still abundant in the early '90s, by 1993, *Bd* had been identified in their population. Severe declines were seen by 1994 and, as mentioned earlier, they were last seen in 1996. This follows the all-too-common pattern seen in many species affected by *Bd.* Abundant populations of frogs are suddenly affected by steep declines and rapid local extinctions. This is quickly followed by range-wide extinction, and areas that were once so densely populated with frogs that it was difficult to avoid them are quickly reduced to frog-barren landscapes.

The pass stubfoot toad *(Atelopus senex)* is yet another lost species of *Atelopus*, just one in a list that is likely to grow. There was nothing particularly special about these little toads. They were not the symbol of a nation. Nor were they the most poisonous or the most colorful. Although, like many of their relatives they could be found in a wide variety of colors. They don't even have a catchy name. They are one of many lost species that will likely slip away almost completely unnoticed by the vast majority of humanity. Despite their seeming insignificance, their loss should not cause us any less pain than the loss of rhinos, tigers, or pandas. So often, we tend to overlook small creatures and the important role they play in the world's ecosystems. We unfortunately, will never know the full role that these 1.5 inch frogs played and can never again study how they fit into their little stream-side world, but each species lost is a world less rich in so many ways no matter how insignificant they might seem.

The pass stubfoot toad, typical of the harlequins, was only found in three locations in central Costa Rica's highland wet and rainforest at altitudes ranging from 1280 to 2040 m (400 to 6000 ft), but it was once abundant. Unfortunately for the stubfoot, their high local endemism and high-altitude habitats made them prime candidates for a devastating chytrid outbreak. While habitat loss and degradation are cited as additional factors in their demise, the scourge of *Bd* was probably the ultimate cause. While not conclusively known, the population going from one of abundance before 1987 to obscurity just a year later bears all the hallmarks of a chytrid outbreak. After decades of extensive and unsuccessful searches to locate any remaining toads, the IUCN declared *Atelopus senex* extinct in 2020.

All of this may lead one to conclude that the fate of the majority of the harlequin toads is extinction. For some of them—maybe many of them—that is the case. However, sometimes a species can surprise us. Some frogs once thought lost have been rediscovered, giving rise to the hope that others may yet exist. This is the case with the Rancho Grande Harlequin Frog *(Atelopus cruciger)*. After a severe collapse in their populations due to a chytrid outbreak, only two individuals could be located in 1986. Once abundant and known from more than 70 locations along the central and northern coastal ranges of Venezuela, these striking yellow and black toads vanished seemingly overnight. For 18 years, not a single toad was found until 2004, when a small population was located in a mountain stream in the Parque Nacional Henri Pittier Cloud Forest. Since then, a handful of other populations have been located. The situation is still tenuous. Chytrid outbreaks can come out of nowhere, and other threats abound, but if these toads can go missing for 18 years and be found again, there is hope that somewhere in the remote forests of Central and South America, more species could be holding on.

Golden Toad
(Incilius periglenes)

The golden toad is another Central American species caught up in the severe declines that have plagued this area of the world for decades. Hailing from the cloud forests of north central Costa Rica, it inhabited very similar habitats to that of its toad cousins in *Atelopus*. Also, like many species of harlequin toads, it had a very limited range, only being found in a 10 sq km (4 sq mi) area of the Monteverde Cloud Forest Preserve. These small toads were known for several interesting reasons. Not unique to them but nonetheless interesting, they showed an extreme color dimorphism between the sexes, with males being a solid yellow to orange. The females, however, would scarcely be thought to be the same species. They exhibited a greenish yellow to black color with striking bright red spots surrounded by yellow, while their undersides showed a solid yellow to flesh color. Also, unlike the stream bank harlequins, these toads would spend the dry months of the year burrowed beneath the forest floor, only emerging to breed during the wet season. Unfortunately, these toads are also known for having one of the most devastating population crashes of any amphibian species.

The golden toad had only been known to science for a little over 20 years. They were discovered in 1966 in their small area of cloud forest, and while they were not visible all of the year, the rains revealed an abundant population. In a survey conducted in 1977, 988 of the toads were counted in a single day. Over the next 10 years, it was common to record 1,500 or more frogs in the 4-month breeding season. Then, between 1987 and 1988, everything changed. In the span of a single year, the population dropped from the typical 1,500 toads to only a handful. By the following year, researchers found only a single toad. Despite exhaustive searches, no trace of the species has been found since 1989. In 2001, the IUCN declared them officially extinct.

Scientists were baffled by the dramatic loss of the species, but the same dramatic population crash seen in the golden toad was also being seen in other amphibian species in Monteverde, including the still critically endangered variable harlequin frog *(Atelopus varius)*. In fact, fully 40% of the frog species of the Monteverde cloud forest disappeared within this same span of time, signaling that there was most likely a common cause. The initial theory proposed was that climate change was to blame. Immediately preceding the collapse was an unusually dry and warm season caused by a strong El Niño event. The result was one of the driest seasons in 100 years. It was thought that this drying event might have been enough to cause the losses seen. Later, after the discovery of the chytrid fungus *Bd*, testing of historically collected specimens showed no presence of *Bd* prior to the collapse in Monteverde, but its presence following it. A wider analysis also allowed researchers to track the spread of chytrid over time, beginning in southern Mexico in 1974 and spreading south into Central and eventually South America. *Bd* reached the Monteverde region of Costa Rica in 1987, just as its amphibians began to collapse.

So chytrid is probably ultimately to blame for the loss of Monteverde's frogs and the extinction of the golden toad, but the impact of *Bd* may not work in isolation. Scientists initially thought that the severe drying event was the culprit in the collapse of the golden toads and others, and it is hard to ignore the event's temporal proximity. It is now believed that climatic events may exacerbate disease transmission in several ways, and while the 1987 El Niño event affecting Costa Rica was not caused by anthropogenic climate change, many more events in the future will be. In the case of Monteverde's amphibians, it's believed that the unusually dry season likely concentrated many of the area's amphibians into smaller and smaller areas as they sought out remaining water resources. Normally, this would have a small overall impact. Resources would be shared, and eventually species would redistribute themselves when the rains once again arrived. Unfortunately, the arrival of *Bd* in Costa Rica coincided with Monteverde's amphibians being concentrated together. Frogs on the move to find water and populations pushed together by the dry conditions may have allowed chytrid to spread rapidly between species. It's impossible to know if the ultimate result of the chytrid outbreak would have been different without this unusually dry season, but it's likely that it accelerated the dramatic losses. As the pace of climate change increases, we will continue to see these abnormal weather variations affect the transmission and distribution of diseases throughout the world. Undoubtedly, there will be other unexpected consequences, many of which will be difficult to predict.

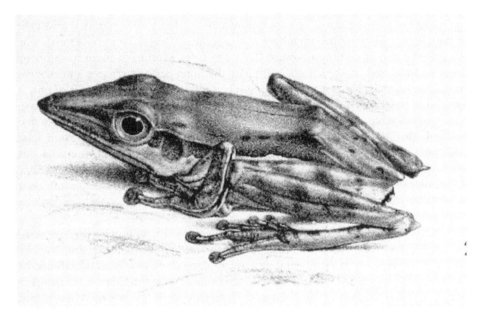

One of the 17 species of extinct shrub frogs from Sri Lanka *Pseudophilautus nasutus.*

Shrub Frogs of Sri Lanka
(Pseudophilautus)

The shrub frogs of Sri Lanka are members of the large and diverse family Rhacophoridae, which includes 8 other genera and over 430 species of these primarily arboreal frogs spread throughout east Asia and sub-Saharan Africa. The members of *Pseudophilautus* occur primarily on the island nation of Sri Lanka, where they have been evolving for some 30 million years, with the rest occurring in the Western Ghats of India. The long evolutionary history of the frogs in Sri Lanka has produced at least 59 species of shrub frog unique to the nation and, not surprisingly, has produced a myriad of shrub frogs of different color and description. So successful have the members of *Pseudophilautus* been that they make up more than 60% of all the amphibians found in the country.

The members of the genus are found in the wet highland forests throughout Sri Lanka. Like the harlequin toads, many species have very limited ranges, making them particularly vulnerable to extinction. Typical of the genus are small to medium size, around 17 mm to 60 mm (0.6 to 2.5 in) in body length, with females being substantially larger than males and colors and patterns varying widely between species. Most of the species are subdued greens to browns, but many exhibit the bright green often seen in tree frogs, with a handful of species showing yellow to orange coloration. Thought to be shared by most members of the genus is the direct development of young, with many species burying eggs in the moist soils of the forest or tree hollows, but at least one is known to attach eggs to leaves. Some of the members of the genus may also be bubble nesters as suggested by their common names. Here, the frogs produce a foam of saliva or other extracts and lay their eggs within. As the foam dries, it creates a protective coating to keep eggs moist and safe. Details of the behaviors and ranges of only a handful of the 100+ species of *Pseudophilautus* throughout the world are known, and much of what is believed of the genus as a whole is inferred from these few accounts. In fact, the number of species of *Pseudophilautus* is in constant flux, with new members being described not only from discoveries in the wild but even from specimens collected more than 100 years ago. The very similar morphologies of many of these frogs and the ever-present issue of what constitutes a separate species continue to make identification and the task of protecting these species difficult.

Of the 112 species of *Pseudophilautus* currently listed by the IUCN, 17 are believed to be extinct, all from Sri Lanka. Of the rest, more than half are listed as either endangered or critically endangered, making them nearly as threatened as the harlequin toads. The reason for the high number of extinctions in Sri Lanka is hard to pin down. Many of the species are known from only a few individuals, and many of these were described in the middle to late 19th or early 20th centuries. Details on where these frogs were originally collected are vague at best, with many simply stating they were collected in "Ceylon" (the old name for Sri Lanka). Without details, no real determination can be made as to why these species have not been seen again, but the remaining species and the threats they face may give us an idea.

The nearly universally accepted reason for the decline of Sri Lanka's shrub frogs, and many other species on the island is deforestation. The loss of forest cover in Sri Lanka in the last 150 years has been dramatic. Before 1900, nearly 90% of the island was covered in primary forest, amounting to more than 5 million hectares (12 million acres). By 1930, this had been reduced to just under 3.5 million hectares. As agriculture and the population grew, forest cover dropped to just 2.3 million hectares (5.6 million acres). Fully 42% of the entire land area of Sri Lanka is currently used for agriculture, and while Sri Lanka still retains about 30% forest cover, only 167,000 hectares, or just 2.58% of the total area of Sri Lanka, is still primary forest. While Sri Lanka has recently committed to increasing forested area and has limited palm oil production in favor of more environmentally friendly crops such as rubber and coconut, a great amount of damage has already been inflicted on the country's biodiversity. As the chytrid fungus depletes the world of many of its amphibians, it is important to remember that habitat loss is still currently the number one threat to biodiversity overall. Thankfully, even though conditions for *Bd* are favorable, chytrid is not thought to be responsible for amphibian declines here, and hopefully that will continue to be the case.

While the majority of the Sri Lankan shrub frogs are in danger of extinction, there is a glimmer of hope. Like the rediscovery of the once lost harlequin toad discussed previously, two species of *Pseudophilautus* were discovered again more than 100 years after they were first described. The webless shrub frog *(Pseudophilautus hypolomas)* was first described in 1876 by the British scientist Albert Günther. For more than 130 years, the species was not recorded again until it was found in 2010 in the Peak Wilderness Sanctuary. Now known from three locations, it has been uplisted from extinct to endangered. The second species rediscovered had been missing for even longer. First described in 1853 by Edward Frederick Kelaart, the starry shrub frog *(Pseudophilautus stellatus)* was not seen again for 160 years until 2013 when researchers located a handful of the frogs in the same sanctuary as the webless shrub frog. Both may have avoided detection for so long due to the remote and difficult terrain of their forest home. Without the protection of this 22,000-hectare (55,000-acre) tract of forest, it is very possible neither of these species would still exist

Southern Gastric Brooding Frog *(Rheobatrachus silus)*

Gastric Brooding Frogs
(Rheobatrachus)

The continent of Australia has seen a myriad of extinctions since humans arrived on its shores, and sadly, many of these extinctions have been of fantastic and unique species found nowhere else. Such is the case of two amphibians like no other in the world. Amphibians always struggle with what to do with their eggs to protect them from predators. Such is the life of small creatures that are food for so many others. Some have solved this by producing large amounts of eggs; some bury them; some hide them on the undersides of leaves, and a few don't lay them at all but develop them internally. All of this is done to increase the chance of survival for their young. The gastric brooding frogs of Australia did lay eggs externally, but what happened next is one of the seemingly least likely ways to raise young. Eggs, once laid, were promptly eaten. Once consumed by the female, the eggs would safely develop inside her stomach, and in about six weeks, out popped fully formed froglets. Unique indeed.

The first of these frogs to be discovered was the southern gastric brooding frog *(Rheobatrachus silus)* in 1972. They inhabited the rocky mountain streams in the forests of the Blackall Ranges of southeastern Queensland, apparently preferring a primarily aquatic lifestyle. The smaller of the two species, they ranged between 33 and 54 mm (1.3-2 in.) in length, with males being substantially smaller than the females. Spending their time foraging for and consuming a variety of invertebrates, both in and out of water, their fairly unremarkable frog lives took quite a turn during the breeding season (at least for females). Once breeding took place, the female would consume her freshly laid eggs. Hormones produced by the eggs would stop the production of gastric acids and, in at least this species, actually change the cell structure of the female gut. The female's stomach transformed into a brood sack solely for the housing of her growing tadpoles. While convenient for her young, this also meant that the female could not feed in the 6-7 weeks it took for the tadpoles to mature. After this period, around 25 froglets would emerge from her mouth, and within 4 days, the female's gut would revert to normal.

Several years after its discovery, the population began to collapse, with the majority of the species disappearing in 1979. The last wild sighting of the southern gastric brooding frog was in 1981, and the last captive individual died in 1983. Extensive searches since the 1980s have been conducted in its range with no sign of the once-common frogs. Scientists had little idea of what caused the collapse of the species, but they did note that it coincided with the decline of another frog that shared the same habitat. This frog, called the Mount Glorious day frog *(Taudactylus diurnus),* also showed a dramatic decline in the same period, suggesting a common cause.

The second species of gastric brooder found was the northern gastric brooding frog *(Rheobatrachus vitellinus)*. Not found until 1984, these larger frogs of the genus were located in the pristine rainforests of Eungella National Park in northeast Queensland. Nearly fully aquatic like their southern cousins, they fed on various small invertebrates such as beetles, caddisfly larvae, and small crayfish and were mostly nocturnal. Like the southern gastric brooding frog, laid eggs were swallowed by the females for development. The presence of the hormone prostaglandin E in the jelly surrounding the eggs shut down production of gastric acids in the female's stomach, but unlike their southern counterparts, this was not accompanied by structural changes in the gut itself. Like the southern species, this also rendered the female unable to eat until her offspring matured. In the only recorded case of a northern gastric brooding frog giving birth, 22 froglets were recorded in the brood, with gestation times likely similar to those of the southern frogs.

Due to the very short amount of time scientists were able to study these frogs and their intriguing physiology, little more is known of the northern gastric brooding frog. Many questions remain unanswered as to how both frogs not only achieved their unique brooding adaptations, but how specifically they were able to carry them out. Sadly, the northern species saw an even more catastrophic decline than the southern. Discovered in 1984, they were still common in their range into March of 1985, but there had been signs of a potential decline. By June of that year, the frogs had vanished from their entire known range, with the species going from common to likely extinct in just four months. Like the southern species, the cause was entirely unknown. The northern gastric brooding frogs lived in pristine rainforest habitat with no significant changes observed that would explain such a dramatic disappearance, but as with the southern species, the decline coincided with the disappearance of another frog species that shared the same habitat. This species was the Eungella torrent frog *(Taudactylus eugellensis)*, a relative of the declining species in the south.

Scientists suspected a common cause for all of these declines, but the solution was not apparent initially. The declines of all these species and the decline or disappearance of 13 frog species in Queensland were eventually attributed, once again, to the chytrid fungus *Batrachochytrium dendrobatidis*. It is now believed that *Bd* entered Australia around southeast Queensland sometime in the mid- to late-1970s. Chytrid spread from here, causing the extinction of up to one-fifth of all amphibians in Australia. There is hope that a small population of the northern species may still exist. Prime habitats within the rainforest of Eungella National Park have not been extensively surveyed, but unfortunately some of these same areas were devastated in the horrible wildfires that plagued Australia in 2019–2020.

Vegas Valley Leopard Frog
(Rana fisheri)

The Vegas Valley leopard frog is the only species of frog known to have gone extinct in modern times in North America—sort of. The interesting story of this frog illustrates the difficulty that scientists and conservationists face as they endeavor to identify and protect species and their habitats. Its story also serves to highlight the human impact on fragile aquatic ecosystems, especially in the arid west of the United States, and the increasing use and importance of genetic profiling to glean valuable information about past and present species.

The Vegas Valley leopard frog once graced the spring fed streams in the vicinity of Las Vegas, Nevada. Isolated by the desert surrounding their habitat, the existence and health of these springs were essential to their survival. First collected in 1891, they were originally believed to be either the same species or closely related to two similar-looking leopard frog species, the relict leopard frog *(Rana onca)* or the widespread and common northern leopard frog *(Rana pipiens)*. Spotted and having the brown to green coloration typical of leopard frogs, these 50-76 mm (2–3 inch) frogs disappeared from their small range sometime prior to 1942. Searches for the frogs in the 1940s noted considerable change in the land surrounding the species' habitat as the growth of the city of Las Vegas encroached. The frogs were declared officially extinct in 1996.

For nearly 70 years, the Vegas Valley leopard frog was feared extinct, however, because of the long-held suspicion that it may not be a unique species in itself, researchers postulated that the species might still exist, but just under a different name. Starting with the assumption that the Vegas Valley frogs may actually be an isolated population of the relict leopard frog, researchers in 2011 used DNA extracted from Vegas Valley frogs collected as far back as 1913 housed at the California Academy of Sciences. When the DNA analysis was completed, the researchers were surprised to find that the relict leopard frogs were only distantly related to the frogs of the Vegas Valley. Expanding their search, they were able to determine that the Vegas Valley leopard frogs were nearly genetically identical to another desert-dwelling leopard frog, the Chiricahua leopard frog *(Rana chiricahuensis)*, proving that the Vegas Valley leopard frog was not extinct after all.

Listed as vulnerable, the closest population of the Chiricahua leopard frog is located 250 miles across the desert from Las Vegas in the state of Arizona. It is believed that the changing climate likely isolated these populations in the past as the western United States warmed and dried after the last interglacial maximum. Thanks to our ability to probe the secrets of DNA, we now know that the Vegas Valley frogs are a case of local extinction, but while thankfully the species as a whole is not extinct, the unfortunate truth is that the extirpation of the frogs in the Vegas Valley is due solely to human causes. In a pattern repeated all over the arid west of the United States, urban expansion and more intensive water use led to the destruction of much of the frogs' habitat. The pumping of groundwater for irrigation depleted the water available to keep desert springs flowing, affecting not only frogs but many species that rely on them. Of the habitat that was left, the introduction of the predatory and much larger American bullfrog may have also played a role in the frogs' disappearance. Continued threats to the species as a whole are habitat destruction from human-associated activities, climate change, and the chytrid fungus *Bd* which was found in a population of dying frogs in Arizona in the 1990s.

So why is the story of the Vegas Valley frog important? Well, it highlights several things. One is the importance of habitat preservation, especially for unique and isolated habitats. The destruction of the springs feeding the home of the Vegas Valley frogs led to a local extinction, but it just as easily could have ended an entire unique species. Many species, especially amphibians, in arid regions have isolated populations, making them more vulnerable to extinction. As climate change and population growth stress water resources, the threat of losing many of these desert-dwelling animals will continue to increase. It will become increasingly important going forward to pay close attention to how we use water and the impacts of that use on natural habitats. With more than 50 golf courses and more than 650,000 people in and around the Las Vegas area, it may be far past time to reevaluate how we use resources in the deserts of the U.S.

Second, this case shows the importance of the growing body of information about the natural world and the creatures that inhabit it. Without DNA analysis, we never would have known that the Vegas Valley frogs still exist, and now we may have the opportunity to reintroduce the species into its former habitat. Now with better information, conservation efforts can be directed toward re-establishing a native species if and when their habitat can be restored. This new information also gives us insight into the history and relationships of multiple species, and the conditions in which they evolved, helping us to make better choices to preserve these species. The more informed our decisions are, the greater the likelihood that we can successfully combat biodiversity loss. This case also demonstrates the enormous difficulty in cataloging the world's species. Species historically have been separated largely on the basis of an animal's morphology, or physical appearance. In this case, the population of frogs once living in the Vegas Valley physically appeared much more similar to other species than to others of their own kind. Genetics now helps us sort things out, but you can see how complicated it all can become. There are numerous instances where populations once thought to be a single species are found to be multiple species, and vice versa.

Knowing the distinctions between species is important to protect biodiversity. Genetic studies may completely upend conservation efforts. For example, a species may be thought to have a relatively large population and therefore to be resistant to environmental threats. All of the members would be treated the same from a conservation standpoint. But what if it is determined that they are not one species but four species? Now they are four separate, small, and potentially vulnerable populations. The strategy for their conservation must now change, and the differences in the species must be explored. These four new species, although outwardly very similar, will all have different behaviors, needs, and roles in the environment. It is only with this sort of knowledge that we can make the best choices to protect biodiversity. Of course, the converse can also happen. In this case, multiple species are found to be just one. This is also valuable knowledge. Resources for conservation are limited. Cases such as this may allow for the reallocation of conservation efforts from a species much more common than believed to one that may need more immediate help.

Wyoming Toad
(Anaxyrus Baxteri)

The Wyoming toad is one of the rarest amphibians in the United States and is considered one of the four rarest amphibians in all of North America. Native to the floodplains and oxbow lakes near the Big and Little Laramie rivers in the Laramie Basin, Wyoming, these toads are thought to be a remnant population of their nearest relative, the Canadian toad *(Anaxyrus hemiophrys),* the closest of which lives more than 750 km (470 mi) away. The climatic changes of the end of the Pleistocene likely separated these toads from the rest of the ancient population. This isolation eventually led to Wyoming having its own unique species of toad. They were first discovered in 1946, with an original range covering 1,820 square kilometers (700 square miles) of the Laramie Basin.

The 44.5–70 mm (1.75–2.75 inch) toads fed primarily on various arthropods, including ants and beetles. They were common throughout their range until their populations began to crash in the mid-1970s. As the toads' population continued to decline by 1984, the situation became increasingly dire, and they were put under federal protection under the Endangered Species Act. For a time, the species was thought to be extinct until a small population was rediscovered in 1987 at Mortenson Lake, Wyoming. By 1989, it was clear that the species was doomed to complete extinction unless quick action was taken. The last known population at Mortenson Lake was dwindling and the last remaining toads were collected in an attempt to save the species. Only 10 toads in total could be located and once collected, the species was believed to be extinct in the wild from that point on. An intensive breeding program was implemented and continues to this day with eight zoos around the nation, one federal fish hatchery, and the University of Wyoming Red Buttes Environmental Laboratory all taking part.

After a captive population was built up, a location for reintroduction was chosen. This was the toads' last stronghold, Mortenson Lake, which became a national wildlife refuge in 1993. While releases over the decades were able to establish breeding populations at this site, there is currently no self-sustaining population despite recent releases of over 10,000 tadpoles and hundreds of adults. The toads are now released at four locations, three on private land and one in Mortenson National Wildlife Refuge, with a wild population of around 60 adults and juveniles. Conservationists are hopeful that eventually a stable population will be established, but population crashes have plagued the recovery effort. What makes this effort all the more difficult is how little we know about these toads. In its own 2015 recovery plan, the USFWS admits that "significant features of the species' life history, behavior, ecological interactions, and habitat needs remain unknown and limit effective management."

One of the suspected initial causes of the Wyoming toad's collapse is habitat loss. The modification and damming of the Laramie River for agricultural irrigation destroyed much of the area where the Wyoming toad once lived. The lack of suitable habitat continues to be a barrier to the species' recovery. Pollutants and pesticides have also been considered factors in the decline, but the primary reason for the toads' collapse, like that of many species of amphibians, was the introduction of the chytrid fungus *Bd*. Lab tests on Wyoming toads collected decades ago show the presence of *Bd* as early as 1965, and *Bd* continues to be considered the most severe threat to the re-establishment of the species. Released toads routinely test positive for the fungus. For example, in 2009, 74% of the 93 wild toads released at Mortenson Lake tested positive for *Bd*, and periodic outbreaks of the disease are thought to be responsible for the repeated population crashes. Unfortunately, these are not the only issues facing the species. The toads' small overall population and resulting low genetic diversity are additional factors that could inhibit their survival by decreasing their adaptive abilities. The members of the breeding program are combating this by boosting captive populations and using selective breeding. While the Wyoming toad still exists, the situation is still very tenuous, and its ultimate survival is by no means guaranteed.

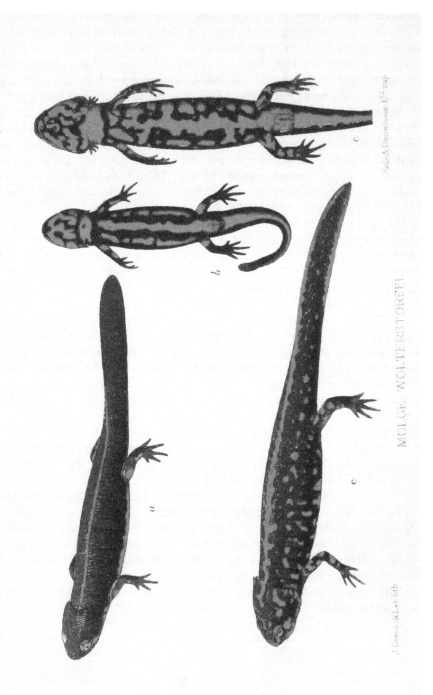

MOLGE WOLTERSTORFFI.

Bale & Danielsson Ld. imp

J. Green del.et lith

Yunnan Lake Newt
(Cynops wolterstorffi)

While extinctions among the salamanders have been fewer than those of their frog relatives by number of species, they have unfortunately suffered as great a loss by percentage of the whole. One of the best documented cases is that of the Yunnan Lake newt. First described in 1905 by the Belgian-British naturalist George Albert Boulanger, the Yunnan lake newt was native only to Kunming Lake (now called Dianchi Lake) in Yunnan Province, China. They were similar in appearance to the rest of their genus (often called fire-bellied newts), which contains 7 additional species, all native to the Asian nations of Japan and China. Interestingly, these newts are actually more closely related to European newts than to others that occur in Asia.

These small 12–16 cm (4.5–6 in) members of Caudata frequented the shallows of the 6th largest lake in China. They were nearly entirely aquatic and retained small external gills of varying sizes. They also possessed parotid glands like those of toads, although there is no information on how toxic they might have been. Once very abundant, it was common to observe thousands of individuals gathered together during the breeding season from April to May of each year. Males, like in many amphibians, were smaller than females and during the breeding season would sport strikingly blue colored tails. Populations remained strong into the 1950s, but by 1979, the newts could no longer be found. Anecdotal evidence suggests that they may have persisted into the mid-1980s. They were listed as extinct by the IUCN in 2004.

Multiple factors likely conspired to bring about the extinction of the Yunnan lake newt. Before the late 1950s, Dianchi Lake was characterized by clear water and a high abundance of aquatic plants. This prime habitat, while nutrient poor, still allowed for a highly diverse ecosystem. At least 10 species of fish were endemic to the lake, as well as the Yunnan newt, but by the 1960s, the health of the lake had rapidly deteriorated. The influx of untreated domestic and industrial wastewater from the nearby city of Kunming (the city would not have a wastewater treatment plant until the 1990s) and the runoff from ever-increasing agriculture fouled the clear waters of the lake. The influx of nutrients caused extensive eutrophication, and as a result, algae growth and low oxygen levels dramatically changed the lake's balance. Gone was the extensive plant life and clear water and in its place toxic blue green algae, human waste, pesticides, and industrial chemicals. By 1994, only two of the ten endemic fish species were left, and Dianchi Lake was one of the most polluted in all of China. Currently, the equivalent of $7.8 billion USD has been spent in an attempt to clean it.

In addition to rampant pollution, species introduced into the lake dramatically altered its ecosystem, putting additional strain on not only the newts but all of the lake's native species. Beginning in the 1950s, the next decade saw 31 exotic species introduced into the lake, including more than 20 different species of fish. Cited as particularly damaging to the newts were grass carp *(Ctenopharyngodon idella)* and the American bullfrog *(Rana catesbeiana)*. As if these factors weren't enough, land "reclamations," especially in the shallow areas on the north part of the lake, reduced habitat and may have particularly diminished prime breeding habitat.

It's difficult to determine which one of these factors was the ultimate cause of the newts' decline. Any one of them alone could have had serious impacts on the newts' populations. Like all amphibians, newts and salamanders are particularly sensitive to pollutants in their environment, and this very likely played a part in their decline. Introduced species are one of the leading causes of extinction worldwide, and this, along with habitat loss, were undoubtedly significant contributors to the newts' disappearance. Unfortunately, what has happened to Dianchi Lake is an example of what has happened, and is still happening, to far too many waterways around the world, imperiling countless species from amphibians to fish to birds to us.

One of the Jalpa false Brook Salamander's Mexican Relatives the Endangered Werler's False Brook Salamander *(Pseudoeurycea werleri).*

Jalpa False Brook Salamander
(Pseudoeurycea exspectata)

First discovered and described in 1954 by L.C. Stuart, the Jalpa false brook salamander was a native of the mountains of the Jalapa region of Guatemala. They were found primarily at middle altitudes of approximately 2500 meters (roughly 8000 feet) in altitude. These small salamanders, measuring just 96 mm in length or just over three and a half inches, inhabited the wet broadleaf deciduous forests of the region. Found commonly on the forest floor in, around, and under rotted logs, it was also one of the few species of salamander found high above the ground inhabiting bromeliads. While all of the initial individuals were collected in the mountains west of the village of Miramundo, Stuart indicates that they may also have been found on some of the isolated volcanic peaks of southeastern Guatemala, although there is no indication as to why he held that belief.

The Jalpa apparently was quite common within the small range that they inhabited. When precisely the population began to deteriorate is not known, but the last sighting of them came in 1976. Despite nearly 20 attempts to locate the species spanning the decades between 1985 and 2018, no individuals have been located. As a result, the IUCN changed their status to "extinct" in 2020. The Jalpa is closely related to two other Guatemalan species: the critically endangered brown false brook salamander *(Pseudoeurycea brunnata)*, and the critically endangered Goebel's false brook salamander *(Pseudoeurycea goebeli)*. Clearly, many of the members of the genus in Guatemala are struggling.

Typical of many of the forests of Central America, deforestation for numerous reasons has played a role in not only the decline of the Jalpa but also that of its related species and many other species of the region. Much of this forest loss is due to agricultural use, not only for small subsistence farming and cattle grazing, but also to support the commercial coffee industry that is prominent in the area. Logging for wood collection and building also plays a part in the reduction of these forests as well as the expansion of human habitation. Current satellite data of the region where the species was first found shows significant fragmentation of the forest from agriculture. Not only does this directly reduce the amount of habitat for the species living there, but it can also significantly change the microclimate of the remaining surrounding forest, making it dryer and less resilient to drought. This fragmentation also creates small islands of habitat. In the case of a small salamander like the Jalpa, this could seriously fragment the population. Smaller, isolated populations are more vulnerable, and for a moisture loving creature like the salamander, a comparatively dry agricultural field is as insurmountable an obstacle as an ocean is to most. Adding to the effects of a degraded habitat, climate change is also playing a role by increasing the length and severity of the dry seasons.

While there is no direct evidence to support the invasion of chytrid fungus as a cause of the Jalpa's decline, it has been suggested in the decline of both the Goebel's false brook salamander and the brown false brook salamander mentioned earlier. The disappearance of the Jalpa does coincide with the movement of chytrid into Guatemala from Mexico in the 1970s, and it certainly could be a factor in their disappearance. Future testing on specimens housed in museums may be able to shed light on whether *Bd* is in fact associated with the extinction of the Jalapa, although it is possible that the Jalpa may have already disappeared prior to the arrival of the fungus.

The likely related slimy salamander *(Plethodon grobmani).*

Ainsworth's Salamander
(Plethodon ainsworthi)

The Ainsworth's salamander could possibly be the only species of salamander known to have gone extinct in North America. I say possibly because the very existence of the species has been filled with controversy. This species is only known from two individuals that were collected near Bay Springs, Mississippi, in June of 1964. The specimens were preserved and labeled as *Plethodon glutinosus,* now known as the northern slimy salamander. It was once believed that all of the slimy salamanders of the eastern U.S. were the same species, but further study eventually separated them into 13 different species. The two specimens in question sat unnoticed in the collection of the Mississippi Museum of Natural Science until 1991, when a researcher named James Lazell found them and recognized some distinctive traits. After sharing his potential discovery with other herpetologists, he was encouraged to formally describe the species, and in 1998, they were described and given the name *Plethodon ainsworthi* after the man who first collected the specimens.

Researchers in 2014 called into question the Ainsworth's status as a unique species. In their opinion, they were in fact the same as another species of slimy salamander called *Plethodon mississippi,* which occurs in the same location that the Ainsworth was collected. The increasingly poor condition of the preserved specimens (now down to only one) makes morphological comparisons difficult, so in order to put the controversy to rest, another team of researchers in 2020 attempted to extract DNA from the samples. Unfortunately, they were unsuccessful in extracting usable DNA but did a thorough review of the salamander's characteristics. In the opinion of the 2020 team, the 2014 researchers were in error, and the species status of *P. ainsworthi* should remain valid. Hopefully, future research will reveal more about the Ainsworth's salamander and its place in the Caudata order.

The best-case scenario would, of course, be finding more of these elusive salamanders. The Ainsworth's were originally found inhabiting the leaf litter near the head of a spring a couple of miles from Bay Springs, in typical woodland habitat for slimy salamanders. To search for any remaining members of the species, Lazell, who described them, contacted the family of the man who originally collected the only two known animals. They were able to point out where they believed the salamanders were originally found. 17 attempts were made to locate the species between 1991 and 1997 in the surrounding area. While these searches turned up several salamander species, the Ainsworth's was not among them. In 2012, searches in the same location by teams from Auburn University and the University of Georgia also failed to locate them.

Because no additional members of the species have been located, they are considered extinct according to the IUCN, but there is an outside chance that they may exist in another location that has not been thoroughly searched. Their similarities to *P. mississippi* could easily cause them to be missed. Reasons for the extinction are hard to pin down with so little known about the species, but it is likely that habitat change would have been the primary cause. The area where they were originally located, while recovering today, was heavily logged in the past for its valuable hardwoods. While other species of salamanders still remain around the spring where the Ainsworth's were found, changes in water quality, temperature, or flow rate due to the loss of tree cover could have been more than the Ainsworth's salamanders could tolerate. This species could have relied on large trees for some part of their life cycle or been particularly reliant on the shade they provided. We will never be certain as to the cause of the Ainsworth's disappearance, but it does provide a cautionary tale. Numerous species of salamander in North America are endemic to a very specific habitat, often around natural springs. Major disruptions to the flow or water quality in these isolated habitats could easily spell disaster. With increased demand for groundwater and the threat of warmer and drier conditions, especially in the western U.S., we must take special care to ensure that the list of extinct North American salamanders does not grow.

7

Reptiles (Reptilia)

Reptiles first appeared around 310 million years ago and quickly became the most dominant land vertebrates for tens of millions of years, beginning with animals like the small *Hylonomus,* which looked like a modern-day lizard. Reptiles were some of the first amniotes (an animal whose young are surrounded by a membrane), an important evolutionary step that allowed them to lay eggs on dry land and eventually led to the amniotic sac that envelops our young. Traditional Linnaean nomenclature distinguishes Reptilia as all amniotes that are not birds or mammals, but some modern organizations place birds with them. In fact, today's crocodiles are more closely related to birds than they are to other modern reptiles, so this is not as odd as it may first seem.

Reptiles evolved some key characteristics that allowed them to occupy a much broader range of habitats than their amphibian cousins. Unlike amphibians, reptiles have a scaly, impermeable skin that is durable and prevents moisture loss. They also developed lungs operated by a diaphragm, which gave them a distinct respiratory advantage over amphibians. Most of all, reptiles did not need a water source to lay their eggs. With leathery shells that contain a waterproof membrane, reptiles were free to lay their eggs away from water without risk (some modern reptiles have done away with laying eggs altogether and bear live young). Like amphibians, reptiles are for the most part endotherms, meaning they take on the temperature of their surroundings, but this apparent disadvantage gives them extremely low energy requirements. Without the need to produce their own heat, most of the food they intake goes to growth, which continues through their usually very long lives. While most amphibians today show only a limited number of body plans, the reptiles' evolutionary advantages once allowed them to diversify into a wide range of shapes and sizes that could range from the small lizard-like creatures that persist today to winged pterosaurs that could take to the air and even huge ocean-going reptiles.

Modern reptiles may not be as diverse as they were in their heyday, but while less diverse in form, there are still more than 11,000 described species, and the total species count may rival that of even birds. Reptilia is made up of four orders: Squamata, which includes snakes, lizards, and geckos; Testudines, which includes turtles and tortoises; Crocodilia, which includes crocodiles, alligators, and caiman; and Rhynchocephalia, which only contains one living member, the tuatara *(Sphenodon punctatus)* of New Zealand. Despite the evolutionary setback 66 million years ago (where unfortunately or fortunately we lost the winged pterosaurs), modern reptiles are still a fantastically diverse group of animals that live and thrive in some of the world's most inhospitable environments, from the open oceans to searing deserts, and possess some impressive physical and physiological adaptations. Reptiles exhibit a very wide range of sizes. The smallest is one of the world's smallest vertebrates and the smallest known amniote, the recently discovered *Brookesia nana* of northern Madagascar. The male of these extremely miniaturized chameleons measures just 21.6 mm (0.8 inches) from his snout to the tip of his tail. Compare this to the largest living reptile, the saltwater crocodile, which can reach 7 meters (23 feet) in length and weigh as much as 1000 kg (2200 lbs).

Among the impressive characteristics of reptiles in general are their long life spans, with many species living 50 years or more, and some, like the giant tortoises, as much as 150 or even 200 years. For example, a Seychelles giant tortoise *(Aldabrachelys gigantea hololissa)* was brought to the British island of Saint Helena as a mature adult in 1882. Named Jonathan, he still lives there. Best estimates of his hatch date are sometime around 1832, making him at least 189 years old. Beyond their long life spans, there are extremely varied adaptations among the members of the class. Some of the most well-known are those of snakes, which are widely feared for being venomous, although only around 20% of all the known snake species are venomous and even fewer are dangerous to humans. Even with the negative emotions surrounding poisonous snakes, few can deny this impressive ability for not only protection but also subduing prey. Their venom is an evolutionary masterpiece of biochemistry, but even more interesting may be the way in which some snakes find prey. Many animals have adapted to a nocturnal lifestyle. Prey such as small rodents, bats, and insects are more active at night, and there is a bounty of food available for those that have developed solutions to working in the dark. Some have done so by developing large, light-sensitive eyes, while others have done so by developing extremely acute hearing or a heightened sense of smell. Snakes fall into this last category and their forked tongues are highly successful in tracking the minute chemical signatures their prey leaves behind, but while being able to track down your prey by smell alone is a very handy adaptation, it doesn't help to capture your dinner that is still shrouded in darkness.

To get around this problem, some snakes have developed a way to see in the dark not by using light (huge bulging eyes would be a bit cumbersome for a snake's lifestyle), but by using heat. There are a couple groups of snakes that can do this: the venomous pit vipers and the constricting boas and pythons. All of these snakes have heat-sensitive pits that allow them to detect the heat given off by another animal. The ability is most highly developed in pit vipers. These nocturnal hunters can detect another animal's heat from a meter away, and their infrared sensing organs can detect temperature differences as small as 0.003 degrees Celsius. The information from these heat-sensing pits forms a heat map of the object they are observing. In the snake's brain, this heat map is combined with visual information coming from the eyes. That's right, pit vipers have thermally enhanced night vision! Researchers say that the thermal information that the snakes receive is as good as or even better than many human-produced infrared devices.

There are numerous species of reptiles that can change color, the most dramatic of which are the well-known chameleons. For centuries, humans pondered just how they were able to do this, but a detailed study in 2015 shed light on this impressive ability. Chameleons change color for a number of reasons. One reason is certainly to help them blend into their environment, but much of the reason they change color is communication, especially in males during breeding for the attraction of a mate or a threat display to a rival. It was long assumed that they did this like some other creatures (notably cephalopods like squid and octopus) using a pigment cell called a chromatophore. This type of cell contains a pigment and can be expanded and contracted to either express the color of the pigment or suppress it. The combination of different pigments and their expression creates the overall color, much like the pixels of a computer screen. However, chameleons use a much different technique. Their skin possesses two separate layers of cells called iridophores. These specialized cells do not contain pigment but rather light reflective crystals. The chameleon can change the spacing of these crystals, which in turn changes their optical qualities and the color of light they reflect. The outer layer is the most adaptive and is better developed in males to produce more vivid color changes. The inner layer is less adaptive, but it is highly reflective in the infrared wavelengths. It's thought that chameleons may be primarily using this layer to regulate their temperature by reflecting or absorbing infrared light. So not only can these impressive little reptiles projectile fire their sticky tongues out of their heads to catch prey and look in two different directions at the same time, they are masters of the physics of light.

The most amazing of all the reptiles, though, has to be the leatherback sea turtle *(Dermochelys coriacea)*. This species of massive marine reptile has been roaming the world's seas for almost a million years, but its evolutionary origins date back more than 100 million. They are the largest of all the sea turtles and one of the largest reptiles that exist, with a typical adult size of 1.5 to 1.8 meters (5–6 feet) in length and a weight of 270–330 kg (600–800 lbs), but they can reach much larger sizes. The largest recorded leatherback was a male (the smaller of the two sexes) and was an astonishing 2.8 meters (9.5 feet) long and over 900 kg (2000 lbs). Leatherbacks lack the hard shells that other sea turtles possess. This is because these turtles are deep-diving specialists. A hard shell would be crushed under the pressure of the ocean depths experienced during their dives. Leatherback turtle dives can reach depths of 1.2 km (4000 ft), deeper than even a typical sperm whale dive. Leatherbacks have numerous adaptations to their cardiovascular system that increase efficiency and allow them to store oxygen in their tissues for these deep dives. They are so well adapted that they have been observed staying under water for more than an hour. Even more impressive than the depths they can reach is how they, as cold-blooded reptiles, deal with the extreme cold at these depths. As it turns out, these reptiles are not truly cold-blooded. Leatherbacks have several adaptations that are typically only seen in mammals or birds, such as cross-current heat exchange in their circulatory system and specialized insulating fat layers. This allows them to handle temperatures that would stun or kill other turtles. Heat produced through metabolic processes can be conserved, which allows these turtles to maintain body temperatures well above the surrounding water—as much as 10–18° C and possibly even more as they dive into colder water.

In addition to this cold hardiness that allows them to range into Arctic waters, these unparalleled members of the turtle order also undertake some of the longest migrations of any animal. Logging thousands of kilometers per year is typical for a leatherback, and they routinely cross the entirety of both the Atlantic and Pacific oceans. For example, turtles that nest in Asia travel all the way to the California coast to forage in its rich waters, a distance of over 11,000 kilometers (7,000 miles). In the Atlantic, a female leatherback tagged in Panama in 2005 spent the next 632 days traveling more than 17,500 km (more than 10,000 miles) around the Atlantic Ocean. Yet more impressive than their stamina are their navigational abilities using Earth's magnetic fields. So sensitive are they to the subtle differences in the field, it's believed that leatherbacks can tell exactly where in the world they are as easily as a ship with a GPS. Turtles with GPS trackers have been shown to have the ability to navigate in a nearly perfect straight line to a new location over thousands of miles of open ocean.

As many as 20% of all reptiles are considered to be at risk of extinction. On the surface, this seems to be better than other vertebrate groups, but reptiles are experiencing many of the same dramatic losses as others. One study estimates that between 1970 and 2012, reptile populations decreased by 54-55% worldwide. Hardest hit are freshwater and marine reptiles, particularly the crocodilians, and both freshwater and marine turtles. Turtles specifically are one of the most threatened groups of animals, with 61% of the total number of described species either endangered or already extinct. Mirroring other groups, reptiles in the tropics are also suffering the greatest declines. Currently, out of the 10,148 species of reptiles assessed by the IUCN, over 1,200 are classified as endangered or critically endangered, and more than 600 are considered vulnerable. While efforts in recent years have dramatically expanded our knowledge, there are still nearly 1,500 species for which data is not sufficient to determine their extinction risk and another 1,500 that have not been assessed at all. Reptiles are historically an understudied group, and this has led to less emphasis on their conservation compared to other groups. Absent for reptiles are the multiple large and well-funded organizations devoted to the protection of other animals, such as birds. Even among herpetologists who study amphibians and reptiles, amphibian conservation often overshadows that of reptiles due to the increased peril that amphibians are currently experiencing.

The general threats to reptiles are largely the same as those shared by all of Earth's biodiversity, with, as is typical, the loss of habitat through deforestation, agriculture, and the draining of wetlands as leading causes of population decline. Turtles face the greatest threat, especially from overharvesting and the collection of eggs. Nearly half of endangered freshwater turtles are threatened due to these activities, and again, more than 60% of all known turtle species are endangered or already extinct. While greater protections for sea turtles now exist, poaching of adults and eggs is still a threat and at one time nearly led to the extinction of all sea turtles. Commercial fishing still poses a significant threat to marine turtles, and large numbers of sea turtles continue to be lost to bycatch from the fishing industry and entanglement in discarded fishing gear. Climate change is and will be a continuing issue for reptiles. Here again, turtles may be the most affected, as the sex determination of many turtle species is based on temperature. In sea turtles, lower temperatures during incubation produce males, while higher temperatures produce females. Rising temperatures are already increasing nest failures and skewing populations toward more females. Desert-dwelling species may also be significantly impacted as temperatures rise beyond even what these specialized species can endure.

Due to the ease of care and popularity of reptiles and reptile products for the fashion industry, there is a very large and poorly regulated international trade in reptiles, and the industry is a significant threat to reptile biodiversity. In the EU alone, between 2004 and 2014, more than 20 million reptiles were imported into its member countries. A recent survey of reptiles for sale on the internet found that over 35% (roughly 2,296 species) of all reptiles are being traded online. 21 percent of these are endangered, and as many as half may be wild-caught. Only around 9% of reptile species are monitored by the Convention on International Trade in Endangered Species (CITES), and these are largely species traded for industry. This leaves the pet trade largely unregulated. For example, Indonesia has had, in recent years, a reported export quota of 3 million tokay geckos *(Gekko gecko)*, all claimed as captive-bred. However, investigations into the country's captive breeding capacity called this into question, and it is likely the majority of geckos exported from Indonesia are wild-caught. Despite outcries for years that many of the tokay geckos traded around the world were threatening wild populations, they didn't receive CITES oversight until 2019. Much like the situation found in the exotic bird trade, many wild-caught reptiles, both legal and illegal, are being laundered through the captive breeding trade. The wildlife trade is also unfortunately endangering newly discovered species. Using descriptions of recent species discoveries, collectors have sought out populations of these newly discovered species to exploit them for their rarity. Multiple species of newly discovered reptiles, endangered reptiles, and even species once believed extinct, have been collected for the wildlife trade using the information contained in formal studies. Entire populations of rare reptile species have been extirpated from the wild, and the threat of scientific research being used to locate these species has even forced some researchers to forgo publishing the location of new discoveries altogether.

Pinta Island Giant Tortoise (Chelonoidis abingdonii)

Giant Tortoises of the Galápagos
(Chelonoidis)

The unique isolation of island habitats has produced many of the world's most distinctive and interesting animals, and this has certainly been true of island reptiles. One of the most recognizable are the giant land tortoises. Only two places in the world now house these creatures: a handful of islands in the western Indian Ocean and the famous islands of the Galápagos in the Pacific. Nearly every island in the Galápagos once had one or more species of giant tortoise. These are all descended from a single ancestor that arrived from the mainland sometime around 3 million years ago. Between 1.6 and 1.5 million years ago, the first of the Galápagos' giant tortoises evolved, eventually radiating into 14 (possibly 15) species, mirroring the familiar radiation of Darwin's finches and becoming the primary large grazers of the islands. At least 2, possibly 3, species of Galápagos tortoises are now extinct, with the third being a likely but undescribed species from the island of Santa Fe.

The Floreana giant tortoise *(Chelonoidis niger)*, was once found on its namesake island of Floreana, one of the most southern of the Galápagos Islands. They likely evolved from an ancestor on Santa Cruz Island around 500,000 years ago. Little is known about the habits of these tortoises, but they were certainly vegetarian and likely subsisted on a typical giant tortoise diet of grasses, shrubs, and cactus. They probably were well adapted to feeding on above-ground vegetation, as suggested by their "saddleback" shaped shell. This trait is shared with several other tortoises of the Galápagos that feed on higher vegetation, with the unique shell shape allowing for maximum extension of the neck upwards. Like other species of Galápagos giant tortoises, they were very large, growing to a maximum of around a meter and a half (4-5 feet) in length and weighing several hundred pounds. There may have originally been a population of more than 8000 of these tortoises on Floreana, but the populations were severely dwindling by the early 19th century. In fact, when Darwin visited the island in 1835, he failed to find any. By the 1840s, only a handful of individuals were known to exist, and by 1850, the species was believed to be extinct.

The second species, the Pinta Island giant tortoise *(Chelonoidis abingdonii)*, once inhabited the most northern island of the Galápagos chain. They were most closely related to the still-living *C. hoodensis,* which surprisingly inhabits the most south-eastern of the Galápagos Islands, some 300 km (186 miles) away. They were first formally described by Albert Günther in 1877, but were known from descriptions as far back as 1798. These huge and docile creatures, also with "saddleback" shells, were up to 2 meters (6 feet) long and could weigh more than 300 pounds. They were vegetarians and fed on a variety of plant life on the dry scrublands of their native island, particularly the tree-like *Opuntia* cactus. Once quite common with an estimated population of at least 2500 adults, records suggest that their population had already crashed by 1867, ten years before they were even formally described. By the mid-20th century, the Pinta was believed to be extinct, but in 1971, a single individual was located. A male, subsequently named Lonesome George, was captured the following year and transferred to the island of Santa Cruz to ensure his survival. In the intervening decades, extensive searches throughout Pinta Island and zoos around the world failed to find any other members of George's species. Unfortunately, Lonesome George died on June 24, 2012, marking the end of his species.

There is little doubt about the cause of the extinction of both of these species and the decline of the remaining Galápagos giant tortoises. Historic descriptions speak of huge populations of tortoises, and sailors visiting the Galápagos began to exploit the animals as early as the 1500s. The tortoises' ability to survive for months—and possibly as much as a year—without food and water made them a durable and attractive food source. Ships visiting the island routinely captured 400–500 animals at a time for use as food and oil. By the late 1600s, it was common for all ships coming through the region to supply themselves with tortoises, and the practice continued well into the 1800s. In a trip to the Galápagos Islands in 1813, captain David Porter reported that the tortoises on San Cristobal Island were already so depleted that his crew failed to find any (although thankfully, they do still survive there). However, he was able to collect some 14 tons of turtles on James Island (now the island of Santiago). By the time Charles Darwin arrived in 1835, there were already permanent settlements on most of the islands. These settlements only increased the threats to the tortoises after centuries of exploitation from the sea. The colony established on Floreana Island in 1829 rapidly wiped out the population of tortoises there, forcing the islanders to travel to other islands to fill the demand for tortoise meat.

As whaling increased in the Pacific, more ships arrived in the Galápagos, and tortoises were a prime target to feed the ships' crews. A study published in 1925 by the director of the New York Aquarium at the time, Charles Haskins Townsend, gives some insight into the impact of these whaling ships. Using ship's logs, he was able to determine that more than 13,000 tortoises (the current total population is estimated at 25,000) were collected between 1831 and 1868 from just 79 vessels. He goes on to note that the American whaling fleet alone in this period was more than 700 vessels, with the majority going to the Pacific, and that this number likely represents only a small fraction of the total take in this period. Townsend estimated that the American whaling fleet took at least 100,000 tortoises subsequent to 1830. It is possible that as many as 200,000 Galápagos giant tortoises were killed during the roughly 200 years of exploitation.

With the increase in human population came not only increased hunting pressure, but also the introduction of new species and devastating changes to the islands' landscapes. By the 1830s, feral pigs were already established on Floreana, and by 1846, more than 2,000 head of cattle were introduced to the island, along with goats, donkeys, dogs, cats, and rats. The increased predation of young tortoises by pigs, dogs, cats, and rats, combined with habitat loss caused by cattle, donkeys, and goats, and the pressures from hunting, left the Floreana giants with little chance. Similar introductions were repeated on numerous islands of the archipelago, and Pinta was no exception. While the population of tortoises there was already nearly gone, it still possessed pristine habitat, but the likely final blow to the species was the introduction of goats in 1959. By 1970, an initial population of three goats had exploded to more than 40,000, completely destroying nearly all of the prime tortoise habitat. It is a testament to the resilience of the Galápagos giant tortoises that, despite centuries of intensive exploitation, dramatic habitat loss, and the introduction of new predators on many of the islands, they still exist at all. The tortoises did receive protection from the government of Ecuador in 1936, and in 1959, all non-inhabited areas of the archipelago became a national park. Protections came too late to save the Floreana or Pinta tortoises, but they were instrumental in protecting the remaining species.

In an unlikely twist of fate, there is potential hope for both of the extinct giants, however. Researchers conducting studies of tortoise populations on the Wolf Volcano in the northern reaches of Isabella Island, were able to determine that some of these tortoises are actually hybrids of different tortoise species, including hybrids of both the Pinta and Floreana giant tortoises. This is an unexpected but fortunate side effect of the early exploitation of the tortoises. It's believed that sailors capturing the tortoises moved some of them to the island inadvertently saving their genes from extinction when the two species interbred. The hope is that, with selective breeding techniques, both of these species may be able to be brought back. While the situation for the giant tortoises of the Galápagos has dramatically improved, even from several decades ago, they still face significant threats. Poaching is still a problem, and local demand for tortoise meat is increasing despite strict protections. The wildlife trade is also a continuing issue, and as recently as March of 2021, smugglers were caught with 185 baby Galápagos tortoises bound for sale—this after more than 100 were stolen from a breeding center in 2018. Tortoise thefts can be lucrative, with hatchling tortoises fetching as much as $5,000 each.

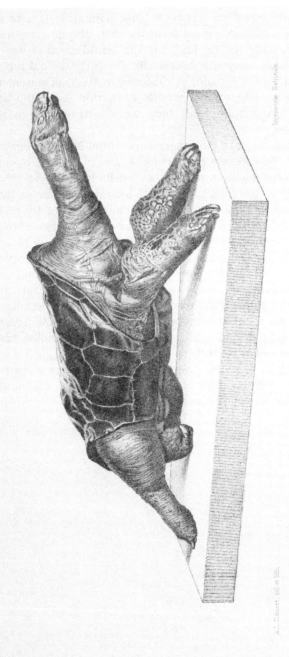

Pl. I.

Centenaire du Muséum.

Testudo (Vosmaeri, Fitzinger.

(Exemplaire des Seychelles.— ¼ gr nat.)

J.-L. Clément del. et lith.

Imprimerie Nationale.

Giant Tortoises of the Mascarene Islands
(Cylindraspis)

Unfortunately, the extinction of two species of Galápagos tortoises was only the most recent in a long line of giant tortoise extinctions. No fewer than 19 species of giant tortoise once existed throughout the world, including in the Canary Islands, the islands of Turks and Caicos, Cuba, and Madagascar. Many of these species went extinct in antiquity due to human predation, but others were able to survive longer. Both species of giant tortoises once found in Madagascar survived until about 1200, and the giants of Turks and Caicos were able to survive up until 1400, all also succumbing to human predation. Giant tortoises are particularly vulnerable to humans. Coming from islands, which are traditionally devoid of large predators, they have little in the way of defense other than sheer size. They are slow and easy for humans to hunt, and they were an attractive source of plentiful, high-quality protein. This combines with an apparent human penchant for eating members of the turtle family going back to our Australopithecine ancestors. With a history closely paralleling the extinctions on the Galápagos Archipelago, the giant tortoises of the Mascarenes are yet another tale of the destructive force of human exploitation. They are also part of a much larger story of human-caused extinctions that includes the famous dodo and many other species covered later.

The Mascarene Islands are composed of the islands of Réunion, Mauritius, and Rodrigues and their surrounding islets. The closest of these lies 700 km (434 miles) east of the coast of Madagascar in the West Indian Ocean. They were once home to an entire genus of giant tortoises consisting of 5 species: the Réunion giant tortoise *(Cylindraspis indica);* two species on the island of Mauritius, the Mauritius giant flat-shelled tortoise *(Cylindraspis triserrata)* and the Mauritius giant domed tortoise *(Cylindraspis inepta)*; and two species from the island of Rodrigues, the Rodrigues giant saddle-backed tortoise *(Cylindraspis vosmaeri)* and the Rodrigues domed tortoise *(Cylindraspis peltastes).* Very little is known about any of these species. Almost none were studied while they were still alive, and no complete specimens are housed in the world's natural history museums, with the exception of the Rodrigues giant. It is interesting to note that here, as in the Galápagos, there are two distinct forms of tortoises, some with more rounded shells and a species with a "saddle-back" shell (this is *C. vosmaeri* shown on previous page) remarkably like those of the species in the Galápagos, a striking similarity considering the giant tortoises of the Mascarene Islands and the giants of the Galápagos are evolutionarily separated by nearly 40 million years.

What we do know from genetic studies is that the giant tortoises of the Mascarenes were a highly evolutionarily divergent group that originated in Africa and that their relationships are much more complex than those of the giants of the Galápagos. For example, one would expect a close relationship between species inhabiting the same islands, and this is true for the two species of Rodrigues. However, the two species on Mauritius are separated by nearly 30 million years of evolution. *C. triserrata* is a direct descendant of the Mascarene tortoises' last common ancestor, but *C. inepta* is surprisingly more closely related to Réunion's *C. indica*. In addition, unlike the Galápagos species, the Mascarene giant tortoises had a much larger size range. The tortoises of Mauritius were very similar in size, with a carapace length of 60–70 cm (20–30 in), but both could grow to 100 cm (40 in), with *C. triserrata* having a flat shell and *C. inepta* having a more rounded shell. On Rodrigues, the domed *C. peltastes*, which measured only 46 cm (18 in), coexisted with the much larger saddle-backed *C. vosmaeri*, which measured 110 cm (43 in). Réunion's domed giant was the largest and could grow to 120 cm, or 4 feet, in length. The largest of the Mascarene tortoises easily weighed hundreds of pounds.

While total population numbers are not known, historical accounts show that the tortoises throughout the island chain were incredibly abundant. Voyagers of the 16th and 17th centuries visiting the island almost universally speak of the countless numbers of tortoises found there. French explorer François Leguat, who for a time lived on the island of Rodrigues, reported in 1691 observing "flocks" of two to three thousand tortoises at a time. So large and dense were these assemblies that apparently one could walk 100 paces on their backs without touching the ground. According to modern estimates, as many as 150,000 to 200,000 tortoises once lived on Rodrigues alone. Despite their original abundance, by the 1720s the population of tortoises on Mauritius proper was already gone. Remnant populations persisted on surrounding islets as late as 1740. The two species on the island of Rodrigues were wiped out by 1800, and the tortoises on Réunion were still abundant in the late 1700s, but by 1840, these too were gone.

There is little question as to the causes of the extinction of these animals. After the discovery of the islands in the 1500s and their abundant tortoises, the unfortunate creatures were relentlessly harvested to supply ships traveling the Indian Ocean and the populations that later settled on the islands themselves. Hundreds were taken at a time, and thousands every year. A tortoise hunting station was set up on Rodrigues in 1735 to supply locals and ships with live tortoises and meat. Soon, 10,000 tortoises per year were being harvested from the islands. Between 1735 and 1771, as many as 280,000 tortoises were butchered or exported out of Rodrigues. Added to this mass exploitation is the introduction of new species from human settlements, including domestic cats, and more destructively, pigs, which devastated tortoise nests by consuming vast numbers of eggs and hatchlings. With adults being harvested by humans and young being destroyed by introduced species, there was little chance of the tortoises' survival.

Day Geckos of Rodrigues Island
(Phelsuma)

The dodo and the giant tortoises of the Mascarene Islands are certainly not the only extinctions in this highly biodiverse island chain. More than 50 species have been lost due to human exploitation of the islands' animals and resources. Losses for reptiles have been particularly severe, and a large percentage of known reptile extinctions worldwide are from the Mascarene Islands. Of the 32 species of reptile currently listed as extinct by the IUCN, 13 are from these three islands and their surrounding islets. Unfortunately, many more species were likely lost before science had a chance to describe them.

Two of these species were among the world's largest geckos. Both in the genus *Phelsuma*, they were also the only two endemic geckos found on Rodrigues and its surrounding islets. The members of the genus *Phelsuma* (known as day geckos for their diurnal habits) are a highly diverse group of lizards, with almost all members of the genus occurring on the islands of Mauritius, Madagascar, and formerly Rodrigues. The smaller and more plentiful of these two lost species was the Newton's day gecko *(Phelsuma edwardnewtonii)*. Accounts of these brightly colored and quite common geckos date back to the late 1600s, with the first being by François Leguat. They were easily identified by their coloration, which was extremely variable and consisted of blues, greens, and yellow with some gray and red thrown in. The explanation for this fantastic variation in color was found by a surprised observer in 1761 when a brightly colored individual was spooked and rapidly changed color to all black. These geckos were evidently color-change specialists. Growing to approximately 20 cm (8 inches) in size but possibly being as large as 30 cm (12 inches), they fed largely on fruit and nectar but also regularly consumed flies. They were found widely, but were particularly fond of inhabiting the island's hurricane and latan palm trees.

Populations of Newton's geckos evidently remained strong for many years, despite growing pressures, and they were still common 100 years after they were first recorded. However, on the main island of Rodrigues, this trend did not hold, and by 1874, they were restricted only to Rodrigues' surrounding islets, particularly Ile aux Fous. The last record of Newton's gecko is of two individuals captured in 1917 from one of Rodrigues' islets, but which does not seem to have been recorded. Despite extensive searches of the main island of Rodrigues and the surrounding islands in the 1960s and again in 2013, no remaining Newton's geckos have been located.

With significant non-native species introductions and severe disruptions to the island's ecosystems beginning in the late 17th century, it's a wonder the Newton's geckos survived until the 20th century. Likely, the introduction of rats to the island was the primary cause of the gecko's demise. Rats had plagued Dutch settlements throughout the Mascarene Islands to such an extent that they caused mass crop failure. On Rodrigues, domestic cats were being introduced to help control the rats as early as the 1720s. Unfortunately for the geckos, this only added another unfamiliar predator, and cats likely contributed to their decline as

BRIT. MUS. N.H.

Pl. XVII.

R. Mintern del. et lith.

Phelsuma newtonii.

Mintern Bros. imp.

well. Habitat loss was also a significant factor in the loss of the Newton's. Forest loss was extremely severe on Rodrigues, and by the late 1800s, almost none of the island's forests remained.

The larger of the two species of Rodrigues geckos was the Linard's giant gecko *(Phelsuma gigas)*. It has the distinction of being the largest species of gecko to exist in modern times. Said to often be the width of a man's arm, these geckos could be as large as 50 cm (20 in) long. By comparison, the largest species of gecko alive today is the New Caledonian giant gecko *(Rhacodactylus leachianus)*, at just 36 cm (14 in). Unlike the brightly colored Newton's gecko, these enormous geckos were a subdued gray and black with only a subtle pale yellow coloring on their underside. Also, unlike the Newton's, they evidently could not change color. They typically ate fruit and nectar, but they were also observed consuming bird eggs. Bucking the description of the day gecko genus, these geckos may also have been at least semi-nocturnal. Like their smaller island mates, these giants seemed to prefer residing in palm trees, particularly the latan.

Also mentioned by Leguat in the late 1600s, the giant geckos were easily found on the main island of Rodrigues until around 1726. By 1761, however, they were extremely rare on the main island but still common on its surrounding islets until the 1840s. By 1874, the Linard's giant gecko was entirely absent from its former haunts, and it is believed that it was likely extinct by that time. The same surveys conducted for the Newton's gecko, mentioned above, also searched for evidence of any remaining Linard's geckos, but unfortunately, these one-of-a-kind giants are almost certainly extinct.

Unlike Newton's gecko and numerous other species of the Mascarene Islands, rats are not suspected as the primary cause of the decline of Linard's giant gecko, but rather the cats introduced to control them. Norway rats, however, may have been the final downfall of the species and were found in abundance on the islet of Ile Frégateby, the last stronghold of the giant gecko, although they weren't found until after the Linard's disappearance. Of course, the giants of Rodrigues also suffered from the decimation of Rodrigues' forests, and there is no doubt that this too played a part in their demise.

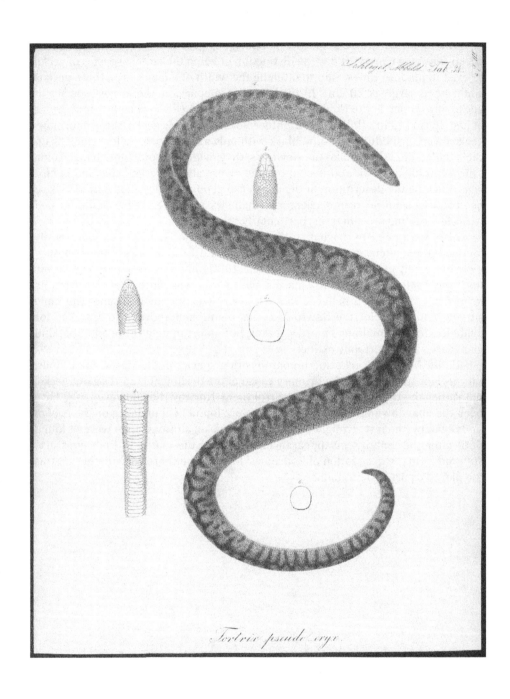

Tortrix pseudo-eryx

Round Island Burrowing Boa
(Bolyeria multocarinata)

Round Island, also in the Mascarene Islands, is located 22.5 km (14 mi) north of the island of Mauritius. Even though it is just 2.19 sq km or less than 1 sq mi, it is one of the largest of the small islands found around Mauritius. Despite its small size, it has been vitally important to some of the rarest Mauritanian species and was the last refuge of an entire family of snakes unique to Mauritius in the family Bolyeriidae. The family consists of just two species, the keel-scaled boa *(Casarea dussumieri),* which can still be found on Round Island, and the Round Island burrowing boa *(Bolyeria multocarinata),* which is now extinct.

Both of these species ranged among several of the small islets near Mauritius, and fossil evidence shows that at one time they also inhabited the main island as well, although there are no written records mentioning them. Very little is known about the burrowing boa, despite it being first described in 1827. What little is known has been determined through morphological studies and the sparse observations of the snakes. The burrowing boas, as their name suggests, were adept at being able to quickly bury themselves in loose soil and leaf litter. Their physical structure, i.e., lack of neck (yes, snakes have necks) and a pointed snout, support these observations and are typical of burrowing snakes. Their preferred habitat was likely the leaf-covered understory of tropical hardwoods and palms. They were usually around 80–150 cm (2.5–5 ft) in length, although some were recorded as long as 180 cm (6 ft). They possessed a particularly distinct jaw structure that they shared with the keel-scaled boa, suggesting not only common ancestry but also that they were, like the keel-scaled boa, lizard-eating specialists.

The original population of the burrowing boa is impossible to determine. Despite human habitation in Mauritius dating back to the 1500s, there are no early mentions of snakes, despite the fact that it is the only island in the Mascarenes that had them. We do know that, although absent on the main island, the burrowing boa was found on several of the surrounding islets along with the keel-scaled boa. They were first collected in 1801 or 1803, although on which islet is not known. By 1881, it is reported that both of the snakes of Mauritius were confined to just Round Island, having been extirpated from all of their other known locations. By the 1900s, ground boas were becoming increasingly rare. They continued to be difficult to find, with only one sighting in 1935. None of the snakes could be located for more than a decade between 1953 and 1967, and in fact, there are only four known sightings in all of the 20th century, with the last in 1975. No other sightings of the Round Island burrowing boa have been recorded, despite the presence of full-time conservation staff on the island beginning in 2002.

What specifically caused the extinction of the ground boa is hard to determine, but it is likely that human pressures are ultimately to blame. Certainly, the boa's initial isolation to a few small islets made them more vulnerable. Then, already driven to extinction on other islets, likely through habitat loss, the introduction of non-native species, and direct elimination by humans, they were restricted to just Round Island. This small remaining population faced continuous challenges. Loss of native plant cover plagued all the islands of the Mascarenes, and Round Island was no exception. As early as 1860, Round Island was experiencing the same extreme degradation that other islands had already seen and was described as already having very little vegetation. Per surveys conducted in 1948, Round Island was nearly devoid of vegetation and was suffering severe erosion and soil loss caused by deforestation and the introduction of goats and rabbits to the island. It is likely that this extreme degradation in habitat was a major factor in the boa's extinction. Despite the fact that the entire island was designated a nature preserve in 1957, and that goats and rabbits were removed in the 1970s and 1980s, it appears that it was too late to save the remaining ground boas.

Christmas Island Whiptail-skink
(Emoia nativitatis)

Another island in the Indian Ocean, the Australian territory of Christmas Island, is found roughly 360 km (223 miles) south of the Indonesian island of Java. It is best known for its abundant land crabs, the most numerous of which is the red land crab *(Gecarcoidea natalis)*, which numbers as many as 45 million and makes up the majority of the island's land crab-driven ecosystem. The island was once inhabited by six native terrestrial reptile species, of which five were unique to the island, including four endemic species of lizard. Unfortunately, recent decades have seen a severe decline in not only reptile species, but in species across the board. Numerous species have been lost in just the last 10 years, despite the island being settled since the 1880s and the majority of the island retaining its historical forest cover.

One of these species, the Christmas Island whiptail-skink, also called the Christmas Island forest skink, was once found island-wide. These diurnal 20 cm (8 in) lizards spent their time eating a variety of terrestrial invertebrates while preferring the sunny openings of the Christmas Island forests. These once common metallic brown skinks had robust populations as late as 1998, with researchers still sighting as many as 80 individuals at a single location. However, just several years later, populations underwent a severe decline. By 2003, they were only found in isolated populations in remote parts of the island, and just two years later, the situation appeared critical. By 2008, only one small population existed on the island, and by 2010, only one individual could be located. Australian legislation listed the forest skink as threatened in 2014, but protections for this species and others have likely come too late. The last known

Christmas Island whiptail-skink, a female named Gump, died in captivity in May of 2014, just 4 months after the passing of protections.

Two of the island's other remaining endemic lizards were last recorded between 2009 and 2013, and are now classified as extinct in the wild due to population crashes similar to the island's whiptail-skinks. Fortunately for these species, the Lister's gecko *(Lepidodactylus listeri)* and the Christmas Island blue-tailed skink *(Cryptoblepharus egeriae)*, there are sufficient numbers in captive populations to continue propagating both species. However, it is unclear what level of success reintroducing these captive animals would have. The ultimate cause of the disappearance of these two species and the extinction of the whiptail-skink remains largely a mystery.

Scientists are the most confident about what has not been the cause of these extinctions. Unlike many cases of species loss, habitat loss is not at fault on Christmas Island. Certainly, early settlement and mining activities disrupted habitats, but high-quality habitat still abounds on the island, with more than 60% of it lying undisturbed and protected. Disease also does not appear to be a culprit, despite the rapid losses mirroring those seen in the world's amphibians. Thorough testing of reptile populations on the island has ruled out viruses, parasites, or heavy metal contamination as potential causes of declines. The island did experience a particularly dry period in the late 1980s through the mid 1990s, but this too does not appear to be a significant cause.

There is evidence that the introduction of non-native predators and competition from other introduced reptiles may be contributing to species decline on the island. However, this evidence is not as straightforward as it is with other animals wiped out by invasive species. Some of the more compelling evidence for the invasive theory is the pattern in which the reptile declines have happened. The declines show a definite pattern of loss proceeding from east to west on the island. This is what we would expect to see if a harmful species was introduced by humans, with the only significant human presence residing in the northeastern part of the island. However, it is unknown what species may be to blame. The introduction of cats and rats on the island likely accounted for some of the losses, but both of these species have been on Christmas Island since at least 1900. Also introduced early on were two invertebrates: a giant centipede species *(Scolopendra subspinipes)* and the yellow crazy ant *(Anoplolepis gracilipes)*, which expanded their ranges in the 1990s, but were likely already widely spread across the island long before reptile declines. It seems unlikely that these species, while damaging to the ecosystems of the island, particularly the effect of the large colonies of crazy ants on the native land crabs, are to blame for the native reptile declines. All of these species interacted on the island for nearly 100 years without a noticeable impact on reptile populations.

In the last 20 to 30 years, several species of introduced reptiles have spread across the island, including the Bowring's skink *(Subdoluseps bowringii)*, the common house gecko *(Hemidactylus frenatus)*, and most notably the wolf snake *(Lycodon capucinus)*, not introduced until the 1980s. Predation of the island's native reptiles by the wolf snake has been confirmed, demonstrating that the snake certainly has impacted populations. A combination of increased predation and competition from newly introduced species and existing non-native predators may have precipitated the recent wave of reptile extinctions. However, this is not well understood. Predation and competition have not collapsed the population of another of the island's native reptiles, the endangered Christmas Island giant gecko *(Cyrtodactylus sadleiri)*, even though predation by the wolf snake, in particular, has been confirmed for this species. Neither have the non-native reptiles on the island shown a decreased susceptibility to predation compared to native species, yet their populations remain strong.

A retrospective assessment recently concluded that the single largest factor in the decline of Christmas Island native reptiles was likely the introduction and subsequent invasion of the island by the wolf snake. This conclusion is based on a consensus among scientists familiar with Christmas Island and the timing of the declines. If this holds true, it is the second reptile extinction attributed to the wolf snake, the other being the extinction of *Gongylomorphus borbonicus,* a skink from the island of Réunion. Also implicated were the island's invasive giant centipedes. However, there is still no explanation as to why these predators do not seem to significantly impact the island's remaining native and non-native lizards. The assessment also concludes that control of these species island-wide is probably not possible, threatening the reestablishment of the blue-tailed skink and the Lister's gecko in the wild. However, enclosures designed to keep predators out have recently seen success in maintaining a captive, semi-wild population of both of these species on the island.

One of the still-living members of the genus, *Leiocephalus carinatus.*

Curly-tailed Lizards of the Caribbean
(Leiocephalus)

The tortoises of the Galápagos were not the only reptiles of the New World impacted by the arrival of humans. Like the islands of the Indian Ocean and the Galápagos, the islands of the West Indies in the Caribbean have seen a number of extinctions. Among them are three species (listed by the IUCN) and a fourth (newly described) of the genus *Leiocephalus,* known as the curly-tailed lizards for their distinctive curling tails. The entire genus is endemic only to the islands of the West Indies and consists of around 29 species; however, they have now been introduced to regions outside their native range, particularly the U.S. state of Florida.

Very little is known about any of the extinct members of *Leiocephalus,* but we can presume something about their behavior based on what we know of their living relatives. In general, curly-tailed lizards are generalists as far as diet is concerned, and some species will eat almost anything. Not surprisingly, insects make up most of their diet, but they also consume various fruits and flowers and even occasionally smaller lizards. They tend to prefer the margins of beaches for their habitat, and likely use their distinctive curly tails to ward off predators and in rival threat displays.

One of the extinct species, *Leiocephalus cuneus,* is only known from fossil evidence and little else. They once inhabited the islands of Anguilla, Barbuda,

Antigua, and possibly Guadeloupe. This species was notable for being by far the largest of the known members of the genus. They had a snout-to-vent length (essentially length minus the tail) of around 20 cm (8 in), making them considerably larger than the largest living curly-tailed lizard *(L. carinatus),* which is around 13 cm (5 in) SVL. When and why this species went extinct is not known. They are believed to have survived into modern times due to a likely account of the species written in 1667.

The Navassa curly-tailed lizard *(Leiocephalus eremitus)* is known only from the small island of Navassa. Navassa Island lies 74 km (46 mi) west of the island of Hispaniola and is just 5.4 sq km (2 sq mi) in area. Despite its discovery in 1504 by members of Columbus' crew, the island remained uninhabited until it was claimed by the U.S. in 1857. Phosphate mining operations were set up on the island in 1865. The species is only known from a single individual that was collected and described in 1868. The species was probably small, with the only known individual having a SVL of just 6.3 cm (2.5 in). No other records of these lizards seem to exist, but the unique traits of the one known individual are distinct enough to conclude that they were a species unique to Navassa. Their extinction is possibly related to the introduction of cats to their island shortly after their discovery.

The Martinique curly-tailed lizard *(Leiocephalus hermineri),* first described in 1837, has not been recorded since its initial discovery, but apparently was quite common on the island in the early 18th century. This species was large, with a total length of 32 cm (12.5 in), and was likely the second largest of the genus after *L. cuneus.* The reason for the extinction of the species is not known, but it is likely a victim of the huge ecological changes that many islands in the region experienced during the 17th and 18th centuries. By 1731, 14% of all the land on Martinique was in sugarcane production, in addition to a wide range of other crops. By the 1780s, the human population had exploded, going from just a few thousand native Caribs before European occupation to thousands of settlers and more than 80,000 slaves. Supporting this population were 19,000 head of cattle and as many as 11,000–12,000 sheep and goats. By the end of the 18th century, 24% of all of Martinique was in crops, and forest cover on the island had dropped from 79% down to just 13.4% of heavily disturbed forest. Of course, the huge expansion of human settlement on the island also brought more than just cattle and sheep, and it is certainly possible that various non-native species could have played a role in the lizard's extinction. The species may also have been affected by a natural disaster. The island was hit with tsunami waves in 1843, produced by an earthquake on the island of Guadeloupe, and waves as high as 2 meters (6 feet) may have inundated the coastal habitats of the already struggling lizards.

A new species, just described in 2021, was found on the island of Guadeloupe. The determination for the new species was made using an individual that was collected and preserved sometime around 1835 and housed in the Natural History Museum of Bordeaux, France, along with various fossil remains from the island. This preserved specimen was named the curly-tailed roquet, or *Leiocephalus roquetus,* after the French term used to describe these lizards. How widely distributed these 26.5 cm (10.5 inch) lizards were is unknown, but they obviously survived into the early 19th century. Reasons for their extinction are also not known, but the history of the island of Guadeloupe parallels that of Martinique. It is possible that *L. roquetus* experienced many of the same pressures as *L. hermineri* of Martinique, mainly habitat loss through deforestation and agriculture and the introduction of non-native predators. We will never know why many of these species are extinct, and we may find more species of the same genus that are no longer living, but while evidence is lacking, it seems probable that the huge impacts from human activities on many of these islands are, at least in part, to blame. These curly-tailed lizards join a large number of species that have been impacted by the massive ecological changes that have occurred across the Caribbean islands since European settlement.

The related and endangered Hispaniolan rhinoceros iguana *(Cyclura cornuta)*.

Navassa Rhinoceros Iguana
(Cyclura onchiopsis)

These iguanas are another native of the small island of Navassa and one of two species of iguanas closely related to the rhinoceros iguanas of the island of Hispaniola, *Cyclura cornuta.* The other is the Mona Island rhinoceros iguana *(Cyclura stejnegeri),* whose small island lies 66 kilometers (41 miles) west of Puerto Rico. For a time, the Navassa and Mona island iguanas were considered subspecies of *Cyclura cornuta*, but they are now considered full species in their own right. The Navassa iguana was first described in 1885 from specimens collected on the island in 1878.

Almost nothing about this species is known apart from the physical description, but it is possible to get a good idea of how the Navassa iguanas lived by looking at the ecology of the rhinoceros iguanas of Hispaniola. Rhinoceros iguanas are large lizards. They can reach total lengths of as much as 140 cm (4.5 feet) and weigh as much as 9 kg (20 lbs). Long-lived, they can live 20 years in captivity and may actually exceed that in the wild. Like most iguanas, they are primarily herbivores, eating a variety of leaves, fruits, seeds, and flowers, but they are also opportunistic carnivores, occasionally consuming insects, crabs, and carrion that they might come across. They lay eggs like most lizards, but their clutch sizes vary greatly, ranging from 5 to 20. The Hispaniola iguanas prefer open scrub habitats, and presumably, the Navassa iguanas favored the same habitat.

Little historical perspective exists on the population of Navassa iguanas, although it is assumed that before human settlement they inhabited most of the island. Even though, as mentioned earlier, Navassa was known as far back as the Columbus expeditions, the island was largely ignored until the middle of the 1800s. The only specimens collected were in 1878, so they were certainly inhabiting the island at that time, but by the early 1900s, the species may already have gone extinct. A lighthouse was built on the island in 1916, but despite being large and easily identifiable, none of the lighthouse keepers report having seen the iguanas.

The lack of information about the species complicates determining what happened to the Navassa iguanas, but it's probable that human impacts were a major factor. Beginning in 1865, an extensive guano mining operation was set up on the island to extract phosphorus for industry. Thousands of years of guano from sea birds had built up on the island, and the removal of this guano severely disturbed the island's plant life. This loss of habitat for feeding and nesting, and potentially the direct exploitation of the iguanas as a food source for the miners, were likely severe blows to the iguana populations. Even if the iguanas managed to survive the mining operations, the rats, feral dogs, and cats later introduced by lighthouse workers could have eliminated the remaining population.

Mining on the island had a dramatic effect on the island's vegetation, and this may have led to the demise of the island's iguanas, but the loss of the iguanas themselves likely contributed to the degradation of the island's ecosystems. In many cases, it is difficult to determine just how the loss of a species impacts the ecosystems in which it is a part, but in this case, there is evidence of the crucial role that the iguanas played on the island. Studies of iguana populations on other islands have shown that their diet makes them effective seed dispersers. Through consuming fruits and their seeds, iguanas carry them across the islands they inhabit, but it has also been shown that the seeds that pass through the iguana's gut germinate faster than seeds that do not. Many species fill this role around the world, and it is an important service animals provide for plants. It is likely that the Navassa iguanas were one of the few, and maybe only, species on the island that could carry out this important service, enriching the environment in which they lived.

8
Fish (Actinopterygii)

T he class Actinopterygii, or ray-finned fish, make up more than 90 percent of the more than 30,000 known species of fish throughout both freshwater and saltwater environments and half of all vertebrate species on Earth. While not the oldest form of fish from an evolutionary standpoint, it is believed that they have been on Earth for between 420 and 430 million years. The earliest known from the fossil record are the members of the genus *Cheirolepis,* dating from the Devonian. By the late Triassic, roughly 230 million years ago, the most dominant group of fishes arose, called the teleosts. These members of Actinopterygii are distinguished by their symmetrical tails and their ability to extend their mouth parts (resulting in the common "fishy face" that we associate with most fish). Nearly all the fish you are familiar with are members of this group, including eels, catfish, tuna, flounder, trout, salmon, cod, cichlids, pufferfish, and even seahorses. They are an incredibly widespread and diverse group with 40 orders, more than 400 families, and 20,000 species.

Members of the class exist nearly everywhere on Earth where water is found from pole to pole in both saltwater and freshwater, and in every ocean from coastal shallows to depths greater than 7,000 meters (23,000 ft). They can be found in high altitude streams and lakes, as well as subterranean caves, and from the Arctic to the Tropics and even in remote desert springs. They have been found in water temperatures ranging from -1.8 to as much as 40 degrees C (29-104°F), pH levels from 4 to more than 10, and oxygen saturations from near zero to completely saturated. There are species even known to tolerate salinity concentrations as high as 90 parts per million, and numerous well-known species split their time between saltwater and freshwater.

The smallest known member of the class is the minuscule *Paedocypris progenetica* from the peat swamps of Southeast Asia. First described in 2006 with its also minuscule, but slightly larger relative *Paedocypris micromegethes.* The male of *P. progenetica* only reaches a maximum size of 10.3 mm (.4 in) and mature females can be as small as 7.9 mm. Not only are they the world's smallest fish, they are also one of the world's smallest known vertebrates. The largest ray-finned fish is the ocean sunfish, or *Mola mola*, found in temperate and tropical seas throughout the world. These rather odd-looking fish can weigh as much as

2,235 kg (4,900 lbs), although one was recently recorded at nearly 6,000 lbs, and while they are not the longest fish due to their dinner plate-like form (think a huge pancake with a single fin top and bottom), they can still be as large as 3.1 meters (10 ft) in length and more than 4 meters (13 ft) tall, nicely demonstrating not only the huge size range of the class but the extremes of form.

With the immense number of different fish species, there are obviously a great number of fantastic adaptations among them. This allows them to survive in an extremely wide variety of aquatic habitats, and the diversity that is displayed in just Actinopterygii alone seems virtually endless. Not only are there fish that dwell within the extreme depths of the ocean, but there are also species that can take to the air. The famous flying fish of the family Exocoetidae can glide hundreds of meters through the air to escape predators. While fish are no doubt aquatic animals, fish leaving their watery habitats is not as abnormal as it may seem. There are a number of species that can be found above water as often as below. Of the Actinopterygii, the mudskippers are the best known. Their lives in the intertidal zone find them skipping about on stiffened fins and breathing through their skin. We are often impressed by the vibrance and color of many fish, but equally impressive are the species that exhibit extreme levels of camouflage, like the reef stonefish *(Synanceia verrucosa),* which is virtually indistinguishable from its surroundings. Not only is it a master of disguise, but it is also the most venomous fish known in the ocean.

Volumes could be written (and have been) about the various adaptations of the members of Actinopterygii, but there are some that standout more than others. One such standout is a group of fish that hails from Amazonia, the electric eels. Once thought to be limited to just one species, there are now several recognized species of the genus *Electrophorus,* with the most common species bearing the shocking name of *Electrophorus electricus.* Called an eel, but more closely related to catfish than eels, they are not the only fish capable of producing and using electric fields. They can, however, use this ability to a much greater extent than any other creature in nature, generating voltage potentials exceeding 800 volts. While they are not lethal to humans, the amount of power they can produce is comparable to being shocked by an electric fence or even a police taser. It is powerful enough to cause paralysis in threats and prey alike, but the electric eels' electrifying abilities are far more impressive than just their ability to deliver a shock.

Electric eels have been known to science since the 1700s, and are credited for inspiring Volta's invention of the battery. Later studied by names such as von Humboldt and Faraday, they not only played pivotal roles in humans' early understanding of electricity and physiology, but they continue to inspire scientific study. More recent studies of these fascinating creatures are giving us insights into exactly how they use electricity. These eels possess three separate electricity-producing organs that work in conjunction to produce power. How they produce these electrical potentials is fairly straightforward and is very much the same way humans produce the electrical signals in our own bodies, but with a much greater possible potential. While known primarily for their high output shocks, eels can also produce low voltage pulses. These pulses are called electric organ discharges, or EODs. Electric eels use EODs for multiple reasons. Low-voltage EOD is used for active electroreception, sensing their surroundings, including threats and predators, using a low-voltage and low-frequency electric field. It's also thought to be used for communication between eels.

High-voltage EODs are used for hunting and defense, the details of which are the most interesting. When encountering a prey item, the eel deploys high-voltage EOD, paralyzing the prey. This paralysis is not simply due to the voltage involved, however. Investigations into the eels' electrical attacks reveal that eels, using an amplification of their own motor neuron signals, can activate the motor neurons of their prey and in this way paralyze their prey by essentially remote controlling their muscles. This same high-voltage system is also used to sense where their paralyzed prey is, increasing strike accuracy.

Alas, a meal is not always easy to find, but the eels have developed a handy way of finding hidden prey. Electric eels not only can sense electrical signals but are also extremely adept at sensing changes in the movement of water around them, such as the change caused by a moving fish. Masters of others' motor neurons, the eels can send out high-voltage EOD pulses that force fish to move, revealing their location. This clever behavior makes it virtually impossible to hide from an electric eel.

Electric eels also have several behaviors that allow them to boost the effect of their EODs. Just like a battery, eels are polarized. Their heads are positive and tails negative. While straight, their long length creates a weaker field with their poles spaced far apart. With small prey, this is of little consequence, and they appear to have little trouble overcoming small fish. However, in the case of larger prey, they may need to increase the intensity of their attack. This is simply done by bringing their two poles closer together, i.e., bringing their tail closer to their head. Theoretically, this curling technique could deliver twice the field strength to the prey, and experimental evidence shows that this is in fact the case. Not only have these eels learned to turn up the power underwater, they have been observed in the wild and in the lab leaving the water to intensify the effect of their attack to ward off predators.

These eels not only understand how to maximize their own electrical output but can also cooperate as a group. Just recently discovered, one species of electric eel, *Electrophorus voltai,* has been observed congregating into groups of up to 100 individuals. At dawn and dusk, these eels set out to hunt, working as a group to round up small fish and then disabling them with coordinated EOD attacks. The observations just published in 2021 are the first known incidences of social hunting among electric eels, demonstrating they might also be shockingly smart.

Anyone who has had the pleasure of watching fireflies light up a warm summer landscape understands the awe that is inspired by creatures that can produce their own light. While bioluminescence is by no means uncommon in the animal world, this doesn't seem to diminish our fascination. Maybe it's because it's an ability that humans don't possess, or maybe because seeing glowing animals is not part of our daily experience. For whatever the reason, it's hard to argue that bioluminescence is not an extremely cool adaptation. Most are familiar with the firefly and other glowing insects, but many might be surprised how common it is in fish. Bioluminescence has evolved no less than 27 times in the ray-finned fishes. As a result, there are many ways in which different species accomplish the task. Some use self-produced chemicals in a wide variety of specialized organs and an equally wide variety of biochemical reactions. Yet others use symbiotic bioluminescent bacteria to produce their light for them, with various structures among different fish to control the light produced. Just as varied as the way fish produce light are the reasons they do. Some use it for camouflage or defense. Some use it to attract prey or to communicate with others, or a combination of some or all of these.

One group of the deep sea anglerfish in the genus *Linophyrne*, have evolved the uncommon use two light sources to attract prey to their gaping tooth filled mouths. Below the chin reside barbs, also called a beard, of various lengths depending on the species. These are illuminated by a protein (luciferin) and enzyme (luciferase) combination that is produced by the fish and contained within an organ called a photophore. When luciferin contacts luciferase, it produces light. The anglerfish can control this reaction to turn their barb light on and off in a mechanism identical to the firefly's. On top of their heads, a different system is deployed. Here, a fleshy ball or "lure" is filled with bioluminescent bacteria. Made from a modified fin spine, these glowing orbs can be moved in various ways. It may be done to attract other fish looking for a meal, to ward off predators, or to attract other angler fish. The structure and size of these lures vary by species, as do the kinds of light-producing bacteria they contain. These bioluminescent bacteria live in a symbiotic relationship with the anglerfish, producing light for the fish and receiving shelter in return. Animals and bacteria having symbiotic relationships are the norm, but close symbiotic relationships such as these typically pass from generation to generation (for example, we inherit our gut bacteria from our mothers).

In anglerfish, there is a mystery to this aspect of their bioluminescence, however. Studies of the anglerfish's bioluminescent bacteria show that they have as much as 50% less genetic information than similar free-living bacteria. As a result, they are highly dependent on their fish hosts. As symbionts, this in itself is not surprising, except that anglerfish are not born with their glowing bacteria. Somehow the fish acquire the bacteria from the vast ocean depths, and somehow the bacteria survive without them. How these feats are respectively accomplished is a mystery to science, as is why the members of *Linophyrne* employ two different systems of illumination. It is clear that there is a vast amount of information we do not know about many fish, and these angler fish are not easy to study. As impressive as their illuminating qualities are, perhaps even more so is the fact that they live and thrive 1,000 meters below the ocean's surface.

Of the more than 23,000 species in Actinopterygii listed by the IUCN, 82 are classified as extinct, and 11 are extinct in the wild. This excludes the cichlids of

Lake Victoria in Africa, previously mentioned, as the IUCN still classifies many of these species as critically endangered and possibly extinct. In the future, as more certain data is collected, the number of extinct members of the class will likely dramatically increase. Including the Lake Victoria species, nearly 1800 species are listed as endangered or critically endangered. Commercial fish stocks in our oceans are monitored, providing a general snapshot of the health of our oceans (and that outlook is generally not good). However, the vastness of the world's oceans makes it extremely difficult to know the population health of the ocean's known fish species, not to mention the countless species yet to be identified. This is especially true in the deep ocean. Because of this, ocean species are often underrepresented in species assessments. In fact, not a single species of strictly marine bony fish has been known to have gone extinct. One species was briefly declared extinct, the smooth handfish *(Sympterichthys unipennis)*, native to the waters off Australia. It is only known from a single specimen collected sometime between 1800 and 1804 and has not been seen since. The species was reclassified as "data deficient" by the IUCN because we know virtually nothing about them that would allow us to determine if they still exist or not. My point here is simply that, as far as marine species go, we have little solid data on how many species could be imperiled or have suffered extinctions. Because of this, it is extremely difficult to get an accurate picture of the state of the Earth's fish diversity as a whole. Among the species listed by the IUCN, more than 4000 species of ray-finned fish are considered data-deficient.

We do largely understand the threats facing fish in general, and not surprisingly, they are many of the same threats that face the majority of the world's biodiversity; many of these have been discussed in previous chapters. In the world's oceans, overfishing is obviously an issue for species that are desired for human dinner plates. Already mentioned, 33% of fish stocks are overfished and 60% are fished at maximum capacity, and the loss of fish biomass in the ocean has been staggering. While regulations are improving the situation among commercial fisheries, an enormous illegal fishing industry threatens numerous fish species with little enforcement of laws in the vastness of the world's oceans. Some may be surprised to see a discussion of habitat loss as a severe issue for marine fish. Obviously, there is not less ocean, but there are very specific habitats within the world's oceans that are critical for the survival of many species, especially when they are young. One such habitat that comes to mind are coral reefs, which are home to thousands of species of fish, among other creatures. The threats to these complex systems have already largely been detailed. Various mechanisms have combined to deteriorate 80% of coral cover and complexity in just the last 50 years in the Caribbean alone, and unfortunately, the threat of warming and acidifying seas is only accelerating the loss. Mangrove forests are essential habitat for many fish species. The total area of mangrove cover has been reduced by a third in the last several decades, and since 1876, thirty percent of the world's seagrass habitats have been lost. Pollution in the world's oceans is also an obvious problem, with an unimaginable amount of plastic, industrial waste, and agricultural runoff entering the oceans every year.

Nearly every human activity impacts the world's freshwater ecosystems, and this brings numerous threats to freshwater fish. Habitat degradation has been, and continues to be, a major threat. Damming and straightening of river courses have cut off migration paths and destroyed vital breeding and feeding habitat for many species. Deforestation and urbanization have changed river flows and dramatically altered water temperatures. The draining of wetlands and groundwater sources for agriculture has had significant impacts on the loss of freshwater habitats. Pollution from industry, urban runoff, and increased sedimentation threaten freshwater resources worldwide. Sedimentation is particularly a problem in areas with large amounts of deforestation; a landscape stripped of its trees can have devastating effects on water quality and freshwater systems. For instance, 60% of Madagascar's fish species are threatened by deforestation as a result of sediments released into aquatic systems. Mass fish kills are still common throughout the world due to accidental or intentional releases of pollutants into waterways, and fish experience detrimental effects on both reproduction and health due to persistent levels of a wide variety of pollutants. The extinction of at least 8 species of European freshwater fish can be linked to pollution and eutrophication of their habitats. The vast majority of wastewater produced worldwide still flows untreated into waterways. Even in countries with a relatively good wastewater treatment record, such as the U.S., failures of obsolete combined sewage and stormwater systems allow an estimated 850 billion gallons of untreated sewage to enter U.S. waters each year.

Invasive species are also a significant threat to freshwater fish species around the world. They can have devastating effects on freshwater systems and are now likely responsible for the extinction of dozens, if not hundreds, of species. The introduction of non-native trout species into the U.S. state of Colorado decimated the populations of four native subspecies of cutthroat trout *(Oncorhynchus clarkii)* there, causing the extinction of one and continuing to threaten the other three. Also in the U.S. west, the introduction of lake trout *(Salvelinus namaycush)* into Yellowstone Lake in Yellowstone National Park continues to threaten native cutthroats there, despite more than 3.5 million lake trout being removed since 1994. This is not the only threat to the fish of Yellowstone. Native to the Mississippi River basin, a smallmouth bass *(Micropterus dolomieu)* was recently caught within a mile of Yellowstone National Park. These aggressive and voracious fish could decimate fish populations that are not adapted to the bass. First introduced into Montana rivers in the 1960s, smallmouth bass were never considered a threat to Yellowstone's cold rivers, but warming waters due to climate change are allowing them to move farther into the Yellowstone system, an unfortunate consequence of multiple human errors.

Overfishing is not unique to marine fish, and many of the world's freshwater fisheries support a large number of humans. Many of these are fished unsustainably. Nearly 10% of the worldwide total of fish caught comes from freshwater sources. Yet, even though this is by no means an insignificant amount, only one-third of countries with significant freshwater fisheries report the number of fish caught in their waters. What data is available shows that some 8.7

million tons of fish are taken from inland waters every year, according to 2002 numbers. This is a fourfold increase in take since data was first available in 1950. Of this, China alone takes in one-quarter of the total, and overall, Asia is the largest consumer of freshwater fish. While data is sparse, there has been a clear depletion of fish stocks in many of Asia's rivers. For example, statistics along the Mekong River show a striking similarity to data from overfished marine waters, with the average size of fish caught decreasing year over year as large fish are depleted. Associated with the Mekong, Tonle Sap Lake, the largest lake in Southeast Asia, has seen total catches decrease dramatically in recent decades. Annual catches have fallen from as much as 100 metric tons per year in the 1980s to less than 5 metric tons by the early 2000s. This, despite increased fishing effort. This trend is repeated in many of the world's freshwater fisheries, particularly in Asia and Africa. However, Asia and Africa are not the only continents to see overfishing in their inland waters. The North American Great Lakes and Pacific Coast salmon fisheries and the Murray-Darling river system of southern Australia all have seen historical collapses of overfished species. In fact, it would be difficult to find any freshwater system that hasn't been overexploited at some point in history.

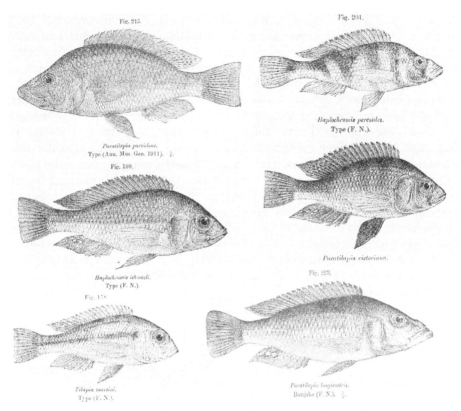

Just some of the likely extinct cichlid species of Lake Victoria
(Note: all of these now reside in the genus *Haplochromis*.)

Cichlids of Lake Victoria
(Cichlidae)

The family Cichlidae is one of the largest families of vertebrates known, with an estimated 2,000–3,000 species globally. Africa and South America have the greatest amount of diversity among these fish and are home to the majority of the world's cichlids. Africa alone has more than 1,000 members of the family, and more than 500 species are endemic to Lake Victoria. The vast majority of these are in the genus *Haplochromis*. These and several other genera of closely related cichlids are referred to as the haplochromine cichlids. Lake Victoria is the second largest freshwater lake in the world and the largest tropical freshwater lake, encompassing an area of more than 68,000 sq km (26,000 sq mi), or the same size as the country of Ireland. So large is the lake that it is bordered by three separate countries: Uganda to the north and west, Kenya in the northeast, and Tanzania, encompassing the lake's southern half. While the evolutionary history of Lake Victoria's cichlid species is still being debated, genetic evidence suggests that all of the lake's endemic cichlids may have evolved from just one or two species, with the first major diversification around 100,000 years ago. However, due to Lake Victoria drying up at the end of the Pleistocene and only refilling around 12,000 years ago, it is likely that most of Lake Victoria's hundreds of species of cichlids arose in a geologic blink of an eye in one of the most amazing species radiations known.

The Lake Victoria cichlids evolved to be able to exploit every conceivable habitat and food source found in their native lake. There are shallow-water and deep-water species, predatory species, algae eaters, mollusk specialists, insectivores, and detritivores. Some prefer rocky-bottom habitats, some mud and sand bottoms, and others troll the open waters of the lake. They display an extraordinary range of specializations, and it seems that no matter the conditions found anywhere in the lake, there was once a cichlid species that could be found there. The true number of species is still unknown, with estimates ranging from only 159 in 1970 to more than 500 in 2000. The total number may be as high as 600. The vast majority are small species, ranging from 6–10 cm (2-4 in), but some species can reach a size of 15–17 cm (6-7 in). Despite knowing that cichlids were widespread throughout the lake and that they inhabited a wide range of habitats, we know little about the ecology of the Lake Victoria cichlids. Just how these fish interacted with and impacted each other and the dozens of other non-cichlid fish native to the lake, as well as the ecological roles that they played, remain poorly understood. There is even little knowledge of their historic distribution.

The dramatic decline of cichlid numbers began in the 1980s. Bottom trawl surveys conducted from 1969–1970 found that 80% of all the deep-water fish found in Lake Victoria were haplochromine cichlids, and the lake was at that time defined by its cichlid-dominated ecosystem. Like many of the world's fish, catch data from fishing operations often provides some of the only population abundance data that is available, and Lake Victoria's cichlids are no exception. Catches from the lake's commercial fisheries found a healthy amount of haplochromine cichlids through the 1970s and into the early 1980s. Catch records from Uganda show catch rates averaging 391.7 kg/h (kilograms per hour) in 1981. Only two years later, however, catches had dropped 48% to 264.7 kg/h. Between 1984 and 1985, the cichlid catch collapsed with dwindling populations, going from 113.9 kg/h to just 17.8 kg/h. By 1986, catches had fallen to effectively zero. On the Tanzanian half of the lake, the populations held up slightly longer but followed a similar pattern. Catch records from this portion of the lake show that fishermen pulled in about 24,000 tons of cichlids in 1983 and were still able to catch 17,000 tons in 1986. After this, catches dropped dramatically. Just 1,500 tons of cichlids were caught in 1987, and catches fell to zero by 1988. Bottom trawl surveys from the Kenyan portion of the lake confirm the lake-wide decline, with deep-dwelling cichlid biomass falling from 35.8 kg/ha (kilograms per hectare) in 1969-1971 to just 0.5 kg/ha in the 1989–1990 survey.

While multiple factors might have contributed to the collapse of the lake's cichlids, the major factor in their decline was most certainly the introduction of the much larger and highly predatory Nile perch *(Lates niloticus)*. These fish can grow to 2 meters (6.5 ft) in length and weigh as much as 200 kg (440 lbs), dwarfing the lake's native cichlids even as young fish. They were first introduced into Lake Victoria sometime in the 1950s, with several subsequent releases through the 1960s. The same historical catch data that shows the decline of the lake's cichlids also shows the rise to dominance of the Nile perch. In Uganda, Nile perch made up just 0.4 percent of the catch of bottom trawl surveys in 1966. Initially restricted to the northern part of the lake in Uganda and Kenya, their populations steadily grew until they exploded beginning around 1980. The catch rate of Nile perch increased by 700% from 0.5 kg/h at the end of the 1960s to 3.5 kg/h in 1981. From 1981 to 1985, catch rates increased by more than 1600%, from 3.5 kg/h to 234.7 kg/h. Surveys from Kenya found the biomass of Nile perch exceeded that of all other fish species between 1977 and 1981, just prior to the disappearance of nearly all of the cichlids in the northern part of the lake. The same scenario played out on the Tanzanian half of the lake just a few years later. In this period, Lake Victoria rapidly switched from a highly species-diverse ecosystem dominated primarily by haplochromine cichlids to a much less diverse system dominated by a single species. As many as 200 of the 500 or so endemic cichlids of the lake may now be extinct, but the huge size of Lake Victoria and limited detailed knowledge of many of its species make definite determinations extremely difficult. What is certain is that the ecosystem within the lake has experienced a dramatic and permanent change, with a huge loss of biodiversity as a result. Eutrophication of the lake has also become an issue as human populations around Lake Victoria grow. Beginning as early as the 1960s, the loss of oxygen in Lake Victoria's waters has dramatically changed the makeup of microorganisms and water clarity. This may have been a factor in the cichlids' decline, although many believe that eutrophication was likely only worsened by the breakdown of the lake's once complex species interactions.

What exists now in Lake Victoria is an entirely different ecosystem, driven by humans' poor decisions. However, all may not be lost for many of the lake's cichlids. While the Nile perch continues to be the predominant fish in the lake, some species of cichlids are recovering, and their ability to diversify, which drove their initial radiation into hundreds of species, is helping them to survive in the new lake environment. Researchers have recorded known species changing their preferred habitats and food sources and even showing physiological changes. For example, one species, *Haplochromis tanaos,* has adapted to the lake's lower light levels by changing the makeup of its retinas. These fish now have fewer blue-light sensitive cones and more red-green-sensitive cones, allowing them to better see in the wavelengths that now dominate their habitat. Another species has adapted to the lower oxygen conditions. Researchers have documented a 70% increase in the gill surface of *Haplochromis pyrrhocephalus* over members of the same species caught in the 1970s. Both of these fish are clear examples of just how far our impact reaches. Not only are we causing the loss of many species, but our actions are having an enormous influence on the ones that remain resulting in dramatic change throughout the world's environments.

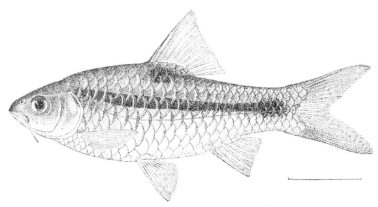

Fig. 5. – Barbodes hemictenus. new species. Type.

One of the Lake Lanao Barb Fish's Philippine relatives, *Barbodes hemictenus*.

Barb Fish of Lake Lanao
(Barbodes)

While the true extent of species loss in Lake Victoria is still not fully understood, there are other lakes where the extent of species loss is clearer. One such lake is the Philippine lake of Lanao. Lanao is the second-largest lake in the Philippines and one of only 20 ancient lakes in the world that have persisted for a million years or more. This 5 million-year-old lake system, a vital fishery for the surrounding human population, was once home to at least 18 endemic species of the minnow and carp family (Cyprinidae) belonging to the genus *Barbodes*. These were joined by as many as 20 other members of the family that reside in the lake.

The members of *Barbodes,* also known as barb fish, are small fish around 10–13.5 cm (4–5 in) in length. They primarily inhabit shallow waters with abundant aquatic vegetation, where they feed on algae and plankton. The origin of Lake Lanao's cyprinids is still being debated. It was once thought that they were an example of an extremely rapid speciation lasting less than 10,000 years due to an incorrect dating of the age of Lake Lanao. Later analysis of the lake's age showed that it was in fact extremely old, and genetic data puts the group's origin between 90,000 and 2 million years ago. There is little detailed population data on most of the lake's cyprinids, and, like Lake Victoria, populations can only be surmised from catch data from the fishing industry. Data shows that there was once a thriving population of cyprinid fishes that rapidly declined in just several decades. Catch data from 1963–1964 shows more than 980,000 kg of cyprinid fish caught in that year; by 1991, this had fallen to just 22,000 kg.

Out of the 18 members of *Barbodes* from Lake Lanao, 15 were listed as extinct by the IUCN in 2020. *Barbodes flavifuscus, Barbodes pachycheilus, Barbodes lanaoensis, Barbodes disa, Barbodes resinus,* and *Barbodes palata* were all last recorded in 1964. *Barbodes truncatulus* in 1973. *Barbodes herrei* in 1974.

Barbodes clemensi was last recorded in 1975 and is thought to have gone extinct within several years of that date, along with *Barbodes palaemophagus,* also missing since 1975. *Barbodes tras* was last seen in 1976. *Barbodes katolo* declined by 85% from 1974–1977 and hasn't been recorded since 1977, along with *Barbodes manalak,* also not recorded since 1977. Rounding out the list, *Barbodes amarus* was last recorded in 1982, and *Barbodes baoulan* was last seen in 1991.

There are two species listed as critically endangered and possibly extinct: *Barbodes lindog* and *Barbodes sirang. B. sirang* was once one of the most plentiful species in Lake Lanao, accounting for as much as half of the total fish catch in the lake. In the 1970s, more than 400 metric tons of these fish were caught every year. By the early 1990s, they made up only 9% of the total fish catch. The last official record of the species was in 2007, but there are reports of sightings as late as 2016. *B. lindog* was also once plentiful but saw its population rapidly collapse by 77% in a single year from 1973 to 1974. By the 1990s, surveys were unable to locate the species, but some were found in catches brought to market in 2008. However, an extensive year-long survey of markets all around the lake conducted in 2016 failed to find any members of the species, and while it is possible that some members of *B. lindog* remain, it is unlikely that they will be able to recover. In recent years, only one of the original 18 species, *Barbodes tumba,* has been found in significant numbers. Many of these observations have been outside of Lake Lanao. Fortunately, it is reported to have a stable population within the outlet of Lanao in the Angus River. Listed as vulnerable, catch data for *Barbodes tumba* within the lake shows that while the species still exists, populations are likely a fraction of what they once were. The catch volume for this species in 2008 was only .05% of what it was in the early 1990s.

So what is happening within the lake that is causing this rash of extinctions? Unlike the case of Lake Victoria, the causes of species loss and decline in Lake Lanao are more complex, but they do have some similarities. The most prominent of these is the introduction of non-native species. Lake Lanao has a long history of species introductions going back as far as 1915. While numerous species were introduced (intentionally or accidentally) throughout the years, there are two specifically cited as contributors to the extinction of the lake's barb fish species. The first of these introductions came in the early 1960s with the introduction of a species in the gobi family called *Glossogobius giuris.* These predatory fish are likely responsible for the loss of the six species of *Barbodes* that were last recorded in the early 1960s. Introduced in the 1970s, the snakehead gudgeon *(Giuris margaritaceus)* has now become the dominant species of fish in Lake Lanao by predating and outcompeting not only the lake's cyprinids but many of its other species.

Other contributors to the barb fish extinctions largely parallel the threats to aquatic ecosystems throughout the world. In so many waters, overfishing and poor fishing practices have severe impacts on fish populations, and this has been true of Lake Lanao as well. The overexploitation of the entire Lake Lanao fishery includes not only unsustainable fishing practices but also destructive practices such as dynamite fishing. Factors such as these have plagued the lake for decades and certainly have played a part, not only in the extinction of many of the lake's cyprinid species, but also in the decline of the total biomass of all species in the lake. Multiple other threats also likely contributed to the loss of Lake Lanao's barb fish. These include the construction of hydroelectric dams and the extraction of water for industrial and agricultural use. Combined, these have severely impacted lake levels and, as a result, have had profound effects on the barb fish's preferred shallow water habitats. Illegal logging and pollution also conspire to foul the waters through the introduction of increased sediments and harmful substances. Whatever specific pressures ultimately combined to wipe out Lake Lanao's barb fish, it is abundantly clear that the tragic loss of so many species is a man-made disaster.

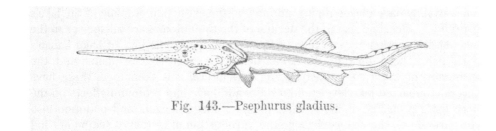

Fig. 143.—Psephurus gladius.

Chinese Paddlefish
(Psephurus gladius)

While the human-caused loss of any species is tragic, I find it even more so when a species that has stood the test of time for far longer than the history of the human race, in this case as much as 50 times longer, is finally relegated to geologic history due to our actions. This is the case with the Chinese paddlefish. One of only two members of the paddlefish family (Polyodontidae) to survive into modern times, it and its closest living relative, the Mississippi paddlefish *(Polyodon spathula)*, evolved from a common ancestor some 100 million years ago, when the two species were likely isolated from each other with the creation of the Atlantic Ocean during the Cretaceous Period. Sadly, these fish, so ancient that they spent millions of years avoiding predation by dinosaurs, eventually outliving them, and surviving the last great extinction event 66 million years ago, met a force greater than a cosmic impactor: humans.

These paddlefish were recently native to the great Yangtze River system in China and its associated lakes, from its upper reaches all the way to the China Sea. Historically, they inhabited the Yellow River and the Yellow Sea as well. Very little is known of their ecology, but they were believed to be migratory and anadromous, meaning they utilized some saltwater habitats during their lives, similar to the better-known salmon. These paddlefish grew to enormous sizes, and they were one of the largest freshwater fish known. They could reach lengths of 7 meters (23 ft) and weights of 450 kg (992 lbs) or more. Unlike their plankton-feeding relatives in the Mississippi, the Chinese paddlefish was a piscivore feeding on a variety of other fish, crabs, and crayfish. While the details of their reproduction are hazy, they migrated between the mouth of the river and the upper reaches for spawning during the spring between March and April. Out of breeding season, adults typically lived in the upper reaches of the river, while juveniles and younger paddlefish inhabited the lower stretches and the tidal beaches of the Yangtze.

Despite being known to the Chinese since antiquity, they were not formally described until 1862. The extent of historical populations is not known, but it's believed that they were not uncommon. As the population around the river grew, so did fishing for not only paddlefish but all species of fish in the Yangtze.

Somewhere around 25 tons of paddlefish were taken out of the Yangtze each year throughout the 1970s. By the 1980s, it was clear that the population of paddlefish was in severe decline. The Chinese government enacted protections in 1983, but despite these protections, the decline continued, and the last official record of the Chinese paddlefish came in 2003. From 2006–2008, an acoustic and netting survey was conducted on a 500-km stretch of the Yangtze in an attempt to locate any remaining paddlefish. Although several acoustic hits suggest that paddlefish may have been present, the survey was unable to capture any individuals.

A more extensive basin-wide survey, the first in more than 40 years, including important tributaries to the Yangtze and both the associated lakes of Dongting and Poyang, ran from 2017–2018. Extensive netting was undertaken, covering the entire basin a total of eight times. Despite recording 332 species of fish, representing 70–80% of the river's entire known fish fauna, not a single paddlefish was recorded. Based on this effort and the lack of confirmed sightings of the paddlefish in the preceding decade, the research team concluded that the paddlefish was now extinct. Statistical analysis of known paddlefish sightings allowed the team to determine that the paddlefish were likely functionally extinct as far back as 1993, and the last members of the species disappeared between 2005 and 2010. The IUCN declared the Yangtze paddlefish extinct in 2022.

Two main impacts conspired to end the extremely long history of this species. Certainly, unregulated and unsustainable fishing practices depleted the populations of these large and slow-maturing creatures. While this uncontrolled fishing was still ongoing, the construction of the Gezhouba dam in 1981 blocked the paddlefish's migration route. With no way for the paddlefish to circumvent the dam, the population and habitat were severely fragmented. While some breeding was known to have taken place after the dam's construction, access to historical spawning grounds was cut off for much of the population. No more than several dozen paddlefish were recorded below the dam after its construction, and by the early 1990s, this had fallen to less than 10. The paddlefish's habitat was further fragmented with the completion of the world's largest dam, the Three Gorges Dam, in 2006. Currently, 157 large dams and more than 1000 moderately sized dams block river flows through the Yangtze basin. In total, there are more than 50,000 dams in the basin. In addition to the impact of fishing and dam construction, pollution from industrial, agricultural, and urban sources has plagued the Yangtze basin for decades. It is likely that these severe pollution problems also played a part in the paddlefish's decline.

Despite the protections that came in 1983, the die was already cast for the paddlefish. While they were no longer fished, the Gezhouba dam, built without fish ladders, had already entirely blocked the fish's migration routes. Captive breeding proved entirely unsuccessful, and with little to no replacement in the population, it was only a matter of time before the wild population succumbed. Realizing the desperate situation, a rescue plan was formed in 2005, but by this time, it was already too late. Numerous other species of fish in the Yangtze basin may be facing a similar fate, and a lack of regular surveys in the basin and sparse knowledge of the status of threatened species in the river continue to make conservation efforts difficult.

The loss of the paddlefish serves to demonstrate two things. First, humans can be a fantastically destructive force, even for a species that has managed to survive for countless generations. We should not assume any species is safe from our actions. Second, inaction when we know a species is in decline can have devastating effects. In this case, no thought was given to the impact of dam construction on the already declining paddlefish (or any other species, for that matter). After construction, decades passed before serious action was considered. Humans could go a long way in limiting biodiversity loss by first considering the impacts of our choices and acting quickly and effectively when we identify a problem. Too often, we are slow to act until it's too late, and unfortunately, examples abound. If different decisions were made, it is possible that one of the world's oldest species would still exist.

The related and critically endangered Devil's Hole Pupfish *(Cyprinodon diabolis)* that exist only in a single small thermal pool in the Nevada desert.

North American Pupfish
(Cyprinodon)

The 120 species of the family Cyprinodontidae, or pupfish, can be found throughout the world. Pupfish are known for their adaptability and high tolerance to extremes of salinity and temperature (some above 40°C or more than 104°F). This is especially true for those of the genus *Cyprinodon* that are found primarily through the Southwest United States, Mexico, and the Caribbean, most with limited to extremely limited ranges. There are a few species that have wider ranges, in particular the sheepshead minnow *(C. variegatus)*, which can be found as far north as Massachusetts in the U.S. and as far south as the Yucatán Peninsula. While wide-ranging species like *C. variegatus* are not currently under threat, the vast majority of the species in *Cyprinodon* are. Out of the 49 currently known species of the genus, 32 (65%) are threatened with extinction, with 20 of these being endangered or critically endangered. Six of the 49 are already extinct or extinct in the wild.

Helping them to survive in marginal and very restrictive habitats is their small size. The largest members of the genus reach a maximum of 9 cm (3.5 in), and many species are as small as 3-5 cm (2–3 in). They also display generally omnivorous feeding habits, and many species survive on whatever is most abundant in their environment. This includes algae, bacteria, detritus such as the scales of other fish, insect larvae, and small crustaceans. The evolutionary history of these petite and often colorful fish continues to be somewhat of a mystery. 30 members of the genus are from the desert southwest of North America and occur in often isolated and remote waterways, begging the question of just how their pupfish ancestors arrived at these locations in the first place. The major groups of *Cyprinodon* arose and diversified beginning around 7-9 million years ago, with the first of the isolated desert species originating 3-5 million years ago and some emerging as little as 250,000–500,000 years ago.

While the relationships between species of the genus are still not well understood, the geologic history of North America does give an idea of how these species became so isolated. Ancient lakes and river courses in the U.S. and Mexico once connected many of the now isolated pupfish habitats. When these waters receded as climatic changes made this part of North America drier and as tectonic shifts changed and blocked water flows, today's *Cyprinodon's* ancestors were trapped in isolated desert waterways and spring systems. These populations eventually became dozens of unique species adapted to those highly specific environments, demonstrating life's amazing ability to persist even in extremely limited habitats.

One of these isolated spring systems is located in the southwest part of the state of Nuevo León, Mexico, and was once home to most of the now extinct species of *Cyprinodon*. Each inhabiting their own spring within the system, five unique species of pupfish once resided here. Occupying the extremely small habitat of Charco La Palma Spring, the La Palma pupfish *(Cyprinodon longidorsalis)* was first discovered in 1984. At the time of discovery, the estimated population was just 50 to 70 individuals within a space of just 10 square meters (110 square feet), perhaps the smallest habitat of any known vertebrate. Despite the limitations, scientists found a small but healthy habitat full of clear water and abundant aquatic plants. During the next several years, conditions within the fish's home deteriorated. Water levels dropped, and the pupfish's spring began to disappear. By 1994, there was almost no water left, and the pupfish were gone. This species is now extinct in the wild, with some individuals surviving in captivity.

Also discovered in 1984, the Charco Azul pupfish *(Cyprinodon inmemoriam)* was already in dire trouble by the time it was first seen. Their home spring, Ojo La Trinidad, had already been reduced by half its historic size, to just 5000 square meters (1.2 acres), and the water quality had deteriorated greatly. Just one month after their discovery, their home had shrunk to just 1000 square meters. By 1985, the spring had dried up completely, resulting in the death of all the species that once lived there, including the pupfish. This species is now entirely extinct.

The Charco Palma pupfish *(Cyprinodon veronicae)* was native to the Ojo de Agua spring in Charco Azul. Discovered the same year as the previous species, described as "brilliantly colored and pugnacious," they had a robust population numbering in the thousands when their spring home was first explored. Even though it appeared that the spring had once covered a larger area, a healthy system of clear pools and a small creek were still present. This situation did not last, however and water levels began to drop, cutting off flow to the spring's small creek by 1985. By 1988, the once-clear waters were increasingly turbid. By 1993, the water had fallen even more and only two pools remained with any water, but the pupfish were still present at the time. By 1997, the entire spring had dried up. While members of the species survive in captivity, it is certain that with the complete destruction of their only known habitat, they are extinct in the wild.

Cyprinodon alvarezi, also known as the Perrito de Potosi, was first discovered in 1961 in its namesake spring of Ojo de Potosi. Like its relatives, the Charco Palma pupfish, it had a robust population. Between 10,000 and 12,000 of the Potosi pupfish could originally be found in their 10,000 square meter (2.5 acre) home. While the environment of Potosi Spring was relatively stable from 1961 through 1983, its endemic fish species were still under threat. The introduction of non-native largemouth bass *(Micropterus salmoides)* sometime prior to 1971 resulted in severe declines in native species in the spring. While *C. alvarezi* persisted despite heavy predation, water levels began to fall dramatically in 1984, with a 90% reduction in the spring's area that year alone. The spring recovered some in later years, but not enough to sustain the Perrito de Potosi. The last sighting of them in the wild was in 1994. They are now extinct in the wild, but still exist in captivity. Also native to this spring, was another pupfish in the genus *Megupsilon,* who is also now extinct. The Catarina pupfish *(Megupsilon aporus)* once had similar populations to the Perrito de Potosi and ultimately suffered a similar fate; however, unlike the Perrito de Potosi, no individuals of the Catarina pupfish still survive.

All of these extinctions ultimately had a common cause. While the Perrito de Potosi had the added issue of an introduced non-native predator, all eventually succumbed to the complete or near-complete destruction of their habitats due to the over-extraction of groundwater for agricultural and domestic use. This extraction cut off the vital source of water that supported the habitats of not only these fish but also many other plant and animal species. Here and around the world, the unsustainable use of groundwater is causing extinctions of not only animals but entire ecosystems and the biodiversity that they support. Especially important in arid environments, groundwater springs may be the only reliable water source for animals of all types, and their destruction can have immediate and permanent impacts on the biodiversity of an entire region. Four of the six critically endangered pupfish listed by the IUCN are threatened due to over-extraction of the water they need to live.

The Santa Cruz pupfish *(Cyprinodon arcuatus)* had by far the widest range of any of the now extinct members of the genus. They inhabited Monkey Spring in Arizona as well as, historically, parts of the upper Santa Cruz river basin in the United States and Mexico. Known as far back as the 1800s, the species was typically recorded as *C. macularius* in early collections. In 2002, further study determined that they were a related but unique species. The true extent of their original range and population is not known, but human-caused changes in the river system as far back as the 1890s had restricted them to Monkey Spring and its associated marsh. Modifications made to water courses in the area disrupted the marsh and led to its draining, but the species remained plentiful in the confines of the spring itself until 1968. Unfortunately, at this time, largemouth bass were introduced into the spring, and the pupfish population rapidly diminished. By 1969, the pupfish were extinct in the wild, with some still surviving in captivity. In 1971, the captive stock failed, and these strikingly pretty and colorful fish were no more.

Despite the fact that these species had been able to survive in extremely limited habitats for hundreds of thousands to millions of years, they were no match for the destructive impact of humans. These cases clearly demonstrate the impact of our careless use of water resources and our thoughtless actions when it comes to modifying natural water systems by not only structural changes but also by introduction. These species are just a few of the thousands impacted in this way. While these issues are still severe, especially in developing countries, there is hope that we are beginning to understand that preserving and restoring natural water systems is critical to our survival as much as it is to other species.

Whitefishes
(Coregonus)

Fish of the salmon family (Salmonidae) are one of the most threatened groups of fish on the planet. Of the 154 species in the family, more than half are threatened with extinction or are already extinct, including 39 species that are endangered or critically endangered and 15 species that are extinct or extinct in the wild. Numerous factors make up the threat to salmonids. Members of the family are valuable food sources and are prone to overexploitation. Some species transition between salt and freshwater, while others inhabit brackish waters or are restricted only to freshwater rivers and lakes. Despite their range of habitats, salmonids are particularly sensitive to water quality and have low tolerance for pollutants and low oxygen levels. The introduction of non-natives into their environments also continues to threaten numerous species. While all of the salmonids have faced challenges, the whitefish have been the most impacted, with nine species of the genus suffering extinction in the last 100 years, both in Europe and North America.

Six of the nine extinct whitefish species were once found in Europe, with the majority being found in large mountain lakes. One species, however, the houting *(Coregonus oxyrinchus)*, lived in the brackish estuaries near the North Atlantic coast, particularly in the Rhine, Schelde, and Meuse river drainages, and at one time even in southern England. The last sighting of this once-common fish was in 1940 in the Rhine River. Pollution and overfishing appear to be the primary causes of their disappearance, but there is controversy surrounding this fish and its status. While still listed as extinct by the IUCN, some scientists believe that a population of whitefish from Denmark is *Coregonus oxyrinchus,* while others believe these fish to be simply a variant of the closely related maraena whitefish *(Coregonus maraena)*. The struggle to determine what constitutes a separate species still continues. Hopefully, genetic testing can clear up the confusion. Even in the preferred outcome of this being a case of local extinction (as is the case with many salmonids around the world, especially in parts of the U.S. Pacific Coast), the loss of a once common species over such a large area demonstrates the negative impact humans are having on Europe's salmonid species. The fate of other species, however, is much more certain.

Numerous lakes in the European Alps have seen the loss of whitefish species endemic to them, and lakes in this region have seen a long history of human-caused impacts going all the way back to ancient times. Sediment cores from some of Europe's lakes show evidence of past eutrophication caused by the influx of sediment into the lakes as a result of deforestation by the Romans. In modern times, the impacts have only increased. One of Europe's largest lakes, Lake Geneva on the border of France and Switzerland, once provided a thriving fishery. Over-exploitation led to the collapse of two species of whitefish, the féra *(Coregonus fera)* and the gravenche *(Coregonus hiemalis).* By the dawn of the 20th century, the population of both fish species was rapidly declining, especially since the introduction of huge drift net operations in 1896. At the same time, other

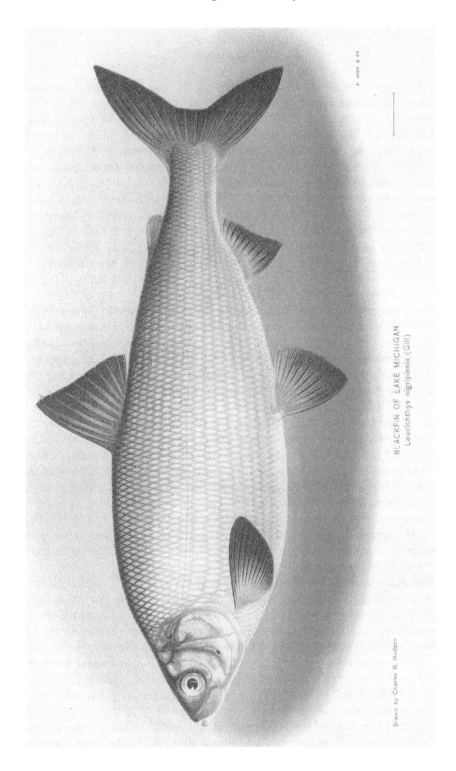

BLACKFIN OF LAKE MICHIGAN
Leucichthys nigripinnis (Gill)

Drawn by Charles B. Hudson

whitefish species were introduced into Lake Geneva in an attempt to bolster fish numbers. By the 1920s, both species were extinct as a result of not only overfishing but also competition and hybridization with non-native whitefish species.

The two species of Lake Geneva were not the first species of the genus lost in modern times. Only described in 1885, *Coregonus restrictus* of Morat Lake in Switzerland was last seen just 5 years later, in 1890. Surveys in the 1950s found no whitefish of any species in the lake, and it is believed that eutrophication prior to the 1950s was responsible for the species' disappearance. In fact, increased levels of sediment and pollution plagued many lakes in the region for decades, most notably from the 1960s into the 1980s, causing extensive eutrophication.

Once supporting a commercial fishery as late as the 1960s, the Lake Constance whitefish *(Coregonus gutturosus)* rapidly declined into extinction in the 1970s. Peaking in 1979, eutrophication decreased oxygen levels in the lake so much that the whitefish's eggs could no longer develop, ending reproduction entirely. *Coregonus bezola,* of the French lake of Bourget, also disappeared. Although it was last officially documented in the late 1800s, fishermen reported that it survived until the 1960s. The cause of this fish's extinction is not known, but the timing of their loss coincides with eutrophication problems elsewhere.

Three species of the genus have disappeared in North America, all from the Great Lakes. The blackfin cisco *(Coregonus nigripinnis)* (shown) was once found throughout the Great Lakes of Michigan, Huron, Ontario, and Superior. They were extirpated from Lake Huron by 1923 and were entirely extinct by the 1960s, with the last known individual caught in Lake Michigan in 1969. The longjaw cisco *(Coregonus alpenae)* was common in Lake Michigan and Lake Huron but rare in Lake Erie. Populations of these fish had already seen severe declines by the early 1900s. They were gone from Lake Erie by 1957 and from Lake Michigan just ten years later. The last of the species was caught in Lake Huron in 1975. The third species, the deepwater cisco *(Coregonus johannae),* saw similar declines, and like the longjaw, their populations were in severe decline by the early 1900s. Also native to Lake Michigan and Lake Huron, they were last seen in 1951 and 1952, respectively.

The declines and eventual extinctions of all three of these species can be attributed to the same set of causes. All three were valuable in the Great Lakes fisheries of the 19th century. Over the decades, unrestricted fishing depleted these and many other fish stocks throughout the Great Lakes. Already in a depleted state or extirpated from their native lakes, the remaining whitefish then came under attack by the non-native sea lamprey *(Petromyzon marinus),* which became established in all the lakes by the 1940s. This parasitic species infiltrated the Great Lakes via the St. Lawrence Seaway, which was constructed to connect the Great Lakes and the Atlantic Ocean. First appearing in Lake Ontario in 1835, the natural barrier of Niagara Falls stopped their progression for a time until improvements in the Welland Canal, which bypasses the falls, allowed them to move farther inland. By 1921, the lampreys were in Lake Erie, and by the 1930s, they had spread to Michigan and Huron. With no natural predators and a high reproductive rate, the sea lamprey populations exploded, precipitating the decline of many of the Great Lakes fishes. As populations of their own species bottomed out, what remained of the lakes' now extinct whitefish disappeared through hybridization by mating with other whitefish species.

New Zealand Grayling
(Prototroctes oxyrhynchus)

For millennia, seasonal runs of anadromous fish returning from the sea to spawn have been a vital part of native communities around the world. These food sources were so important that many cultures incorporated them into their mythologies and religions. Much like many of the once famous and sustaining salmon runs of the Pacific Northwest of North America, the New Zealand grayling was an important part of the many species of anadromous fish the Māori utilized. Called graylings by Europeans, who thought they looked like the grayling from Europe, the Māori called them upokororo, among several other names. They were once the most common and widespread species of fish throughout New Zealand, and they exemplify the cost of species loss not only in terms of biodiversity but the loss of cultural heritage.

Not related to the graylings of the Northern Hemisphere, the New Zealand grayling is related to the smelts of the family Retropinnidae, along with its closest relative, the Australian grayling *(Prototroctes maraena)*. These lovely and subtlety colored silvery fish could once be found in shoals numbering in the thousands on their midsummer migrations up New Zealand's rivers. Primarily thought to feed on algae, they may also have eaten a variety of small insects. They were typically 25-30 cm (10-12 in) in length, but have been reported to grow as large as 50 cm (20 in). Details of their full lifecycle are not known, but like other anadromous fish, they migrated between the ocean and freshwater environments to breed.

Prior to the 1860s, the upokororo was common and abundant in many of New Zealand's rivers and streams on both the North and South islands. They were so common, in fact, that they were often caught and used to cover gardens as fertilizer. Their immense shoals could be so dense that they were known to shut down the water wheels of mills along the rivers. Beginning in the 1870s, there were signs of decline in some rivers, while others still maintained large shoals in the thousands. By the late 1870s, it was clear that the population was undergoing a severe contraction. In the three years between 1875 and 1878, the population of the Maitai River alone dropped to almost nothing. By the turn of the century, they were absent from many of the rivers where they were once common, and now they were isolated to only a handful of rivers in the North Island and just one in the South. The last known graylings were caught in the North Island in 1923 (though there may have been sightings as late as the 1950s). In 1953, the New Zealand government enacted protections for the species, but this came far too late to have any impact.

The reasons for a species' extinction are not always straightforward, and the case of the New Zealand grayling certainly is not. However, new theories about the loss of these fish may help us save other species. Like most of the species we have seen, humans were probably ultimately to blame for the species' disappearance. The timing of their collapse coincides with increased pressures from the expansion of European colonization of New Zealand, and there are several specific factors for which Europeans were responsible. One factor was the

RETROPINNA OPOKORORO. Hector.

massive amount of land use change surrounding the grayling's freshwater habitats. Previously, we have looked at the effects of deforestation on water quality and water temperature, and this may have greatly impacted the grayling's ability to utilize waterways. Another factor was the introduction of non-native trout into the waters of New Zealand beginning in the 1870s. Increased fishing may have also played a part in diminishing the grayling's numbers.

These are all common reasons for species declines, but in the case of the grayling, it was not clear how these factors impacted populations found in remote rivers that had not experienced degradation or been introduced to non-native trout. How could either of these factors affect fish not exposed to them? Here, an understanding of the species' behavior helps to explain how the entire species was impacted and may give insights into declines seen in other animals. Many anadromous fish species exhibit a behavior called natal-homing. This means they return to the rivers where they were born. For these species, effects on one particular river would only affect the population native to that river. If the graylings followed this behavior, it seems unlikely that they would have seen population drops in remote, pristine rivers. Researchers studying the grayling's demise believe they know why they disappeared all across their range. They did not return exclusively to their natal rivers but, when returning from the ocean, would ascend whatever river they happened to come upon. In time, this exposed the entire population to the effects of deforestation and competition with non-native trout.

This seems unlikely to have such a severe impact, but researchers have been able to show why this is so devastating. The rivers that are no longer suitable for reproduction and/or have high rates of predation are called sinks. As the population of fish cycles through these sinks, reproduction and survival of adults decrease, eventually to a point where the species cannot be maintained. Modeling of the grayling populations without these sink rivers shows that the species could have lost as much as 30% of its population each year with no ill effects. However, if just 5% of the rivers they utilized were sinks, they could only sustain a 5% loss of population each year. It is likely that the existence of too many sink rivers and too large a loss of population each year drove the rapid decline of the species. Even with some rivers not impacted directly, the species had little chance of survival.

Often, our view of species extinction and a species' needs is too simplistic. We want to associate a direct cause with a direct effect, but seeing the whole picture is vitally important to stem the tide of species loss. There is no one-size-fits-all approach. In the case of the grayling, strict protections of pristine rivers (something that anyone would assume would have a positive benefit) would have done little to save the species. It's possible that restoration of rivers and fishing bans may have been able to save the fish. The unfortunate extinction of the grayling demonstrates how knowledge about what a species needs for survival is vitally important. As we move forward with ever greater challenges, and as we must decide what to protect and what to restore, our understanding of what habitats species use and how they use them must guide our decisions..

9
Mammals (Mammalia)

Whether it's the giant panda, tigers, our ape cousins, or any number of high-profile species, mammals are often foremost in our thoughts when it comes to saving species. I certainly believe this is because we relate to them to a greater degree because they are the most like us. Our attraction to our fellow mammals is apparent. We keep 137 million dogs and cats as pets in the U.S. alone. Clearly, we feel a kinship with animals that are warm and fuzzy. Beyond the comforting aspect of a warm, furry body near us, we are attracted to our fellow mammals because we can see many things in them that we see in ourselves. Many mammals show a high degree of intelligence, form close and caring attachments to their young, and can display a range of emotions that we can recognize. Our closest relatives in the animal kingdom, the great apes, can often seem so very much like us. More than any other group of animals, mammals can often evoke compassion for the plight of the natural world. "Heartless" is the human who can look into the eyes of a baby orca curiously approaching your boat or an orangutan trying to defend its home from loggers and not feel the urge to protect these animals.

Many may be surprised at just how ancient the origins of mammals are. Our distant "true" mammal ancestors date back at least 178 million years and could go back more than 200 million years, but some mammal traits began to appear in our proto-mammalian ancestors as much as 300 million years ago. While dinosaurs were dominating the world, mammals were quietly going about their business, diversifying to a surprising extent. Within several million years of their emergence, some were showing adaptations once thought to have arisen only recently. These included webbed feet, like we see in modern beavers; strong digging legs and claws, like those of the badger; and even the first known gliding mammals that date back 160 million years. While still relatively small-bodied in these early years, mammals were much more variable than the small, shrew-like animals we once thought them to be. Although scientists are not yet clear on the entire picture of early mammal evolution, the mass extinction 66 million years ago that wiped out the dinosaurs gave mammals the opportunity to become the dominant large life forms on the planet, spawning the ancestors of the animals we are so familiar with today and, of course, us as well.

Mammals in name are defined by how we rear our young, with all of them feeding on milk produced from the mother's mammary glands, but there are other defining characteristics. Mammals also have hair, although some have very little, are warm-blooded, and share a distinctive jaw structure and inner ear construction. The class of Mammalia is divided into 3 subclasses containing 27 separate orders. These subclasses divide mammals based on how their young come about. The most familiar to us would be the one of which we are a part, Eutheria, or the placental mammals. This includes all mammals that, like us, give birth to live young that are supported in the womb by a placenta. It currently consists of 19 orders, the four largest of which are Rodentia (40% of all mammals and include mice, rats, squirrels, porcupines, and beavers, etc.), Chiroptera (bats, 22% of all mammals), Eulipotyphla (shrews, moles, and hedgehogs, 8%), and Primates (monkeys, lemurs, and apes, also 8%). The second of these subclasses is Metatheria. It contains all of the marsupial mammals that bear young at a very early developmental stage and typically rear them in a pouch. This subclass consists of 7 orders, the most familiar of which are Diprotodontia, which includes Australia's kangaroos, wombats, wallabies, and koalas, and Didelphimorphia, which includes the opossums of the New World and North America's only marsupial, the Virginia opossum *(Didelphis virginiana).* The third subclass is Prototheria and includes species that have maybe the most surprising way for a mammal to bear young: they lay eggs. These egg-laying mammals are all members of a single order, Monotremata, the monotremes. This ancient order that harkens back to the early days of mammal evolution only consists of 5 living species: the enigmatic platypus *(Ornithorhynchus anatinus)* and 4 species of echidna, 1 in the genus *Tachyglossus* and 3 in the genus *Zaglossus.*

According to the American Society of Mammalogists' Mammal Diversity Database, there are currently (as of June 2023) 6544 described species of mammals that are currently alive on our planet. While not the most species-rich group of animals, on land they occupy a fantastically large range of the planet's ecosystems, surviving above the Arctic Circle, through temperate and tropical regions, and into the great heights of the world's mountain ranges. Marine mammals exist in all of the world's oceans, from pole to pole. The only significant absences in the world's habitats are on the remote oceanic islands, which were often nearly devoid of mammals, especially land mammals, until their introduction by humans. The vast majority of mammal species are small-bodied, but mammals exhibit an enormous size range. The world's smallest known mammal is the bumblebee bat *(Craseonycteris thonglongyai)* of Thailand, which measures just 29–33 mm (1.14–1.3 in) and weighs a mere 2 g (0.07 oz). The largest is the blue whale *(Balaenoptera musculus),* whose females average 27 meters (88.5 feet) long but can reach lengths of 33.5 meters or more than 109 feet. These enormous animals can weigh as much as 190,000 kg, or more than 410,000 lbs. That's more than 200 tons, or more than twice the weight of even the largest known dinosaurs, or 95 million times more massive than the bumblebee bat!

Mammals display an amazing amount of diverse adaptations, and the class is home to the fastest living land animal, the cheetah *(Acinonyx jubatus),* the largest living land animal, the African elephant *(Loxodonta africana)*, and the largest living animal ever, the aforementioned blue whale. Mammals have adapted to survive in some of the planet's harshest environments. Both the musk ox *(Ovibos moschatus)* and the Arctic wolf *(Canis lupus arctos)* that live in the Arctic climes of the Northern Hemisphere can tolerate temperatures lower than -46°C (-50° F). The dromedary camel *(Camelus dromedarius)* of Africa possesses a myriad of anatomical and physiological adaptations that allow these animals to tolerate the extreme heat of their desert home. They thrive in an environment that often exceeds 48°C (120°F) and can go without drinking for two weeks. The Bactrian camel of Mongolia *(Camelus bactrianus)* survives both the heat and the cold, living in an environment where temperatures range from -40°C to 40°C (-40°F to 104°F). Mammals have managed to master both the skies with more than 1,400 species of bats and the environments of the world's oceans with 90 species of whales and dolphins. Humans are arguably the most socially advanced of the mammals and likely possess the greatest level of intelligence (although intelligence in our case clearly doesn't necessarily equate to good sense), but in physical abilities we are bested by nearly every other member of our class. Humans, however, have not cornered the market on mammal intelligence. Both cetaceans (whales and dolphins) and our ape cousins are highly intelligent, have complex communication abilities, and the ability to engage in abstract thought. For example, both gorillas and chimpanzees can learn and communicate in human sign language, and dolphins have excellent planning and problem-solving skills.

While cetaceans are certainly highly intelligent creatures, their intelligence may not be the most impressive of their abilities. All whales and dolphins have numerous adaptations that have evolved for their aquatic lives. All of the animals in this group can dive to impressive depths and have complex mechanisms to regulate oxygen in their bodies, adaptations that they share with other deep diving mammals like pinnipeds (seals and sea lions). These deep-diving mammals can have blood volumes per mass four times greater than those of land animals, and they can have twice the hemoglobin concentration and 10 times the myoglobin concentration of humans. They can collapse their lungs to prevent gas exchange of nitrogen into their blood (the cause of "the bends" in human divers), and they have special mechanisms within their bodies to deal with the immense pressure of water at depth. Most of these animals can dive to several hundred meters without any issue, but others are deep dive specialists. Sperm whales *(Physeter macrocephalus)* routinely dive to 450–900 meters (1,500–3,000 feet) in their search for squid, but have been recorded diving at more than 2,000 meters (6,500 feet), holding their breath for more than an hour. But as impressive as this is, there is one species that can top even that.

The Cuvier's beaked whale *(Ziphius cavirostris)* may be the deepest diver of any mammal. In 2014, researchers published over 3700 hours of dive data for this little-studied species. They found that these whales typically dive to around 1,400 meters (4,600 feet), staying underwater for nearly 70 minutes at a time. However, they also recorded a dive that would have been thought impossible for an air-breathing animal to make. One individual dove to a depth of 2,992 meters (9,816 feet), staying down for 137.5 minutes—both records. To put into perspective how impressive this is, the pressure nearly 2 miles below is 400 times that at the surface, equivalent to more than 4,400 psi. What adaptations these whales have to dive so deep for so long are not known. While most deep-diving mammals operate at or below their Aerobic Dive Limit (the amount of time a diving mammal can stay submerged before producing lactic acid), beaked whales typically exceed this by a factor of two, and the record dive exceeded the whale's theoretical ADL by a factor of four. Clearly, we have a lot more to learn about these amazing animals, but the Cuvier's abilities are unquestionably impressive.

Many different animals have come up with varying ways of being able to operate in the dark. The typical solution is large, light-sensitive eyes, and there are many mammals that have excellent night vision. However, some mammals have developed a novel way of being able to see in even complete darkness. Just as surprising as this adaptation itself is that several very disparate groups of mammals use this same technique to navigate their worlds. It is certainly one of the most interesting of the adaptations that have evolved among the group, and a fantastic example of convergent evolution. While echolocation is not limited exclusively to mammals (there are two species of bird known to use it) there are many mammals that use it, including the familiar bats and cetaceans, but also several species of shrew and several of their relatives on Madagascar, the tenrec. There is even a primate that uses echolocation, the aye-aye *(Daubentonia madagascariensis)*, a species of nocturnal lemur also found on Madagascar. Even humans have the ability to a limited extent. This ability is most highly developed in the bats and cetaceans that echolocate.

When it comes to echolocating mammals, bats are probably many people's first thought. Not all bats use echolocation, but the vast majority (950+ species) do. Not only can they use it to navigate in complete darkness, they can track and capture prey as small as a mosquito in mid-flight using sound alone. The concept of echolocation (also called biosonar) is fairly straightforward. Just like in man-made sonar, a high-intensity sound is produced, which propagates away from the source and reflects off an object. The time it takes for this reflected sound to come back determines the distance. More than that, the different aspects of an object will reflect sound in slightly different ways. This will cause subtle differences in when the reflected sound arrives at the receiver in human devices or at a bat's ears. These subtle differences allow for a 3-dimensional reconstruction of an object.

Bats are shockingly good at echolocation and have multiple techniques they use to probe their surroundings. First off, bats are really loud, especially considering that most bats are quite small animals. They can produce calls as loud as 140 dB. By comparison, a jet at takeoff registers 120 dB! Most bats also use what is called "frequency modulation." Varying the frequency of their calls, typically ranging in the 20 kHz to 100 kHz range (human hearing maxes out at 20 kHz), allows them to better pick out the separate frequencies reflecting off objects, which creates less interference (the ultrasonic range of their calls is also why we don't hear how loud they are). It might be surprising that a bat's auditory system doesn't vary that much from those of a typical mammal, and they can tune in on specific frequencies much the same way we can pick out a particular instrument in a symphony, although they are, of course, much better at it. Bats have the ability to discern not only frequencies but also minute differences in the timing of arriving sound waves (called delay resolution). The better the delay resolution, the more clear the image. Bats put human sonar devices to shame in this regard. Studies done show that the big brown bat *(Eptesicus fuscus)* can easily discern reflected sound waves arriving just 0.4 milliseconds apart. At this resolution, they can tell the distance to an object within 0.07 mm or just two one-thousandths of an inch. At the limit of their abilities, their delay resolution can approach 10 nanoseconds. This ultra-fine ability to discern frequency and delay allows them to build a highly detailed 3D image of their surroundings. It's so fine that it's believed that they can even discern between different species of plants. Combining the frequency modulation, intensity, call frequency, direction, and even the projection width of their ultrasonic calls, bats can avoid obstacles and other bats, all while honing in on flying prey entirely by sound. So refined are the bat's abilities that the United States Navy has spent significant amounts of money researching them in an attempt to improve their own sonar systems.

Mammals are one of the best studied groups of animals next to birds, so their decline has been well documented. In the last 500 years, just over 100 species of mammal are thought to have gone extinct, according to the American Society of Mammalogists. Nearly 6,000 species have been evaluated for their risk of extinction. Of these, 776 species are listed by the IUCN as endangered or critically endangered, with another 557 listed as vulnerable. More than a quarter of all mammals are currently considered to be at risk of extinction. However, this data may not give a clear picture of how bad the situation is for mammals. It is estimated that for every species that has gone extinct, there are 10 that have seen serious declines in abundance. Even in species of low concern, ranges and populations are contracting. In an analysis of 177 different mammalian species for which detailed information is available, all lost 30% or more of their historical ranges, and more than 40% have seen severe population declines. If this data is representative of all mammals, it may only be a matter of time before we see a large increase in the number of species considered endangered or critically endangered. Our fellow primates are one of the most imperiled groups of mammals; 60% of the over 500 species are at risk of extinction, and 75% of primates have declining populations.

Declines in mammal populations have been observed throughout the world, but they are most severe on the continents of South America, Asia, and Africa, especially in the tropical regions of these continents. Some areas of the world are now nearly devoid of the mammal fauna they once had. For example, the Atlantic Forest biome in South America has lost 62% of its mammal abundance, and the Caatinga shrub forest of Brazil has lost 75%. Broad research encompassing the entirety of the Neotropics (the tropical regions from Mexico through Central and South America) has shown a significant drop in the prevalence of mammals throughout the region. Using occurrence data, the researchers constructed a "defaunation index" (DI) ranging from 0 (completely intact mammal communities) to 1 (complete absence of mammals). For the entirety of the Neotropics, 8 separate orders of mammals had a DI of 0.6 or above. In other words, two-thirds of these animal communities are absent at the levels they should be, and they include a wide range of animals, from rodents and rabbits to undulates, big cats, and primates. Other continents are seeing similar decreases. For example, as mentioned in Chapter 3, there has been a 59% decrease in mammal populations *within* protected areas in Africa in the last 40 years.

The causes of these dramatic declines vary. Disease, invasive species, and increased wildfires are all contributors, with climate change a looming but not yet primary threat. Currently the largest drivers worldwide of mammalian declines are habitat loss and hunting. Logging and agricultural use are the main reasons for habitat loss and are responsible for the largest threats to mammal species in much of tropical Asia, for example. Expansion of palm oil and other agriculture and legal and illegal logging are dramatically reducing the forests of many Asian nations, and the forests of Southeast Asia are disappearing at a rate of 1.6 million hectares (3.9 million acres) every year. Of course, land conversion and deforestation impact mammals everywhere, and the loss of suitable habitat will be an ever-increasing threat as climate change begins to significantly change the world's landscapes.

Illegal subsistence hunting, hunting for the illegal wildlife trade, and legally sanctioned overhunting are having devastating effects on mammal populations worldwide, although once again Asia, Africa, and South America are seeing the largest impacts. Hunting is having such a large impact that it is even changing the makeup of mammal populations on a continental scale. The same Neotropical study mentioned before found a dramatic decrease in the body mass distribution of mammals in the Neotropics, falling from 14 kg to just 4 kg, demonstrating the loss of large-bodied mammals in the region. Humans are continuing the ancient tradition of hunting the world's large fauna into extinction. In all of the world's tropics, hunting has caused a more than 40% decline in the range of mammals, and populations have declined by as much as 80%. The declines in recent decades in Africa are nearly entirely due to hunting, either for food or for the illegal wildlife trade. While hunting comes in multiple forms, certainly the most egregious is the illegal wildlife trade. The hunting and sale of the world's wildlife, valued at as much as 20 billion USD per year, has imperiled the survival of the world's elephants, rhinos, and big cats. While these species receive the majority of attention, the most trafficked mammal in the world is the pangolin, which is killed for its unique keratinized body scales for many of the same stupid reasons as rhino horn. Native to Asia and Africa, there are eight species of pangolin, all of which are threatened by the wildlife trade. It is estimated that between 1977 and 2014, more than 800,000 pangolins have been harvested for their scales, and pressure has only increased. In 2019 alone, 195,000 pangolins were killed for the wildlife trade.

While the largest threats to mammals currently are in South and Central America, Africa, and Asia, it's important to remember that North America and Europe have already experienced a mass defaunation of their mammals over the last several hundred years, with several species going extinct and many narrowly avoiding extinction. Protections through habitat preservation and strict hunting regulations and enforcement have allowed many of the species to recover, although nowhere near their original abundance. Some of the successes in North America and Europe may serve as a model for other countries seeking to preserve their wildlife. Unfortunately, despite some success in these parts of the world, it is becoming clear that not enough land is protected to ensure the survival of some of their most iconic species, and regulations may be moving in the wrong direction. The gray wolf *(Canis lupus)* in the United States is a prime example. Despite an extensive reintroduction effort spanning decades, the gray wolf lost federal protections in 2020. Since then, legal wolf hunts in numerous states have claimed hundreds of wolves. Protections were reinstated to some wolves by a 2022 court order, but the situation remains tenuous. Predators are essential to restoring and maintaining natural landscapes, but unfortunately, long-held prejudices against wolves and other predators throughout the world persist, and the centuries-old persecution of predators continues today.

Several notable mammal extinctions occurred early in the modern period, including the extinction of the Aurochs *(Bos primigenius)* of Europe, the large ancient species of cattle that gave rise to present-day domestic cattle. Once ranging from Asia to Europe and North Africa, habitat loss and hunting had restricted them to parts of Eastern Europe by the 13th century. By 1564, the population had been reduced to only 38 known animals, and the last known living Aurochs died in 1627 in the Jaktorów Forest of Poland.

On the other side of the world, an entire family of island-dwelling shrews once lived in the West Indies. The family Nesophontidae once consisted of at least six species of shrews, all in the genus *Nesophontes.* Sub-fossil evidence suggests that they all survived until the arrival of Europeans, when they were most likely wiped out by the introduction of rats. The West Indies were also home to several species in the primate family, with at least one species that may have survived into modern times. The Jamaican monkey *(Xenothrix mcgregori)* was a slow-moving, sloth-like monkey that may have survived as late as the 1700s. Humans appear to be the primary cause of their extinction as well.

Rodents have seen the greatest number of extinctions of any group of mammals in the last 500 years. There are 38 species listed as extinct on the IUCN Red List, with the vast majority being island endemics. Of these, 14 are from the islands of the Caribbean; 12 are from Australia; 3 are from the Galápagos Islands; 2 are from Christmas Island; and 1 is from Indonesia. In nearly all cases, the human-facilitated introduction of non-native species was the primary cause of, or at the very least, a significant contributor to, the extinction of these island species. For many of these species, particularly those of the Caribbean, the introduction of European species of rats was catastrophic to populations of native rodents. On the island continent of Australia, feral cats were widespread across the country by the 1890s and proceeded to have a devastating effect on native rodents there, as well as many other species.

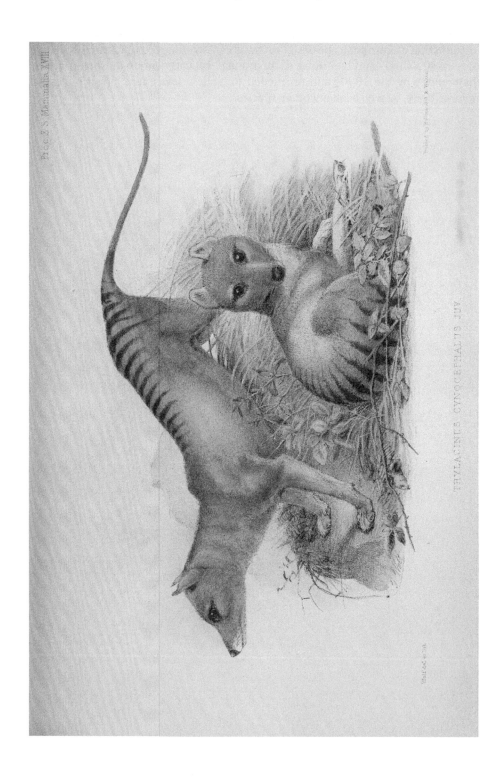

Thylacine
(Thylacinus cynocephalus)

We'll begin our look at mammals with what I believe is one of the most fascinating animals lost in recent history, the thylacine. Also called the Tasmanian tiger or the Tasmanian wolf, the thylacine was neither. It was actually a pouch-bearing marsupial shaped by evolution into the form of a canine. Despite its uncanny dog-like appearance, it has no relation to the canine family but rather is related to the carnivorous marsupials of the order Dasyuromorphia. Its closest living relative is the endangered numbat *(Myrmecobius fasciatus),* a small insectivorous marsupial that resembles a pointy-faced squirrel. The family Thylacinidae once contained nine genera and over a dozen species, with the thylacine being the only one to survive into the recent past. In modern times, they were restricted to the island of Tasmania, which lies 240 km (150 mi) off the southern coast of Australia, but were widespread on the mainland and in New Guinea a couple thousand years ago. Europeans first noticed their prints as early as 1642, but early sightings were scarce. They were formally described in 1807, a few years after the European settlement of Tasmania.

These pouched, tiger-striped, dog-like animals hunted the island's wallabies, kangaroos, and small game. Elusive and shy, they preferred to hunt at night, early morning, or late evening. About the size of a coyote *(Canis latrans)*, they were the largest marsupial carnivore to live in the modern world. They probably weighed between 15 and 30 kg (33 and 60 lbs), with newer research showing that the lower limit of the range was likely more typical. Females gave birth to 2-4 young, which were carried in a rear-facing pouch with her for up to 3 months. They may or may not have made burrows or lairs when breeding. While the anatomy and some behaviors of these animals are known from individuals housed in zoos and collected specimens, very little is known about their ecology. Much of what we do know is speculation based on the reports of hunters and ranchers. Seen as vermin, much like the much maligned coyote of North America, no formal studies of thylacines in the wild were ever conducted.

At the beginning of the colonization of Tasmania in 1803, it is estimated that the island had between 2000 and 4000 thylacines. After the introduction of sheep to the island, ranchers feared that their sheep may be at risk from the striped native hunters, and they were aggressively hunted for the next 100 years. How much of an impact the thylacines actually had on livestock is not known, but it is likely that the threat was largely or completely exaggerated. Modern research on the thylacine's jaw structure suggests that their weak jaws would not have allowed them to kill prey as large as a sheep and that they probably could only hunt smaller game.

As early as 1830, bounties were offered for killing thylacines, and a state-sponsored bounty system was in place from 1886–1908. Over the two decades of the state system, bounty payments for 2,182 thylacines were made. These, in addition to the thylacines killed for privately offered bounties, sport, and the 450 or more collected for museum collections, decimated their populations. While no formal studies tracked populations, the number of thylacines brought in for bounty probably mirrored the population. Based on this data, the population of the thylacine probably collapsed between 1905 and 1908. The last of the various bounties were offered in 1914. Soon after, it became clear that thylacines were in dire trouble, and calls were made to protect the animals. They received partial protection in 1929 and full protection in 1936. Unfortunately, this protection came too late. The last captive thylacine died in a Hobart zoo in 1936. While some wild thylacines may have remained, it is believed that they too died out sometime between 1936 and 1943, but may have held on as late as 1956.

The concerted effort to kill these animals was a significant factor in their extinction, but there is evidence that the isolated population was already suffering from low genetic diversity. The intense persecution and its resulting population decline only exacerbated this issue. The enormous expansion of sheep ranching in Tasmania led to more than just the hunting of thylacines. Landscape changes from intense grazing also removed food for wallabies and kangaroos. This led to a severe decline in the thylacine's preferred prey. According to reports, a large portion of the island's landscape was nearly devoid of these animals by the early 20th century. Ultimately, disease may have struck the final blow. Animals suffering from a still-unidentified disease were widely reported in the early years of the 20th century. A condition similar to canine distemper or possibly mange was becoming increasingly prevalent in the population and affected both wild and captive populations. For example, the Melbourne Zoo lost 16 thylacines to disease between 1901 and 1903. How these animals were infected hundreds of kilometers away from wild populations is not known, but it's clear that disease was killing thylacines in the years before their population collapsed. While some point to disease as the cause of the thylacines' extinction while ignoring the concerted effort to exterminate them, it is clear that disease (likely also introduced by humans) only finished what humans started.

The thylacine is still being discussed today. It is prominent not only for its unique traits and as a fascinating case of convergent evolution but also in the on-going discussion of recent animal extinctions. They are one of the very few extinct animals for which moving pictures exist. The haunting movies of these unique animals while they still lived bring a realism that is lacking with so many other species. It is one thing to understand intellectually that something like a T-Rex or a giant ground sloth once lived, and it is entirely another to see it actually move. These movies allow for a connection that still images, drawings, and even your imagination can't convey, moving them from abstract ideas from the past to real, living, breathing creatures. I believe this is one of the reasons thylacines continue to captivate us. These images serve to remind us that all of the animals that humans have had a part in eliminating were actually real. They are not just scientific descriptions or pictures in books, but living things. This brings with it the desperate hope that they still exist, and there have been numerous reported "sightings" of the thylacine. Most of these are misidentifications or the product of overactive imaginations, but they serve to show that hope remains that we did not eliminate this fascinating creature.

Bluebuck
(Hippotragus leucophaeus)

The bluebuck is the only known species of large African mammal to have gone extinct in modern times, although there are several subspecies that have, including the western black rhino *(Diceros bicornis longipes)*, the functionally extinct northern white rhino *(Ceratotherium simum cottoni)*, and the quagga *(Equus quagga quagga)*, a type of zebra that once lived alongside the bluebuck. The bluebuck was native to the extreme southern tip of South Africa and, in modern history, was limited to a very small range of just 4300 sq km (1660 sq mi). However, fossil evidence indicates that at one time they were much more widespread. The bluebuck split off from its closest relative, the sable antelope *(Hippotragus niger)*, sometime around 2.8 million years ago. They were once migratory, but as the sea levels rose during the beginning of the Holocene, they lost this migratory route, isolating their population to their modern distribution. Due to the restriction of their range, they were already declining by the time Europeans arrived on the Cape.

The bluebuck was known to Europeans as far back as 1679, but the first real description of the animals did not come until 1719, and a formal description came just decades before their extinction in 1766. They were a large antelope, standing nearly 120 cm (4 ft) tall at the shoulder, with horns as long as 61 cm (2 ft). Though smaller bodied than their relative the sable, they still reached weights of 135-180 kg or 300-400 lbs. Their name comes from the bluish hue of their coat. While other members of the genus typically feed in mixed grass and shrubland, the bluebuck was a grass specialist requiring high-quality grasslands for feeding. Unfortunately, very little else is known about the bluebuck. Its ecology was never studied while the animal was alive, an all too common issue for many extinct species. Only a handful of museums contain any specimens. However, enough materials exist to do some genetic analysis.

When Europeans arrived at the Cape, the bluebuck was already uncommon. Only a population of around 400 animals was estimated to exist at the beginning of colonization. Genetic analysis confirms that the population was likely small and shows that the bluebuck was suffering from very low genetic diversity. Due to the lack of available specimens, this determination was made with the remains of only 4 animals, and it is possible but unlikely that this could have skewed the results. By the 1770s, the species was becoming increasingly rare, and it is believed that the last individual was probably shot sometime around 1800.

There is a possibility that some animals may have remained in parts of their historic range. At least one author believes that a journal from 1853 describes seeing bluebuck, which, at the time, was misidentified as the similar-looking roan *(Hippotragus equinus)*, in the current province of Free State. This sighting would suggest that a small, separate population, isolated from the known one in the southern Cape, may have existed. Fossil evidence confirms that Free State was once part of the bluebuck's range. If this is correct, the species may have survived

The Blue-Buck, ♂ and ♀.
HIPPOTRAGUS LEUCOPHÆUS.

Published by R.H.Porter.

into the late 1850s or even later, but no other sources indicate bluebuck was present at the time.

There is little doubt that the bluebuck was already a suffering species when Europeans arrived in the Cape area, and given the intense pressures brought by the newcomers to South Africa, they stood little chance of survival. You may recall some of the severe impacts of hunting and land use change in the Cape area from earlier. Many of the Cape's large fauna were wiped out by hunting by the 1790s, and the expansion of the grazing of sheep and cattle not only competed against the remaining local fauna, but changed the landscape. Due to these pressures, the bluebuck and the quagga both suffered extinctions, and numerous other species were extirpated from the Cape's habitats. While many of these species avoided extinction by surviving in other areas of South Africa, the bluebuck likely only occurred in a single isolated range and could not avoid the pressures put on its population. Human-caused habitat loss and hunting undoubtedly ended a species that had been in decline for some time, but this may have just been an acceleration of a process that was inevitable.

Canis antarcticus

Falkland Islands Wolf
(Dusicyon australis)

The story of the wolves of the Falkland Islands is one of mystery, a mystery that perplexed not only Charles Darwin when he visited the islands in 1833 and again in 1834, but also generations of naturalists since. Confused by what process would allow the Falkland Island wolves to colonize these islands but not a single other terrestrial mammal. Just how did a mammal of this size, probably as large as 20 kg (44 lbs), make it to islands isolated some 480 km (300 miles) east of the mainland of Patagonia? Numerous theories were proposed over the years. Some believed that the wolf was once a domesticated animal brought to the islands by ancient humans. Others thought a group of these wolves were somehow transported by ice or logs that swept them to the islands. Certainly, finding a population of canines on an isolated, windswept archipelago hundreds of miles from the nearest continent was unique in history. Of course, large mammals rarely inhabit islands simply because they lack a good way to get there, but apparently no one told these wolves about that.

Genetic studies of the few specimens that remain in the world's natural history museums may have shed some light on the problem. The genetic relationship of the Falklands wolves to other canines was a mystery in itself, but one that had the possibility of providing information on the origins of these unique creatures. Earlier studies had shown that their closest living relative was the maned wolf *(Chrysocyon brachyurus)* of South America. However, the maned wolves and the wolves of the Falklands are separated by nearly 7 million years of evolution, leaving the specific origins of *D. australis* elusive. In 2013, researchers were able to determine the wolves' closest relative was an extinct canine from the mainland called *Dusicyon avus.* More importantly for the Falkland wolves' origin story, they were able to determine that the Falkland wolves split off from *Dusicyon avus* sometime around 16,000 years ago. This date is important for two reasons. One, it likely eliminates the possibility that humans introduced the Falklands wolves, and two, it may explain how they came to reside there. The date closely aligns with a glacial peak that dramatically lowered sea levels compared to today. This left a narrow and shallow 20-km-wide straight between the island and the mainland. Freezing of the shallow strait in the winter likely allowed the Falkland wolves' ancestors to reach the islands. When temperatures and sea levels rose, it trapped the wolves' ancestors on the islands and eventually gave rise to the wolves that Darwin observed in 1833. Why no other mammal made it this way is unknown. There was probably little incentive for them to follow the ice bridge to the islands, whereas these plucky predators likely came in search of food discovering an abundance of seabirds and marine mammals.

The Falkland Island wolf is not only known for its surprising existence, but is now known for being the only canine known to suffer an extinction in modern times. Commonly called wolves, they were more like foxes in appearance and behavior. Darwin commonly referred to them as foxes and described them as possessing a wolf-like head but otherwise appearing like a tall, stout fox. They were about the size of a North American coyote, but with shorter legs and a more substantial build. These solitary hunters were found throughout the islands and primarily fed on penguins and other birds, as well as visiting pinnipeds. It seems they would eat nearly anything, including fish, crabs, and even insects. Unfortunately, a detailed study of the wolves never occurred. Nothing is known of their reproductive habits or offspring. It does appear as though they used burrows commandeered from penguins nesting on the islands.

Their original population is also unknown. Europeans first saw them as early as 1690, but the island continued to be uninhabited until 1765. The species was not formally described until 1792, but by this time it was already suffering from the pressure of humans. As early as the first expedition to claim the Falklands in 1765, the wolves were being killed, and five were shot almost immediately after the expedition made landfall. According to Darwin, by the time he visited in the 1830s, the wolf population had already been significantly reduced. Unfortunately, the Falklands wolves had little fear of humans, making them easy to approach and kill. Many were taken for the fur trade, and the killing of the wolves only increased as the islands became ever more populated with sheep. By the 1860s, large commercial operations raising sheep were established on the islands and quickly became the leading industry, and, threat or not, the wolves were eliminated to protect the sheep. The last Falkland Islands wolf was killed in 1876.

The demise of the wolves of the Falkland Islands, disappointing as it may be, is not surprising. Humans have a longstanding tradition of eliminating predators wherever they go. While animals like the gray wolf *(Canis lupus)* were widespread enough to avoid complete extinction, even under heavy persecution, the wolves of the Falklands could not avoid the takeover of their islands by humans. Seen as a threat to man and his assets, with the added bonus of having a useful fur coat, the human inhabitants of the Falklands had no qualms about killing these animals, and they did just that until they were no more. Just as unfortunate as the historical persecution of wolves and other predators is that the common attitude toward them has changed little since these wolves' extermination.

Extinct Bandicoots of Australia
(Peramelemorphia)

The mammals of Australia have been the hardest hit of any in the world, and the continent has suffered more mammal extinctions than any other. Since European settlement in 1788, roughly 30 species of Australian mammals have disappeared, among them numerous species of rodents, at least 4 species of bandicoot (which are highlighted here), and 4 species of wallaby, including 2 species of hare wallaby that you will meet next. Making up their own order, Peramelemorphia, there are currently 26 known species of bandicoot in 8 genera alive today that inhabit Australia, New Guinea, and the island of Tasmania. Distantly related to shrews, these small to medium-sized marsupials are typically nocturnal and omnivorous. The bandicoot order is divided into 3 families consisting of the long-nosed and short-nosed bandicoots (Peramelidae), the pig-footed bandicoots (Chaeropodidae), and the bilbies or rabbit-eared bandicoots (Thylacomyidae). Extinctions have been recorded in all three families, with one of them now completely extinct.

The family Chaeropodidae was once thought to contain just one species, the southern pig-footed bandicoot *(Chaeropus ecaudatus),* first described in 1838. In 2019, a new analysis of specimens and their DNA revealed the existence of two species, with the second given the name *Chaeropus yirratji*. The southern species, *C. ecaudatus,* inhabited the dry grass and scrub of the southwest of Australia, whereas *C. yirratji* likely preferred the sandy deserts of central Australia. Together, the family once covered a large portion of the continent. Unique to this family of bandicoots were the structure of their feet, from which their common name is derived. They walked on two hoof-like toes on their front legs, similar to a pig, and a single toe on the back, like that of a horse or deer (this can be seen in the illustration on the following page). Thin legged and clumsy when walking, they evidently could bound quite quickly if needed, much like an antelope in miniature. These small animals, measuring 23–23 cm (9–10 in), fed on a variety of foods, primarily plants, but also ate a variety of insects. Nocturnal, they would spend their days in a burrow dug out of the ground or a nest in a hollow log, depending on habitat. Offspring were commonly limited to two, but they may have had as many as four. Despite their widespread distribution, there is little information on how common pig-footed bandicoots were. They were apparently common in the southwest (probably *C. ecaudatus*) in the middle of the 19th century, but by the 1890s they were absent from the region. They survived longer in the central deserts of the continent (likely *C. yirratji*), with the last specimen collected in 1901, but reports show them surviving possibly as late as the 1950s. Unfortunately, both species are now certainly extinct, and with them, we have lost the entire family of these unique little animals.

The lesser bilby, or yallara *(Macrotis leucura)*, was one of two species in the family Thylacomyidae. The only other is the still-living greater bilby *(Macrotis lagotis).* The lesser bilby once ranged throughout Australia's central deserts. First described in 1887, they are most closely related to the bandicoots of the

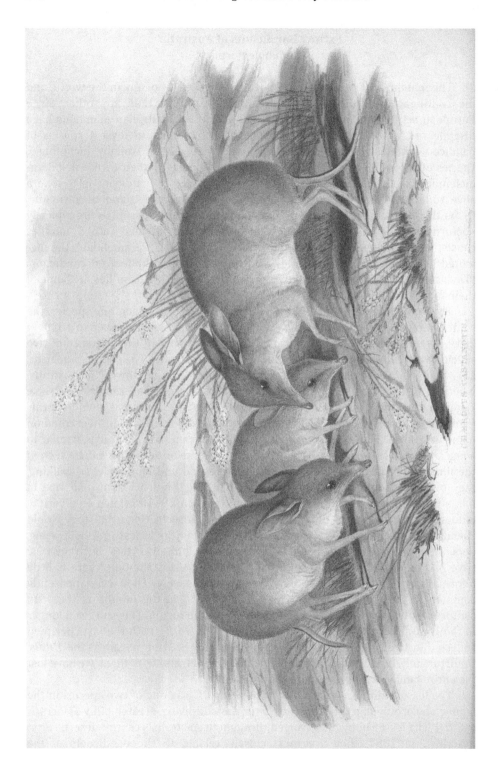

Chaeropodidae. While they were different in appearance from their pig-footed cousins, they did share the trait of peculiar feet, with three stout clawed toes with two very small toes on their front feet and a three-toed back foot. Typical of bilbies, they had long rabbit-like ears, a light sandy-colored coat, and very long tails. These 32–44 cm (12–17 in) animals were excellent diggers and made extensive dens built into sand dunes. Omnivorous and strictly nocturnal, they primarily consumed small mammals and insects, such as termites, beetles, and ants, but also fruits and seeds. These unassuming animals were impressive survivalists. They were so well adapted to their desert environment that they could avoid drinking entirely and obtained all the moisture they required from their food. A typical litter was 1 to 3 young that would stay in their mother's rear-facing pouch for around 75 days. The lesser bilby was once probably common throughout its range but had already been extirpated from parts of it by the 1920s. The last specimens of the species were collected in the 1930s. Eyewitness accounts from the Aboriginal community tell us they were still living in the western deserts in the 1960s but likely went extinct shortly thereafter.

The desert bandicoot *(Perameles eremiana)* was a member of the family Peramelidae, which contains the long-nosed and short-nosed bandicoots. These small bandicoots, just 18-28 cm (7-11 in) and about 250g (half a pound), were also once common throughout the central deserts of Australia. First described in 1897, very little is known about their ecology. We do know that they were likely omnivorous but fed primarily on ants, termites, and beetles. They were also nocturnal and made shallow burrows lined with vegetation, where they spent their days sleeping out of sight of predators. Their closest living relatives are the western barred bandicoots *(Perameles bougainville)*, which formerly were widespread through the southwest of Australia but now are limited to only a handful of reintroduction sites on the mainland of the continent. When the population of the desert bandicoot began to collapse is not known. The last specimen formally collected was in 1943, and surveys of Aboriginal communities support the idea that the species was absent from at least some of its range by the late 1940s, while it likely persisted in other parts of the range until the 1960s.

All three of these species experienced the same causes of extinction, and unlike pressures elsewhere, nearly all the mammals of Australia have seen dramatic declines due to the introduction of non-native predators. For these species, the primary driver of their extinctions appears to be the introduction of domestic cats and the later introduction of the European red fox *(Vulpes vulpes)*. Cats were first brought to Australia in 1788 and probably first became feral sometime around 1820 in the city of Sydney, but were absent from the interior of Australia until the 1880s. By 1890, feral cats roamed 90% of the continent. Deliberately introduced for hunting, the red fox was in Australia as early as 1845. By 1870, they were established in the wild after numerous introductions in the intervening decades. Slower to spread than the cat, foxes could still be found in all but the most northern areas of Australia by the 1950s. Faced with these new, highly efficient novel predators, the continent's small to medium-sized terrestrial mammals took a severe hit. Many populations saw widespread declines within decades of the fox appearing in their ranges. Another introduced species, the rabbit, also may have played a part in changing the habitats upon which the bandicoots depended.

Despite many of Australia's endangered small mammals having sufficient areas of land protected in parks and preserves, Australia continues to see its native mammal fauna disappear. Changes in habitat and continued pressure from introduced species make recovery efforts very difficult. There have been successes in reintroducing some species, but these attempts are only successful in areas with predator-proof fencing, highlighting just how damaging these introduced species still are to the ecosystems of Australia. There are 15 species of small mammals endemic to the Australian mainland that are currently classified as endangered or critically endangered. For all of these, introduced predators are the primary threat to their survival.

Hare Wallabies
(Lagorchestes)

The family of Macropodidae includes kangaroos, wallabies, pademelons, and quokkas. Of this family, collectively known as macropods, wallabies have been the hardest hit and are the only group to have seen multiple extinctions since the European colonization of Australia. There have been at least four extinctions overall: one in the genus *Onychogalea,* one in the genus *Macropus,* and two in the genus *Lagorchestes.* There were once 4 members of the genus *Lagorchestes,* also called the hare wallabies, that ranged across the Australian continent. Named for their similarities to the European hare, there are still two species that are extant: the rufous hare wallaby *(Lagorchestes hirsutus)* and the spectacled hare wallaby *(Lagorchestes conspicillatus).* The hare wallabies were once the most plentiful and widespread of any of the macropods, but unfortunately, they suffered the same devastating declines that many of Australia's small mammals have experienced.

The eastern hare wallaby (*Lagorchestes leprorides,* shown on the following page) was once found throughout the southeastern regions of Australia. They were first described in 1841 and were known for being extremely fleet-footed. Not only were they fast and agile, but they were incredibly good jumpers and could jump as high as 2.4 meters (8 ft) into the air. About 50 cm (20 in) long from head to tail, they were strictly nocturnal and could often be found during the day in a shallow scrape excavated beneath a saltbush or similar cover. They preferred an open grassland environment, but nothing is known about their feeding habits. It is believed that they only had one offspring at a time, but there is very little recorded about this species other than a physical description and the few details listed above. They were reportedly quite common throughout their range up until the 1850s. The last eastern hare wallaby collected was a female in 1889 in New South Wales, and it appears that she may have been one of the last of her species. When exactly these wallabies disappeared is unknown, but it is presumed to be near the date of the last collection.

The precise cause of the extinction of these once abundant animals is unknown. Likely, a combination of predation from feral cats and land use changes led to the extinction of the eastern hare wallaby. Increased cattle and sheep grazing within their range would have not only competed directly with the wallabies for food but would have forced changes in the makeup of the grasslands they depended on. Domesticated cats were introduced to the southeast part of Australia very early on, and once feral, they would have been widespread in the area by the middle of the 1800s.

The central hare wallaby, or kuluwarri (*Lagorchestes astomatus),* is only known to science from a single skull found near Lake Mackay in 1931. It is the basis for the species description published in 1943. Everything we know of these animals in the wild comes from the Aboriginal community. Based on their encounters with these animals, they once roamed a large area stretching from the Tanami desert in north central Australia to the Great Sands and Gibson deserts in western Australia. Obviously well adapted to desert life, they fed on grasses,

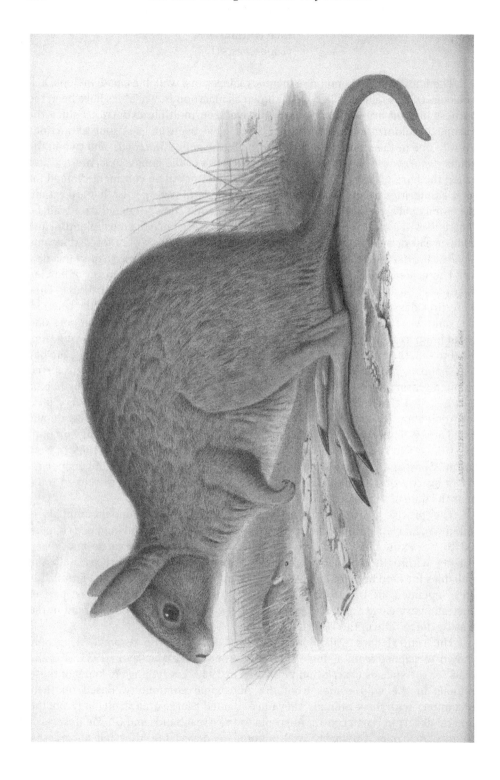

seeds, leaves, and the fruit of the desert quandong and made short, grass-lined burrows in the hummocks of spinifex grass. Based on the skull dimensions, Finlayson, who described the species, believed it was the smallest member of the genus. The species was described by Aboriginals as being similar in size to the boodie or burrowing bettong *(Bettongia lesueur)*, which has a body length of 37–44 cm (14–17 in). It is believed that this species gave birth to only one offspring at a time, but may have occasionally had twins. Once common, these wallabies were absent from portions of their range by the 1940s, and the last members are believed to have survived into the 1960s.

The extinction of the central hare wallaby was, once again, likely due to predation from feral cats and introduced foxes that have impacted so many of Australia's mammals. Habitat change was also most certainly a contributing factor. The extinction of these wallabies parallels the extirpation of their relative, the rufous wallaby, from most of the mainland of Australia in the 1930s. One of the only two surviving members of the genus, these wallabies now survive only on islands off the coast and protected reintroduction sites on the mainland. There was a single wild population in the Tanami desert until the 1990s, but this population was wiped out by foxes. Lending good evidence to the impact of foxes on Australia's wildlife and particularly hare wallabies, the only species of *Lagorchestes* that has not seen devastating population declines is that of the spectacled wallaby, whose range largely occurs north of the range of the fox.

Male   Young   Female

Caribbean Monk Seal
(Neomonachus tropicalis)

Marine mammals certainly have not escaped the extinctions of the modern era, and several species have disappeared in just the last 70 years. The earliest recorded extinction of a marine mammal goes back as far as 1768 with the disappearance of the Steller's sea cow *(Hydrodamalis gigas).* These manatee relatives from the Bering Sea were hunted into extinction within decades of their discovery by Europeans. Currently, there are more than 30 species of marine mammals that are threatened, including multiple species of whales, dolphins, seals, and sea lions.

The Caribbean monk seal was one of only three species of monk seals known to exist. The others are the still extant but endangered Hawaiian monk seal *(Neomonachus schauinslandi)* and the Mediterranean monk seal *(Monachus monachus).* The monk seals of the Caribbean are the only tropical species of marine mammal that have been driven to extinction. Known to people native to the West Indies for thousands of years, Europeans first came into contact with these animals in 1494, when they were sighted by the Columbus expedition. They were mentioned occasionally in natural history publications for the next several hundred years, but they were not formally described until 1849. Little interest was given to the animals beyond their commercial value, so there is little information on the Caribbean monk seal's ecology, despite a long history of human interactions. For example, unknown to science is exactly what these seals ate. Their physical characteristics suggest they were general feeders, and it is likely they ate a variety of foods, including algae, fish, mollusks, cephalopods, and crustaceans.

What we know of the species largely comes from accounts of sailors, the few animals that were kept in captivity, and animals that were killed for museum collections. They could grow to be between 200 and 244 cm (6.8–8 ft) long and weigh 70–200 kg (154–440 lbs) as adults. They once ranged widely across the entirety of the Caribbean region, from as far east as the islands of the Lesser Antilles and Guyana, as far north as the coasts of Florida and Georgia, as far west as the coasts of central Mexico, and as far south as the Gulf Coast of Costa Rica. Once a common sight throughout their range, estimations put their original populations between 200 and 300 thousand animals. Populations remained robust through the early 1700s, but by the later half of the 19th century, they were a rare species. By the 20th century, the seals had disappeared from much of their range as their population contracted to the west. The last known seal to be killed in U.S. waters was in 1922, and the last reliable sighting of a Caribbean monk seal was in 1952 near the Serranilla Bank between Honduras and Jamaica. Despite decades of repeated aerial surveys, no remnant populations of Caribbean monk seals have been located, and they were declared extinct by the IUCN in 2008.

While there is evidence that native Caribbean peoples did occasionally kill and consume monk seals, the real threat from human predation did not arrive until European settlement. From the very outset of contact, Europeans hunted these seals, with eight being killed upon their discovery in 1494. Initially, the impact of European hunting was much too small to affect populations, but as European influence in the Caribbean grew, so did the hunting of its monk seals. Valued for their blubber and skins, seals were killed and rendered into oil for lubrication, lamp oil, and cooking oil. Their skins were made into covers, belts, and bags. As early as the 1640s, the Dutch were sending out hunting parties to procure oil to lubricate the machinery of their sugar plantations. Reports show that Spanish and British sealers were frequenting the Yucatán by the 1670s. By 1700, the plantation owners of Jamaica were sending hunters to the islands of the Bahamas, resulting in hundreds of seals being killed each night during their breeding season. Despite the heavy losses, the seals' populations initially held up well to the huge take, but after 200 years of heavy exploitation, populations collapsed in the 1850s. Ironically, as the seals became increasingly rare, the demand from museums and collectors only increased. One of the last remnant populations in Mexico was wiped out in 1911 for museum collections. Here, as many as 200 seals were killed in a devastating blow to the seals' survival.

Despite being protected by Jamaica in 1945, becoming a species of international concern in 1949, and eventual listing under the U.S. Endangered Species Act, protections came much too late for the Caribbean monk seal. By this time, centuries of relentless hunting had depleted their populations beyond recovery. While other factors contributing to the species' decline may have come into play (such as the loss of beach habitat and reduction of food resources), there is little doubt that humans are the ultimate cause of the Caribbean monk seals' extinction, hunting them out of existence.

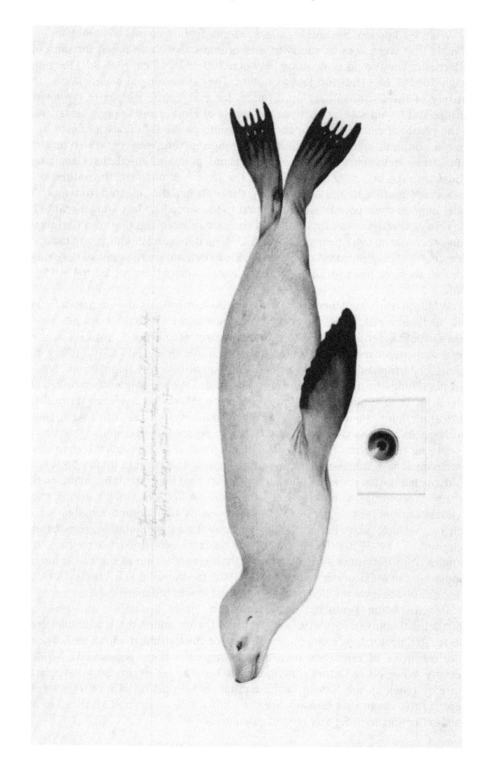

Japanese Sea Lion
(Zalophus japonicus)

The Caribbean monk seal is not the only member of the pinnipeds to see their populations zeroed out in the recent past. Unfortunately, the Japanese sea lion suffered a similar fate. One of only three members of the genus *Zalophus*, these sea lions were once considered a subspecies of the California sea lion *(Zalophus californianus)*, but genetic research shows that these two species diverged some time around 2 million years ago, along with the third member of *Zalophus*, the endangered Galápagos sea lion *(Zalophus wollebaeki)*. The Japanese members of the genus once roamed the northwest Pacific, from Russia's coasts south to the Korean Peninsula and the waters surrounding Japan, with their population centered on the islets of Ulleungdo Island and the Liancourt Rocks in the Sea of Japan.

The ecology of the Japanese sea lion was little studied while the animals were alive, but it is assumed that breeding and feeding behaviors closely resembled those of their California cousins. Like the California species, the Japanese sea lions showed a large size difference between the sexes, with females being around 1.6 m (5 ft) from head to tail and around 100 kg (220 lbs). Males, however, could be 2.3 to 2.5 meters (7.5 to 8 ft) in length and weigh as much as 560 kg (1,200 lbs). They likely fed on a variety of fish and squid. They were frequently seen resting on rocky outcroppings, in caves, and on sandy beaches, with the latter preferred for breeding and rearing small pups. Like the California sea lion, they typically had one pup, which would continue to be fed milk for six months to a year after birth.

Although not described by western science until the later part of the 19th century, there is good archeological evidence that the Japanese sea lion was well known and was hunted by the peoples surrounding the Sea of Japan going back at least several thousand years. It is not believed that these early hunters impacted the populations of the Japanese sea lions to any great extent. However, the limited human impact on the Japanese sea lions did not last, and in 1904, commercial hunting of the animals began. Recent population modeling efforts determined that there were likely 30,000 to 50,000 Japanese sea lions throughout their range at the start of commercial hunting. Like the Caribbean monk seal, the Japanese sea lions were a valuable source of oil and skins. In just the first year of commercial hunting, 3,200 sea lions were killed. By 1908, the population had already been halved, and just a decade after the start of commercial hunting, it had fallen by 70%. The next decades saw less and less sea lions being killed as populations continued to plummet. By the last sighting near the Liancourt Rocks in 1951, there were roughly 50–60 individuals left. The species was likely extinct within years of this last sighting. Numerous surveys attempting to locate any remaining populations of Japanese sea lions have failed to find any individuals. Unconfirmed reports of sightings as late as 1975 are thought to be misidentifications. The IUCN classified the species as extinct in 1994.

Once again, so little is known about this species that the reasons for its extinction are somewhat difficult to determine. It is certainly obvious that the beginning of commercial hunting played a significant role in the loss of these animals, and this is the most widely accepted cause. There may very well be other reasons that contributed to the loss of the Japanese sea lion. It has been shown that the effects of El Niño and La Niña patterns significantly affect the birth and survival rates of young California sea lions, and it is possible that similar weather patterns or some other unknown pressure could have affected the Japanese sea lions, resulting in less resilience in the face of intense hunting pressure. However, since no other probable causes of decline have been discovered, it is likely safe to assume that the Japanese sea lion, like numerous other species, would still be with us if commercial hunting of the animals had not taken place.

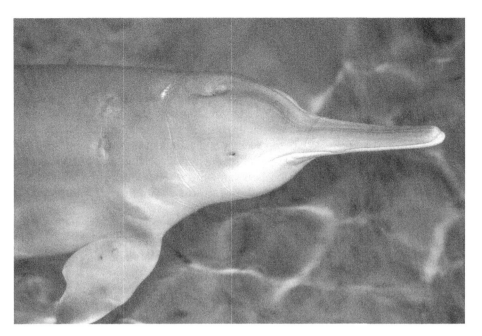

Baiji
(Lipotes vexillifer)

The baiji, or Yangtze River dolphin, was one of only a handful of freshwater cetaceans known to science. Only 7 species remain: 4 species of dolphin in South America, 2 in Asia, and 1 species of porpoise, the Yangtze finless porpoise *(Neophocaena asiaeorientalis)*, a critically endangered species itself that once shared the Yangtze River with the baiji. The baiji, once revered in China, is now known for a number of unfortunate distinctions. It was the largest species of animal to suffer extinction in the 50 years since the disappearance of the Japanese sea lion and the only cetacean known to have been driven to extinction by humans. Not only this, but it was the last remaining member of an entire family of dolphins, the Lipotidae (the fourth loss of a mammal family in the last 500 years). While the origins of these and other river dolphins have been long debated, it is believed that their ancient ancestors were stranded in the river systems they inhabited millions of years ago by climatic changes. The baiji had no living relatives at the time of its extinction but was distantly related to the river dolphins of the Amazon, sharing a common ancestor with these dolphins some 16 million years ago.

The baiji once swam throughout the middle and lower regions of the Yangtze River, with their range extending over some 1900 km (1180 miles) of river, as well as Dongting Lake and China's largest freshwater body, Poyang Lake. They were also observed to briefly inhabit the nearby Qiantang River south of the Yangtze after a large flood in 1955 allowed some of the dolphins to migrate into a different river basin. Little is known of the ecology of these elusive animals. Like other dolphins, their diet consisted almost entirely of fish. Feeding in often-murky shallows and mud bottoms, the baiji used its excellently developed echolocation abilities to navigate and capture its prey. Typical of river dolphins, they were smaller-bodied than their ocean-dwelling relatives and possessed highly elongated snouts. Females were larger than males, weighing between 64 and 167 kg (141-368 lbs) and measuring 185-253 cm (6-8.3 ft) long. Males were typically 42–125 kg (92–275 lbs) in weight and around 141-216 cm (4.6-7 ft) in length. Like other cetaceans, they were gregarious, typically found in pairs and groups of up to ten individuals. Little is known of their reproductive habits, but like other large mammals, they reproduced slowly, with females having a single calf once every two years.

They were first described in 1919 by Gerrit Miller, and his description contains an account from Charles Hoy, the man who provided the specimen Miller used in his description. Hoy described seeing large numbers of dolphins around Dongting Lake and said they were commonly seen in the area. The original population of the baiji might have been as many as 5000 individuals, and as of the early 20th century, it is clear that they were still relatively abundant. However, the first scientific survey of their populations, conducted between 1979 and 1981, only found 400 animals. By the mid 1980s, this number had been further reduced to just 300 animals, and the population remained in free fall. By the beginning of the 1990s, the population was estimated at just 100. Seeing the need for a more definite count, a comprehensive search was mounted from 1997–1999 across the baiji's entire range. The results were certainly disheartening. The survey was only able to locate 13 animals in total, 12 adults and a single calf. After this date, the only confirmed sightings of the baiji were a stranded individual found in 2001 and a single animal photographed in 2002. In 2006, a team of researchers from across the world conducted an extensive acoustic survey of the Yangtze River to listen for the calls of any remaining baiji. Even though a 1669 km (1037 mile) length of river was searched twice, not a single dolphin could be located. This led the research team to conclude that the baiji was at least functionally extinct. Despite no confirmed observations for 20 years, the IUCN lists them as critically endangered, but they are now almost certainly extinct.

There were a multitude of solely human impacts that led to the extinction of the baiji. While fishing on the Yangtze River has taken place for thousands of years, the impact on the river's dolphins dramatically increased as industrializa-tion and population growth took hold. The mass deployment of long lines containing thousands of hooks to snag fish, gill nets, and fyke nets killed significant numbers of dolphins through entanglement. These techniques were responsible for at least half of the baiji deaths through the 1970s and 1980s. The later introduction of electro-fishing, a process in which electric current is passed through the water to kill fish, also took a toll. An estimated 40% of baiji deaths through the 1990s were caused by this practice. While many of these methods were banned by the Chinese government, enforcement was difficult, so many continued. A survey conducted in 2006 found more than a thousand cases of illegal fishing on the Yangtze just between the cities of Yichang and Shanghai. The Yangtze is also home to extensive shipping operations, and strikes from ships were known to have killed and injured numerous dolphins. During the 2006 population survey, no fewer than 19,830 large shipping vessels were recorded on the Yangtze. This equates to one large ship every 100 meters along the entire 1669-kilometer survey route. Yet other factors degraded and reduced the habitat of the baiji, including numerous dams that not only disturbed the natural flows of the river but blocked the dolphins from vital habitats. Pollution throughout the Yangtze basin has been and continues to be a significant environmental issue. Runoff from agriculture and industry combine to severely pollute the Yangtze's waters. While the baiji still inhabited these waters, at least 12 billion cubic meters of untreated industrial wastewater entered the river every year.

Much like the loss of the Yangtze paddlefish, China certainly missed the opportunity to save the baiji. Despite recommendations by China's own scientists as early as 1986 that a captive breeding program or a monitored breeding program in special preserves may be necessary to ensure the survival of the baiji, nothing was done to further this idea. A conservation action plan for the increasingly endangered dolphins was not approved until 2001. Even if this plan had been fully funded, with only a dozen or so remaining animals, it was probably already too late to save the species. Recognizing that the situation on the Yangtze had gotten out of hand, China imposed a 3-month annual fishing ban in the Yangtze beginning in 2003 in an attempt to improve the river's condition. With this not resulting in significant improvement, the government enacted a 10-year fishing moratorium on all of the Yangtze and its tributaries beginning in 2021. Not only this, but more than 6,000 industrial polluters in the Yangtze basin have been shut down in recent years. Hopefully these efforts can significantly improve this enormous river system and the outlook for not only its more than 400 species of fish but also the still-surviving and critically endangered Yangtze finless porpoise.

The still extant Samoan flying fox *(Pteropus samoensis)*.

Flying Foxes
(Pteropus)

Population losses and extinctions have spanned every order of mammal, and the order of Chiroptera is no exception. Currently, there are nine species of bat that are known to have gone extinct. All of these extinctions are from the mid-19th century onward, and all are from species that are native to islands. While island endemics currently account for all known bat extinctions, the first extinction of a bat species from a major continent is likely to occur in the coming years. For example, in North America, there are 3 species of bat that have seen a 90% or greater decline in their populations. Once very common, the little brown bat *(Myotis lucifugus),* the northern long-eared bat *(Myotis septentrionalis),* and the tricolored bat *(Perimyotis subflavus)* all have suffered devastating losses due to a non-native fungal disease called White Nosed Syndrome. The fungus called *Pseudogymnoascus destructans* infects bats during their winter hibernation and results in increased activity in the bats. Unable to replace energy reserves and fluids, the bats ultimately succumb to starvation and dehydration. Bats on the whole are jeopardized by a litany of factors. Worldwide, more than 200 species of bats are threatened, including 23 that are critically endangered.

Hardest hit among all the bats are the members of the genus *Pteropus,* also known largely as flying foxes. There are currently 63 recognized species in the genus, with more than half (37) being threatened and six, which are covered here, believed to already be extinct. One other, the Aru flying fox *(Pteropus aruensis)* from Indonesia, is considered possibly extinct. Common to the genus are its members' large size (the group contains many of the largest species of bats), a largely fruit-based diet, although many occasionally eat insects, and dog-like faces with large eyes (hence the fox moniker). Species vary in nocturnal and diurnal habits, and unlike many bat species, they rely on eyesight for navigation and cannot echolocate. The genus is widespread in the Old World tropics, with species found in tropical climes ranging from East Africa to South and Southeast Asia, as well as many South Pacific islands and Australia. These bats play key roles in the environments they inhabit, particularly on the often remote islands where they are found, as pollinators and seed dispersers. Even though flying foxes often occur in large groups, their low reproductive rates make them vulnerable to population declines.

For many of the extinct members of the genus *Pteropus,* there is, at best, sparse information about their ecologies, life cycles, and behaviors. Species are frequently known to science by only a few or even a single specimen. It is possible that many of these species were on the brink of extinction well before they were known to western science, but why some of these species are now gone and others in the same genus still persist, even in the same ranges, is often not well understood. One of the flying foxes we probably know least about is the large Palau flying fox *(Pteropus pilosus).* Once native to the Pacific islands of Palau, it is only known from two specimens that were collected sometime before 1874. These large bats were described by Knud Andersen in 1908, but even in the original description, almost no information is given about this species apart from a very basic physical account. What is known is that these were the largest bats found on the islands of Palau and were even larger than the single species of flying fox that is still extant in Palau, a subspecies of the Marianas flying fox *(Pteropus mariannus pelewensis),* which has an impressive wingspan of up to 10.6 cm (3.5 feet). The hunting of flying foxes is common in many of the places they inhabit, and they are often the largest mammals found on remote island chains. This continues to threaten *P. m. pelewensis* in Palau, and hunting by humans likely played a role in the demise of *P. pilosus.* Due to its larger size, it is possible that historically, *P. pilosus* was hunted to a much greater extent than its smaller relative. The last individuals collected in 1874 may have been two of only a handful left by this time.

Close to Palau are the islands of the Marianas, the largest of which is Guam, the namesake of the still extant Marianas flying fox *(Pteropus mariannus)* mentioned above. Guam once had a second species of flying fox thought to be endemic to the island called the Guam flying fox, or the little Marianas fruit bat *(Pteropus tokudae).* Smaller than the Marianas flying fox, they had a maximum wingspan of about 70 cm (27 in) and weighed 152 g (5 oz), about a third the mass of their larger relative. They were first discovered in 1931 and formally described in 1934. Little is known of these bats, but it is likely that they preferred to forage on the fruits and flowers of the evergreen shrubs of northern Guam. The Guam flying foxes were evidently never common, at least in modern times, but were hunted and considered a delicacy by the native Chamorro people. The last known adult individual, a female, was shot by a hunter in 1968, and no other known sightings have occurred since this date. The United States listed the bats as endangered in 1984 and took steps to protect the species if they were located again. Unfortunately, it is nearly certain that the Guam flying fox is extinct. Hunting of these bats was probably the major driver of population declines, but as with many species lost on the island, the introduction of the brown tree snake or other invasive species could have played a role, as well as habitat loss and degradation of the species' natural environment.

The islands of Samoa once had four species of flying foxes from the genus *Pteropus.* Two of these still reside on these and other islands in the Pacific: the Samoan flying fox *(Pteropus samoensis)* and the insular or Pacific flying fox *(Pteropus tonganus).* The two extinct species are rather a mystery, and were only formally described in 2009 from specimens collected in the 19th century. The two species are probably the smallest and largest species of flying fox to occur on the islands of Samoa. The smaller of these two bats is the rather unoriginally named small Samoan flying fox *(Pteropus allenorum).* Only known from a single individual collected on the island of Upolu in 1856 and subsequently donated to the Academy of Natural Sciences of Philadelphia in 1857. These bats had a wingspan of around 60 cm (24 in), compared to the 86 cm (34 in) span of *P. samoensis.* Based on morphological studies it appears these bats may be closely related to *Pteropus fundatus* of Vanuatu. These same studies give clues to the ecology of these bats, and the small Samoan flying fox shares features with other flying foxes that feed primarily on small fruits and nectar. With only one known specimen and no information about this species in the wild, it is impossible to even speculate why and when they became extinct, but nearly all modern extinctions on islands around the world have a human component.

The second species once found on Samoa is known from only two skulls housed in the Smithsonian's National Museum of Natural History that were collected sometime between 1839 and 1841 by the U.S. Exploring Expedition. Studies of the skulls of the large Samoan flying fox *(Pteropus coxi)* show a more robust build than the two remaining extant species. It is possible that they may have been even larger than *P. tonganus,* which has a wingspan of over 100 cm (39 in) and may have been the largest of all of the bats to occur in Polynesia. The skull morphology of these bats also reveals similarities to the so-called "monkey-faced bats" of the Solomon Islands and Fiji and suggests that, like them, the large Samoan flying fox may have fed on hard nuts and fruits that other bats may not have been able to consume. The reasons for the extinction of these bats are as elusive as those of the small Samoan flying fox, but it is possible that the bats' large size made them prime targets for human hunters. It is likely that both of these bats have been extinct for 100 years or more. However, an eyewitness account from a botanist working in Samoa in the 1980s suggests there was still a very large species of flying fox living at that time that may have been *P. coxi.* If true, these bats may have persisted until recently.

Yet another little-known species of flying fox comes from the Percy Islands off the Queensland coast of Australia. The Percy Island flying fox *(Pteropus brunneus)* is only known to science from a single male individual that was collected on South Percy Island. When exactly this individual was collected is disputed, but it was likely sometime between 1854 and 1874. It was formally described in 1878 and is notably similar to the extant little red flying fox *(Pteropus scapulatus),* but smaller. It's believed that the Percy Island flying fox shared a similar range, not only on the Percy Islands but possibly on the Queensland mainland. It is also believed that both of these bats shared a similar ecology. It is likely that the Percy Island flying fox, like the other flying foxes of Australia, was nocturnal and fed primarily on flowers but also consumed fruits, sap, and insects. The species was reported as once being common, but the population declined into extinction sometime in the 1890s. The causes leading to their extinction are unknown, but it is assumed that pressures commonly faced by Australian flying foxes were shared by the Percy Island flying foxes. In particular, habitat loss and degradation due to agricultural expansion and the grazing of livestock were likely the primary factors in their decline. In fact, grazing within the bats' suspected range peaked in 1894, closely coinciding with their disappearance. Disease has also been suspected in the declines of other flying fox species and may have been introduced into the Percy Island population from domestic animals or humans.

The devastation of the biodiversity on the Mascarene Islands also extended to a species of flying fox. The lesser Mascarene flying fox *(Pteropus subniger)* once inhabited the islands of Mauritius and Réunion. One of three species of flying foxes native to the Mascarene Islands, the other two, the black-spined flying fox *(Pteropus niger)* and the golden bat *(Pteropus rodricensis)*, are still extant but endangered. Flying foxes were noted as early as 1598 on the islands, but different species were not distinguished until much later. The lesser Mascarene flying fox, while known for nearly two centuries, was not described until 1792. These small flying foxes with a 60 cm (24 in) wingspan were once quite common, especially in the early part of the 18th century. The species was nocturnal, feeding on flowers, leaves, fruits, and possibly tree sap. They were particularly known for roosting in caves, rock clefts, or hollow trees. Their morphology suggests they could tolerate cooler temperatures than the other Mascarene flying foxes, and it is likely they preferred the higher habitats of Réunion Island. By the middle of the 19th century, these bats were becoming increasingly rare. The Réunion population completely disappeared sometime in the 1860s, while the population of Mauritius likely disappeared between 1864 and 1873. The last known individual collected was on the island of Mauritius in 1864. There is a long history of hunting flying foxes on the Mascarene Islands, both before and after European settlement, and losses from hunting have caused catastrophic losses in the populations of all of the islands' flying foxes. It is thought that the increased hunting pressure after European settlement was the primary driver of the extinction of the lesser Mascarene flying fox.

The related common pipistrelle *(Pipistrellus pipistrellus)*.

Christmas Island Pipistrelle
(Pipistrellus murrayi)

The Christmas Island pipistrelle is the most recent species of bat to suffer extinction and probably the only bat species to go extinct in the last 50 years, as well as one of the most recent of any mammal to suffer extinction. It is one of the alarmingly numerous extinctions to occur on Christmas Island that have been observed in recent years. Unlike many of the extinct flying foxes, about which we know little, these bats were well known and well studied, with detailed population information available. Their extinction demonstrates that, even with population monitoring and high-quality information, the extinction of a species can occur quickly without proper intervention. Their loss serves as a warning that acting too slowly on biodiversity loss will see species lost forever.

The genus *Pipistrellus* contains 25 extant species of bats that are common and widely distributed throughout the world. The Christmas Island pipistrelle was unique to the island but shared the typical traits of the genus, such as small size, an insectivorous diet, nocturnal behavior, and the use of echolocation for hunting and navigation. These tiny 3-4.5 g (0.1-0.15 oz) bats fed on a wide range of small flying insects throughout Christmas Island, including moths, beetles, and flying ants. They preferred roosting in areas of primary and secondary rainforest in a variety of places, including under palm fronds and under the bark of dead trees, in groups of up to 50 individuals. They typically fed along the more open forest margins. Females in the colony would simultaneously give birth to a single pup that would nurse for about 4 weeks.

The population of the Christmas Island pipistrelle is well known throughout the history of human habitation on the island, and they were very common throughout from the onset of colonization in the 1890s until at least the mid 1980s. Being the only bat species on the island that used echolocation, ultrasonic monitors could be employed to accurately monitor pipistrelle populations. Studies in the early 1990s were the first to indicate that the species was declining and that the bats' range was in contraction to the west. Data from these early studies suggested a 33% drop in the population overall. By 1998, the pipistrelles could no longer be found in the northeastern portion of the island. From 1998 to 2004, the population continued to rapidly decline, losing between 55 and 65 percent of its remaining numbers. By 2007, it had disappeared from 90% of its former range. Monthly surveys of the remaining bats from 2006 to 2009 saw an additional 99.4% drop in population. By January 2009, only four individuals could be located on the far western side of the island. At this time, the total estimated population of the Christmas Island pipistrelle was as few as 20 individuals. Three weeks of acoustic monitoring in August of the same year detected only one individual. After the 29th of August 2009, this single remaining bat was last recorded, and despite multiple surveys, including an entire island-wide search in 2019, no remaining pipistrelles could be located. In 2017, the species was listed as extinct by the IUCN.

The exact cause of the extinction of the pipistrelles on Christmas Island is not well understood, but the timing of the bat population declines and westward range contraction closely mirrors that of the now extinct reptiles on the island. This suggests that there is likely to be a common cause. As with their reptile island mates, habitat loss has been ruled out as a significant factor, with researchers noting that 75% of the island was still covered in high-quality habitat at the time of the bats' disappearance. Likewise, the impact of feral cats, rats, the island's non-native predatory giant centipedes, or the invasion of yellow crazy ants is not thought to be significant in the bats' decline. Disease is also unlikely to have simultaneously impacted both reptile and mammal species. The likely candidate responsible for the decline of the island's pipistrelles is the same one suspected for its reptiles: the non-native wolf snake that was first recorded on the island in 1987. While predation by the wolf snake is presumed to be the most likely cause of the decline of some of the island's reptiles and the Christmas Island pipistrelle, there is no conclusive evidence of such. It is still debated whether the wolf snake could have caused such dramatic declines in so many species in just 20 years, while other species suffered little or no impact. Hopefully further investigations can reveal more definite causes of the recent extinctions on Christmas Island, and with this knowledge we can save not only the species on Christmas Island but species elsewhere as well.

Just as tragic as the extinction of the pipistrelle was the Australian government's inaction in the face of the bats' plight. The bats were listed as endangered in 2001 by the Australian government, and a recovery plan for the species was forthcoming by 2004. By 2006, it was clear to conservationists that drastic action, including a captive breeding program, may be needed to save the species. Unfortunately, the move toward a captive breeding program was not initiated until the population had dropped to only an estimated 20 individuals in January of 2009. More unfortunately, instead of immediately implementing the capture of the remaining pipistrelles, the government decided that a feasibility study first needed to be done, despite a longstanding body of knowledge about the captive breeding of similar species. A recommendation to capture the remaining population of Christmas Island pipistrelles came in June of 2009, and in July the government decided to actually do it. Months of talking wasted valuable time, and the last individual disappeared the following month. Why Australia waited until the very last months of the species' existence to attempt the capture of the remaining bats, after years of known declines, is hard to explain. It is a clear example of how conservation attempts can be thwarted by the inefficiency of government. While conservation programs are largely successful, timing is critical. With the increasing threats to the world's biodiversity, the consequence of inaction will be devastating. We would do well to remember the words of pioneering bird conservationist Rosalie Barrow Edge: "The time to protect a species is when it is still common."

10
There is Hope

"No important change in ethics was ever accomplished without an internal change in our intellectual emphasis, loyalties, affections, and convictions."

-Aldo Leopold

U p until this point this book has been, inarguably, more than a little depressing. I hope that you have learned some things about this beautiful world we live in and some of the amazing creatures that we share it with, but perhaps you feel, like I often felt while researching and writing this, a profound sense of hopelessness. If this is the case, I certainly cannot blame you. The impact of humanity on the natural world has been extreme, to say the least, and continues to be. The problems we face are now so large and daunting, and we have made so little progress. Nevertheless, let me try to convince you (and possibly myself) that there is a chance. Despite the cataclysm developing around us, there are signs of hope. There really are ways out of this mess with a better future for humans and all of the other organisms on Earth. The path will be hard. Sacrifices will have to be made, and all of humanity is going to have to get on board. All of us, no holdouts, including you and me. We will need both a bottom-up approach from everyday citizens and a top-down approach from Government, but with hard work, perseverance, the power of the human mind, and a little luck, it can be done. Here we'll take a look at some of the real-life solutions to save biodiversity, stabilize our climate, and change our relationship with nature. It is by no means a complete list of issues that need to be addressed; rather, it is a highlight of major areas where we can focus effort and resources. I have certainly left things out, but I believe progress in these areas will bring about meaningful, lasting, and positive change.

Agriculture

It is clear that feeding the human population has the largest impact on biodiversity of anything that we do. If we have any chance of saving the majority of it, we need to revolutionize agriculture. From the mass use of pesticides and fertilizers to deforestation and water utilization, agriculture's threat to biodiversity comes in many forms, not to mention its impact on an ever-warming climate. Rapid solutions are necessary, and it has become clear that what has become the standard model in agriculture is not sustainable. The good news is that there are both low-tech and high-tech solutions that can not only lessen the impact we have but even help to restore nature. Combining Earth-friendly and farmer-friendly practices with some high-tech solutions has a real chance of getting us where we need to be.

First, the low-tech solutions Some may be surprised to learn that many of these practices have been around for a long time—in some cases, thousands of years. Many ancient cultures realized and understood that soil health was vitally important to their ability to feed themselves, but along the way, many of these practices fell by the wayside with the invention of synthetic fertilizers. We believed synthetic fertilizers were a godsend. Farmers now had a tool to supercharge their crops. Depleted and marginal agricultural lands were restored to production and returned yields like never before. The subsequent invention of pesticides then got rid of unwanted weeds, insects, and diseases. Gone were the days of failed crops and poor returns. Or so we thought. Unfortunately, while fueling the Green Revolution and drastically increasing the world food supply, synthetic fertilizers and modern agricultural practices were not the silver bullet we thought them to be. While modern agriculture has delivered on the promise of more food, it has done so at a significant environmental cost, not to mention the rising monetary costs of the massive amount of chemical inputs required to grow crops.

In the Green Revolution, we ignored how nature maintains the abundance of plant life on Earth and implemented our own system. This came at the expense of nature's system and of the most important thing agriculture needs: soil. Today's conventional agriculture has led to the depletion of soils throughout the world, leading to the abandonment of as much as 400 million hectares (988 million acres) of farmland. One of the main culprits in soil loss is tillage. Tillage exposes soil to the air, releasing carbon, increasing erosion, reducing water absorption, and disturbing the complex microbiome of the soil. The overuse of fertilizers and pesticides further strips the soil of its microbial life and has a litany of other harmful effects on water, wildlife, and human health. As a result, much of the quality topsoil of the world's best agricultural lands is gone. The answer to the soil problem and many other issues related to today's chemical-intensive agriculture is regenerative farming. While this term means different things to different people, there is clear evidence that a crop growing system that integrates the elimination of tillage, the growing of cover crops, and the use of complex crop rotations can restore soil health, sequester carbon, reduce irrigation, and largely reduce or eliminate the need for synthetic fertilizers and pesticides. These demonstrated practices can maintain and even exceed the yield of traditional agriculture. Better yet, these practices have been shown to work throughout the world.

In his book, *Growing a Revolution,* geologist and writer David Montgomery makes the case for this "new" type of agriculture, and the case is compelling. He visits the Rodale Institute, which has been researching regenerative techniques for more than 40 years, the No-Till Center in Ghana, which is bringing these techniques to the farms of Africa, and talks with farmers themselves who are using the system. Time and time again, he sees that these techniques work in restoring the vital fungal and microbial systems that tillage destroys, reducing erosion, restoring water uptake, and increasing the carbon content of the soil through the use of cover crops that return nutrients and organic matter to the land. All this while weeds are controlled with nearly zero pesticides, soils are kept cool, and the cycle of crop diseases and pests is disrupted by crop rotations, making pesticides often entirely unnecessary.

The key to the system is restoring soil health and allowing the complex interplay of mycorrhizal fungi, soil bacteria, and plants to reestablish itself. Western regenerative farmers have seen their yields maintained or even increase over conventional practices and the benefit is even greater in poorer nations. Some African farms have seen productivity increase by a factor of four using these techniques. Regenerative farmers also see their land outperform their neighbors' in times of drought and flood. Instead of erosion and flooded fields, regenerative farmers watch as their fields absorb flooding rains, helping to "climate proof" their land. Because their fields absorb and retain water, they see a dramatic reduction in the amount of irrigation their fields require (increasing soil carbon from 1% to 3% can double the amount of water the soil can hold) and better resilience in times of drought. Intercropping (planting other harvestable crops within the main crop) and the reduction of inputs have allowed regenerative farmers to have more to sell with less cost, and, unlike many in conventional agriculture, they are actually making money. All this while seeing the biodiversity on their lands explode with the return of pollinators and wildlife. Less fuel, less chemicals, and higher profits, a win for farmers and the rest of nature.

This type of agriculture could also be huge in our fight against climate change. The average soil carbon content of North American farmland has dropped from 6% to just 3%, and severely deteriorated land can be as low as just a half percent, but regenerative farmers see their soil carbon levels increase. Farms that started with depleted soils as low as 1% have seen their soil bounce back to a healthy level. Land under conventional agriculture can lose as much as 0.5 to 1 percent of its carbon per year, but regenerative techniques can *increase* soil carbon by 0.2 to 0.4 percent per year. Normal, healthy soils have a typical total carbon content of 6–8%, and regenerative farmers have been able to restore their soils not only to this level but to 10% or more.

Of course, growing crops is not the only detrimental practice in agriculture, and the raising of livestock, especially cattle, not only takes up huge amounts of land but also degrades grazing lands. Certainly, human consumption of meat needs to decrease dramatically, but regenerative grazing can reduce the impact of the meat we do eat, all while increasing carbon sequestration and increasing the health and diversity of grazing lands. Used alone or in combination with regenerative crop production (grazing cattle on crop fields is a handy way to naturally fertilize the soil), regenerative grazing could be a game changer for cattle production. Instead of feedlots supported by conventional crop production, animals feed off the land for the benefit of both by ironically *increasing* grazing intensity. On the surface, this sounds silly. Cattle grazing has depleted lands around the world, so increasing grazing sounds disastrous. Many now practicing regenerative grazing thought the same thing, but it's not as crazy as it sounds. The world's grasslands support an immense number of wild large grazers without the issue of overgrazing, so nature shows us it is possible. The problem with cattle is how they graze, and it's this behavior that is at the heart of the issue. Herds of wild grazers are tightly packed for protection and move a lot. Because of this, they tend to graze indiscriminately, grabbing whatever they can before they move on. Domestic cattle like to stay in one place. They spread out and are picky eaters. They tend to eat only the plants they like. With no competition from other cattle, they deplete these plants, reducing the diversity of the grassland. Because only some plants are grazed, the system that builds soil carbon doesn't work. As a result, soils deteriorate.

To reverse this, regenerative grazing forces cattle together by grazing them in much smaller areas. This increases the competition between individuals, so they graze on whatever they can get a hold of, and the increased trampling creates a natural mulch that increases moisture retention. After a couple of days they're moved to another area. They might not graze this patch again for a year. While they are gone, the grass explodes to life. The intense mowing spurs the plants to force carbon-rich exudates into the soil. Soil bacteria and mycorrhizal fungi use these exudates to reward the plants with the nutrients they need. Farmers have seen growth double on their lands grazed in this way, as well as the return of a complex mix of native plant life. Some are able to graze twice the cattle per acre compared to their conventional neighbors and have seen the soil carbon levels in their soils increase from as low as 2% to a healthy 6% and even as high as 10%. Once again, we see increased yields for farmers and increased biodiversity for nature, all while sequestering carbon.

The positives of regenerative agriculture seem almost too good to be true, but there is excellent data showing it works. The world-wide implementation of these techniques could have an unbelievably positive impact on biodiversity and (at least for decades to come) turn our entire agricultural system from a net source of carbon to a carbon sink. In addition, regenerative farming can help eliminate the need for agricultural expansion, especially in poorer nations and the tropics. It will also reduce the need for irrigation, keep nutrients in the field and not in our waterways, and allow pollinators to thrive. So why has there not been a much wider adoption of these techniques? As is typical, industry and its common partner, Government, have pushed hard to stifle its growth. Only around 30% of the entire cropland in the U.S. is no-till, and of this, very few farmers practice all 3 components of a successful regenerative system. Government backed programs still largely support conventional agriculture and often inhibit the ability of farmers wanting to transition to regenerative farming. Farmers desperately need financial support in the first few years needed to begin to repair their soils, and governments have not yet adapted to the necessity of change. Of course, in government, change is largely dictated by the billion-dollar industries and their political donations, and the agrochemical industry is certainly no fan of an agricultural system that largely eliminates the use of their products. In poor nations, the problem is more one of education. Many already cannot afford to use pesticides and fertilizers, but do not have exposure to regenerative techniques, and many may struggle to find or afford seeds for cover crops.

Also inhibiting wide adoption is the fact that regenerative farming does not offer the same one-size-fits-all solutions that conventional farming does. While the techniques have been shown to work anywhere in the world, specifics like what type of cover crops work best and the number and type of crops in rotation will all vary from area to area and farm to farm. Farmers that do not have experienced regenerative farmers nearby may have to experiment more to find the right mix for their land, and experimentation costs time and money for already cash strapped farmers. It is not surprising that the uncertainty and dramatic departure from traditional techniques of regenerative farming may make farmers new to the system uneasy, especially when their livelihoods are on the line. Support from governments at the local and national level could help alleviate these fears. More regional research into regenerative agricultural practices from government backed programs and universities could help farmers get off to a good start. Research needs to quickly transition from conventional techniques that support big business to techniques that support the soil, the environment, and the farmer. Far too little funding has gone to this in the past.

There is a second low-tech solution related to regenerative grazing called "wild-land farming." This could be another useful technique that combines agriculture with the rewilding of the land. Here, instead of forcing cattle to act wild, landscapes are restored with their native wild grazers. In the U.S., a company called Wild Idea is raising bison on 300,000 acres of American prairie by letting the bison do what they have been doing for thousands of years. This not only provides a sustainable source of meat, but unlike domestic cattle, the bison's natural behavior enhances the landscape, increasing diversity and soil carbon with little to no input from humans. Bison are even harvested and processed right on the land. This is agriculture that hardly looks like it. Humans get to harvest animals, as they've been doing for thousands of years, and the natural landscape is being restored for the benefit of the climate and biodiversity. The growth potential in North America is huge. There are millions of acres of former prairie available for more bison, and maybe in the near future there will once again be millions of bison roaming the American west for the benefit of us and the prairie.

This concept isn't just for North America, and Europe has a lot of potential to bring back some of its long-lost landscapes. A prime example is the Knapp Estate in Sussex, England. Farmed intensively since WWII, the poor soil quality doomed traditional operations. After decades of losses, the decision to change the operation came in 2000. After selling off what remained of the dairy herds and machinery, a rewilding project was started to restore the land. Now, instead of plowing the land and grazing dairy cattle, the 3,500-acre farm raises a mix of animals to restore an ancient assembly of English animals. Now herds of old

English longhorns, Exmoor ponies, Tamworth pigs, and red and fallow deer roam the property as stand-ins for the wild animals that once roamed England. The entire property is now a nature preserve and farm in one. The herds are sustainably harvested and sold as high-quality organic meats, and the landscape has recovered to such a great extent that people now pay to come see wildlife and even go camping. It is now one of the best places in all of England to find a collection of rare native plants, insects, bats, and birds. Projects like this have the dramatic potential to change the landscape of Europe, which has lost so much of its native biodiversity while still providing agricultural output. If implemented on a wide scale, efforts such as these could change entire landscapes while providing humans with valuable food resources all over the world.

While the regenerative movement is all about working with nature, the high-tech solutions are very much the opposite. As pleasant as lovely diverse farms buzzing with bees and birds sound, regenerative farms will still take up a huge amount of land. As the human population grows, we need to be able to produce more food in less space, and the high-tech solutions developed in the land-constrained Netherlands could be the model for how to do this. Unbelievably, this tiny nation is the world's second largest exporter of food after the United States, despite having just 0.4% of the land area. The Dutch solution has been advanced greenhouses. The pinnacle of these are fully automated plant-growing factories that can produce the same amount of food as conventional agriculture on one-tenth the land. Greenhouses have some distinct advantages. The climate can be finely controlled to maximize growth, and they can grow crops year-round. They can also finely control the amount of water and nutrients plants receive to maximize efficiency. Best of all, they can be put anywhere, especially in urban areas. They can even be built as a vertical farm that maximizes growing space in dense urban environments, potentially allowing us to grow a large amount of food *within* our cities.

Of course, growing food indoors year-round does require energy for heating and lighting in temperate climates, and water consumption is always an issue. While not all of the greenhouses in the Netherlands are fully sustainable, there are some that show how it can be done by using strictly renewable energy sources such as solar and wind-produced electricity for lighting and biogas and geothermal sources for heating. Water is collected from rain and then recycled throughout the system. Even better is that the technologies and methods for sustainable greenhouses already exist and could simply be copied to new locations. The largest barrier to these systems is cost. High-tech and complicated automated greenhouses, by their nature, are going to have high building and operational costs, and they are not a likely solution for poorer nations. However, they could have a significant benefit by maximizing food production in wealthier nations, especially nations with large populations and little land, and within the world's large urban centers.

What You Can Do:

Especially in wealthy nations, the consumer has a lot of power when it comes to what is bought and sold. That is why billions of dollars are spent on advertising to influence your decisions. One of the largest impacts you can have is what you choose at the grocery store. Not only buying less meat but carefully selecting the meats you do buy can have a huge impact, not only on your personal impact but also on how the market produces meat. Research the products available at your store. The producers who are doing a good job are happy to tell you all about it in detail. The others might throw around words like "sustainable" or "free range," but delve into what this actually means. "Natural" is a commonly used term that has no substance; be wary when you see this; there are all kinds of things you could consider "natural" that aren't a good thing.

Ideally, you would buy most of your foods from operations that practice regenerative agriculture, but since there is no government-backed certification for this (unlike organic foods), this could be very difficult unless you have local producers you are familiar with in your area. Organic certified food growers are not necessarily practicing regenerative agriculture. They often rely on lots of tillage to control weeds, but are still better for the environment and you (compared to conventional growing) by reducing your and nature's intake of pesticides and the use of synthetic fertilizers. In a collaboration between industry and science, the Rodale Institute and the clothing manufacturer Patagonia, along with others, started the Regenerative Organic Certified program in an attempt to fill the certification void. This non-profit organization allows farmers practicing regenerative agriculture to apply for certification, much like the certifications already in place for traditional organic farms. Look for the Regenerative Organic logo for products that are certified. Currently, there are a limited number of farms certified, but with a huge company like Patagonia focusing on buying re-generatively produced hemp and cotton for their clothing, expect to see more regenerative products hitting the market as more companies look to source the most responsible raw materials for manufacturing and food. You can help move this forward by seeking out regenerative certified goods and contacting your favorite brands to tell them that regeneratively produced goods are important to you.

For people with land, especially many of us in the U.S. with ample yards, there is one way to know for sure how your food is produced, and that's to grow some of it yourself. Consider putting in your own no-till garden. You'll be surprised at how many vegetables you can grow. Get your neighbors involved, or get together with your city and start a regenerative community garden. Sharing resources and crops increases variety and builds community. While the impact seems small, allied countries during WWI and then again in WWII were able to bolster their food supplies significantly with "victory" gardens. In the U.S. alone, Americans raised an estimated 9–10 million tons of fruits and vegetables at the peak during the Second World War. There's no reason something like this can't be done again. Yes, it can take some work, but I think many will find solace and a new appreciation for the wonders of nature by reconnecting with the land.

Lobby your government and vote. This is a suggestion you'll see over and over again. With enough pressure from the public, they eventually have to act; all the corporate money in the world cannot overcome a populace bent on change. Tell your politicians to support laws and incentives for regenerative agriculture. You might have to first explain to them what it is. You may also have to explain to them that their job is representing what's best for the People, and that includes what's best for the environment. After all, we sort of need it to function properly. If you live in an area with large agricultural production, politicians are quick to appear friendly to farmers. See where they stand on regenerative agriculture and its impact on farmers' bottom lines. You'll quickly be able to determine whether they support what's best for the farmers or what's best for the ag industry.

What Government Can Do:

The U.S. already spends about 20 billion dollars a year subsidizing agriculture, and the vast majority of that money goes to support conventionally grown grain crops. Subsidies of this nature should be freed up to promote regenerative agriculture and high-density growing operations. The money is clearly already there; it just needs to be used better. Farmers could be incentivized to convert to regenerative systems by getting grants or low-interest loans to cover the first few years of operation, and governments could make sure crop insurance covers these systems in case of catastrophic loss. Farmers could also be paid for how much carbon they are storing, getting bonus money for every percent increase in soil carbon they see. Each nation could also set up regional regenerative research and outreach centers that would bring government agencies and universities together to determine the best practices for that region. Farmers could then take this information and apply it to their own farms. Essentially, the government pays for the trial and error so the farmer doesn't have to. For expensive greenhouse operations, governments could give hefty tax breaks to lower costs and encourage their implementation. Governments can also get people involved in producing their own food by restarting and promoting the "victory garden" concept; maybe call them "climate gardens." The U.S. and other nations made a huge effort to promote this during both world wars through outreach and programs to encourage home gardens. There seems to be no reason why we shouldn't start these initiatives again. This time, the focus can be on regenerative techniques and the positive benefits of growing your own food.

In wealthy nations, we must be encouraging and incentivizing farmers away from conventional agriculture. In poor nations, education and financial help to get farmers to use regenerative techniques will be key, and it's in these countries where it could have the greatest benefit in increasing food production. Poor countries can use what resources they have to promote regenerative systems, but wealthy nations already in the transition have a role to play. Wealthy governments could use their new research centers to spawn sister centers in poor nations to help rapidly expand regenerative farming around the world. Remember, we all have to work to get out of this together, and wealthy nations have the resources to help poorer nations make the changes we need to see in the limited time we have. The good news is that there will be less industry pushback in poorer nations since many poor farmers can't afford their products anyway.

Of course, the conventional ag industry will have serious issues with all of this. They stand to lose a lot of money, and programs may have to be implemented to help soften the blow for people working in the industry (let me be clear, I'm talking about the everyday employees, not people whose salaries are in the millions of dollars; they'll be fine). Our governments are going to have to somehow deal with this and other industries as we make radical changes in the coming years. Exactly what that looks like, I'm not sure, but industry money and influence are significant barriers to change, and at the end of the day, the choice needs to be made on where the money should go, to farmers themselves or big industry.

Energy and Climate Change

While climate change has not been a significant factor in recent extinctions, severe climate related impacts are just on the horizon. Even in the best case scenarios we stand to lose countless species, including much of the world's shallow water coral reefs and many of the species they support. While our changes to agriculture could eliminate as much as a quarter of global emissions and even sequester billions of tons of CO_2, it still will not be enough. Agriculture needs to change rapidly for many reasons, but in regards to climate, humans' use of fossil fuels is the largest issue. Globally, nearly 40% of carbon emissions come from electricity, heating, and transportation, and in the U.S., over 50% of emissions come from transportation and generating electricity alone.

To solve our fossil fuel problem, we first need to generate electricity without fossil fuels, and then we need to use that electricity for much of our transportation. By doing this, you have already cut the CO_2 output of one of the world's largest emitters, the U.S., by nearly half. The technologies to do this already exist. They are well developed and are not only improving but also becoming dramatically cheaper—in some cases, cheaper than their fossil fuel counterparts. So, how do we generate electricity without fossil fuels? There are many ways this is possible, but the most promising to meet the majority of the world's needs is solar energy. It turns out the enormous fusion powered ball we call the sun puts out a lot of energy, and it's been powering most of the life on earth for billions of years. Even the energy we liberate from fossil fuels ultimately originated from the sun. At any one time, the Earth receives about 173,000 trillion watts of energy from the sun, more than 10,000 times the world's total energy use. It is by far the most abundant source of energy we can tap. Even using current technology, we can easily meet the world's current electricity demands using solar alone.

The most common solar systems are called photovoltaics (PV). These convert sunlight directly into electricity and are a common sight in many neighborhoods, and will likely be the majority of the solar installed as we transition away from fossil fuels. There is huge potential for PV systems, but also some issues. One plus is that the sun provides plenty of energy we can harness. A 2021 study concluded that we could meet the world's electricity demands by placing PV systems on just 50% of the world's total rooftop area. The study's authors assumed that 100% of the roof area would be available, so this estimate is certainly low, but it demonstrates the enormous potential power generation just on existing roofs. The largest issue with solar is that, obviously, some areas are going to benefit from it more than others. The sunny areas of the western United States are far more productive than, say, the cloudy skies of the UK. Also obvious is that sometimes it's night. While technological advancements in solar panels themselves will improve efficiency (most solar panels convert about 20% of the light they receive into electricity, but this may be improved to as much as 40%), the storage of the energy they produce is still a large barrier to their wide implementation. Solutions include storing excess energy by pumping water uphill during the day and releasing it through turbines to generate it at night, or using electric motors to lift weights that are released to reverse the process when power is needed. The most efficient option is to store the electricity in batteries.

A quick note on batteries. We are going to need a lot of them in the future, and limitations in current battery technology must be resolved. These are primarily that they wear out, and are composed of hard to come by elements like lithium. Scientists are working on both of these. Solid-state technology is soon coming to market. These batteries have no liquid components so they are safer, more durable, and have a much higher energy density. Additionally, many labs have already developed batteries that utilize all kinds of different materials. Where the technology eventually goes is hard to tell, but there are a lot of solutions being explored to make batteries with increased energy densities and lower costs. While battery technology is a barrier now, I don't think it will be in the future.

So why don't we just put solar panels and batteries on everyone's house? Why not, indeed? In the U.S., especially in the west, many, if not most, people could cover their current electricity use with a solar PV system. With ample battery storage, they could run their households not just overnight but for several days without using any energy from the grid. In poorer nations, even very small PV systems could cover their needs and, in many communities, bring electricity to them for the first time. The largest barrier here is cost (and the monopolies of power companies in the U.S.). While the price per watt of solar energy has come down 90% in the last decade, installing a system to cover your needs, especially when adding a battery system, still can cost tens of thousands of dollars. This is a big investment for the average person and totally out of reach for the poor. I'll discuss this more when I talk about the government's role, but quick thought—

put fossil fuel subsidies into clean energy. The U.S. alone directly gives 20 billion dollars of federal and state money to subsidize the fossil fuel industry each year. That would buy a lot of solar panels.

There is one solution that may solve most of the drawbacks of solar, and that is space-based solar. Currently, it's not a technology we could take to scale, but theoretically, space-based solar stations could continually collect light without the 30% loss due to the earth's atmosphere, the threat of cloudy days, or the sun ever setting. Once collected, the energy would then be beamed, in the form of microwaves, to an Earth-based collection plant. Here, the energy would be converted back into electricity and sent into the grid. While it sounds fantastical, we can do this with current technology, and we know solar panels work well in space. Nearly all of our satellites, which are essential for so many things from communication to navigation and weather, and the International Space Station all run on solar power. The idea is viable enough that the U.S. Air Force is planning to have a space-based solar test platform in place in the next couple of years. Space is expensive, and there certainly will be technological barriers to overcome. While this likely will not represent a significant part of clean energy production in the near term, space-based solar has enormous potential for the future.

While for the most part solar can meet our energy needs, if our reliance on fossil fuels has taught us anything, it has taught us that going all in on a single energy source might not be the best idea. Diversification in where we get our energy is key to a stable green energy supply in the future. Part of this future will certainly contain wind energy. Already a significant player in renewables, wind, and especially offshore wind, can help bridge the energy gap in places that see less sun. A quarter of the UK's energy is already being produced by a combination of on-shore and offshore wind turbines. In the U.S., wind is quickly becoming the second-largest source of electricity, although it accounts for just 8% of the total. Farmers in the Great Plains of America have been able to capitalize on the windy, wide-open expanses and gain extra income by allowing wind projects on their grazing and croplands. Unlike solar, the small footprint of a wind turbine allows them to integrate well into agricultural lands. In the future, regenerative farms and even wild grasslands may not only be restoring soil and sequestering carbon but also helping to produce our electricity. There is plenty of wind in the world's oceans, and offshore wind farms can produce ocean-friendly energy without taking up space on land or displacing sea life. There are, of course, drawbacks to wind energy that might limit where we place large installations. The quickly rotating blade tips of a modern wind turbine make it extremely difficult for birds to avoid. Consideration of this, especially along migration paths, is essential to minimize losses. Detailed environmental studies should eliminate wind projects in areas where losses will be unacceptably high.

Hydroelectric power is already the most widely used renewable in use today, making up nearly 20% of the total electricity produced worldwide. Of course, building dams has many negative environmental impacts, and going forward the expansion of traditional hydroelectric power is probably a step backward when talking about conserving biodiversity. However, new designs in hydro-technology, such as ultra-fish-friendly shaft power plants that do not dramatically alter the river course or its surroundings, may be the way forward for countries that have lots of rivers and little sun. In remote or developing areas with the right topography, low-impact, small-scale hydroelectric could be a plentiful source of green power. These systems do not dam rivers, but simply divert some of the flow to a small power plant at a lower elevation, then return the water to its normal course. While a source of carbon-free power, climate change itself may limit our ability to use hydropower. The years-long drought in the western U.S. has already threatened to render several major hydropower stations useless.

Geothermal energy is common in some countries, and there is no reason it couldn't be implemented worldwide. Geothermal is an excellent way to generate power by just using the heat generated in the Earth, and it is by far the most efficient way to heat a structure, whether it be a residential home, an industrial complex, or a greenhouse operation. For those not familiar with geothermal, let me explain. It turns out that if you dig really deep into the Earth, it gets hot down there; the middle is molten, explaining things like thermal springs and volcanoes. Geothermal systems essentially use wells drilled deep into the Earth to collect some of this heat and bring it to the surface. Unfortunately, drilling deep wells is expensive, and this is the largest barrier to wide implementation. It's most cost effective in areas that have thermal features close to the surface, eliminating the need for deep wells. There are also shallow geothermal systems available for residential applications that use the ground's stable temperatures just a few feet below the surface, warming in the winter and cooling in the summer. These systems are by far the most efficient way to heat and cool your house. Cost is still a significant barrier, but the technology is there and it works. There is also discussion that abandoned oil and gas wells could be converted to be used for geothermal energy. There are thousands of these wells throughout the world. With most of the work already done, this could be a cost-effective way to expand this clean energy source.

The most controversial of all the carbon free ways to generate electricity is by using nuclear energy. However, it may be a necessary evil. We need to transition off fossil fuels extremely rapidly, and we might not be able to solve the storage problems that come with renewables in the time we have. The huge advantage of nuclear plants is that they can operate at scale, controlling their output like a traditional power plant. They also easily integrate with existing power grids. There are serious concerns with traditional fission power, and rightly so. Accidents like the Chernobyl explosion and the more recent issues in Fukushima, Japan, highlight the dangers of a highly radioactive power source, not to mention the issue of disposing of spent nuclear fuel that can continue to be dangerous for generations. New technologies can reduce this risk with safer plants that can reprocess spent fuel from older-style reactors while producing power.

The holy grail of nuclear power is, of course, fusion power. These systems could theoretically produce much more power than a traditional nuclear power plant without generating any radioactive waste. Once operational, they could produce a nearly infinite amount of clean power. A major breakthrough in fusion power technology could solve the world's energy problems almost overnight. Many naysayers point out that decades of work still have not produced a working fusion reactor. While this is true, there has been progress despite funding issues. For example, the U.S. puts about 500 million dollars into magnetic confinement fusion research each year, which sounds like a lot, but they give 20 billion dollars to oil and gas companies just for existing.

While rather large technological barriers exist, with sufficient effort and investment, there is no reason we could not see an operational fusion reactor within a decade. Remember, the United States went from no manned space program to sending astronauts to the moon in just 8 years. Accomplishing this took 40,000 people at NASA and roughly 120 billion dollars in today's money. We are nowhere near making the investment to make fusion happen, thus the slow results. Note that 120 billion dollars over a decade would be dramatically less than what we would give in subsidies to fossil fuels, with the result being unlimited clean power. Maybe it's time once again for a moonshot moment. This time, instead of leaving Earth, we focus on saving it. Along the way, humanity gains a technology so transformative it would make going to the moon seem insignificant.

As I mentioned earlier, the goal of green electricity is twofold. It allows us to eliminate the emissions from fossil fuel production of electricity and many of the emissions from the transportation sector by powering our ground transportation with electricity. While electric cars are still a niche product, they are becoming more mainstream every day, and most of the major auto manufacturers are already pouring billions of dollars into developing electric cars. Battery technology improvements will decrease charging times and increase ranges. With a dramatic increase in the number and efficiency of charging stations, electric cars are becoming more practical with less hassle. The largest issues preventing the conversion to electric cars are price and charging. People used to putting gas in their cars are used to filling their tanks and being on the go. Many worry about getting where they need to go in a timely manner. This will continue to be an issue, but the fact is, nearly all of the driving people do is close to home. Rarely do people take long trips, and in the rare instance they do, good planning can overcome most of the issues. As rapid charging stations expand, this will become easier still. Soon you'll be able to add plenty of range as you eat lunch or stop at an attraction on your drive. As manufacturers convert more of their production to electric cars, prices will eventually come down, and it's likely that the electric version of a car may be only marginally higher than that of the gas version. Government incentives should continue even as prices decline. Conversion to electric cars will be much more rapid if they actually cost less than fossil fuel-powered cars.

Cars, of course, aren't the only form of transportation. Public transportation systems are perfect for electrification. In large cities, many of the subway and train systems are already electric, and electrification is perfect for buses that are constantly starting and stopping. In development now are chargers that can be embedded in the roadway itself. Technology like this could allow buses to charge as they follow their routes, eliminating the need to take them out of service to charge. The same technology could be used for mail trucks that follow the same route each day. Of course, the goal is to electrify as much of our transportation as possible, and that also means the trucks we use for shipping and delivery. Delivery trucks work well when electrified. They travel short distances and usually return at night to a central location, which simplifies them being charged each day. Long-haul trucks are more difficult, but range issues may be solved by installing batteries into the trailers hauling goods. At night, the truck and trailer could be charged. When they arrive at their destination, a fresh, pre-charged trailer comes with the outbound load. This would take coordination between trucking companies and their customers, but it certainly could be done. Another solution would be swappable battery packs. Tesla already has a system in place that can robotically change out a car's battery pack while you wait. Truck stops could use a similar system that takes about the same amount of time as filling the truck with fuel.

While the electrification of the majority of our ground transportation is certainly doable, the electrification of other forms of transportation will likely never be practical. Making air travel and ocean-based shipping carbon neutral will be two of the largest challenges we will face. Both of these, especially shipping via fleets of enormous container ships, account for the majority of transportation emissions globally. Sea based shipping alone contributes more CO_2 to the atmosphere each year than the nation of Germany. It is also likely we will need to power many of the world's existing fossil-fuel cars for years to come. The most practical solution is likely the use of carbon-neutral fuel sources as more or less direct replacements for fossil fuels. Biofuels are one solution, but as of yet are still typically more carbon intensive in the long run than using fossil fuels. Advances in this area could provide a significant source of climate-friendly fossil fuel replacements. Hydrogen is also emerging as a new fuel of choice. Clean burning with water as the main by-product, it not only can be burned directly, but also can be used in a hydrogen fuel cell to produce electricity. Hydrogen-fueled passenger trains are already in use in Germany on some of their non-electrified lines, and aircraft manufacturer Airbus is working on having the first hydrogen powered commercial aircraft in the skies by 2035. Outside of transportation, hydrogen may also represent a replacement for natural gas using existing natural gas infrastructure. Wide adoption of hydrogen as an alternative fuel source is still hampered by the energy required to produce it. The most common way is electrolysis, which passes electricity through water, breaking the oxygen and hydrogen bonds. This can be accomplished using green electricity sources, thus providing a carbon-neutral way to convert electricity into an easily transportable multi-use fuel. However, producing hydrogen may not be necessary with some geologists now believing that there may be vast stores of accessible hydrogen within Earth's crust, but this remains to be seen.

Maybe the most practical solution for the direct replacement of fossil fuels may be by making them in a carbon neutral way. One novel idea is to produce hydrocarbon-based fuels by pulling CO_2 out of the air. Here, CO_2 is extracted from the air and assembled via a catalytic process into many of the hydrocarbon-based fuels we are familiar with. While this will not remove CO_2 permanently from the atmosphere, it will prevent more from entering by replacing extracted fossil fuels. These carbon-neutral fuels could have a huge impact in the fight to become global net-zero emitters, and there are multiple companies working on the technology right now. Completely carbon-neutral natural gas, jet fuel, and gasoline have already been produced, and companies are looking to scale up to full production. Like many emerging technologies, the largest barrier is cost, and it will be extremely difficult without substantial subsidies for these fuels to compete with fossil fuel sources. However, wide adoption of these fuels could rapidly help us to decarbonize our transportation without the need for advanced technologies. Both shipping and air travel could convert to these fuels with no modification to existing fleets, and while less efficient than electrification for ground transport, they could provide a vital bridge to reducing emissions as electrified transport comes online.

While these carbon-neutral fuels could be a real game changer for global shipping, there is a relatively simple solution to the carbon cost of traversing the world's oceans, by returning to a power source used for thousands of years, wind. There are several companies already providing shipping on sail-powered cargo ships. One of these companies, Sailcargo, is currently using a 137 ft square-rigged schooner called the *Vega,* originally built in 1909. Starting in 2023, carrying 80 tons, it will make regular trips ferrying coffee between Columbia and New Jersey. She will later be joined by the *Ceiba* that is currently being built. This sail and electric hybrid ship will be able to carry 250 tons to ports around the world. Another company, TransOceanic Wind Transport, plans to have two new cargo sailing ships, capable of hauling 1,100 tons of freight each, sailing routes by 2024. Under construction now, these ships will be joined by as many as 30 others by 2030. While right now these ships are primarily small and of traditional sailing designs, the future could bring much larger and more technologically advanced designs to the seas. Already in development, the Oceanbird concept ship will utilize an advanced hull design and wing-type sails. At more than 650 ft long, it will be capable of transporting 7,000 cars across the ocean. Sailing ships will likely never be able to carry the amount of goods of a huge modern container ship, but these smaller vessels may have an important role to play in making shipping on the high seas a much more sustainable endeavor.

Making energy generation, transportation, and agriculture all carbon neutral could reduce human carbon emissions by 65-75%, a huge step in keeping the climate stable for us and the rest of the biosphere. Advances in technology will make this easier and cheaper, but the good news is there is no need to wait for major technological leaps to make many of the changes we need. We can start making significant changes immediately. Of course, we will need to do more work to get to zero. Cutting our remaining emissions will likely need radical new technologies. One of the most difficult challenges may be the elimination of emissions from the production of vital materials such as steel and concrete. These two materials alone account for 16% of global CO_2 emissions. One solution could be the production of carbon nanomaterials. These materials could replace steel and concrete in buildings at a lighter weight and higher strength. If made from natural gas, they can eliminate the emissions from the production of other materials, while providing hydrogen without CO_2 emissions. While more difficult to do, it's possible that these materials could even be produced from CO_2 in the air, reducing atmospheric CO_2, providing high strength materials, and permanently fixing carbon within their structures.

Whatever solutions ultimately become the most widely adopted remain to be seen. Likely, a combination will be deployed in various ways, especially for energy production and transportation, but it is clear that the solutions are there. Many are not yet ready to be deployed at scale, but with significant investment, some could be available in just a matter of years.

What you can do:

Take responsibility for your own emissions and work to zero. Look at the biggest sources of your emissions and reduce or eliminate them. There are various carbon calculators available on the internet that can help you see where your emissions are coming from. Making large financial investments won't be possible for everyone, but if you can afford it, put solar panels on your house, buy an electric car, make your house more energy efficient, upgrade your heating and cooling systems to a heat pump, and convert to electric appliances. The good news is that, financially, all these things will save you money in the long run. Fly as little as you can, but if you have to, either you or your company can invest in offsets for the emissions.* Look at what you buy, how it's produced, and if what you purchase is actually necessary. Most of us have a garage or basement full of crap we didn't really need, and all of it has associated emissions. While on this subject, do you really need to buy an electric car? Do you actually need a car at all? Riding a bike is a much better choice; there are no emissions from burning fossil fuels to move it or the emissions from producing the car. In fact, buying an e-bike may be the best overall solution. Using the energy that you can generate from PVs in one square meter of land can get you around 1000 miles in an electric car, but over 20,000 on an e-bike. With the surge of people working from home and future improvements in public transportation and car sharing services, many might find it's not worth the cost or hassle to own a vehicle, especially if you live in a large city. When you want to take a long trip, you can simply rent a car. You can afford this because you didn't have to pay to purchase, register, maintain, or store a car of your own. Car-loving Americans might find this difficult. To them I ask, do you really need 2 cars? Or three? (We have a lot of cars.)

Your money talks. Invest in green companies, divest from fossil fuels, and financially support organizations that are working on climate solutions. Lastly, push your government representatives to eliminate subsidies for fossil fuels and put that money into reducing carbon emissions, including investments in solar, wind, fusion research, public transportation, and incentives for people like yourself to decarbonize their lives. Demand more from your governments. They are not doing nearly enough, nearly fast enough. For example, governments around the world are still approving fossil fuel-fired power stations, even coal-burning stations. With a typical lifespan of 40 years, we cannot meet emissions goals by building new fossil fuel plants. Approving such projects this late in the game shows either apathy or stupidity from those in government. In most of the world, we are the ones that vote for who runs our countries, and voting at the local level through the national level for candidates who are serious about climate and the environment is crucial.

*Note on offsets: Research these closely. Many are little more than a scam. You giving money to a company that owns a protected patch of forest that will absorb CO_2 anyway does not offset what you're doing. Try to invest in companies that are striving to take *more* CO_2 out of the atmosphere with your money, i.e., reforestation projects, rewilding projects, carbon sequestration projects, or the like. Also, if you could just "offset" all of your emissions, emissions wouldn't be a problem in the first place. Also note, any program that actually might make a difference won't be cheap.

What government can do:

Subsidize clean and carbon-neutral energy and end the enormous subsidies on fossil fuels, which are a significant amount. Subsidies to fossil fuels worldwide are valued at around 345 billion dollars, including direct money, tax breaks, and other perks. The broader impact of these subsidies when considering environmental costs might be costing us as much as 5.9 trillion dollars, according to the IMF. Instead of subsidizing fossil fuels, subsidy programs must expand to help people install PV systems, buy electric cars, upgrade heating and cooling systems, etc. through direct government grants and low-interest loans, not just tax credits. Some of this is already being done, but more needs to be done to make green choices cheaper and more accessible than the fossil fuel alternatives. Regulation in the energy sector needs to promote green energy rather than discourage it. Multiple states in the U.S. have policies or allow rules that discourage or prevent people from installing rooftop solar. People should have the freedom to generate their own power if they so wish, and our governments have a role to play in making sure that our energy providers cannot prevent people from doing so.

Governments should also get serious about expanding green infrastructure by focusing money into improving power grids, public transportation, electrifying their vehicle fleets, and improving building efficiency. The U.S. has taken the first steps in funding these types of improvements with an infrastructure bill passed in 2021 that provides 7.5 billion dollars for installing electric car chargers, $3 billion to support battery manufacturing, $5 billion dollars for electric transit buses, $5 billion dollars for green school buses, and $65 billion dollars to upgrade the U.S. electrical grid. Governments must also adopt much stronger climate mandates and create frameworks to enforce them. They should start with themselves in reducing emissions by forming actual plans to eliminate emissions; not just goals that can be ignored. All of the countries that have signed on to the Paris Agreement, save one, are behind schedule.

A carbon tax will be necessary to incentivize abandoning fossil fuels. Most companies will continue business as usual until it is economically prohibitive not to change. A tax on the carbon businesses emit will force them to confront their emissions for the sake of their bottom line. In an ideal world, this wouldn't be necessary, but whoever tells you that businesses will "do the right thing" even if it costs them money is naive or lying. How many businesses have had products they knew were killing their customers but kept selling them anyway? The focus of business is making money. While some will make the choice to reduce emissions voluntarily, the vast majority will not. Money collected for carbon taxes must be put directly into carbon-reducing programs, rewilding and reforestation. Implementing these taxes will not be popular, but should be done as soon as possible to push change.

The most impactful thing governments can do is begin to transition their economies off of an infinite growth model and reduce or eliminate the use of GDP as an indicator of economic health. I'll discuss this more a bit later, but it's clear that building and consuming more for the sake of economic growth is not going to allow us to reduce our emissions sufficiently. How our economies are structured also impacts much more than just our greenhouse gas emissions.

Fighting climate change is going to have to be a global effort, and the world's governments are going to have to get on the same page. If the idea of leaders all around the world agreeing on something and then actually acting on it seems far-fetched, take heart. While little has been done to curb carbon emissions, world governments have actually been able to work together in the past on other issues. In 1987, amidst wide support, the Montreal Protocol banned the sale and production of 100 ozone depleting substances. It was ratified by *every* member of the U.N.; all 198 of them. Seeing the threat to the Earth's protective ozone layer, nations came together to curb this threat. Moving to carbon neutrality is certainly going to be a bigger challenge, but if the nations of the world could come together once, it's at least possible they could do it again.

Protection of Land, Species, and Rewilding

The world's biodiversity and climate need natural spaces. We can make huge inroads in saving the former while stabilizing the latter by protecting and expanding the Earth's wildlands. Currently only 17% of the world's land is protected in some way, and this will not be nearly enough to keep biodiversity and its vital functions intact. Many suggest that the lofty goal of setting aside 50% of the world's land masses and a targeted 30% of the world's oceans will be necessary to stem the tide of species loss and revive the oceans. In fact, recently published research shows that we must retain a minimum of 44% of the Earth's terrestrial area in natural landscapes to maintain Earth's current biodiversity. The world should set this as a goal and aggressively work toward it. Living things need space, and giving them the space they need may be the easiest and most beneficial thing humanity can do.

The best news on this front is that we know that these things can not only be done, but can be successful. The world's national parks and wildlife preserves, the forest restorations of Costa Rica, and legislation like the U.S. Migratory Bird Act and the Endangered Species Act attest to this. We must simply continue these long-standing efforts, but now with a renewed effort to expand protected areas, restore degraded landscapes, and increase the enforcement of the laws that protect wildlife.

Yes, humans have had devastating negative impacts on nature, but we have also learned to protect it. There are thousands of examples, large and small, that demonstrate this. We can use these past examples to guide our new push to save biodiversity. Here are just some of the examples of what we have been able to accomplish.

Protection of lands is not a new concept. The history of wildlife preserves goes back at least to the Middle Ages, but what is new is the reason for protecting lands and wildlife. For most of history, preserves simply existed to secure forests and wildlife for the aristocracy. These private preserves protected lands from mass exploitation but primarily served to keep resources for the rich and away from the poor. That all changed with the creation of the world's first national park. In 1872, Yellowstone National Park was created in the United States, not as a hunting preserve for the rich but to protect the amazing landscapes and its wildlife for the public and their future generations. This new concept, to protect land for its own sake—not for exploitation but so that wild lands remained wild —was revolutionary. Since this first park, nations around the world have realized the importance of protecting part of their natural heritage. Just since 2010, over 21 million sq km (8 million sq miles) of land have been preserved, an area larger than Russia, continuing the legacy of Yellowstone. While not all are protected at the level of a national park, these newly protected areas demonstrate the continued commitment to preserve the Earth's remaining wild places.

While the protected lands we have now are not enough, they lay the groundwork for expansion. The key to this is not only expanding protected lands but also connecting these lands to each other. Even at over 2 million acres, Yellowstone is still too small to support its wealth of large vertebrates. It's often the case that even large national parks and protected areas are too small to permanently ensure the protection of the landscapes and wildlife they are meant to protect. Protected areas can act just like islands, but connecting adjacent lands through wildlife corridors can allow species to migrate, find new breeding partners, and set up new populations. This becomes even more essential as climate change forces species to move around. As we move to protect 50% of our land, we can also ensure that these protected lands are not in isolation but part of continent-wide networks. An example of this is the Rocky Mountain Wildway, an effort by dozens of organizations to connect protected lands along the Rocky Mountain Range from Alaska to Mexico. When fully realized, wildlife will have access to more than 6,000 miles of North America through three countries.

If we are to set aside 50% of our land for nature, we'll need to protect all of the world's remaining wilderness, but we are also going to have to restore vast amounts of land to restore its native biodiversity. This, too, is possible. Due to unrestricted logging and the expansion of agriculture, by the 1980s, Costa Rica's forest cover was reduced to just 25%, a far cry from the 75% forest cover it enjoyed just 40 years before. Seeing their dwindling forests, the government decided to take action, taking control of logging and implementing a system that pays landowners to protect and restore forests. In just 30 years, the country was able to double its rainforests, and in doing so, it has become a model for other countries.

We repeatedly see that with a little help, nature can rebound to an amazing extent. One of the most impressive examples of this is Gorongosa National Park in Mozambique. First established as a hunting preserve in the 1920s, the area became a national park in 1960. African wildlife thrived here, from herds of grazers such as antelope, buffalo, and wildebeest to hippos and elephants, as well as a slew of Africa's top predators such as the iconic lion, leopard, and the now-rare African wild dog. Unfortunately, a civil war ravaged the country for more than 20 years. By the time it ended in 1992 and hunting in the then-abandoned national park was finally stopped, 95% of the park's large animals were gone. Thanks to conservation efforts, most recently a collaboration between the U.S.-based non-profit Carr Foundation and the Mozambique government, Gorongosa is returning to its pre-war splendor. By 2010, a survey of nine key species showed a 50% recovery compared to prewar numbers, and by 2019, these same species had recovered by nearly 95%. Once extirpated from the park, reintroduced African wild dogs are now thriving once again. Following the reintroduction of 15 dogs into the park in 2018 and another 15 a year later, the population has exploded. As of June 2020, the population exceeded 100 individuals. Now with four separate packs and the majority of the park still to be populated, Gorongosa could be at the heart of the recovery of these critically endangered animals. If we can bring back a landscape as degraded as Gorongosa and double the rainforest of Costa Rica in just a few decades, we can do the same anywhere. We just need to have the will.

We do not always have to take part in active restoration, however. Nature has an amazing ability for recovery, and in many cases, just allowing land to return to its wild state all on its own could be the best answer. The best example of this is certainly the Chernobyl Exclusion Zone (CEZ). In 1986, the world's worst nuclear accident irradiated a huge swath of northern Ukraine. To protect people from the long-term effects of the radiation, a 2,800 sq km (1,000 sq mi) zone was closed to human habitation. What happened over the next 30 years was unintended and unexpected. Nature flourished. Despite high levels of radioactive contamination, the remnants of Ukraine's wild past have repopulated this landscape in the absence of humans and their actions. In the decade after the accident, the populations of red deer, roe deer, elk, and wild boar all exploded. Forests regrew, and wolves returned. In fact, wolf populations in the CEZ are seven times higher than the surrounding areas. Now the CEZ is the third largest wildlife preserve in Europe and is home to more than 60 species now rare in Europe, including the Eurasian lynx, brown bear, and European bison. It has even become a haven for the endangered Przewalski's horse, introduced into the zone in 1998. Concerns linger about the lasting effects of radiation on the wildlife of Chernobyl, but the amazing recovery of nature proves that if nature can return there, it can return anywhere. Some landscapes will certainly need our help to recover, and we can speed the process of recovery by planting trees and recovering grassland diversity by reintroducing species lost to the land. Helping these landscapes recover quickly can maximize their contribution to reducing climate change and restoring necessary habitats for species on the brink. As we undertake these directed recoveries, it is comforting to know that much of the land we set aside will come back on its own.

As we protect and restore our world's wild spaces, we can also transform our urban spaces into places that promote and protect biodiversity. While they will never be as rich as true wilderness, our own cities and towns could still be rich with life if we only made that a priority. The good news is that there are many things that can be done within our own communities to make this happen. Already, more and more cities around the world are embracing initiatives to plant more trees, expand urban forests and green spaces, create community and rooftop gardens, and embrace new building techniques that integrate nature within their structures, creating "vertical forests" within the urban landscape. One of the first constructions in the "vertical forest" concept is in Milan, Italy. Called Bosco Vertical, these high-rise apartment blocks contain more than 800 trees, 5,000 shrubs, and more than 15,000 plants. Described as a "home for trees that also houses humans and birds," this ingenious design allows for 30,000 square meters (7 acres) of woodland to occupy just 3,000 square meters (.74 acres) of urban land. Not only does this provide a lush and beautiful living space that benefits pollinators and birds, but it also helps to regulate the building's temperature and humidity while filtering pollutants. Projects like Bosco Vertical are planned for cities throughout the world, and the concept, realized in new constructions and added to existing ones, could dramatically transform our urban landscapes from lifeless concrete jungles to something that actually resembles a jungle.

While integrating biodiversity into our buildings may be a valuable tool for the future of urban construction, there are much less technical ways to expand nature within our cities. Most cities have disused land that could be converted to parks or green space for the enjoyment of humans and wildlife. In New York City, after a push from the community, an abandoned raised railway was turned into a nearly one and a half mile long raised park. Called the High Line, the old railway now is home to 120 species of plants attracting bees, birds, and millions of visitors each year. Paris has its own version of the High Line called the Coulée Verte, or Green Course. It follows 2.9 miles of the former tracks of the Vincennes railway line and was one of the first urban greenways to repurpose disused rail paths for urban green space. These and many other projects like them show the potential to bring nature back to our urban landscapes by converting unused and obsolete infrastructure into valuable pockets of biodiversity within our cities.

Of course, just as vital as protecting our lands is protecting our oceans. Here again, there are success stories. Overfishing has depleted our oceans, but protecting key habitats such as reefs, mangroves, and seagrass plains could restore nature and healthy fish stocks for people. The key is setting aside critical habitats in strict no-take preserves. One project off the coast of the Baja Peninsula in the Gulf of California in Mexico has done just that. Due to years of overfishing, the waters of Cabo Pulmo contained just a shadow of the diversity they once did. The local community banded together and lobbied the Mexican government to protect the area. The result was the establishment of Cabo Pulmo National Park in 1995 as the first no-take preserve in the Gulf of California and the revitalization of the area's ocean ecosystem. In just the 10 years between 1999 and 2009, the fish biomass within the protected area grew by an astonishing 463%. Even more impressive, the biomass of top predators grew by over 1,000%. Absent from the area for years, sharks once again swam the reef. As life in the protected zone exploded, fish overflowed into the fishing zones, revitalizing the area's fisheries. Not only did wildlife and fisherman benefit, but new opportunities for the local community arrived as tourism increased with people flocking to see the thriving reef system. The local community continues to be a vital stakeholder, promoting and enforcing the area's protections.

This idea of conservation is in no way new. The practice of closing key areas to fishing has been practiced in Palau for generations. This isolated nation in the middle of the Pacific has relied on its local fish populations for more than 4,000 years, so management of its fisheries has always been a priority. The traditional practices that have served them so well for so long continue today. The Palauan government does not hesitate to close one of the country's reefs to fishing immediately if fish stocks begin to wane. This, combined with seasonal closures, limitations on exports, and the closure of 80% of Palau's territorial waters to fishing, allow them to maintain an excess of fish for their own needs and creates a vital refuge for Pacific reef species. Using examples like these, protecting just one third of ocean habitats as strict no-take preserves could recover the majority of the ocean's fish populations in just 30 years. Some initially will resist these fishing restrictions. However, given time this would not only revitalize our world's oceans, but also allow fishermen to sustainably catch more fish than they have in generations.

While we can and should protect and restore every bit of land possible, we can improve this effort by identifying and prioritizing the location and type of habitats we should protect and restore. The only way to maximize our ability to do this is to dramatically increase our knowledge of the world's biodiversity by identifying its species, their habitat requirements, and the interactions between species that maintain the Earth's living systems. Only by gaining this knowledge can we ensure that the majority of Earth's species have the adequate space and the necessary habitats to thrive. While more emphasis is needed in government and academia, we are seeing progress. The availability of data on the natural world is expanding. Much of the knowledge we do possess is becoming more accessible thanks to organizations like the Global Biodiversity Information Facility. GBIF compiles huge amounts of biodiversity data and allows researchers to access occurrence data for species around the world. Since 2007, the amount of data available just through GBIF has grown by over 1,000%. Even more good news for those wishing to help add to our knowledge base of species and where they occur, is the emergence of "citizen scientist" based programs such as eBird and iNaturalist where non-professional enthusiast observers as well as professionals can log their observations of when and where they come upon species where they live. eBird, operating since 2002, was one of the early leaders in harnessing amateur observations for data collection. Those in the birding community tend to be serious enthusiasts in their hobby, many spending years or even decades detailing when, where, and what species they were observing. In the past, most of this valuable data was not accessible by anyone but the observers themselves. eBird's online format changed that and now collects over 100 million observations every year worldwide. These types of programs are generating large amounts of valuable data and are growing. The occurrence data collected by volunteer observers accounted for only 11% of the data coming into GBIF in 2007, by 2020, this had increased to 65%. Best of all, anyone can participate and add their own valuable piece to the puzzle.

The importance of protecting and restoring our wildlands and waters is paramount, but with the protection and restoration, we must address the extremely prevalent and extremely damaging issue of invasive species. Removing invasive species and preventing the spread of new ones will be a critical part of maintaining the Earth's biodiversity. Little progress has been made on this front globally. Although the elimination of problem species in specific protected areas has been successful in reestablishing stable plant and animal communities, most of these projects have been small-scale. Many invasive species issues (especially in our waterways) may be extremely difficult, if not impossible, to eliminate. Mitigation programs are vital to give native species a chance, and additional effort is desperately needed to prevent yet more invasive species from being introduced. Invasive species get introduced into the world's environments in many different ways, but at their root, international trade is the biggest culprit. Stricter biosecurity measures and the adoption of larger penalties for violations of these measures are necessary. The world's economies must come together to form a unified front. Another major issue is the exotic species trade and, far too often, species once housed as pets are naively released into the wild. While I understand the fascination of wanting to own some of these amazing creatures, it is time to end the exotic pet trade. There are few, if any, benefits to the animals themselves, and serious negative impacts to many of the species traded and to the environment as a whole. It's hard to argue for any legitimate reason for private citizens to own rare or exotic species of animals.

There have been numerous successes around the world in eliminating some invasive species. Though we have a long way to go, there is hope on this front. Already mentioned are the elimination of goats and other introduced species on some of the Galápagos Islands, and the rats of Alaska's Rat Island have now been gone for over a decade after an extensive eradication campaign. With the rats gone, seabirds devastated by predation returned, they in turn fed on mollusks, which were devastating the island's kelp beds. Just 11 years after the elimination of the rats, the island's ecosystem now looks like other islands that have never had them. While these types of restorations aren't as publicized as some, lots of successful work has been done. Since the 1950s, there have been more than 900 successful invasive animal eradications on more than 800 of the world's islands. Large scale efforts are also underway on several continents, with the European Union now requiring member states to control or eradicate 37 non-native species, the United States incentivizing the unlimited capture of several species of invasive fish, and Australia committing to reducing its feral cat population by 2 million. The problem is overwhelmingly large, and unfortunately, to protect biodiversity, we must kill plants and animals that are doing nothing but what evolution has built them to do. This is an extremely sad outcome, but we have little other choice. I hope that in the future, humans can do a better job and we can eliminate the need to wipe out invasive species that are only there because of us.

While, setting aside lands and waters in parks and preserves and restoration of habitat and reintroduction of species is vitally important, these initiatives are only successful because of a framework of laws that ensure that wildlife is protected. Without these laws, our protected lands would be only in name, and our efforts could largely be for naught. This continued commitment to making and enforcing laws that protect biodiversity will remain critical. Prime examples are the Migratory Bird Act and the Endangered Species Act in the United States. The former, enacted in 1918, prohibited the hunting, taking, capturing, killing, or selling of over 1,000 species of migratory birds without a permit and, with it, the elimination of the commercial trade in these species. This pioneering law is responsible for saving numerous species from extinction and continues to work today to protect North America's birds. The Endangered Species Act, passed in 1973, built a framework to protect species in peril both nationally and internationally through the protection of habitat, the prohibition of trafficking, and recovery and reintroduction programs for listed species. It has been one of the most successful conservation laws ever. 99% of the species protected under the ESA have avoided extinction, and it's likely responsible for saving nearly 300 species of plants and animals from extinction so far, including bald eagles,

California condors, and gray whales. It is a testament to what governments can accomplish when committed to a good cause.

National and international laws have already saved numerous species from extinction, most famously the majority of the world's whale species, and while animals like tigers, rhinos, elephants, and the world's species of great apes are still critically imperiled, many of them would already be extinct if not for the protections extended to them. Going forward, increased enforcement of existing laws and new international agreements to shut down the illegal animal trade, logging, and fishing industries will have an enormous impact on the fight to preserve biodiversity.

What you can do:

Restoring wild spaces can begin in your own backyard by planting a mix of native pollinator-friendly and bird-friendly plants. You can help limit the dispersal of invasive plants by making sure what you are planting is either native, or a non-invasive species. Plant a tree. Sure, planting a single tree seems somewhat pointless, but if we could get everyone in the world to plant a single tree, we'd have 8 billion more trees. If you don't have a place to put a tree, pay someone to plant one somewhere else. Even better, pay them to plant a lot of trees. There are many reforestation programs; there is likely one in your own region. Support organizations that protect and restore our forests, grasslands, wetlands, and oceans. There are many reputable nonprofits doing great work, and they need funding to continue this work. If you don't have the money to donate, volunteer your time with one of these organizations.

Become a citizen scientist. There are numerous programs available to help add to our knowledge base of the living world, continuing the long tradition of nonprofessional scientists making vital contributions to life science. Plus, it's a great way to become more intimately involved in your own local environment. As always, lobby your local, state, and federal governments and tell them you want more land protected in national parks, wilderness areas and wildlife preserves, and green spaces in your communities. Tell them that expanding no-take preserves in coastal waters should be a priority. Lobby them to support expanding, strengthening, and funding laws that protect wildlife. Despite the success of the Endangered Species Act, only an estimated 3.5% of the funding deemed necessary by scientists for the species under ESA protection is actually allotted. Vote for candidates who support these positions at every level.

Again, pay attention to what you buy. If you're buying foods that use unsustainable palm oil and your furniture is made out of tropical hardwoods, you are part of the problem. Choose to not be a part of the problem. What you use and how much you use determines your personal impact on the loss of wildlands, from paper and wood products, to the types and origin of the food you eat and beyond. Research your choices and see what sort of impact they have. Choose the least damaging options or consider going without. There's a good reason I keep bringing this up. What we consume drives markets, and if we demand low impact, environmentally friendly products, that's what the market will provide. If we stop consuming certain things, those markets will become unprofitable and disappear. There is immense power in what we choose to buy, and consumption ultimately drives all of humanity's impacts on the environment.

What Government can do:

Governments have a large role to play in making the laws that protect resources and wildlife and have the power to make huge strides in helping to preserve 50% of our land and 30% of the ocean. Focus should be placed on the expansion of national parks and preserves while addressing the needs of people affected by these decisions by working closely with landowners and residents of protected lands to set up programs so that humans and wildlife can share resources to the benefit of both. Engage fishermen to protect coastal waters while providing them with support when affected by closures. This will be critical in expanding protected habitats. Expand funding for research to learn about the natural world and expand educational and job opportunities for those wanting to do this work. Wealthy governments should look seriously at financial incentives for poorer nations to preserve and restore their natural resources instead of exploiting them. This is important for halting the loss of rainforests and other vital habitats. Wealthy nations already give billions of dollars in aid to other countries for defense and humanitarian purposes, so this differs little from those programs already in place. Preservation of these lands is also necessary for the fight against climate change, and wealthy nations are the largest contributors. It's time for the largest emitters to pony up and help fight the global problem that they largely created. Financially incentivizing the protection of natural landscapes is an essential part. People in developing nations don't want to chop down their forests, but like all of us, they are simply trying to support their livelihoods. Let's make sure they have a better option.

Pollution

Pollution comes in many forms, from pesticides and fertilizers from agriculture, to human and industrial waste, the immense amount of trash we throw away, the cars we drive, and a myriad of other sources. Some of the solutions we've already talked about will help eliminate some of these sources. Revolutionizing agriculture may largely eliminate the need for fertilizers and pesticides on an industrial scale and prevent them from killing pollinators and polluting our waters. Moving to electrified transportation, clean power generation, and carbon-neutral fuels will eliminate not only the emissions from cars, trucks, and power plants, but also oil production and refining, cleaning our air in the process. Many may remember just how rapidly air quality improved as people stopped driving during the COVID-19 pandemic lockdowns. These changes will do little to impact pollution from industrial manufacturing, human waste, and the enormous amount of trash humans discard every day. However, there are solutions to these things too. We can implement some of them easily, meaning that we have the current technologies to prevent this pollution from entering the environment. Others will be much more difficult, and new materials and fundamental changes to the way we produce and consume goods will be necessary.

Water pollution is still a huge issue among nations, both wealthy and developing. Trash from our cities, pollution from industrial sources, and human waste will all continue to enter our waterways without solutions. Thankfully, there are solutions, and some are surprisingly simple. Take trash as an example. When rainwater hits our urban areas, it collects and flows through our streets and parking lots, taking with it trash and debris. This inevitably ends up in our waterways. Stopping much of this trash and debris can be as simple as installing a removable net where stormwater is being channeled, capturing trash, and allowing water to flow unimpeded. If widely implemented, along with other types of debris capture, we could significantly reduce the amount of trash entering our waterways and our oceans. Stormwater also picks up pollutants. Taking a cue from nature, more and more cities are understanding the value of wetlands to slow runoff and clean stormwater. Integrating man-made wetlands into stormwater systems allows pollutants and sediments to settle out, provides habitat green space for wildlife and people, restores the vital functions that wetlands provide, and takes stress off of combined stormwater sewer systems.

Human waste entering our waterways is still an enormous problem for humans and the ecosystem. 6 in 10 people living in the world do not have access to proper sanitation, and much of this waste ends up polluting waterways. Wealthy nations have solved much of this by building extensive sewer systems and waste treatment plants, but despite their infrastructure, the U.S., U.K., and EU all still have many cities with shared systems for human waste and stormwater. When heavy rains overwhelm these systems, they release untreated sewage into waterways. There are several ways to help eliminate this issue, and one is by building networks of artificial wetlands like the ones just mentioned. Separating these combined systems is also an option, but comes at a high cost. Also costly, but a potential solution is the storage of stormwater underground. Here, tunnels are bored beneath urban areas, acting as huge cisterns to capture rainwater until it can be treated. The city of Milwaukee in the U.S. has done this with excellent results. Their system has prevented 141 billion gallons of pollution from reaching Lake Michigan and has reduced overflows of its combined sewage system from an average of 50 to 60 overflows a year to just over 2.

Because of the cost and complexity of large, centralized waste systems, few developing nations can afford them. They may also be less practical than other options. One idea envisions decentralizing waste management, and one U.S. company called Epic CleanTec has developed and fielded a system that treats wastewater onsite. Their system can recycle 95% of its water and reuse it for non-potable purposes. Solid waste is sterilized and can be mixed with soil for a high-quality fertilizer. The system not only recovers waste for a useful purpose but also dramatically reduces water usage, an enormous plus for drought-stricken places like California. Using a similar system, the Salesforce building in San Francisco saves 30,000 gallons of water a day by recycling its water. Systems like this are ideal for large office buildings or apartment complexes and could reduce costs and increase the efficiency of waste management systems. Other solutions, especially in countries with little to no infrastructure, are much less high-tech, and one organization has revived and modernized an age-old idea. Called Sanergy, they have revived the idea of collecting what the Victorians called "night soil" and turning it into a valuable material. Working in the infrastructure-less parts of Nairobi, Kenya, Sanergy collects over 13,000 tons of human waste each year from lavatories they provide in poor neighborhoods, turning that waste into a safe and useful organic fertilizer that local farmers can use. Hoping to expand around the world, their system could be an inexpensive and scalable way to provide developing countries with a solution to human waste and its polluting effects.

Both of these systems hint at the ultimate solution to our waste problems. We need to stop thinking in straight lines. In nature, nothing is wasted. The end of one process feeds the next. These endless cycles of energy and nutrient transfer sustain all of Earth's biosphere. The reason we pollute so much is that much of what we produce and the by-products of that production are simply discarded. We need to stop the linear process of producing a good, using it, and then throwing it away. Simply, we need to recycle, but not the way we do it now. We need to recycle everything. This will take a serious change in how humans do business. First, we will need to make products that can be entirely recycled, and second, our industries will need to combine processes so that the waste of one industry becomes the raw materials for the next. We need to form a circular economy where we waste nothing, just like nature.

One example of how this could work in industry is the Kalundborg Symbiosis in the Netherlands. Here, a complex of 13 public and private companies shares resources such as water, materials, and energy. The outputs of one company become the inputs for another. This not only reduces energy use, CO_2 emissions, water use, and waste, but also saves money. Elsewhere, companies are beginning to look harder at the full life cycle of their products and are focusing on making their products fixable, upgradeable, or fully recyclable with the goal of eliminating end-of-use waste. Others are looking to take things that have already been discarded and turn them into new products. A major player in this revolution is a Taiwanese company called Miniwiz. Miniwiz is the brainchild of Arthur Huang, a passionate promoter of circular manufacturing who believes in a zero-waste future. His company now produces more than 1,200 products, all manufactured from waste from agriculture, construction, and consumer sources. Through innovation in materials science and careful consideration about the eventual fate of their own products, Miniwiz is demonstrating that a circular economy is a real possibility.

Of course, one of our biggest problems is what to do with all that plastic waste. Companies like Miniwiz are helping to solve that issue by taking plastic out of the environment and turning it into durable, long-use materials for building and other applications. The issue still remains that, unlike glass or metals, when things made of plastic come to the end of their lives, there is a limit to how many times they can be recycled. In the future, this may no longer be true, and it turns out nature may have solved this problem for us. A bacteria called *Ideonella sakaiensis* was first discovered in Japan in 2016 near a plastic recycling plant. What was special about these particular bacteria was that they were breaking down and feeding on PET plastics. Scientists were able to isolate the enzymes that the bacteria used to do this and then set about designing new enzymes that could be even more efficient. Just recently, scientists at the University of Texas at Austin have used advanced AI to develop the best one yet. Their new PETase is twice as efficient as the next-best enzyme. With it, they can degrade over 50 types of PET plastic. So efficient is it that, at a temperature of 50°C (122°F), it was able to completely degrade a plastic cake pan in just 48 hours. The discovery of enzymes such as this could be revolutionary in how we recycle plastics. Because they cause a complete breakdown of the plastic polymer, the material can be re-polymerized into new plastic, and plastics recycled in this way would be infinitely recyclable. Eventually, we may be able to recycle all types of plastic this way, taking them out of the environment and into a circular system that reutilizes them perpetually.

Using this new discovery, we would be able to keep plastics out of our oceans and landfills and even reclaim them from the environment, vastly reducing the issue of microplastic pollution. This is undoubtedly a huge start. However, we must first address our huge recycling problem. Making plastics that are infinitely recyclable will be great, but we barely recycle the plastics we can now. This is driven by the convenience of throwing away single-use plastics, poor recycling systems, and the fact that it's simply cheaper for companies to buy virgin material. For single-use applications such as packaging, where recycling them is either too difficult or too costly, new alternatives are needed. Ultimately, we might find that the continued use of traditional plastics, especially for food packaging, is too harmful to continue. We may also find that our recycling efforts cannot scale fast enough to prevent the buildup of plastic in our environment. In either case, replacements for the most common types of plastic are necessary. I see our ultimate approach as two-fold, with the ultimate goal of producing no new traditional plastic, ever. First, we need the total replacement of everyday plastic items like food containers, bottles, packaging, disposable cups, etc. with compostable and biodegradable materials, be they plant-based bioplastics or other earth-friendly materials. Second, we must begin recycling all traditional plastics into more permanent applications. This shift will not be easy, but it needs to happen as fast as possible, and the ability to do this exists. Hopefully in the near future, with the combination of a true circular path for traditional plastics and the wider use of bio-plastics and alternative materials, we can finally solve the plastic problem. Of course, as with other issues, there will be industries that will try hard to curb any reduction in plastic use or production, including the oil companies that supply the raw materials, the plastic producers themselves, and the industries that use the most plastic, particularly the food and beverage industry. Keep in mind the latter is often telling you they care about plastic waste as they use more every year.

As we transition away from fossil fuels, the internal combustion engine, and fossil fuel power generation, our air will improve, but this will all take time. There are things we could replace in short order, however. One of the most polluting things that we could rapidly replace is gasoline powered lawn equipment. Shockingly, the amount of ozone creating pollutants produced by small engines is actually more than produced by our cars. According to the U.S. EPA, hour for hour, our lawnmowers, trimmers, and leaf blowers produce 11 times more pollution than driving a car. Spurred on by this data, the state of California in the U.S. is banning the sale of new gasoline power equipment starting in 2024. The good news for anyone wanting to switch to cleaner options, a full range of electric power equipment is available from numerous manufacturers. Air pollution from manufacturing will continue to cause problems, but there is hope that continued and improved regulation worldwide can help to eliminate the majority of factory emissions. Unfortunately, one of the increasingly large contributors to our air quality, forest fires, is little in our control. Even more reason to change how human society is doing things rapidly.

We are coming up with novel ways to help fight air pollution, though. One company called Airlite produces a paint that not only does not pollute itself but actually cleans the air by combating air pollution. Using light and the paint's catalytic surface, it can convert nitrogen and sulfur oxides, benzene, formaldehyde, and carbon monoxide into non-reactive salts. Even better, these salt compounds create a mineral film that helps reduce radiant heating, saving energy on air conditioning. Lab tests show that Airlite's paint can reduce air pollution by 88%, but it doesn't just work in the lab. The paint's first real-world test came when it was put inside Rome's Umberto I road tunnel. Amazingly, even in a highly polluted situation like this, it was shown to reduce pollution in the tunnel by 51%. 100 square meters of surface painted with Airlite eliminates the same amount of pollution as 100 square meters of forest, and wide application in the world's cities could have a profound effect on local air pollution levels.

Certainly we have other pollution problems to be addressed, and we will likely struggle for years to reduce and eliminate the thousands of toxic chemicals society uses for an enormous range of applications. While some of these may not have alternatives, we may find upon closer inspection that the benefits of many commonly used chemicals are not worth the damage they do. PFAS come to mind, with the realization that maybe sticky pans and less stain-resistant clothing are a far better option than the toxic effects of these chemicals.

Let me close this section by bringing up an issue that's close to all of us and one that affects biodiversity by reducing valuable habitat, polluting our waterways, and using a huge amount of water. I'm talking about turf lawns. Americans alone apply 70 million pounds of fertilizers and 126 million pounds of pesticides to their lawns each year. In addition, they use an estimated 9 billion gallons of water each *day* to irrigate these lawns. While regenerative agriculture will reduce the bulk of fertilizer and pesticide use, a significant source of this pollution is in the hands of homeowners. Changing our practices surrounding our lawns by replacing much of our turf grass with native plant species would not only dramatically reduce pollution and save water, but open up a surprising amount of habitat. Just in the U.S., turf grass occupies some 163,813 sq km (63,000 sq mi) of land. This is more than the combined land area used to raise corn, wheat, and fruit trees, or an area larger than the state of Georgia. No one is advocating ripping up all of our sports fields or park open spaces, but converting a significant portion of this turf and normalizing and promoting lawns that use natural plantings could transform these monocrop landscapes into rich tapestries of native plant species. This benefits humans as well as countless species of insects, birds, and small animals.

What you can do:

Infinite recycling of plastics, while necessary, is still a long way off. We need to reduce our use immediately, and the best way to help is to buy as little of it as possible. That means no single-use plastic water or soda bottles. In fact, you should be appalled that these even still exist. Move to better storage options by eliminating single-use plastic bags for things like food storage. There are excellent silicone replacements on the market, and if it needs to be disposable, there are compostable versions available. In that vein, consider switching to compostable trash bags if your community offers composting. If composting is not an option, use a bag made of plant-based materials. It probably won't break down in a landfill (little does), but it won't pollute the environment if it does. One of the most difficult tasks in this regard may be identifying plastic in things that you think little about. For example, few of us would realize that most dryer sheets are made of sheets of polyester plastic unless we were told. The goal here is to eliminate plastic use of any kind when possible. Not an easy task, I know.

Recycle and dispose of all the items you use properly, especially batteries, lightbulbs, electronics, chemicals, and appliances. Recycling is good, but not using something in the first place is better. For example, you can buy a single-use plastic bottle and then put it in the recycling bin. Many assume that if something is placed in a recycling bin, it will actually be recycled, but this is often not the case, especially with plastics. If you have to buy a single-use container, aluminum bottles or cans or glass containers are a better choice and have a much higher likelihood of being recycled. About 50% of the aluminum we use gets recycled, compared to around 25% of PET plastics and less than 10% of all plastics.

Once again, what you buy makes a difference. The clothing we wear creates an enormous amount of waste. Don't buy for fashion, but for functionality and longevity. Good quality clothing lasts longer and has to be replaced less. Buy clothing made out of natural fibers such as cotton, wool, and hemp, preferably from growers that practice regenerative agriculture. If you are buying clothing made of synthetics, buy ones made from recycled materials. When done with clothes, donate them locally to be resold if they are in good condition, or drop them off somewhere that recycles fabrics. Consider the entire lifecycle of what you buy. How long will it last, can it be repaired, if not, is it recyclable, and of course, do I really need it? Support companies that promote circular manufacturing and do not support companies with poor environmental records. Buy recycled products whenever you can to reduce total waste. Everything you buy with recycled content saves new materials from being produced and then eventually discarded.

Buy electric lawn equipment, your lungs will thank you. If you use landscaping services, use those who only use electric equipment. Better yet, get rid of your turf lawn. You won't need a mower any longer, and you can eliminate your use of pesticides and fertilizers all together while saving water, especially in arid climates. Plant a selection of native plants to promote biodiversity. While you are redoing your landscaping, paint your house. Airlite is available retail, and you could fight air pollution inside and outside your house. Lobby your governments at every level to strengthen pollution laws where you live. Suggest they install trash traps in your stormwater system, and promote the reduction of pesticide and fertilizer use on public and private lands in your community. Demand clean air and water. If your community does not have a composting program, lobby your community leaders to get one started. Volunteer your time to help clean up trash where you live. There are many organizations out there that do this work, and many communities have trash pickup days you can help with. Bring a bag with you on your daily walk and pick up what you come across. All of us chipping in a little bit would go a long way in keeping trash out of our waterways. Simple changes like reducing or eliminating take-out foods, or ordering from restaurants that have Earth friendly packaging can go a long way in fighting waste, but are often overlooked.

What Government can do:

Pass and enforce pollution laws on municipal waste and industry, and tax companies for wasteful practices if they operate in countries with more lax laws. Much of the reason wealthy nations are cleaner is because instead of meeting the standards of their own countries, companies just moved their dirty operations to other countries. Governments, especially in wealthy nations, need to deal with their own trash problems and stop sending waste to other countries. Relocating your pollution is not a solution. Promote circular manufacturing by giving tax breaks to companies that are working to make it happen. Tax virgin materials such as steel, aluminum, and especially plastics to make it more cost-effective to use recycled inputs. Set mandates for recycled content for produced goods. Ban the use of traditional single-use plastics. Bans such as these for things like straws and plastic shopping bags are already in place in some locations, but they should be expanded to include single-use bottles, plates, utensils, and takeout containers. Where needed, replace these with compostable and biodegradable options. Scotland is implementing such a ban right now, restricting the sale of many of the most problematic types of single-use plastics. This follows a 2018 EU ban on the sale of multiple single-use plastics that went into effect in 2021. Moves like these may spur other countries to do the same. To make the transition to better waste management, governments also need to make sure that recycling and composting services are available to everyone. Many communities simply do not have these services, and we can't begin the transition to zero-waste societies without this first step.

Get serious about water pollution. This starts with municipalities taking a serious look at their stormwater and sewer systems to ensure that they are preventing waste from entering our waterways. National governments can help by ensuring funds are available to upgrade and fix failing systems. Internationally, more focus and funds must be given to ensure that developing nations have solutions to their waste problems in order to protect the world's waterways.

Strict regulations on agricultural and domestic use of fertilizers and pesticides, along with the promotion of regenerative agriculture, should be implemented to protect aquatic life and pollinators. Countries that have not already done so should strictly regulate or ban the use of neonicotinoid pesticides. Beyond pesticides, a thorough, unbiased accounting of the thousands of commonly used chemicals and their effects on the environment needs to occur. Particularly environmentally persistent chemicals such as PFAS should be a top priority for elimination. Of course, keeping pollutants out of our environment is an imperative, but we also must recognize the damage already done and commit to undoing it. There are thousands upon thousands of former industrial sites, military facilities, mines, and dump sites around the world that retain alarming amounts of pollution that continue to threaten ecosystems and public health. Our governments need to make identifying and cleaning up these sites a priority and properly fund programs to deal with them. Hold industry accountable; they should be the ones to pay and not taxpayers. They were, after all, the ones who profited from the pollution they created.

Consumption and the Economy

While thankfully we do have solutions for many of our environmental challenges, we cannot hope to eliminate these issues if we do not deal with a fundamental flaw in many of our societies, the need for more. More of everything. More cars, more clothes, more gadgets, larger houses, and more stuff with which to fill them. We live in a throwaway society where we have normalized waste so much that we even throw out huge amounts of food. We buy the latest fashions, the newest colors, we buy things we already have 10 of, because it's "new." Our media and our society constantly bombard us with the message that we need more and that we are in some way deficient if we don't buy what they're schlepping. Sure, I too like "stuff," but we all need to be acutely conscious of the impact of acquiring that "stuff." Is it something that really brings value to my life?

Does it have functionality and longevity? Is it in some way truly valuable to me, or am I buying something that has little meaning, that has no real function, or that will just shortly be thrown away? Am I perpetuating a destructive cycle of waste for brief personal enjoyment? These are questions that we need to be asking ourselves.

Driving this consumerism is the way our economies are constructed. In short, to keep them growing, we need to endlessly consume more. Much of this has been driven by using the idea of GDP, or gross domestic product, as a measure of economic success. Unfortunately, this measure only takes into account the total output of an economy. The more that is produced and consumed, the higher the GDP, the higher the GDP, the stronger the economy. There is a fatal flaw in using this measurement. It assumes that producing more is always better, and this breeds wastefulness. For example, buying a quality product and using it for ten years is worse with respect to GDP than buying a similar, poorly produced product every year. The more we buy, then throw away, the more that is produced, and the higher the GDP. This model, which has been used in some form for centuries, does not, however, take into account how that production may actually be detrimental. GDP does not have a conscience. Good or bad, if it adds value to the economy, it counts toward GDP. GDP is, of course, just a number. It, in itself, is not the issue. The issue is our governments' overuse of it as a barometer of national success and its use to such an extent that they have, for decades, largely promoted GDP growth and the consumerism that supports it over all else. For example, the U.S. Federal Government's broad support of advertising to push consumer demand dates back at least to the Hoover administration, or nearly a century. Such ingrained thinking may be the hardest change we have to make in this regard, but the long-term health of the natural world and, by extension, humanity depends on it. There is little hope for a stable and prosperous future if our economic systems continue to undermine the environment.

How do we change this? Even Nobel Prize-winning economist and designer of the modern GDP, Simon Kuznets, realized that GDP should not be the be-all-end-all in gauging progress, stating in 1934 that "The welfare of a nation can scarcely be inferred from a measurement of national income." The solution is new metrics for success. Our economic policies need to consider the full picture, including the environmental costs of our consumption. GDP traditionally equates to monetary wealth, but wealth is of little value when your populace no longer has enough water or food and your environment has collapsed. We need to begin looking at national success not just as the amount of money being made but how well the people of the nation are doing. A nation can be wealthy monetarily but still have serious environmental problems, an unhealthy populace, poverty, and crippling inequalities. A much better system would not look at just money but at the well-being of life within the nation. After all, shouldn't that be the goal—to make sure *all* the inhabitants of a nation are thriving?

The small Asian nation of Bhutan shines as an example of how this can be accomplished. Instead of focusing on GDP, they instead focus on GNH or Gross National Happiness. The GNH index is composed of four main pillars: good governance, sustainable socio-economic development, cultural preservation, and environmental conservation. (Notice that last one? How the environment is doing is a pillar of how they judge success.) The four pillars are broken down further into nine domains that include psychological well-being, health, education, time use, cultural diversity and resilience, good governance, community vitality, ecological diversity and resilience, and living standard. These are further broken down into 33 indicators relating to how the population is doing with respect to the nine domains. These indicators are used to adjust government policy to increase the well-being of the people of Bhutan. What may be even more surprising about this system is that the government of Bhutan asks its people how they are doing and then listens to them. As skeptical as many of us may be about this, it's hard to argue with their success. Using these policies, they have been able to reduce their poverty level from 36% in 2007 to less than 10%, all while seeing an average growth in GDP of 7.5% per year, while also maintaining 72.5% forest cover (in fact, a minimum of 60% forest cover is mandated by their constitution) and its status as the only carbon-*negative* country in the world.

Bhutan is a small and non-industrialized nation, and it's clear that their policies would not magically turn somewhere like the U.S. into a carbon-negative country, but just think of the progress that could be made if the well-being of its environment and citizens was central to its economic policies. There are signs that the idea of GNH is catching on. Several years ago, New Zealand's then Prime Minister, Jacinda Ardern, announced that her country would begin using a GNH index as one of the official indicators of success in New Zealand. Just like in Bhutan, this indicator would influence government policy. First influencing the budget in 2019, it's still too early to tell what impact the GNH index will have on the economy, people, and environment of New Zealand, but there is promise that this sort of thinking could expand around the world, finally moving nations' focus to the things that are most important.

What you can do:

At the risk of sounding like a broken record, you guessed it, take a look at your own consumption. Once again, what we consume drives markets, and we have a surprising amount of power by voting with our dollars. More than just what you buy, look at the impact of all of your consumption. From energy and water use to how much you drive and what you throw away, everything we do has a consequence. Our goal is to eliminate as much of that consequence as possible. More importantly, look at what drives your consumption. Is it need or hype? Try to break free from society's constant message that you need more. It's time to stop "keeping up with the Joneses," unless maybe your neighbor is Ed Beagley Jr. (for those who may not know, he and Bill Nye have had a good-natured feud for years about who's house is more environmentally friendly). As always, vote, and try to encourage those you vote for to adopt new measures of economic success.

Infinite growth is impossible; nothing does it, and our economies are no exception. We need to be finding ways to move beyond this idea.

What Government can do:

Move away from indicators such as GDP as the only measure of economic success and begin to move our economies away from an infinite growth model. This change will not come easily, but it's becoming increasingly clear that how our economies operate now is not sustainable, either socially or environmentally. Begin to use a GNH or similar index and focus less on monetary wealth and more on making sure needs are met. We need stable economies, but economies that operate at the expense of the majority of the populace and the environment are inherently not stable. Simply, we need a different way. What that path ultimately looks like will evolve in the coming decades. While many of us may not live to see a change in such a fundamental part of society, now is the time to realize the inherent flaws in the system and start the process of change.

Changing our relationship.

While things like giving up GDP for GNH may signal a shift in the way we think, a much larger change must take place if we are to secure Earth's biodiversity and ultimately humanities place among it. Humanity needs a fundamentally different relationship with the planet. One that sees its value, not in what we can exploit from it, but as our life giving home. The only home we have and likely ever will. This shift—call it an "Earth-centric" or "Earth-first" philosophy—would make what is good for the planet and its life the number one priority in human decision-making. It would see Earth, and its biodiversity, as a function of our own well-being, along with the full realization that better off our home, the better off we are. Seeing how nature provides for us physically, psychologically, even spiritually, would inevitably harbor a much deeper appreciation for Earth's life, and with it a deeper connection. With that connection, humanity will learn to take care of its most important asset.

As this type of mindset becomes ingrained in our cultures, human behavior changes. The Earth, now seen by most as an essential provider, a critical part of human well-being, and a primary source of all that humans need, is now the most important concern of humanity. Gone is the idea of exploiting nature; replacing it is the idea of being just one part of a larger system, one where humanity gives back as much as it receives. In this world of new thinking, people in their daily lives make decisions to protect the life around them through the choices they make in what to eat, the resources they use, and the lifestyle they lead, knowing that all of this has an impact not just on the whole, but ultimately on them personally. The thought is ever present, and their actions become as automatic as the choices they make to protect and care for their own families. Humans now understand that this "Earth-first" way of thinking is essential for the care of humanity and its interests, and this way of thinking does not diminish their lives but enriches it and ensures the prosperity of not only humanity but all life on Earth. We become a species, not obsessed with wealth or status, but one of well-being. This shift in priorities and the realization that humans need—actually need—the life around us could usher in a fundamental change in humanity to the benefit of everything.

What you can do:

Unfortunately, humans are a long way off from Earth-centered thinking on a large scale, but the shift begins with each one of us. Be mindful. In each individual decision you make, you should consider the impact of that decision on the environment. Consider your consumption, your concept of need, and try to stick to the necessary. You might have to abandon some things, but you may also realize you really don't mind. As society progresses, these decisions will become easier. For example, right now, it's impossible to not use plastic in some way, no matter how hard you try. As alternatives become more widely available, it will become much easier to leave plastic behind. Remind yourself why you are doing this. Reconnect with nature in whatever way you can, whether in your backyard, a local park, or deep in a wilderness area. We are often so immersed in our daily lives that we lose touch with the natural world. We can go days without experiencing the birds in our trees, the way the wind makes the leaves on those trees flutter, the bees visiting our flowers, or the coolness of the grass on our bare feet. It's not that these things aren't there, we are just too occupied with other things to notice. Try your best each day to experience something in the natural world, even for a brief time. Try to eat lunch outside each day, or start your morning with coffee on the patio or a walk.

What government can do:

While individuals, informed by their conscience and the best information they can obtain, can choose each day the best path forward to live in harmony with nature, governments need more structured direction. One way to put an Earth-first emphasis on how they operate is to introduce the planetary boundaries concept into their policy making to quantify and address the major issues surrounding the degradation of the environment. First developed by Earth System scientists John Rockström, Will Steffen, and others, the planetary boundaries framework quantifies the limits of human activity to ensure that the Earth keeps the stability that human beings have been enjoying for the last 10,000 years. It looks at 9 different factors: climate change, ocean acidification, chemical pollution, fertilizer use, freshwater use, land conversion, biodiversity loss, air pollution, and ozone layer depletion, and sets a boundary for each. For example, the boundary for climate change is an atmospheric CO_2 concentration < 350 ppm. Not all of the factors yet have a defined boundary, work is still being done to put a number on these, but the concept breaks down the complexities of our environmental issues to a focus of just 9 factors, allowing lawmakers to focus on the big picture. The details of policy will of course be more complex, but used as an integrated part of how our governments do business, the idea could have a huge impact.

Ideally, planetary boundaries would be required by law to be considered first in any of our governments' decisions, from the setting of policy to introducing and passing laws to government purchasing all the way to what food is served in government cafeterias. For example, will a particular decision reduce CO_2 emissions, sequester carbon, or have a positive or negative impact on pollution? If the impact is negative with respect to a boundary, another option must be considered. Positive or negative, the impact must be quantified with respect to planetary boundaries before all other considerations. This type of Earth-first governance would refocus government decisions on what's truly best for all of us: a functional and stable environment. Wide adoption of this sort of governance would ensure that all countries in the world are working to make the best decisions for the planet. Policy should be focused on bringing factors like atmospheric CO_2, fertilizer use, and biodiversity loss back within their acceptable limits, while preventing others from increasing beyond their established boundaries, ultimately bringing humanity back to living within our biological means.

The solutions outlined here are just some of the solutions to some of the seemingly endless problems humans need to address. The challenge of changing how humanity interacts with our world is daunting, to say the least. Instead of facing these challenges, many have simply given up. They claim that the task is impossible—that there is no point because not everyone in the world is on board —while ironically making themselves one of those people. They cannot make a difference, so do nothing. While I agree the task we are facing is enormous, like any challenge, the first step is to begin the work. We've all been there. We have all faced something that we weren't sure we could accomplish. Whether it was finishing War and Peace, making it to the top of a mountain, that work project that you thought would never end, your college degree, your military service, or writing a book, there was probably a time that you thought you just couldn't do it. You just couldn't see how it would end. Saving the earth from ourselves is no different. You just show up. Each day, you do the work. Sure, you'll get dis-couraged. You'll wonder what the point is. You'll want to just say, "The hell with it." You'll screw up. Your judgment will lapse. You are, after all, only human. Even as huge as all of this is, if we put in the work, there will be results. Will you personally save the world? Of course not, but that's not the goal. The goal is that *you* do the right thing, and if there are enough people like you, then there's no telling what we can accomplish.

The human race is now at a crossroads. The choices we make today will determine the path that we and the planet take. On one path, humans live up to their potential, taking what we have learned and using this knowledge to manage Earth's precious resources. By doing this, we usher in a new era for humanity where we make sure all life has an opportunity to thrive, including our fellow man. On this path, we build a future where human potential is nurtured and we break free from the stifling notion of ever-increasing economic growth. In the end, we value our well-being over the attainment of wealth and learn to live at peace, not only with our world but with each other.

On the other path, we don't change, or we don't change enough, or fast enough. We allow concerns about economic growth, the loss of monetary dominance, and the struggle for political power to blind us to the real danger. The Earth's biodiversity collapses, and the climate swings out of control. As the world shifts into a different ecological regime, all the stability that humans have enjoyed for thousands of years disappears. Coastal cities are flooded, forests burn, land becomes uninhabitable, millions of people are displaced. This shift puts stress on already stressed resources. Rains fail, habitats change, and temperatures swing wildly. Food webs in the ocean and on land begin to break down. The loss is staggering. The areas where the bulk of food is grown around the world may no longer support agriculture. As landscapes shift from wet to dry and from dry to wet, humans scramble to find where they can survive, but it will take hundreds of years, maybe thousands, before these new landscapes are fully established, before Earth settles into the new normal. Agriculture on a large scale collapses. Billions starve even with modern farming techniques. Without consistent rain and defined seasons, there is just nothing we can do. Long before this, panic would have set in. Shortages of food and water spark wars. As the shortages intensify, society begins to break down. The areas that still support agriculture and have access to fresh water begin to hoard resources. On this path, money means nothing. Water and food are the most valuable assets. Humans are now facing the most grave situation our species has ever seen. We have paid the price for our actions, and the rest of the world's life along with us.

Both of these scenarios read like the summary of some futurist's book. I wish the situation were not that dire, but it is. Dramatic change will come and within decades, not generations. Whether through us taking charge of our own destiny and that of the planet, or through our inaction, the world will end up a very different place. We will be the reason. For humans, more than just our survival is at stake. The Earth is our home, and even if we manage to survive in a depleted world, what have we lost? Human beings have a deep connection to nature, even if we don't realize it. With every habitat diminished and every organism lost, humans lose a part of ourselves. A part of our culture, our history, and the natural world that not only gave rise to us but also maintains us both physically and psychologically. Through our inaction, we risk more than a world we can't live in. We risk a world we don't want to live in.

Recommended Reading

Image Credits

Bibliography

Recommended Reading

Attenborough, David. *A life on our planet: My witness statement and a vision for the future*. Random House, 2020.

Audubon, John James. *Audubon and His Journals*. 1897. Reprint. Dover, 1960.

Berners-Lee, Mike. *There Is No Planet B: A Handbook for the Make Or Break Years-Updated Edition*. Cambridge University Press, 2021.

Brusatte, Steve. *The rise and reign of mammals*. HarperCollins, 2022.

Carson, Rachel. *Silent Spring*. Mariner, 1990.

Cheke, Anthony, and Julian P. Hume. *Lost land of the dodo: the ecological history of Mauritius, Réunion and Rodrigues*. Bloomsbury Publishing, 2010.

Ellis, Erle C. *Anthropocene: a very short introduction*. Vol. 558. Oxford University Press, 2018.

Figueres, Christiana, and Tom Rivett-Carnac. *The future we choose: the stubborn optimist's guide to the climate crisis*. Vintage, 2021.

Fuller, Errol. *Extinct Birds revised edition*. Comstock, 2001.

Gates, Bill. *How to avoid a climate disaster: the solutions we have and the breakthroughs we need*. Knopf, 2021.

Kolbert, Elizabeth. *The sixth extinction: An unnatural history*. A&C Black, 2014.

Lenton, Timothy. *Earth system science: a very short introduction*. Vol. 464. Oxford University Press, 2016.

Leopold, Aldo. *A Sand County almanac, and sketches here and there*. Oxford University Press, USA, 1989.

Lewis, Meriwether, William Clark, and Anthony Brandt. *The Journals of Lewis and Clark*. Washington, D.C.: National Geographic Adventure Classics, 2002.

Montgomery, David R. *Growing a revolution: bringing our soil back to life*. WW Norton & Company, 2017.

Nijhuis, Michelle. *Beloved Beasts: Fighting for Life in an Age of Extinction*. WW Norton & Company, 2021.

Richards, John F. *The Unending Frontier: An Environmental History of the Early Modern World*. University of California Press, 2003.

Rockstrom, Johan. *Big world, small planet: Abundance within planetary boundaries*. Yale University Press, 2015.

Seneff, Stephanie. *Toxic Legacy: How the Weedkiller Glyphosate Is Destroying Our Health and the Environment*. Chelsea Green Publishing, 2021.

Weidensaul, Scott. A World on the Wing: The Global Odyssey of Migratory Birds. WW Norton & Company, 2021.

Wilson, Edward O. *Half-earth: our planet's fight for life*. WW Norton & Company, 2016.

Wilson, Edward O. *The diversity of life*. WW Norton & Company, 1999.

Image Credits

Birds

Passenger Pigeon, William Pope, 1835. Courtesy of the Toronto Public Library. https://www.torontopubliclibrary.ca/detail.jsp?Entt=RDMDC-894-1-1&R=DC-894-1-1&searchPageType=dao

Great Auk, Robert Havell after John James Audubon,1836, Courtesy of the National Gallery of Art,   Washington.

Ivory-billed Woodpecker, John James Audubon, 1851, John James Audubon Letters and Drawings, 1805-1892, MS Am 21 (31), Houghton Library, Harvard University.

Carolina Parakeets, John James Auduboun, 1833, Courtesy of the New York Historical Society.

Huia (male and female) *Heteralocha acutirostris*,1888, John Gerrard Keulemans, from *A History of the Birds of New Zealand*. Licensed under CC BY-SA 3.0 NZ, Courtesy of New Zealand Electronic Text Centre.

Maui-nui ʻakialoa, 1893, John Gerrard Keulemans, from *The Avifauna of Laysan* by Lionel Walter Rothschild. Image from the Biodiversity Heritage Library. Contributed by the Smithsonian Libraries. www.biodiversitylibrary.org

Moho nobilis, 1893, John Gerrard Keulemans, from the *Avifauna of Laysan* by Lionel Walter Rothschild. Image from the Biodiversity Heritage Library. Contributed by the Smithsonian   Libraries. www.biodiversitylibrary.org

Ara tricolor, 1801, Jacques Barraband, from *Histoire naturelle des perroquets* by François Le Vaillant. Image from the Biodiversity Heritage Library. Contributed by the Missouri Botanical Garden. www.biodiversitylibrary.org

Corvus tropicus (Corvus hawaiiensis), 1890, Fredrick William Frohawk, from *Aves Hawaiienses : the birds of the Sandwich Islands* by Scott B Wilson. Image from the Biodiversity Heritage Library. Contributed by the Smithsonian Libraries. www.biodiversitylibrary.org

Melamprosops phaeosoma, Paul E. Baker, courtesy of the US Fish and Wildlife Service.

Ara spixi (Cyanopsitta spixii), 1878, Joseph Smith, from *The Proceedings of the Zoological Society of London*. Courtesy of the Internet Archive. www.archive.org.

Amphibians

Golden Coqui, George Dewey, Courtesy of the US Department of Fish and Wildlife.

Panamanian Golden Frog *(Atelopus zeteki)*, 2008, Brian Gatwike, Licensed under CC BY 2.0.

Bufo periglenes (Incilius periglenes), Charles H. Smith, Courtesy of the US Fish and Wildlife Service.

Pseudophilautus nasutus, Albert Charles Lewis Günther, 1868, from *The Proceedings of the Scientific Meetings of the Zoological Society of London.* Image from the Biodiversity Heritage Library. Contributed by the Natural HIstory Museum Library, London. www.biodiversitylibrary.org

Rheobatrachus silus, 2014, Benjamin Healley, Licensed under CC BY 4.0.

Chiricahua leopard frog, Jim Rorabaugh, Courtesy of the US Fish and WIldlife Service.

Wyoming Toad, Sara Armstrong, Courtesy of the US Fish and WIldlife Service.

Molge wolterstorffi (Cynops wolterstorffi), 1905, George Albert Boulanger, from *Proceedings of the Zoological Society of London*. Image from the Biodiversity Heritage Library. Contributed by the Smithsonian Libraries. www.biodiversitylibrary.org

Pseudoeurycea werleri, 2008, Jorge Armín Escalante Pasos. Licensed under CC BY-SA 4.0.

Reptiles

Testudo abingdonii (Chelonoidis abingdonii), Albert Charles Lewis Günther, 1877, from *The Gigantic Land-Tortoises (Living and Extinct) in the Collection of the British Museum.* Image from the Biodiversity Heritage Library. Contributed by the Smithsonian Libraries. www.biodiversitylibrary.org

Testudo vosmaeri (Cylindraspis vosmaeri), 1893, Muséum national d'histoire naturelle. From *Centenaire de la fondation du Muséum d'histoire naturelle* 10 juin 1793 - 10 juin 1893. Image from the Biodiversity Heritage Library. Contributed by the Smithsonian Libraries. www.biodiversitylibrary.org

Phelsuma edwardnewtonii, George Albert Boulanger, 1885, from *Catalogue of the lizards in the British museum (Natural history)*. Image from the Biodiversity Heritage Library. Contributed by the Cornell University Library. www.biodiversitylibrary.org

Tortrix Pseudo-eryx (Bolyeria multocarinata), 1700-1880, Iconographia Zoologica, courtesy of the Special Collections of the University of Amsterdam.

Lygosoma nativitatis (Emoia nativitatis), 1900, from *A Monograph of Christmas Island (Indian Ocean)*. Image from the Biodiversity Heritage Library. Contributed by the Smithsonian Libraries. www.biodiversitylibrary.org

Leiocephalus carinatus, 2014, Bramans. Licensed under CC BY-SA 4.0.

Rhinoceros Iguana *(Cyclura cornuta),* 2010, Martin Pettitt. Licensed under CC BY 2.0.

Fish

Cichlidae, 1915, George Albert Boulanger, from *Catalogue of the fresh-water fishes of Africa in the British museum (Natural history)*. Image from the Biodiversity Heritage Library. Contributed by the Smithsonian Libraries.
www.biodiversitylibrary.org

Barbodes hemictenus, 1907, David Starr Jordan, from *Fishes from Islands of the Philippine Archipelago*, Bulletin of the Bureau of Fisheries, vol. 27. Image from the Biodiversity Heritage Library. Contributed by the Smithsonian Libraries.
www.biodiversitylibrary.org

Psephurus gladius, 1880, Albert Charles Lewis Günther, from *An Introduction to the Study of Fishes*. Image from the Biodiversity Heritage Library. Contributed by the Smithsonian Libraries. www.biodiversitylibrary.org

Devil's Hole pupfish *(Cyprinodon diabolis)*, 2012, Olin Feuerbacher, courtesy of the US Fish and Wildlife Service.

Leucichthys nigripinnis (Coregonus nigripinnis), 1911, Charles Bradford Hudson, from *Review of the Salmonid Fishes of the Great Lakes with Notes on the Whitefishes of Other Regions*, Bulletin of the Bureau of Fisheries vol 29, courtesy of of the Freshwater and Marine Image Bank.

Retropinna opokororo (Prototroctes oxyrhynchus), 1870, James Hector, from *Transactions and Proceedings of the New Zealand Institute* Vol 3. Image from the Biodiversity Heritage Library. Contributed by the Smithsonian Libraries.
www.biodiversitylibrary.org

Mammals

Thylacinus cynocephalus, 1850, from *Proceedings of the Zoological Society of London Illustrations 1848-1860*, vol I. Image from the Biodiversity Heritage Library. Contributed by the Harvard University, Museum of Comparative Zoology, Ernst Mayr Library. www.biodiversitylibrary.org

Hippotragus leucophaeus, 1899, Joseph Wolf and J. Smith, from *The Book of Antelopes* vol. IV. Image from the Biodiversity Heritage Library. Contributed by the Smithsonian Libraries. www.biodiversitylibrary.org

Canis australis (Dusicyon australis), 1838-1839, George R. Waterhouse, from *The Zoology of the Voyage of H.M.S. Beagle... during the years 1832-1836*. Image from the Biodiversity Heritage Library. Contributed by the Natural History Museum Library, London. www.biodiversitylibrary.org

Chaeropus castanotis (Chaeropus ecaudatus),1863, H.C. Richter and John Gould, from *The Mammals of Australia* vol.1. Image from the Biodiversity Heritage Library. Contributed by the Smithsonian Libraries. www.biodiversitylibrary.org

Lagorchestes leporides,1863, H.C. Richter and John Gould, from *The Mammals of Australia* vol. 2. Image from the Biodiversity Heritage Library. Contributed by the Smithsonian Libraries. www.biodiversitylibrary.org

Monachus tropicalis (Neomonachus tropicalis),1890, J.A. Allen, from *The West Indian seal* (Monachus tropicalis Gray). Bulletin of the AMNH vol II 1887-1890, article 1. Image from the Biodiversity Heritage Library. Contributed by the American Museum of Natural History Library. www.biodiversitylibrary.org

*Zalophus californianus japonicus (Zalophus japonicus),*1823-1829, Kawahara
   Keiga, Courtesy of the Naturalis Biodiversity Center, Netherlands.
Chinese River Dolphin, 2020, Roland Seitre, courtesy of the Institute of
   Hydrobiology, Chinese Academy of Sciences.
*Pteropus whitmeei (Pteropus samoensis),*1874, Edward R Alston, from *Proceedings
   of the Zoological Society of London.* Image from the Biodiversity Heritage
   Library. Contributed by the Natural History Museum Library, London.
   www.biodiversitylibrary.org
Pipistrellus pipistrellus, 2011, Gilles San Martin, Licensed under cc-by-sa-2.0.

Bibliography

Evolution, Extinction, and Humans

Betts, H.C., Puttick, M.N., Clark, J.W. et al. Integrated genomic and fossil evidence illuminates life's early evolution and eukaryote origin. *Nat Ecol Evol* 2, 1556–1562 (2018).

Dodd, MS, Papineau, D, Grenne, T et al. (5 more authors) (2017) Evidence for early life in Earth's oldest hydrothermal vent precipitates. *Nature*, 543 (7643). pp. 60-64. ISSN 0028-0836

Badyaev A, Hill G. Avian Quick-Change Artists. *Natural History Magazine.* June 2002.

Duncan EJ, Gluckman PD, Dearden PK. Epigenetics, plasticity, and evolution: How do we link epigenetic change to phenotype? *J Exp Zool B Mol Dev Evol.* 2014 Jun;322(4):208-20. doi: 10.1002/jez.b.22571. Epub 2014 Apr 9. PMID: 24719220.

Bossdorf O, Richards CL, Pigliucci M. Epigenetics for ecologists. Ecol Lett. 2008 Feb;11(2):106-15. doi: 10.1111/j.1461-0248.2007.01130.x. *Epub* 2007 Nov 15. PMID: 18021243.

Hunter, Philip. "The great leap forward. Major evolutionary jumps might be caused by changes in gene regulation rather than the emergence of new genes." *EMBO reports* vol. 9,7 (2008): 608-11. doi:10.1038/embor.2008.115

Day T, Bonduriansky R. A unified approach to the evolutionary consequences of genetic and nongenetic inheritance. *Am Nat.* 2011 Aug;178(2):E18-36. doi: 10.1086/660911. PMID: 21750377.

Lind, M.I., Spagopoulou, F. Evolutionary consequences of epigenetic inheritance. *Heredity* 121, 205–209 (2018). https://doi.org/10.1038/s41437-018-0113-y

McNew, S.M., Beck, D., Sadler-Riggleman, I. et al. Epigenetic variation between urban and rural populations of Darwin's finches. BMC Evol Biol 17, 183 (2017). https://doi.org/10.1186/s12862-017-1025-9

Bartlett, Rick, et al. "Abrupt global-ocean anoxia during the Late Ordovician–early Silurian detected using uranium isotopes of marine carbonates." *Proceedings of the National Academy of Sciences* 115.23 (2018): 5896-5901.

Shen, Shu-zhong, et al. "Calibrating the end-Permian mass extinction." science 334.6061 (2011): 1367-1372.

Burgess, Seth D., James D. Muirhead, and Samuel A. Bowring. "Initial pulse of Siberian Traps sills as the trigger of the end-Permian mass extinction." *Nature Communications* 8.1 (2017): 1-6.

Chapman, Timothy, et al. "Pulses in silicic arc magmatism initiate end-Permian climate instability and extinction." *Nature Geoscience* 15.5 (2022): 411-416.

AMNH. End of the Line - The demise of the Trilobites. *American Museum of Natural History*. Accessed 10 March 2021. https://www.amnh.org/research/paleontology/collections/fossil-invertebrate-collection/trilobite-website/trilobite-localities/end-of-the-line-the-demise-of-the-trilobites

Davies, J. H. F. L., et al. "End-Triassic mass extinction started by intrusive CAMP activity." *Nature communications* 8.1 (2017): 1-8.

Blackburn, T. et.al. Zircon U-Pb Geochronology Links the End-Triassic Extinction with the Central Atlantic Magmatic Province. *Science* 340, 941–945. doi:10.1126/science.1234204

Dunhill, Alexander M., et al. "Impact of the Late Triassic mass extinction on functional diversity and composition of marine ecosystems." *Paleontology* 61.1 (2018): 133-148.

Reid, Walter V. "*Millennium ecosystem assessment.*" (2005).

Siraj, A., Loeb, A. Breakup of a long-period comet as the origin of the dinosaur extinction. *Sci Rep* 11, 3803 (2021).

Collins, G.S., Patel, N., Davison, T.M. et al. A steeply-inclined trajectory for the Chicxulub impact. *Nat Commun* 11, 1480 (2020).

Kring, David A. "The Chicxulub impact event and its environmental consequences at the Cretaceous–Tertiary boundary." *Palaeogeography, Palaeoclimatology, Palaeoecology* 255.1-2 (2007): 4-21.

Ceballos, Gerardo, Paul R. Ehrlich, and Peter H. Raven. "Vertebrates on the brink as indicators of biological annihilation and the sixth mass extinction." *Proceedings of the National Academy of Sciences* 117.24 (2020): 13596-13602.

Cattau, C.E., Fletcher Jr, R.J., Kimball, R.T. et al. Rapid morphological change of a top predator with the invasion of a novel prey. *Nat Ecol Evol* 2, 108–115 (2018). https://doi.org/10.1038/s41559-017-0378-1

Ryding S, Klaassen M, Tattersall GJ, Gardner JL, Symonds MRE. Shape-shifting: changing animal morphologies as a response to climatic warming. *Trends Ecol Evol*. 2021 Aug 19:S0169-5347(21)00197-X. doi: 10.1016/j.tree.2021.07.006. Epub ahead of print. PMID: 34507845.

.

Biodiversity

Griffiths, Huw & Anker, Paul & Linse, Katrin & Maxwell, Jamie & Post, Alexandra & Stevens, Craig & Tulaczyk, Slawek & Smith, James. (2021). Breaking All the Rules: The First Recorded Hard Substrate Sessile Benthic Community Far Beneath an Antarctic Ice Shelf. *Frontiers in Marine Science*. 8. 642040. 10.3389/fmars.2021.642040.

Fiala, G., Stetter, K.O. Pyrococcus furiosus sp. nov. represents a novel genus of marine heterotrophic archaebacteria growing optimally at 100°C. *Arch. Microbiol.* 145, 56–61 (1986). https://doi.org/10.1007/BF00413027

Szewzyk, U et al. "Thermophilic, anaerobic bacteria isolated from a deep borehole in granite in Sweden." *Proceedings of the National Academy of Sciences of the United States of America* vol. 91,5 (1994): 1810-3. doi:10.1073/pnas.91.5.1810

Fisher, C., MacDonald, I., Sassen, R. et al. Methane Ice Worms: Hesiocaeca
    methanicola Colonizing Fossil Fuel Reserves. Naturwissenschaften 87, 184–
    187 (2000). https://doi.org/10.1007/s001140050700

Motta, P.C. Butterflies from the Uberlândia region, Central Brazil: species list and
    biological comments, Braz. J. Biol. 62 (1), Feb 2002. https://doi.org/10.1590/
    S1519-69842002000100017

Roskov Y., Ower G., Orrell T., Nicolson D., Bailly N., Kirk P.M., Bourgoin T., DeWalt
    R.E., Decock W., van Nieukerken E.J., Penev L. (eds.) (2020). Species 2000 & ITIS
    Catalogue of Life, 2020-12-01. Digital resource at www.catalogueoflife.org.
    Species 2000: Naturalis, Leiden, the Netherlands. ISSN 2405-8858.

Mora C, Tittensor DP, Adl S, Simpson AGB, Worm B (2011) How Many Species Are
    There on Earth and in the Ocean? PLoS Biol 9(8): e1001127. https://doi.org/
    10.1371/journal.pbio.1001127

Kenneth J. Locey, Jay T. Lennon, Scaling laws predict global microbial diversity
    Proceedings of the National Academy of Sciences May 2016, 113 (21) 5970-5975;
    DOI: 10.1073/pnas.1521291113

Schluter, D., Pennell, M. Speciation gradients and the distribution of biodiversity.
    Nature 546, 48–55 (2017). https://doi.org/10.1038/nature22897

Slik, J W Ferry et al. "An estimate of the number of tropical tree species."
    Proceedings of the National Academy of Sciences of the United States of America
    vol. 112,24 (2015): 7472-7. doi:10.1073/pnas.1423147112

Raven, Peter & Gereau, Roy & Phillipson, Peter & Chatelain, Cyrille & Jenkins,
    Clinton & Ulloa, Carmen. (2020).The distribution of biodiversity richness in the
    tropics. Science advances. 6. 10.1126/sciadv.abc6228.

G.W. Beccaloni, K.J. Gaston. Predicting the species richness of neotropical forest
    butterflies: Ithomiinae (Lepidoptera: Nymphalidae) as indicators. Biological
    Conservation, Volume 71, Issue 1, 1995, Pages 77-86,ISSN 0006-3207, https://
    doi.org/10.1016/0006-3207(94)00023-J.

Jessup, David A., et al. "Southern sea otter as a sentinel of marine ecosystem
    health." EcoHealth 1.3 (2004): 239-245.

Estes, James A., and John F. Palmisano. "Sea otters: their role in structuring
    nearshore communities." Science 185.4156 (1974): 1058-1060.

Sharps, Jon C., and Daniel W. Uresk. "Ecological review of black-tailed prairie dogs
    and associated species in western South Dakota." The Great Basin Naturalist
    (1990): 339-345.

Whicker, April D., and James K. Detling. "Ecological consequences of prairie dog
    disturbances." BioScience 38.11 (1988): 778-785.

Martínez-Estévez, Lourdes et al. Prairie dog decline reduces the supply of
    ecosystem services and leads to desertification of semiarid grasslands. PloS
    ONE vol. 8,10 e75229. 9 Oct. 2013, doi:10.1371/journal.pone.0075229

KN Shoemaker, K Novak, A Nicholas, T Abbott Species Status Assessment Report
    for the White-tiled prairie dog (Cynimys lecurus) - 2017 -
    scienceapplications.org
    https://doi.org/10.7717/peerj.2354

Gustafson, E. J., de Bruijn, A., Lichti, N., Jacobs, D. F., Sturtevant, B. R., Foster, J., Miranda, B. R., and Tidwell, J H, and G L Allan. "Fish as food: aquaculture's contribution. Ecological and economic impacts and contributions of fish farming and capture fisheries." *EMBO reports* vol. 2,11 (2001): 958-63. doi:10.1093/embo-reports/kve236

Şekercioğlu, Çağan H. Analysis: the economic value of birds. *The Cornell Lab*, 12 June 2017.
https://www.allaboutbirds.org/news/analysis-the-economic-value-of-birds/

Fuller RA, Irvine KN, Devine-Wright P, Warren PH, Gaston KJ. Psychological benefits of greenspace increase with biodiversity. *Biol Lett.* 2007 Aug 22;3(4):390-4.
https://doi.org/10.1098/rsbl.2007.0149.

Seto, Karen C., Burak Güneralp, and Lucy R. Hutyra. "Global forecasts of urban expansion to 2030 and direct impacts on biodiversity and carbon pools." *Proceedings of the National Academy of Sciences* 109.40 (2012): 16083-16088.

Colvin, B.A., M.W. Fall, L.A. Fitzgerald, and L.L. Loope, 2005. Review of Brown Treesnake Problems and Control Programs: Report of Observations and Recommendations (PDF | 262 KB)(link is external). Published at the request of the U.S. Department of Interior, Office of Insular Affairs for the Brown Treesnake Control Committee.

Pace, M. L. D. L. Strayer, D. Fischer, and H. M. Malcom. 2010. Recovery of native zooplankton associated with increased mortality of an invasive mussel. *Ecosphere* 1(1):art3. doi:10.1890/ES10-00002.1

Kaufman, Les. "Catastrophic Change in Species-Rich Freshwater Ecosystems." *BioScience*, vol. 42, no. 11, 1992, pp. 846–858. JSTOR, www.jstor.org/stable/1312084. Accessed 10 May 2021.

F. Witte, J. H. Wanink & M. Kishe-Machumu (2007) Species Distinction and the Biodiversity Crisis in Lake Victoria, *Transactions of the American Fisheries Society*, 136:4, 1146-1159, DOI: 10.1577/T05-179.1

Dalgleish, H. J. 2017. The implications of American chestnut reintroduction on landscape dynamics and carbon storage. *Ecosphere* 8(4):e01773. 10.1002/ecs2.1773

Templeton, Alan R., et al. "Disrupting evolutionary processes: the effect of habitat fragmentation on collared lizards in the Missouri Ozarks." Proceedings of the National Academy of Sciences 98.10 (2001): 5426-5432.

WWF. 10 Facts about cane toads. *WWF Australia*. 26 September 2021.
https://www.wwf.org.au/news/blogs/10-facts-about-cane-toads#gs.w2j7ui

Government of Australia. The cane toad (*Bufo marinus*) - fact sheet. Feb 2010.
https://www.environment.gov.au/biodiversity/invasive-species/publications/factsheet-cane-toad-bufo-marinus

Emslie, R. 2020. *Diceros bicornis. The IUCN Red List of Threatened Species* 2020: e.T6557A152728945. https://dx.doi.org/10.2305/IUCN.UK.2020-1.RLTS.T6557A152728945.en.
Downloaded on 10 May 2021.

Cerling, Thure E., et al. "Radiocarbon dating of seized ivory confirms rapid decline in African elephant populations and provides insight into illegal trade." *Proceedings of the National Academy of Sciences* 113.47 (2016): 13330-13335.

Chase MJ, Schlossberg S, Griffin CR, Bouché PJC, Djene SW, Elkan PW, Ferreira S, Grossman F, Kohi EM, Landen K, Omondi P, Peltier A, Selier SAJ, Sutcliffe R. 2016. Continent-wide survey reveals massive decline in African savannah elephants. *PeerJ* 4:e2354

Pecl, Gretta T., et al. "Biodiversity redistribution under climate change: Impacts on ecosystems and human well-being." *Science* 355.6332 (2017): eaai9214.

The Beginnings

Broughton, J.M., Weitzel, E.M. Population reconstructions for humans and megafauna suggest mixed causes for North American Pleistocene extinctions. Nat Commun 9, 5441 (2018). https://doi.org/10.1038/s41467-018-07897-1

Sandom, Christopher et al. "Global late Quaternary megafauna extinctions linked to humans, not climate change." Proceedings. B*iological sciences* vol. 281,1787 (2014): 20133254. doi:10.1098/rspb.2013.3254

Lister, Adrian & Stuart, Anthony. (2007). Patterns of Late Quaternary megafaunal extinctions in Europe and northern Asia. *CFS Courier Forschungsinstitut Senckenberg.* 259. 289-299.

Yadvinder Malhi, Christopher E. Doughty, Mauro Galetti, Felisa A. Smith, Jens-Christian Svenning, John W. Terborgh, Megafauna and ecosystem function *Proceedings of the National Academy of Sciences* Jan 2016, 113 (4) 838-846; DOI: 10.1073/pnas.1502540113

van der Kaars, S., Miller, G., Turney, C. et al. Humans rather than climate the primary cause of Pleistocene megafaunal extinction in Australia. Nat Commun 8, 14142 (2017). https://doi.org/10.1038/ncomms14142

Bustos, David, et al. "Footprints preserve terminal Pleistocene hunt? Human-sloth interactions in North America." *Science Advances* 4.4 (2018): eaar7621.

Prates, L., Perez, S.I. Late Pleistocene South American megafaunal extinctions associated with rise of Fishtail points and human population. *Nat Commun* 12, 2175 (2021). https://doi.org/10.1038/s41467-021-22506-4

Saltré, F., Chadoeuf, J., Peters, K.J. et al. Climate-human interaction associated with southeast Australian megafauna extinction patterns. *Nat Commun* 10, 5311 (2019). https://doi.org/10.1038/s41467-019-13277-0

Becerra-Valdivia, L., Higham, T. The timing and effect of the earliest human arrivals in North America. Nature 584, 93–97 (2020). https://doi.org/10.1038/s41586-020-2491-6

Laborde, Campo. "A Late Pleistocene giant ground sloth kill and butchering site in the Pampas." *Science Advances* 5.3: 1-10.

Surovell, Todd A., et al. "Test of Martin's overkill hypothesis using radiocarbon dates on extinct megafauna." Proceedings of the National Academy of Sciences 113.4 (2016): 886-891.

Allentoft, Morten Erik, et al. "Extinct New Zealand megafauna were not in decline before human colonization." *Proceedings of the National Academy of Sciences* 111.13 (2014): 4922-4927.

Perry, George LW, et al. "A high-precision chronology for the rapid extinction of New Zealand moa (Aves, Dinornithiformes)." *Quaternary Science Reviews* 105 (2014): 126-135.

Holdaway, R., Allentoft, M., Jacomb, C. et al. An extremely low-density human population exterminated New Zealand moa. *Nat Commun* 5, 5436 (2014). https://doi.org/10.1038/ncomms6436

Schnitzler, A.E. (2011), Past and present distribution of the North African–Asian lion subgroup: a review. *Mammal Review*, 41: 220-243. https://doi.org/10.1111/j.1365-2907.2010.00181.x

Blumenthal, Janice M., et al. "Cayman Islands sea turtle nesting population increases over 22 years of monitoring." *Frontiers in Marine Science* (2021): 461.

White, H Bryant et al. "Trapping and furbearer management in North American wildlife conservation." *The International journal of environmental studies* vol. 72,5 (2015): 756-769. doi:10.1080/00207233.2015.1019297

Obbard, Martyn & Jones, James & Newman, R.A. & Booth, A. & Satterthwaite, A.J. & Linscombe, G. Furbearer Harvests in North America, 1600–1984. 1987.

Cressey, D. World's whaling slaughter tallied. *Nature* 519, 140–141 (2015). https://doi.org/10.1038/519140a

Defebaugh, James Elliott. History of the Lumber Industry of America. United States, *American lumberman*, 1907.

Rauner Library. Why wolves don't roam Dartmouth. *Dartmouth*, 24 Sept. 2013. https://raunerlibrary.blogspot.com/2013/09/why-wolves-dont-roam-dartmouth.html

U.S. Bureau of the Census. *Historical Statistics of the United States, Colonial Times to 1957*. Washington, D.C., 1960 https://www2.census.gov/library/publications/1960/compendia/hist_stats_colonial-1957/hist_stats_colonial-1957-chK.pdf

Pongratz, J.,, Reick, C., Raddatz, T., and Claussen, M. A reconstruction of global agricultural areas and land cover for the last millennium. *Global Biogeochem.* Cycles, 2008,d 22, GB3018, doi:10.1029/2007GB003153.

USDA. US Census for Agriculture 1954 Vol2. *United States Department of Agriculture*. 1956.

Entomological News, and Proceedings of the Entomological Section of the Academy of Natural Sciences of Philadelphia. United States, *Entomological Rooms of the Academy of Natural Sciences*, 1890.

De Voe, Thomas F. *1811-1892. The Market Assistant: Containing a Brief Description of Every Article of Human Food Sold In the Public Markets of the Cities of New York, Boston, Philadelphia, And Brooklyn; Including the Various Domestic And Wild Animals, Poultry, Game, Fish, Vegetables, Fruits &c., &c. With Many Curious Incidents And Anecdotes.* Cambridge, 1867.

Rangarajan, Mahesh, *India's Wildlife History*. Delhi, 2001.

Edgar N. Barclay. *Big game shooting records: together with biographical notes and anecdotes on the most prominent big game hunters of ancient and modern times.* H. F. & G. Witherby, 1932

MacCleery, Douglas W. American Forests: A History of Resiliency and Recovery. *U.S. Department of Agriculture, Forest Service*, 1993.

O'Driscol, Bill. A century ago, Pennsylvania stood almost entirely stripped of trees. *Pittsburgh City Paper* 19 Aug 2015.
https://www.pghcitypaper.com/pittsburgh/a-century-ago-pennsylvania-stood-almost-entirely-stripped-of-trees/Content?oid=1848219

Taylor D. The Coal Industry 1700–1850. In: *Mastering Economic and Social History*. Macmillan Master Series. Palgrave, London, 1988. https://doi.org/10.1007/978-1-349-19377-6_6

Bruce C. Netschert and Sam H. Schurr, *Energy in the American Economy, 1850-1975: An Economic Study of Its History and prospects.* John Hopkins University Press, 1960

Ritchie, Hannah. The death of UK coal in five charts. *Our World in Data*, 28 January 2019.
https://ourworldindata.org/death-uk-coal

U.S. Energy Information Administration. U.S. field production of crude oil. *EIA* 5 July 2022.
https://www.eia.gov/dnav/pet/hist/LeafHandler.ashx?n=pet&s=mcrfpus2&f=a

Davis, Stacy C., and Robert G. Boundy. Transportation Energy Data Book: Edition 39. *Oak Ridge National Laboratory*, 2020, https://doi.org/10.2172/1767864.

Davis, Stacy C., and Robert G. Boundy. Transportation Energy Data Book: Edition 33. *Oak Ridge National Laboratory*, 2016.
https://tedb.ornl.gov/wp-content/uploads/2019/03/Edition33_Full_Doc.pdf

Boden, Tom; Andres, Bob. Global CO2 emissions from fossil-fuel burning, cement manufacture, and gas flaring: 1751-2014. *Carbon Dioxide Information Analysis Center*, 3 March 2017.
https://cdiac.ess-dive.lbl.gov/ftp/ndp030/global.1751_2014.ems

Ritchie, Hannah; Roser, Max. Atmospheric concentrations. *Our World Data*, 2020
https://ourworldindata.org/atmospheric-concentrations

— What the history of London's air pollution can tell us about the future of today's growing megacities. *Our World Data*, 20 June 2017.
https://ourworldindata.org/london-air-pollution

Cliff I. Davidson (1979) Air Pollution In Pittsburgh: A Historical Perspective, *Journal of the Air Pollution Control Association*, 29:10, 1035-1041, DOI: 10.1080/00022470.1979.10470892

Concord River Greenway. History: river as sink and sewer. *Lowell Parks and Conservation Trust*, accessed 15 Aug. 2021
https://lowelllandtrust.org/greenwayclassroom/history/sinksewer.htm#ftn-1

U.S. Bureau of Census. Compendium of the Tenth Census 1880. U.S. Government Printing Office, 1883.

https://www.census.gov/library/publications/1885/dec/1880-compendium.html

U.S. Bureau of Census. Preliminary report of the eighth census 1860. U.S. Government Printing Office, 1862
https://www2.census.gov/library/publications/decennial/1860/statistics/1860d-20.pdf

Thurstan, R., Brockington, S. & Roberts, C. The effects of 118 years of industrial fishing on UK bottom trawl fisheries. *Nat Commun* 1, 15 (2010). https://doi.org/10.1038/ncomms1013

IEA. World total coal production 1971-2020. *IEA*, Paris, 13 Aug 2021
https://www.iea.org/data-and-statistics/charts/world-total-coal-production-1971-2020

IEA. Coal-Fired Power. *IEA*, 2020
https://www.iea.org/reports/coal-fired-power

Lester R. Brown. *World On the Edge: How to Prevent Environmental and Economic Collapse.* New York: W.W. Norton & Company, 2010

U.S. Energy Information Administration. Global liquid fuels. *EIA,* 7 July 2022.
https://www.eia.gov/outlooks/steo/report/global_oil.php

Ian D. Craigie, Jonathan E.M. Baillie, Andrew Balmford, Chris Carbone, Ben Collen, Rhys E. Green, Jon M. Hutton, Large mammal population declines in Africa's protected areas, *Biological Conservation*, Volume 143, Issue 9, 2010, Pages 2221-2228, ISSN 0006-3207, https://doi.org/10.1016/j.biocon.2010.06.007.

Gehui Wang, Renyi Zhang, Mario E. Gomez, et. al, Persistent sulfate formation from London Fog to Chinese haze, *Proceedings of the National Academy of Sciences* Nov 2016, 113 (48) 13630-13635; DOI: 10.1073/pnas.1616540113

US Environmental Protection Agency. Office of Water Planning and Standards. Fish Kills Caused by Pollution-Fifteen-Year Summary 1961-1975. 1978.

Blake more, Erin. The shocking river fire that fueled the creation of the EPA. *History*, 1 Dec 2020.
https://www.history.com/news/epa-earth-day-cleveland-cuyahoga-river-fire-clean-water-act

China Coal, *worldometer,* accessed 27 July 2022.
https://www.worldometers.info/coal/china-coal/

Buntaine, Mark T., Bing Zhang, and Patrick Hunnicutt. "Citizen monitoring of waterways decreases pollution in China by supporting government action and oversight." Proceedings of the National Academy of Sciences 118.29 (2021): e2015175118.

Wong, Edward. Nearly 14,000 companies in China violate pollution rules. *The New York Times,* 13 June 2017.
https://www.nytimes.com/2017/06/13/world/asia/china-companies-air-pollution-paris-agreement.html

Where we are Now

UN Office for Disaster Risk Reduction. "The Human Cost of Disasters: An Overview of the Last 20 Years (2000–2019)."(2020).

Samenow, Jason; Livingston, Ian. Canada sets new all-time heat record of 121 degrees amid unprecedented heat wave. *Washington Post*, 29 June, 2021. https://www.washingtonpost.com/weather/2021/06/27/heat-records-pacific-northwest/ #:~:text=Lytton%2C%20British%20Columbia%2C%20hit%20110.8%20degr ees%2C%20the%20highest,mark%20of%20109.9%20from%201900%2C%2 01931%20and%201941.

Breeden, Aurelien. U.K. Heat Wave: Britain Sets New Record on a Second Day of Scorching Temperatures. *The New York Times*, 20 July 2022. https://www.nytimes.com/live/2022/07/19/world/uk-europe-heat-fires-weather

Arrhenius, Svante. "XXXI. On the influence of carbonic acid in the air upon the temperature of the ground." *The London, Edinburgh, and Dublin Philosophical Magazine and Journal of Science* 41.251 (1896): 237-276.

Frants, Benjamin. What big oil knew about climate change, in its own words. *The Conversation*, 28 Oct. 2021. https://theconversation.com/what-big-oil-knew-about-climate-change-in-its-own-words-170642

IPCC (2014): Climate Change 2014: Synthesis Report. Contribution of Working Groups I, II and III to the Fifth Assessment Report of the Intergovernmental Panel on Climate Change. EXIT [Core Writing Team, R.K. Pachauri and L.A. Meyer (eds.)]. *IPCC*, Geneva, Switzerland, 151 pp.

IPCC, 2021: Climate Change 2021: The Physical Science Basis. Contribution of Working Group I to the Sixth Assessment Report of the Intergovernmental Panel on Climate Change[Masson-Delmotte, V., P. Zhai, A. Pirani, S.L. Connors, C. Péan, S. Berger, N. Caud, Y. Chen, L. Goldfarb, M.I. Gomis, M. Huang, K. Leitzell, E. Lonnoy, J.B.R. Matthews, T.K. Maycock, T. Waterfield, O. Yelekçi, R. Yu, and B. Zhou (eds.)]. Cambridge University Press, Cambridge, United Kingdom and New York, NY, USA, In press, doi:10.1017/9781009157896.

Bongaarts, John. "IPBES, 2019. Summary for policymakers of the global assessment report on biodiversity and ecosystem services of the Intergovernmental Science-Policy Platform on Biodiversity and Ecosystem Services." (2019): 680-681.

Stein, Theo, Despite pandemic shutdowns, carbon dioxide and methane surged in 2020. *NOAA*, 7 April 2021. https://research.noaa.gov/article/ArtMID/587/ArticleID/2742/Despite-pandemic-shutdowns-carbon-dioxide-and-methane-surged-in-2020

Blunden, J. and T. Boyer, Eds., 2022: "State of the Climate in 2021". Bull. Amer. Meteor. Soc., 103 (8), Si–S465, https://doi.org/ 10.1175/2022BAMSStateoftheClimate.1

Gingerich, P. D. (2019). Temporal scaling of carbon emission and accumulation rates: Modern anthropogenic emissions compared to estimates of PETM onset accumulation. *Paleoceanography and Paleoclimatology*, 34, 329– 335. https://doi.org/10.1029/2018PA003379

Steffen W, Rockström J, Richardson K, Lenton TM, Folke C, Liverman D, Summerhayes CP, Barnosky AD, Cornell SE, Crucifix M, Donges JF, Fetzer I, Lade SJ, Scheffer M, Winkelmann R, Schellnhuber HJ. Trajectories of the Earth System in the Anthropocene. *Proc Natl Acad Sci U S A*. 2018 Aug 14;115(33):8252-8259. doi: 10.1073/pnas.1810141115. Epub 2018 Aug 6. PMID: 30082409; PMCID: PMC6099852.

Briner, J.P., Cuzzone, J.K., Badgeley, J.A. et al. Rate of mass loss from the Greenland Ice Sheet will exceed Holocene values this century. *Nature* 586, 70–74 (2020). https://doi.org/10.1038/s41586-020-2742-6

Bromaghin, J.F., McDonald, T.L., Stirling, I., Derocher, A.E., Richardson, E.S., Regehr, E.V., Douglas, D.C., Durner, G.M., Atwood, T. and Amstrup, S.C. (2015), Polar bear population dynamics in the southern Beaufort Sea during a period of sea ice decline. *Ecological Applications*, 25: 634-651. https://doi.org/10.1890/14-1129.1

Takahashi, Atsuhiro, Tomo'omi Kumagai, Hironari Kanamori, Hatsuki Fujinami, Tetsuya Hiyama, and Masayuki Hara. " Impact of Tropical Deforestation and Forest Degradation on Precipitation over Borneo Island". *Journal of Hydrometeorology* 18.11 (2017): 2907-2922. < https://doi.org/10.1175/JHM-D-17-0008.1>. Web. 12 Apr. 2021.

Gaveau, D., Sheil, D., Husnayaen et al. Rapid conversions and avoided deforestation: examining four decades of industrial plantation expansion in Borneo. *Sci Rep* 6, 32017 (2016). https://doi.org/10.1038/srep32017

Ancrenaz, M., Gumal, M., Marshall, A.J., Meijaard, E., Wich , S.A. & Husson, S. 2016. *Pongo pygmaeus* (errata version published in 2018). *The IUCN Red List of Threatened Species* 2016: e.T17975A123809220. https://dx.doi.org/10.2305/IUCN.UK.2016-1.RLTS.T17975A17966347.en. Downloaded on 12 April 2021.

Marcelo C.C. Stabile, André L. Guimarães, Daniel S. Silva, Vivian Ribeiro, Marcia N. Macedo, Michael T. Coe, Erika Pinto, Paulo Moutinho, Ane Alencar,

Solving Brazil's land use puzzle: Increasing production and slowing Amazon deforestation. *Land Use Policy*, Volume 91, 2020, 104362, ISSN 0264-8377, https://doi.org/10.1016/j.landusepol.2019.104362.

Baden, Andrea L.,Lemurs are the world's most endangered mammals, but planting trees can help save them, *The Conversation*, 23 December 2019. https://theconversation.com/lemurs-are-the-worlds-most-endangered-mammals-but-planting-trees-can-help-save-them-127878

Ghislain Vieilledent, Clovis Grinand, Fety A. Rakotomalala, Rija Ranaivosoa, Jean-Roger Rakotoarijaona, Thomas F. Allnutt, Frédéric Achard,

Combining global tree cover loss data with historical national forest cover maps to look at six decades of deforestation and forest fragmentation in Madagascar. *Biological Conservation*,Volume 222, 2018,Pages 189-197,ISSN 0006-3207, https://doi.org/10.1016/j.biocon.2018.04.008.

Thoman, R. L., J. Richter-Menge, and M. L. Druckenmiller, Eds. Arctic Report Card 2020, *NOAA*, 2020. https://doi.org/10.25923/mn5p-t549.

Hall-Spencer, Jason M., et al. "Volcanic carbon dioxide vents show ecosystem effects of ocean acidification." *Nature* 454.7200 (2008): 96-99.

Eakin, C.M., Liu, G., Gomez, A.M., De la Couri, J.L., Heron, S.F., Skirving, W.J., Geiger, E.F., Marsh, B.L., Tirak, K.V., Strong, A.E. . Unprecedented three years of global coral bleaching 2014–17. Sidebar 3.1. [in State of the Climate in 2017]. *Bulletin of the American Meteorological Society* 99(8), 2018, S74–S75.

Glenn De'ath, Katharina E. Fabricius, Hugh Sweatman, Marji Puotinen, 27–year decline of coral cover and its causes. *Proceedings of the National Academy of Sciences*, Oct 2012, 2012. 08909; DOI: 10.1073/pnas.1208909109

Stuart-Smith, R.D., Brown, C.J., Ceccarelli, D.M. et al. Ecosystem restructuring along the Great Barrier Reef following mass coral bleaching. *Nature* 560, 92–96 (2018). https://doi.org/10.1038/s41586-018-0359-9

Hughes, Terry P., et al. "Emergent properties in the responses of tropical corals to recurrent climate extremes." *Current Biology* 31.23 (2021): 5393-5399.

Gaskil, Melissa, The Current State of Coral Reefs, *PBS Nature*,15 July 2019. https://www.pbs.org/wnet/nature/blog/the-current-state-of-coral-reefs/

Queste, B. Y., Vic, C., Heywood, K. J., & Piontkovski, S. A. (2018). Physical controls on oxygen distribution and denitrification potential in the north west Arabian Sea. *Geophysical Research Letters*, 45, 4143– 4152. https://doi.org/10.1029/2017GL076666

Lachkar, Z., Lévy, M., & Smith, K. S. (2019). Strong intensification of the Arabian Sea oxygen minimum zone in response to Arabian Gulf warming. *Geophysical Research Letters*, 46, 5420– 5429. https://doi.org/10.1029/2018GL081631

Woodcock, B., Isaac, N., Bullock, J. et al. Impacts of neonicotinoid use on long-term population changes in wild bees in England. *Nat Commun* 7, 12459 (2016). https://doi.org/10.1038/ncomms12459

Martin S. Warren, Dirk Maes, Chris A. M. van Swaay, Philippe Goffart, Hans Van Dyck, Nigel A. D. Bourn, Irma Wynhoff, Dan Hoare, Sam Ellis. The decline of butterflies in Europe: Problems, significance, and possible solutions. *Proceedings of the National Academy of Sciences* Jan 2021, 118 (2) e2002551117; DOI: 10.1073/pnas.2002551117

Habel, J.C., Ulrich, W., Biburger, N., Seibold, S. and Schmitt, T. (2019), Agricultural intensification drives butterfly decline. *Insect Conserv Divers*, 12: 289-295. https://doi.org/10.1111/icad.12343

David L. Wagner, Eliza M. Grames, Matthew L. Forister, May R. Berenbaum, David Stopak. Insect decline in the Anthropocene: Death by a thousand cuts. Proceedings of the *National Academy of Sciences* Jan 2021, 118 (2) e2023989118; DOI: 10.1073/pnas.2023989118

Dirzo, Rodolfo & Young, Hillary & Galetti, Mauro & Ceballos, Gerardo & Isaac, Nick & Collen, Ben. Defaunation in the Anthropocene. *Science*, 2014, 345. 401-6. 10.1126/science.1251817.

Alavanja MC. Introduction: pesticides use and exposure extensive worldwide. *Rev Environ Health*. 2009;24(4):303-309. doi:10.1515/reveh.2009.24.4.303

Aktar MW, Sengupta D, Chowdhury A. Impact of pesticides use in agriculture: their benefits and hazards. *Interdiscip Toxicol.* 2009;2(1):1-12. doi:10.2478/v10102-009-0001-7

Zhang, Luoping, et al. "Exposure to glyphosate-based herbicides and risk for non-Hodgkin lymphoma: a meta-analysis and supporting evidence." *Mutation Research/Reviews in Mutation Research* 781 (2019): 186-206

Boretti, Alberto, and Lorenzo Rosa. "Reassessing the projections of the world water development report." *NPJ Clean Water* 2.1 (2019): 1-6.

Hladik, Michelle L., and Dana W. Kolpin. "First national-scale reconnaissance of neonicotinoid insecticides in streams across the USA." *Environmental Chemistry* 13.1 (2015): 12-20.

Palmer, Cynthia. Neonicotinoid insecticides found in congressional cafeteria food, *American Bird Conservancy*, July 2015
https://abcbirds.org/wp-content/uploads/2015/07/Congressional_Dining_Hall_Report_July_2015.pdf

Sydney A. Cameron, Jeffrey D. Lozier, James P. Strange, Jonathan B. Koch, Nils Cordes, Leellen F. Solter, Terry L. Griswold. Patterns of widespread decline in North American bumble bees. *Proceedings of the National Academy of Sciences,* Jan 2011, 108 (2) 662-667; DOI: 10.1073/pnas.1014743108

Crall, James. Glyphosate impairs bee thermoregulation. *Science,* 376, 6597, (1051-1052), (2022). /doi/10.1126/science.abq5554

Farina, Walter M., et al. "Effects of the herbicide glyphosate on honey bee sensory and cognitive abilities: Individual impairments with implications for the hive." *Insects* 10.10 (2019): 354.

Motta, Erick VS, et al. "Oral or topical exposure to glyphosate in herbicide formulation impacts the gut microbiota and survival rates of honey bees." *Applied and environmental microbiology* 86.18 (2020): e01150-20.

Benbrook, C.M. Trends in glyphosate herbicide use in the United States and globally. *Environ Sci Eur* 28, 3 (2016). https://doi.org/10.1186/s12302-016-0070-0

DiBartolomeis, Michael, et al. "An assessment of acute insecticide toxicity loading (AITL) of chemical pesticides used on agricultural land in the United States." *PloS ONE* 14.8 (2019): e0220029.

Development Report. *npj Clean Water* 2, 15 (2019). https://doi.org/10.1038/s41545-019-0039-9

University of Arizona. Groundwater pumping has significantly reduced US stream flows: The new study has important implications for managing US water resources. *ScienceDaily,* 20 June 2019.
https://www.sciencedaily.com/releases/2019/06/190620100007.htm

Castelvecchi, Davide. "Rampant groundwater pumping has changed the tilt of Earth's axis." *Nature* (2023).

Robins, Jim, Crisis on the Colorado, *Yale Environment 360*, Yale School of the Environment, January-February 2019.
https://e360.yale.edu/series/crisis-on-the-colorado

Salvatore Pascale, Sarah B. Kapnick, Thomas L. Delworth, William F. Cooke. Increasing risk of another Cape Town "Day Zero" drought in the 21st century*Proceedings of the National Academy of Sciences* Nov 2020, 117 (47) 29495-29503; DOI: 10.1073/pnas.2009144117

Michigan State University. "Number of people suffering extreme droughts will double." *ScienceDaily,* 11 January, 2021. www.sciencedaily.com/releases/2021/01/21011112

McCartney, Matthew; Sally, Hilmy. 2007. "Managing the environmental impact of dams." In Ranade, P. S. (Ed.). *Rivers, dams and development: Issues and Dilemmas.* Punjagutta, Hyderabad, India: Icfai University Press. pp.88-104.

Hill, Megan, How a dying river came roaring back to life, *The Saturday Evening Post,* 22 April, 2021. https://www.saturdayeveningpost.com/2020/04/how-a-dying-river-came-roaring-back-to-life

E360 Digest, Extreme weather events have increased significantly in the last 20 years,*Yale Environment 360*, Yale School of the Environment, 13 October 2020. https://e360.yale.edu/digest/extreme-weather-events-have-increased-significantly-in-the-last-20-years

Worm, Boris, et al. "Impacts of biodiversity loss on ocean ecosystem services." science 314.5800 (2006): 787-790.

Pacoureau, N., Rigby, C.L., Kyne, P.M. et al. Half a century of global decline in oceanic sharks and rays. *Nature* 589, 567–571 (2021). https://doi.org/10.1038/s41586-020-03173-9

Fairclough, Caty, Shark finning: sharks turned prey, *Smithsonian*, August 2013. https://ocean.si.edu/ocean-life/sharks-rays/shark-finning-sharks-turned-prey

Kimberlee K. Barnes, Dana W. Kolpin, Edward T. Furlong, Steven D. Zaugg, Michael T. Meyer, Larry B. Barber, A national reconnaissance of pharmaceuticals and other organic wastewater contaminants in the United States — I) Groundwater. *Science of The Total Environment,*Volume 402,Issues 2–3,2008,Pages 192-200,ISSN 0048-9697, https://doi.org/10.1016/j.scitotenv.2008.04.028.

Küster, Anette, and Nicole Adler. "Pharmaceuticals in the environment: scientific evidence of risks and its regulation." *Philosophical transactions of the Royal Society of London.* Series B, Biological sciences vol. 369,1656 (2014): 20130587. doi:10.1098/rstb.2013.0587

Massarsky A, Trudeau VL, Moon TW. β-blockers as endocrine disruptors: the potential effects of human β-blockers on aquatic organisms. *J Exp Zool A Ecol Genet Physiol.* 2011 Jun 1;315(5):251-65. doi: 10.1002/jez.672. Epub 2011 Mar 1. PMID: 21370487.

Kostich MS, Batt AL, Lazorchak JM. Concentrations of prioritized pharmaceuticals in effluents from 50 large wastewater treatment plants in the US and implications for risk estimation. *Environ Pollut.* 2014 Jan;184:354-9. doi: 10.1016/j.envpol.2013.09.013. Epub 2013 Oct 3. PMID: 24095705.

Stephanie Tamschick, Beata Rozenblut-Kościsty, Maria Ogielska, Andreas Lehmann, Petros Lymberakis, Frauke Hoffmann, Ilka Lutz, Werner Kloas,

Matthias Stöck. Sex reversal assessments reveal different vulnerability to endocrine disruption between deeply diverged anuran lineages. *Scientific Reports*, 2016; 6: 23825 DOI: 10.1038/srep23825

Veronika Kivenson, Karin L. Lemkau, Oscar Pizarro, Dana R. Yoerger, Carl Kaiser, Robert K. Nelson, Catherine Carmichael, Blair G. Paul, Christopher M. Reddy, and David L. Valentine. Ocean Dumping of Containerized DDT Waste Was a Sloppy Process. *Environmental Science & Technology*, 2019 53 (6), 2971-2980,DOI: 10.1021/acs.est.8b05859

Xia, Rosanna, Stunning DDT dump site off L.A. coast much bigger than scientists expected, *L.A. Times*, April 26 2021. https://www.latimes.com/environment/story/2021-04-26/ddt-waste-barrels-off-la-coast-shock-california-scientists

Shaddick, G., Thomas, M.L., Mudu, P. et al. Half the world's population are exposed to increasing air pollution. *npj Clim Atmos Sci* 3, 23 (2020). https://doi.org/10.1038/s41612-020-0124-2

Jerrett M, Burnett RT, Pope CA 3rd, et al. Long-term ozone exposure and mortality. The *New England Journal of Medicine.* 2009 Mar;360(11):1085-1095. DOI: 10.1056/nejmoa0803894. PMID: 19279340; PMCID: PMC4105969.

Turner MC, Jerrett M, Pope CA 3rd, et al. Long-Term Ozone Exposure and Mortality in a Large Prospective Study. *American Journal of Respiratory and Critical Care Medicine.* 2016 May;193(10):1134-1142. DOI: 10.1164/rccm.201508-1633oc. PMID: 26680605; PMCID: PMC4872664.

Keiser, David, Gabriel Lade, and Ivan Rudik. "Air pollution and visitation at US national parks." *Science advances* 4.7 (2018): eaat1613.

Burke, Marshall, et al. "The changing risk and burden of wildfire in the United States." *Proceedings of the National Academy of Sciences* 118.2 (2021): e2011048118.

Yu, P., Davis, S. M., Toon, O. B., Portmann, R. W., Bardeen, C. G., Barnes, J. E., et al. (2021). Persistent stratospheric warming due to 2019–2020 Australian wildfire smoke. *Geophysical Research Letters*, 48, e2021GL092609. https://doi.org/10.1029/2021GL092609

Food Wastage Footprint (Project). Food wastage footprint: impacts on natural resources: summary report. *Food & Agriculture Org*, 2013. http://www.fao.org/news/story/en/item/196402/icode/.

UN Environmental Programme, Worldwide food waste, accessed 10 July, 2021 https://www.unep.org/thinkeatsave/get-informed/worldwide-food-waste

Stockstad, Erik, Common tire chemical implicated in mysterious deaths of at-risk salmon, *Science*, 3 Dec 2021. https://www.sciencemag.org/news/2020/12/common-tire-chemical-implicated-mysterious-deaths-risk-salmon

Tian, Zhenyu, et al. "A ubiquitous tire rubber–derived chemical induces acute mortality in coho salmon." *Science* 371.6525 (2021): 185-189.

Cousins, Ian T., et al. "Outside the Safe Operating Space of a New Planetary Boundary for Per-and Polyfluoroalkyl Substances (PFAS)." *Environmental Science & Technology* (2022).

Pelch, Katherine E., et al. "PFAS health effects database: Protocol for a systematic evidence map." *Environment international 130* (2019): 104851.

Jesse A. Goodrich, Douglas Walker, et. al. Exposure to perfluoroalkyl substances and risk of hepatocellular carcinoma in a multiethnic cohort, *JHEP Reports*, 2022, 100550, ISSN 2589-5559, https://doi.org/10.1016/j.jhepr.2022.100550.

Li, Fan, et al. "Short-chain per-and polyfluoroalkyl substances in aquatic systems: Occurrence, impacts and treatment." *Chemical Engineering Journal 380* (2020): 122506.

World Economic Forum, Ellen MacArthur Foundation and McKinsey & Company. "The New Plastics Economy — Rethinking the future of plastics." 2016.

Cox, Kieran D., Covernton, Garth A., Davies, Hailey L., Dower, John F., Juanes, Francis and Dudas, Sarah E. (2019) Human Consumption of Microplastics. *Environmental Science & Technology*, 53 (12). pp. 7068-7074. DOI 10.1021/acs.est.9b01517.

Geyer, Roland, Jenna R. Jambeck, and Kara Lavender Law. "Production, use, and fate of all plastics ever made." *Science advances* 3.7 (2017): e1700782.

Cable, Rachel & Beletsky, Dmitry & Beletsky, Raisa & Wigginton, Krista & Locke, Brendan & Duhaime, Melissa. (2017). Distribution and Modeled Transport of Plastic Pollution in the Great Lakes, the World's Largest Freshwater Resource. *Frontiers in Environmental Science*. 5. 10.3389/fenvs.2017.00045.

Kosuth, Marry, et al. "Synthetic polymer contamination in global drinking water." *Orb media* (2017).

Hirt, N., Body-Malapel, M. Immunotoxicity and intestinal effects of nano- and microplastics: a review of the literature. *Part Fibre Toxicol* 17, 57 (2020). https://doi.org/10.1186/s12989-020-00387-7

Marko D. Prokić, Tijana B. Radovanović, Jelena P. Gavrić, Caterina Faggio, Ecotoxicological effects of microplastics: Examination of biomarkers, current state and future perspectives. *TrAC Trends in Analytical Chemistry*, Volume 111,2019,Pages 37-46,ISSN 0165-9936, https://doi.org/10.1016/j.trac.2018.12.001.

Campanale C, Massarelli C, Savino I, Locaputo V, Uricchio VF. A Detailed Review Study on Potential Effects of Microplastics and Additives of Concern on Human Health. *Int J Environ Res Public Health*. 2020 Feb 13;17(4):1212. doi: 10.3390/ijerph17041212.

Antonio Ragusa, Alessandro Svelato, Criselda Santacroce, Piera Catalano, Valentina Notarstefano, Oliana Carnevali, Fabrizio Papa, Mauro Ciro Antonio Rongioletti, Federico Baiocco, Simonetta Draghi, Elisabetta D'Amore, Denise Rinaldo, Maria Matta, Elisabetta Giorgini,Plasticenta: First evidence of microplastics in human placenta. *Environment International*,Volume 146, 2021,106274,ISSN 0160-4120, https://doi.org/10.1016/j.envint.2020.106274.

Leslie, Heather A., et al. "Discovery and quantification of plastic particle pollution in human blood." *Environment International* (2022): 107199.

Fournier, S.B., D'Errico, J.N., Adler, D.S. et al. Nanopolystyrene translocation and fetal deposition after acute lung exposure during late-stage pregnancy. *Part Fibre Toxicol* 17, 55 (2020). https://doi.org/10.1186/s12989-020-00385-9

UN Department of Economic and Social Affairs, World population prospects 2019: highlights, June 2019.
https://population.un.org/wpp/Publications/Files/WPP2019_10KeyFindings.pdf

Wibowo, M.C., Yang, Z., Borry, M. et al. Reconstruction of ancient microbial genomes from the human gut. *Nature* 594, 234–239 (2021). https://doi.org/10.1038/s41586-021-03532-0

Birds

Field, D.J., Benito, J., Chen, A. et al. Late Cretaceous neornithine from Europe illuminates the origins of crown birds. *Nature* 579, 397–401 (2020). https://doi.org/10.1038/s41586-020-2096-0

Balter, Michael. When modern birds took flight. *Science*. 348, 617-617 (2015) doi:10.1126/science.348.6235.617
   https://www.science.org/doi/abs/10.1126/science.348.6235.617

Butchart, Stuart HM, et al. "Which bird species have gone extinct? A novel quantitative classification approach." *Biological Conservation* 227 (2018): 9-18.

Rosenberg, Kenneth V., et al. "Decline of the North American avifauna." *Science* 366.6461 (2019): 120-124.

Li, Y., Miao, R. & Khanna, M. Neonicotinoids and decline in bird biodiversity in the United States. *Nat Sustain* 3, 1027–1035 (2020). https://doi.org/10.1038/s41893-020-0582-x

BirdLife International. State of the world's birds: taking the pulse of the planet. Cambridge, UK: *BirdLife International*. 2018.

— (2021) Species factsheet: *Emberiza aureola*. Downloaded from http://www.birdlife.org on 24/09/2021.

— Assessing the scope and scale of illegal killing and taking of birds in the Mediterranean, and establishing a basis for systematic monitoring. Cambridge, UK: *BirdLife International*. 2015.

— (2021) Species factsheet: *Garrulax rufifrons*. Downloaded from http://www.birdlife.org on 24/09/2021.

— (2008) The illegal parrot trade remains a problem in Latin America. Downloaded from http://www.birdlife.org on 27/09/2021

David Tsz Chung Chan, Emily Shui Kei Poon, Anson Tsz Chun Wong, Simon Yung Wa Sin, Global trade in parrots – Influential factors of trade and implications for conservation, *Global Ecology and Conservation*, Volume 30, 2021, e01784,ISSN 2351-9894, https://doi.org/10.1016/j.gecco.2021.e01784.

IUCN 2021. *The IUCN Red List of Threatened Species*. Version 2021-2. <https://www.iucnredlist.org>

Lévêque, Lucile et al. "Characterizing the spatio-temporal threats, conservation hotspots and conservation gaps for the most extinction-prone bird family

(Aves: Rallidae)." *Royal Society open science* vol. 8,9 210262. 8 Sep. 2021, doi:10.1098/rsos.210262

Hume, Julian P. "The history of the Dodo Raphus cucullatus and the penguin of Mauritius." *Historical Biology* 18.2 (2006): 69-93.

Passenger Pigeon

Eric J. Guiry, Trevor J. Orchard, Thomas C.A. Royle, Christina Cheung, Dongya Y. Yang, Dietary plasticity and the extinction of the passenger pigeon (*Ectopistes migratorius*), *Quaternary Science Reviews*, Volume 233, 2020, 106225,ISSN 0277-3791, https://doi.org/10.1016/j.quascirev.2020.106225.

Hung, Chih-Ming, et al. "Drastic population fluctuations explain the rapid extinction of the passenger pigeon." *Proceedings of the National Academy of Sciences* 111.29 (2014): 10636-10641.

Bucher E.H. (1992) The Causes of Extinction of the Passenger Pigeon. In: Power D.M. (eds) Current Ornithology. *Current Ornithology*, vol 9. Springer, Boston, MA. https://doi.org/10.1007/978-1-4757-9921-7_1

Yeoman, Barry. Why the passenger pigeon went extinct. *Audubon*, May-June 2014. https://www.audubon.org/magazine/may-june-2014/why-passenger-pigeon-went-extinct

National Museum of Natural History. The passenger pigeon. *Smithsonian*, March 2001. https://www.si.edu/spotlight/passenger-pigeon

Ehrlich, Paul R.; David S. Dobkin, and Darryl Wheye. The passenger pigeon. *Stanford University*, 1988. https://web.stanford.edu/group/stanfordbirds/text/essays/Passenger_Pigeon.html

Ellsworth, Joshua W., and BRENDA C. McCOMB. "Potential effects of passenger pigeon flocks on the structure and composition of presettlement forests of eastern North America." *Conservation Biology* 17.6 (2003): 1548-1558.

Great Auk

Thomas, Jessica E., et al. "Demographic reconstruction from ancient DNA supports rapid extinction of the great auk." *Elife 8* (2019): e47509.

Grieve, Symington. *The Great Auk, Or Garefowl (Alca Impennis, Linn.): Its History, Archæology, and Remains.* T.C. Jack, 1885.

Sven-Axel Bengtson, Breeding Ecology and Extinction of the Great Auk (*Pinguinus impennis*): Anecdotal Evidence and Conjectures, *The Auk*, Volume 101, Issue 1, January 1984, Pages 1–12, https://doi.org/10.1093/auk/101.1.1

Birkhead, Tim. *Great Auk Islands; a Field Biologist in the Arctic.* United Kingdom, Bloomsbury Publishing, 2010

Ivory-billed Woodpecker

An Alternative Hypothesis for the Cause of the Ivory-billed Woodpecker's Decline, *The Condor*, Volume 110, Issue 4, 1 November 2008, Pages 808–810, https://doi.org/10.1525/cond.2008.8658

BirdLife International (2021) Species factsheet: *Campephilus principalis.* Downloaded from http://www.birdlife.org on 04/10/2021.

Kodikara, S, Demirhan, H, Wang, Y, Solow, A, Stone, L. Inferring extinction year using a Bayesian approach. *Methods Ecol Evol.* 2020; 11: 964– 973. https:// doi.org/10.1111/2041-210X.13408

Hasbrouck, Edwin M. "The Present Status of the Ivory-Billed Woodpecker (*Campephilus Principalis*)." *The Auk*, vol. 8, no. 2, 1891, pp. 174–86, https:// doi.org/10.2307/4068072.

Lammertink, M., & Estrada, A. (1995). Status of the Ivory-billed Woodpecker *Campephilus principalis* in Cuba: Almost certainly extinct. *Bird Conservation International*, 5(1), 53-59. doi:10.1017/S095927090000294X

Tanner, James T. *The Ivory-Billed Woodpecker.* United States, Dover Publications, 2003.

Franklin, Jerry F. "Structural and functional diversity in temperate forests." *Biodiversity.* National Academy Press, 52.1 (1988).

Carolina Parakeet

Hasbrouck, Edwin M. "The Carolina Paroquet (*Conurus Carolinensis*)." *The Auk*, vol. 8, no. 4, 1891, pp. 369–79, https://doi.org/10.2307/4068141.

Burgio, KR, Colin J. Carlson, Alexander L. Bond, Margaret A. Rubega, Morgan W. Tingley. The two extinctions of the Carolina parakeet. *bioRxiv* 801142; doi: https://doi.org/10.1101/801142

Burgio, KR, Carlson, CJ, Tingley, MW. Lazarus ecology: Recovering the distribution and migratory patterns of the extinct Carolina parakeet. *Ecol Evol.* 2017; 7: 5467– 5475. https://doi.org/10.1002/ece3.3135

Pere Gelabert, Marcela Sandoval-Velasco, Aitor Serres, et al. Evolutionary History, Genomic Adaptation to Toxic Diet, and Extinction of the Carolina Parakeet, *Current Biology*, Volume 30, Issue 1, 2020, Pages 108-114.e5,ISSN 0960-9822, https://doi.org/10.1016/j.cub.2019.10.066.

Begum, Tammana. Reviving the cold case of the Carolina parakeet extinction. *Natural History Museum* (UK), 27 July 2021. https://www.nhm.ac.uk/discover/news/2021/july/reviving-the-cold-case-of-the-carolina-parakeet-extinction.html

Wikisource contributors. "Ornithological Biography/Volume 1/Carolina Parrot." *Wikisource* , 18 Feb. 2011. Web. 1 Oct. 2021.

Huia

Galbreath, Ross. "The 1907 'last generally accepted record of huia (Heteralocha acutirostris) is unreliable." *Notornis* 64 (2017): 239-242.

Buller, WL. *A History of the Birds of New Zealand.* Van Vorst, 1888.

Salvador, Rodrigo Brincalepe, et al. "Historical distribution data of New Zealand endemic families Callaeidae and Notiomystidae (Aves, Passeriformes)." Check List 15 (2019): 701.

Dussex, Nicolas, et al. "Complete genomes of two extinct New Zealand passerines show responses to climate fluctuations but no evidence for genomic erosion prior to extinction." *Biology letters* 15.9 (2019): 20190491.

Houston, David C. "The Maˉori and the Huia." *Ethno-ornithology*. Routledge, 2012. 71-76.

Moorhouse, R. J. (1996) 'The extraordinary bill dimorphism of the Huia (Heteralocha acutirostris): Sexual selection of intersexual competition?'. *Notornis*, 1996. vol 43, pp.19–34.

Hawaiian Honeycreepers.

Pyle, R.L., and P. Pyle. 2017. The Birds of the Hawaiian Islands: Occurrence, History, Distribution, and Status. *B.P. Bishop Museum*. Version 2, 1 January 2017.
http://hbs.bishopmuseum.org/birds/rlp-monograph

Atkinson, Carter T., and Dennis A. LaPointe. "Introduced avian diseases, climate change, and the future of Hawaiian honeycreepers." *Journal of Avian Medicine and Surgery* 23.1 (2009): 53-63.

Henshaw, Henry Wetherbee. *Birds of the Hawaiian Islands: being a complete list of the birds of the Hawaiian possessions, with notes on their habits*. T.G. Thrum, 1902.

Banko, Winston E. "History of endemic Hawaiian birds: Part I: species accounts: forest birds:'Akialoa, Nukupu'u &'Akiapōlā'au." (1984).

Smith, Katherine F., Dov F. Sax, and Kevin D. Lafferty. "Evidence for the role of infectious disease in species extinction and endangerment." *Conservation biology* 20.5 (2006): 1349-1357.

Lerner, Heather RL, et al. "Multilocus resolution of phylogeny and timescale in the extant adaptive radiation of Hawaiian honeycreepers." *Current Biology* 21.21 (2011): 1838-1844.

'O'o Birds of Hawaii

Fleischer, Robert C., Helen F. James, and Storrs L. Olson. "Convergent evolution of Hawaiian and Australo-Pacific honeyeaters from distant songbird ancestors." *Current Biology* 18.24 (2008): 1927-1931.

Banko WE. History of endemic Hawaiian birds: part I: population histories, species accounts: forest birds: 'Elepaio, 'Ō'ō, & Kioea. Honolulu (HI): Cooperative National Park Resources Studies Unit, University of Hawaii at Manoa, Department of Botany. CPSU/UH *Avian History Report*, 7a and 7b, 1981

Pyle, R.L., and P. Pyle. The Birds of the Hawaiian Islands: Occurrence, History, Distribution, and Status. *B.P. Bishop Museum*,Version 2. 1 January 2017. http://hbs.bishopmuseum.org/birds/rlp-monograph

Elphick, Chris S., David L. Roberts, and J. Michael Reed. "Estimated dates of recent extinctions for North American and Hawaiian birds." *Biological Conservation* 143.3 (2010): 617-624.

Cuban Macaw

Wiley, James W., and Guy M. Kirwan. "The extinct macaws of the West Indies with special reference to Cuban Macaw, Ara tricolor." *Bulletin of the British Ornithologists' Club* 133.2 (2013): 125-156.

Johansson, U.S., Ericson, P.G.P., Blom, M.P.K. and Irestedt, M. The phylogenetic position of the extinct Cuban Macaw Ara tricolor based on complete mitochondrial genome sequences. *Ibis* (2018): 160: 666-672. https://doi.org/10.1111/ibi.12591

Williams, Matthew I., and David W. Steadman. "The historic and prehistoric distribution of parrots (Psittacidae) in the West Indies." *Biogeography of the West Indies.* CRC Press, 2001. 175-190.

Gala, Monica, and Arnaud Lenoble. "Evidence of the former existence of an endemic macaw in Guadeloupe, Lesser Antilles." *Journal of Ornithology* 156.4 (2015): 1061-1066.

Lambert, Meghan. "Forestry management in Cuba: An environmental history of the 20th century." (2008).

Hawaiian Crow

Sakai, Howard F., and James R. Carpenter. "The variety and nutritional value of foods consumed by Hawaiian Crow nestlings, an endangered species." *The Condor* 92.1 (1990): 220-228.

Tomich, P. Quentin. "Notes on nests and behavior of the Hawaiian Crow." (1971).

Work, Thierry M., Donna Ball, and Mark Wolcott. "Erysipelas in a free-ranging Hawaiian crow (Corvus hawaiiensis)." *Avian diseases,* 1999 :338-341.

Jønsson, Knud A., Pierre-Henri Fabre, and Martin Irestedt. "Brains, tools, innovation and biogeography in crows and ravens." *BMC evolutionary biology* 12.1 (2012): 1-12.

Massey, J. Gregory, et al. "Characteristics of Naturally Acquired Plasmodium Relictum Capistranoae Infections in Naive Hawaiian Crows (Corvus Hawaiiensis) in Hawaii." The Journal of Parasitology, vol. 82, no. 1, *The American Society of Parasitologists*, 1996, pp. 182–85, https://doi.org/10.2307/3284139.

Rutz, Christian, et al. "Discovery of species-wide tool use in the Hawaiian crow." *Nature* 537.7620 (2016): 403-407.

Po'ouli

BirdLife International (2021) Species factsheet: *Melamprosops phaeosoma.* Downloaded from http://www.birdlife.org

VanderWerf, Eric A., et al. "Update on Recovery Efforts for the Po'ouli." *'Elepaio: Journal of the Hawaii Audubon Society* 63.4 (2003): 25-30.

Baldwin , P.H. and T.L.C. Casey. 1983. A preliminary list of foods of the Po'ouli. 'Elepaio 43:53-56

Citation: Pyle, R.L., and P. Pyle. 2017. The Birds of the Hawaiian Islands: Occurrence, History, Distribution, and Status. *B.P. Bishop Museum*, Version 2, 1 January 2017. http://hbs.bishopmuseum.org/birds/rlp-monograph/

Spix's Macaw

Juniper, A. & Yamashita, Carlos. (1991). The habitat and status of Spix's Macaw *Cyanopsitta spixii. Bird Conservation International* 1. 1-9. 10.1017/ S0959270900000502.

Marcuk, V., Purchase, C., de Boer, D. et al. Qualitative description of the submission and agonistic behavior of the Spix's Macaw (Cyanopsitta spixii, Spix 1824), with special reference to the displacement displays. *J Ethol* 38, 253–270 (2020). https://doi.org/10.1007/s10164-020-00650-6

Tavares, Erika Sendra, et al. "Phylogenetic relationships and historical biogeography of neotropical parrots (Psittaciformes: Psittacidae: Arini) inferred from mitochondrial and nuclear DNA sequences." *Systematic Biology* 55.3 (2006): 454-470.

BirdLife International (2021) Species factsheet: *Cyanopsitta spixii*. Downloaded from http://www.birdlife.org

Amphibians

AmphibiaWeb. 2021. <https://amphibiaweb.org> University of California, Berkeley, CA, USA.

Hime, Paul M., et al. "Phylogenomics reveals ancient gene tree discordance in the amphibian tree of life." *Systematic biology* 70.1 (2021): 49-66.

Petranka, J.W., Eldridge, M.E. and Haley, K.E. (1993), Effects of Timber Harvesting on Southern Appalachian Salamanders. *Conservation Biology*, 7: 363-370. https://doi.org/10.1046/j.1523-1739.1993.07020363.x

Scheele, Ben C., et al. "Amphibian fungal panzootic causes catastrophic and ongoing loss of biodiversity." *Science* 363.6434 (2019): 1459-1463.

Rittmeyer EN, Allison A, Gründler MC, Thompson DK, Austin CC (2012) Ecological Guild Evolution and the Discovery of the World's Smallest Vertebrate. *PLoS ONE* 7(1): e29797. https://doi.org/10.1371/journal.pone.0029797

Costanzo, Jon P., et al. "Hibernation physiology, freezing adaptation and extreme freeze tolerance in a northern population of the wood frog." *Journal of Experimental Biology* 216.18 (2013): 3461-3473.

Joven, Alberto et al. "Model systems for regeneration: salamanders." *Development* (Cambridge, England) vol. 146,14 dev167700. 22 Jul. 2019, doi:10.1242/ dev.167700

Martin A. Schlaepfer, Craig Hoover, C. Kenneth Dodd, Challenges in Evaluating the Impact of the Trade in Amphibians and Reptiles on Wild Populations, *BioScience*, Volume 55, Issue 3, March 2005, Pages 256–264, https://doi.org/ 10.1641/0006-3568(2005)055[0256:CIETIO]2.0.CO;2

Kemp, T.S. *Amphibians: A Very Short Introduction*, Oxford University Press, 2021

Hughes, Alice C., Ben Marshall, and Colin Strine. "Gaps in global wildlife trade monitoring leave amphibians vulnerable." *bioRxiv* (2021).

Scheele, Ben C et al. "Amphibian Fungal Panzootic Causes Catastrophic and Ongoing Loss of Biodiversity." SCIENCE 363.6434 (2019): 1459–1463. Print.

Ribeiro, Luisa P., et al. "Bullfrog farms release virulent zoospores of the frog-killing fungus into the natural environment." *Scientific reports* 9.1 (2019): 1-10.

Martel, An, et al. "*Batrachochytrium salamandrivorans* sp. nov. causes lethal chytridiomycosis in amphibians." *Proceedings of the National Academy of Sciences* 110.38 (2013): 15325-15329.

National Wildlife Health Center. *Batrachochytrium salamandrivorans (Bsal). USGS*, 10 April 2018. https://www.usgs.gov/centers/nwhc/science/batrachochytrium-salamandrivorans-bsal?qt-science_center_objects=0#qt-science_center_objects

Golden Coqui Frog

Drewry, George E., and Kirkland L. Jones. "A New Ovoviviparous Frog, Eleutherodactylus Jasperi (Amphibia, Anura, Leptodactylidae), from Puerto Rico." Journal of Herpetology, vol. 10, no. 3, *Society for the Study of Amphibians and Reptiles*, 1976, pp. 161–65, https://doi.org/10.2307/1562976.

Burrowes, Patricia A., Rafael L. Joglar, and David E. Green. "Potential causes for amphibian declines in Puerto Rico." *Herpetologica* 60.2 (2004): 141-154.

Rios-Lopez, Neftali, and Richard Thomas. "A new species of palustrine Eleutherodactylus (Anura: Leptodactylidae) from Puerto Rico." *Zootaxa* 1512.5 (2007): 1-64.

AmphibiaWeb 2020 *Eleutherodactylus jasperi*: Puerto Rican Golden Frog <https://amphibiaweb.org/species/2988> University of California, Berkeley, CA, USA. Accessed Nov 10, 2021.

Brooks, Thomas, and Michael Leonard Smith. "Caribbean catastrophes." *Science* 294.5546 (2001): 1469-1471.

Harlequin Toads

AmphibiaWeb 2019 *Atelopus zeteki*: Panamanian Golden Frog <https://amphibiaweb.org/species/91> University of California, Berkeley, CA, USA. Accessed Nov 23, 2021.

Waddle, Anthony W., et al. "Amphibian resistance to chytridiomycosis increases following low-virulence chytrid fungal infection or drug-mediated clearance." *Journal of Applied Ecology* 58.10 (2021): 2053-2064.

IUCN SSC Amphibian Specialist Group. 2020. *Atelopus chiriquiensis. The IUCN Red List of Threatened Species* 2020: e.T54498A54340769. https://dx.doi.org/10.2305/IUCN.UK.2020-3.RLTS.T54498A54340769.en. Downloaded on 23 November 2021.

AmphibiaWeb 2010 *Atelopus chiriquiensis*: Chiriqui Harlequin Frog <https://amphibiaweb.org/species/40> University of California, Berkeley, CA, USA. Accessed Nov 23, 2021.

La Marca, Enrique, et al. "Catastrophic population declines and extinctions in Neotropical harlequin frogs (Bufonidae: Atelopus) 1." *Biotropica: The Journal of Biology and Conservation* 37.2 (2005): 190-201.

AmphibiaWeb 2009 *Atelopus senex* <https://amphibiaweb.org/species/79> University of California, Berkeley, CA, USA. Accessed Nov 24, 2021.

IUCN SSC Amphibian Specialist Group. 2020. *Atelopus senex. The IUCN Red List of Threatened Species 2020*: e.T54549A54358350. https://dx.doi.org/10.2305/

IUCN.UK.2020-3.RLTS.T54549A54358350.en. Downloaded on 24 November 2021.

AmphibiaWeb 2014 *Atelopus cruciger*: Rancho Grande Harlequin Frog <https://amphibiaweb.org/species/43> University of California, Berkeley, CA, USA. Accessed Nov 24, 2021.

Cheng, Tina L., et al. "Coincident mass extirpation of neotropical amphibians with the emergence of the infectious fungal pathogen Batrachochytrium dendrobatidis." *Proceedings of the National Academy of Sciences* 108.23 (2011): 9502-9507.

Golden Toad

Anchukaitis, Kevin J., and Michael N. Evans. "Tropical cloud forest climate variability and the demise of the Monteverde golden toad." *Proceedings of the National Academy of Sciences* 107.11 (2010): 5036-5040.

Pounds, J. Alan, and Martha L. Crump. "Amphibian declines and climate disturbance: the case of the golden toad and the harlequin frog." *Conservation Biology* 8.1 (1994): 72-85.

AmphibiaWeb 2010 *Incilius periglenes*: Sapo Dorado <https://amphibiaweb.org/species/253> University of California, Berkeley, CA, USA. Accessed Nov 29, 2021.

Shrub Frogs of Sri Lanka

Ellepola, Gajaba, et al. "Molecular species delimitation of shrub frogs of the genus Pseudophilautus (Anura, Rhacophoridae)." *PloS ONE* 16.10 (2021): e0258594.

Bahir, Mohomed M., et al. "Reproduction and terrestrial direct development in Sri Lankan shrub frogs (Ranidae: Rhacophorinae: Philautus)." *The Raffles Bulletin of Zoology* 12 (2005): 339-350.

Stuart, S.N., Hoffmann, M., Chanson, J.S., Cox, N.A., Berridge, R.J., Ramani, P., and Young, B.E. (eds.). *Threatened Amphibians of the World.* Lynx Edicions, Barcelona, Spain; IUCN, Gland, Switzerland; and Conservation International, 2008.

Information on amphibian biology and conservation. [web application]. Berkeley, California: *AmphibiaWeb*. 2021. https://amphibiaweb.org/.

Reddy, C. Sudhakar, et al. "Assessment and monitoring of deforestation and forest fragmentation in South Asia since the 1930s." *Global and Planetary Change* 161 (2018): 132-148

Mapa, R. B., et al. "Land use in Sri Lanka: past, present and the future." *Proceedings of the 17th World Congress of Social Science (WCSS), Bangkok, Thailand.* 2002.

Manamendra-Arachchi, K., and Pethiyagoda, R. (2005). "The Sri Lankan shrub-frogs of the genus Philautus Gistel, 1848 (Ranidae: Rhacophorinae), with description of 27 new species." *Raffles Bulletin of Zoology*, Supplement 12, 163-303.

Butler, Rhett. Statistic: Sri Lanka. *Mongabay*, accessed 23 Nov. 2021.

https://rainforests.mongabay.com/deforestation/forest-information-archive/
Sri_Lanka.htm

Gastric Brooding Frogs

AmphibiaWeb 2016 *Rheobatrachus vitellinus*: Northern Gastric Brooding Frog
<https://amphibiaweb.org/species/3544> University of California, Berkeley,
CA, USA. Accessed Dec 2, 2021.

Geyle, Hayley M., et al. "Red hot frogs: identifying the Australian frogs most at risk
of extinction." *Pacific Conservation Biology* (2021).

Jean-Marc Hero, Keith McDonald, Ross Alford, Michael Cunningham, Richard
Retallick. 2004. *Rheobatrachus vitellinus*. *The IUCN Red List of Threatened
Species* 2004: e.T19476A8897826. https://dx.doi.org/10.2305/
IUCN.UK.2004.RLTS.T19476A8897826.en. Downloaded on 02

Vegas Valley Leopard Frog

Hekkala, Evon R., et al. "Resurrecting an extinct species: archival DNA, taxonomy,
and conservation of the Vegas Valley leopard frog." *Conservation Genetics* 12.5
(2011): 1379-1385.

AmphibiaWeb 2011 *Rana fisheri*: Las Vegas Valley Leopard Frog <https://
amphibiaweb.org/species/6859> University of California, Berkeley, CA, USA.
Accessed Dec 6, 2021.

Linsdale, Jean M. "Amphibians and Reptiles in Nevada." Proceedings of the
American Academy of Arts and Sciences, vol. 73, no. 8, *American Academy of
Arts & Sciences*, 1940, pp. 197–257, https://doi.org/10.2307/25130182.

Bradley, Gregory A., et al. "Chytridiomycosis in native Arizona frogs." *Journal of
wildlife diseases* 38.1 (2002): 206-212.

Wyoming Toad

Odum, R. Andrew, and Paul Stephen Corn. "Wyoming Toad (*Bufo baxteri*)." (2002).

Vincent, Kim & Abbott, Tyler. First Revised Recovery Plan for Wyoming Toad.
2015.

Gagliardi, Robert. Wyoming toad recovery sees success in southeast. *Wyoming
FIsh and Game Department*, 31 Aug. 2020.https://wgfd.wyo.gov/News/
Wyoming-toad-recovery-sees-success-in-southeast

Yunnan Lake Newt

AmphibiaWeb 2001 *Cynops wolterstorffi*: Kunming Lake Newt <https://
amphibiaweb.org/species/4246> University of California, Berkeley, CA, USA.
Accessed Dec 9, 2021.

Xiangcan, Jin, et al. Lake Danchi. *Lakenet*, Feb 2006.
http://www.worldlakes.org/uploads/11_lake_dianchi_27february2006.pdf

Jalpa False Brook Salamander

Stuart, L.C. Descriptions of some new amphibians and reptiles from Guatemala.
Proceedings of the Biological Society of Washington: 159-178, 1954.

—. 1963. A checklist of the herpetofauna of Guatemala. *Miscellaneous Publications, Museum of Zoology, University of Michigan*: 1-150.

IUCN SSC Amphibian Specialist Group. 2020. *Pseudoeurycea exspectata. The IUCN Red List of Threatened Species* 2020: e.T59376A54381158. https://dx.doi.org/10.2305/IUCN.UK.2020-2.RLTS.T59376A54381158.en. Accessed on 27 July 2022.

Ainsworth's Salamander

Lazell, James. "New Salamander of the Genus Plethodon from Mississippi." Copeia, vol. 1998, no. 4, *American Society of Ichthyologists and Herpetologists* (ASIH), Allen Press], 1998, pp. 967–70, https://doi.org/10.2307/1447343.

AmphibiaWeb. 2021. <https://amphibiaweb.org> University of California, Berkeley, CA, USA. Accessed 14 Dec 2021.

Pierson, Todd W., et al. "Preservation-induced morphological change in salamanders and failed DNA extraction from a decades-old museum specimen: implications for *Plethodon ainsworthi*." *Journal of Herpetology* 54.2 (2020): 137-143.

Reptiles

Maddin, Hillary. 310 million-year-old tree fossils to reveal new ancient animals, *The Conversation*, 16 July 2019. https://theconversation.com/310-million-year-old-tree-fossils-to-reveal-new-ancient-animals-120195?xid=PS_smithsonian

Glaw, Frank, et al. "Extreme miniaturization of a new amniote vertebrate and insights into the evolution of genital size in chameleons." *Scientific reports* 11.1 (2021): 1-14.

Campbell, Angela L., et al. "Biological infrared imaging and sensing." *Micron* 33.2 (2002): 211-225.

Gracheva, Elena O., et al. "Molecular basis of infrared detection by snakes." *Nature* 464.7291 (2010): 1006-1011.

Zyga,Lisa. Snakes' heat vision enables accurate attacks on prey. *Phys.org*, 31 August 2006. https://phys.org/news/2006-08-snakes-vision-enables-accurate-prey.html

Saha, Anwesha, et al. "Tracking global population trends: Population time-series data and a living planet index for reptiles." *Journal of Herpetology* 52.3 (2018): 259-268.

Teyssier, Jérémie, et al. "Photonic crystals cause active colour change in chameleons." *Nature communications* 6.1 (2015): 1-7.

Dutton, Peter & Bowen, Brian & Owens, David & Barragán, Ana & Davis, Scott. (1999). Phylogeography of the leatherback turtle (*Dermochelys coriacea*). *Journal of Zoology* 248. 10.1017/S0952836999007116.

James, Michael C., and N. Mrosovsky. "Body temperatures of leatherback turtles (*Dermochelys coriacea*) in temperate waters off Nova Scotia, Canada." *Canadian Journal of Zoology* 82.8 (2004): 1302-1306.

Lovich, Jeffrey E., et al. "Where have all the turtles gone, and why does it matter?." *BioScience* 68.10 (2018): 771-781.

Auliya, Mark, et al. "Trade in live reptiles, its impact on wild populations, and the role of the European market." Biological Conservation 204 (2016): 103-119. *Zoology* 82.8 (2004): 1302-1306.

Safina, Carl. *Voyage of the Turtle: In Pursuit of the Earth's Last Dinosaur.* Henry Holt and Company, 2007.

Fossette, Sabrina, et al. "Atlantic leatherback migratory paths and temporary residence areas." *PLoS ONE* 5.11 (2010): e13908.

Putman, Nathan F., et al. "Longitude perception and bicoordinate magnetic maps in sea turtles." *Current Biology* 21.6 (2011): 463-466.

Giant Tortoises of the Galápagos

Cayot, L.J., Gibbs, J.P., Tapia, W. & Caccone, A. 2016. *Chelonoidis abingdonii. The IUCN Red List of Threatened Species* 2016: e.T9017A65487433. https://dx.doi.org/10.2305/IUCN.UK.2016-1.RLTS.T9017A65487433.en. Accessed on 27 December 2021.

Poulakakis, Nikos, et al. "Colonization history of Galapagos giant tortoises: Insights from mitogenomes support the progression rule." *Journal of Zoological Systematics and Evolutionary Research* 58.4 (2020): 1262-1275.

Günther, A.C.L.G. *The Gigantic Land-Tortoises (Living and Extinct) in the Collection of the British Museum.* Taylor and Francis, London, 1877.

van Dijk, P.P., Rhodin, A.G.J., Cayot, L.J. & Caccone, A. 2017. *Chelonoidis niger. The IUCN Red List of Threatened Species* 2017: e.T9023A3149101. https://dx.doi.org/10.2305/IUCN.UK.2017-3.RLTS.T9023A3149101.en. Accessed on 28 December 2021.

Poulakakis, Nikos, et al. "Historical DNA analysis reveals living descendants of an extinct species of Galápagos tortoise." *Proceedings of the National Academy of Sciences* 105.40 (2008): 15464-15469.

Galapagos Conservancy. Outrage at massacre of giant tortoises in Galápagos. *Galapagos.org*, 13 Oct. 2021. https://www.galapagos.org/newsroom/outrage-at-massacre-of-giant-tortoises-in-galapagos/

Townsend, C.H. The Galapagos tortoises in their relation to the whaling industry: a study of old logbooks. *Zoologica*, 1925 4(3): 55–135.

Giant Tortoises of the Mascarene Islands

Rhodin, Anders GJ, et al. "Turtles and tortoises of the world during the rise and global spread of humanity: first checklist and review of extinct Pleistocene and Holocene chelonians." (2015): 1-66.

Kehlmaier, C., Graciá, E., Campbell, P.D. et al. Ancient mitogenomics clarifies radiation of extinct Mascarene giant tortoises (Cylindraspis spp.). *Sci Rep* 9, 17487 (2019). https://doi.org/10.1038/s41598-019-54019-y

Hume, Julian Pender, et al. "Discovery of the first Mascarene giant tortoise nesting site on Rodrigues Island, Indian Ocean (Testudinidae: Cylindraspis)." *Herpetology* Notes 14 (2021): 103-116.

Austin, Jeremy J., and E. Nicholas Arnold. "Ancient mitochondrial DNA and morphology elucidate an extinct island radiation of Indian Ocean giant tortoises (Cylindraspis)." *Proceedings of the Royal Society of London.* Series B: Biological Sciences 268.1485 (2001): 2515-2523.

Grant de Vaux, Charles. *The History of Mauritius, Or the Isle of France, and the Neighbouring Islands: From Their First Discovery to the Present Time ; Composed and Principally from the Papers Amd Memoirs of Baron Grant, who Resided 20 Years in the Island.* United Kingdom, Nicol, 1801.

Day Geckos of Rodrigues Island

Cole, N. 2021. *Phelsuma edwardnewtonii. The IUCN Red List of Threatened Species* 2021: e.T17432631A17432636. https://dx.doi.org/10.2305/IUCN.UK.2021-2.RLTS.T17432631A17432636.en. Accessed on 03 January 2022.

— 2021. *Phelsuma gigas. The IUCN Red List of Threatened Species* 2021: e.T16925A166929864.https://dx.doi.org/10.2305/IUCN.UK.2021-2.RLTS.T16925A166929864.en. Accessed on 03 January 2022.

Bour, R., Frétey, T. and Cheke, A.S. 2014. Philibert Marragon (1749–1826) and the Mémoire sur l'Isle de Rodrigue (1795). *Bibliotheca Herpetologica* 10(2): 5-32.

See also: *Lost Land of the Dodo* below.

Round Island Burrowing Boa

Cole, N. 2021. *Bolyeria multocarinata. The IUCN Red List of Threatened Species* 2021: e.T2864A13483086. https://dx.doi.org/10.2305/IUCN.UK.2021-2.RLTS.T2864A13483086.en. Accessed on 12 January 2022.

`Cheke, A.S. and Hume, J.P. *Lost Land of the Dodo: an ecological history of Mauritius, Réunion and Rodrigues.* Yale University Press, 2008.

Christmas Island Whiptail-skink

Andrew, P., Cogger, H., Driscoll, D., Flakus, S., Harlow, P., Maple, D., Misso, M., Pink, C., Retallick, K., Rose, K., Tiernan, B., West, J. and Woinarski, J.C.Z. 2016. Somewhat saved: a captive breeding programme for two endemic Christmas Island lizard species, now extinct in the wild. *Oryx*: 1-4. doi:10.1017/S0030605316001071.

Smith, M.J., Cogger, H., Tiernan, B., Maple, D., Boland, C., Napier, F., Detto, T. and Smith, P. 2012. An oceanic island reptile community under threat: the decline of reptiles on Christmas Island, Indian Ocean. *Herpetological Conservation and Biology* 7(2): 206-218.

Woinarski, John, and Hal Cogger. "Australian endangered species: Christmas Island Forest Skink." *The Conversation*, 19 Sept. 2013.

Woinarski, J., D. Driscoll, and H. Cogger. "Vale Gump: the last known Christmas Island Forest Skink." *The Conversation*, 7 Aug. 2014.

http://theconversation.com/vale-gump-the-last-known-christmas-island-forest-skink-30252.

Cogger, Harold G., and Ross Sadlier. The terrestrial reptiles of Christmas Island, Indian Ocean. *Australian Museum*, 1981.

Emery, Jon-Paul, et al. "The lost lizards of Christmas Island: A retrospective assessment of factors driving the collapse of a native reptile community." *Conservation Science and Practice* 3.2 (2021): e358.

Curly-tailed Lizards of the Caribbean

Breuil, Michel. "The terrestrial herpetofauna of Martinique: Past, present, future." *Applied Herpetology* 6.2 (2009): 123-149.

Boulanger, G. A. *Catalogue of the lizards in the British Museum* (Natural History), 2nd. ed., 1885.

Powell, Robert. "*Leiocephalus eremitus.*" *Catalogue of American Amphibians and Reptiles* (CAAR) (1999).

Inchaustegui, S., Landestoy, M. & Powell, R. 2021. *Leiocephalus eremitus* (amended version of 2016 assessment). *The IUCN Red List of Threatened Species* 2021: e.T11388A207443416. https://dx.doi.org/10.2305/IUCN.UK.2021-3.RLTS.T11388A207443416.en. Accessed on 14 January 2022.

Bochaton, Corentin, Laurent Charles, and Arnaud Lenoble. "Historical and fossil evidence of an extinct endemic species of Leiocephalus (Squamata: Leiocephalidae) from the Guadeloupe Islands." *Zootaxa* 4927.3 (2021): 383-409.

Powell, R. 2016. *Leiocephalus cuneus* (errata version published in 2017). *The IUCN Red List of Threatened Species* 2016: e.T75306422A115482357.

Pregill, G.K. 1992. Systematics of the West Indian lizard genus *Leiocephalus* (Squamata: Iguania: Tropiduridae). *Museum of Natural History Miscellaneous Publication* (University of Kansas) 84: 1-69.

Etheridge, R. (1964) Late Pleistocene lizards from Barbuda, British West Indies. *Bulletin of the Florida State Museum*, 9, 46–75.

Navassa Rhinoceros Iguana

Powell, Robert. "Herpetology of Navassa Island, West Indies." *Caribbean Journal of Science* 35 (1999): 1-13.

—"*Cyclura onchiopsis.*" *Catalogue of American Amphibians and Reptiles* (CAAR) (2000).

—. 2011. *Cyclura onchiopsis. The IUCN Red List of Threatened Species* 2011: e.T173001A6955940. https://dx.doi.org/10.2305/IUCN.UK.2011-1.RLTS.T173001A6955940.en. Accessed on 19 January 2022.

Egnatios-Beene, J. 2002. "*Cyclura cornuta*" (On-line), *Animal Diversity Web*. Accessed January 18, 2022 at https://animaldiversity.org/accounts/Cyclura_cornuta/

Fish

Lu, Jing, et al. "The oldest actinopterygian highlights the cryptic early history of the hyperdiverse ray-finned fishes." *Current Biology* 26.12 (2016): 1602-1608.

Jonna, R. 2021. "*Actinopterygii*" (On-line), *Animal Diversity Web*. Accessed March 02, 2022 at https://animaldiversity.org/accounts/Actinopterygii/

Kottelat, M., R. Britz, H.H. Tan and K.-E. Witte, 2005. Paedocypris, a new genus of Southeast Asian cyprinid fish with a remarkable sexual dimorphism, comprises the world's smallest vertebrate. *Proc. Royal Soc.* Biol. Sci. 273:895-899.

Griffin, B. 2011. "*Mola mola*" (On-line), *Animal Diversity Web*. Accessed March 03, 2022 at https://animaldiversity.org/accounts/Mola_mola/

Catania, Kenneth C. "The astonishing behavior of electric eels." *Frontiers in Integrative Neuroscience* (2019): 23.

Bastos, Douglas A., et al. "Social predation in electric eels." *Ecology and evolution* 11.3 (2021): 1088-1092.

Davis, Matthew P., John S. Sparks, and W. Leo Smith. "Repeated and widespread evolution of bioluminescence in marine fishes." *PloS ONE* 11.6 (2016): e0155154.

Baker LJ, Freed LL, Easson CG, et al. Diverse deep-sea anglerfishes share a genetically reduced luminous symbiont that is acquired from the environment. *Elife*. 2019;8:e47606. Published 2019 Oct 1. doi:10.7554/eLife.47606

Arthington, Angela H., et al. "Fish conservation in freshwater and marine realms: status, threats and management." *Aquatic Conservation: Marine and Freshwater Ecosystems* 26.5 (2016): 838-857.

Lynch, Abigail J., et al. "The social, economic, and environmental importance of inland fish and fisheries." *Environmental Reviews* 24.2 (2016): 115-121.

J. David Allan, Robin Abell, Zeb Hogan, Carmen Revenga, Brad W. Taylor, Robin L. Welcomme, Kirk Winemiller, Overfishing of Inland Waters, *BioScience*, Volume 55, Issue 12, December 2005, Pages 1041–1051, https://doi.org/10.1641/0006-3568(2005)055[1041:OOIW]2.0.CO;2

Cichlids of Lake Victoria

Marshall, Brian E. "Guilty as charged: Nile perch was the cause of the haplochromine decline in Lake Victoria." *Canadian Journal of Fisheries and Aquatic Sciences* 75.9 (2018): 1542-1559.

Outa, Nicholas Otieno, et al. "A review on the status of some major fish species in Lake Victoria and possible conservation strategies." *Lakes & Reservoirs: Research & Management* 25.1 (2020): 105-111.

Verheyen, Erik & Salzburger, Walter & Snoeks, Jos & Meyer, Axel. (2003). Origin of the Superflock of Cichlid Fishes from Lake Victoria, East Africa. *Science* 300. 325-9. 10.1126/science.1080699.

Nagl, Sandra, et al. "The Origin and Age of Haplochromine Fishes in Lake Victoria, East Africa." Proceedings: Biological Sciences, vol. 267, no. 1447, *The Royal Society*, 2000, pp. 1049–61, http://www.jstor.org/stable/1571453.

Barb Fish of Lake Lanao

Ismail, Gladys B., David B. Sampson, and David LG Noakes. "The status of Lake Lanao endemic cyprinids (Puntius species) and their conservation." *Environmental biology of fishes* 97.4 (2014): 425-434.

Guerrero III, R. D. "Saving the last cyprinid in Lake Lanao [Philippines]: how we lost most of the endemic fishes in Lake Lanao and what we can do to save the remaining one." *Agriculture* (Philippines) (2018).

Republic of the Philippines. "Native fish species of Lake Lanao vanishing fast". *National Research Council* (Philippines), 15 Oct. 2018. https://nrcp.dost.gov.ph/previous-issues/386-native-fish-species-of-lake-lanao-vanishing-fast-nrcp-research

Metillo, EPHRIME B., and CARMELITA O. Garcia-Hansel. "A review on the ecology and biodiversity of Lake Lanao (Mindanao Is., The Philippines)." IAMURE International *Journal of Ecology and Conservation* 18 (2016): 17-66.

Torres, A.G., Guerrero, R.D. III, Nacua, S.S., Gimena, R.V., Eza, N.D., Kesner-Reyes, K., David, E.B., Bactong Jr., M.A., Villanueva, T.R., Alcantara, A.J. & Rebancos, C.M. 2020. Barbodes sirang (errata version published in 2021). *The IUCN Red List of Threatened Species* 2020: e.T18898A192625918. https://dx.doi.org/10.2305/IUCN.UK.2020-3.RLTS.T18898A192625918.en. Accessed on 22 March 2022.

Abdulmalik-Labe, Onaya P., and Jonas P. Quilang. "Genetic diversity among the endemic barb Barbodes tumba (Teleostei: Cyprinidae) populations from Mindanao, Philippines." *Journal of Threatened Taxa* 11.7 (2019): 13822-13832.

Chinese Paddlefish

Zhang, Hui, et al. "Extinction of one of the world's largest freshwater fishes: Lessons for conserving the endangered Yangtze fauna." *Science of the Total Environment* 710 (2020): 136242.

Fan, Xiang-guo, et al. "A review on conservation issues in the upper Yangtze River–a last chance for a big challenge: Can Chinese paddlefish (Psephurus gladius), Dabry´s sturgeon,(Acipenser dabryanus) and other fish species still be saved?." *Journal of Applied Ichthyology* 22 (2006): 32-39.

Zhang, H., et al. "Is there evidence that the Chinese paddlefish (Psephurus gladius) still survives in the upper Yangtze River? Concerns inferred from hydroacoustic and capture surveys." *J. Appl. Ichthyol* 25.2 (2009): 95-99.

Wei, Qiwei, et al. "Biology, fisheries, and conservation of sturgeons and paddlefish in China." *Environmental Biology of Fishes* 48.1 (1997): 241-255.

Shen, Yanjun, et al. "Phylogenetic perspective on the relationships and evolutionary history of the Acipenseriformes." *Genomics* 112.5 (2020): 3511-3517.

North American Pupfish

Froese, R. and D. Pauly. Editors. 2022. *FishBase*. World Wide Web electronic publication. www.fishbase.org, version (02/2022).

Minckley, W. L., Robert Rush Miller, and Steven Mark Norris. "Three new pupfish
    species, Cyprinodon (Teleostei, Cyprinodontidae), from Chihuahua, Mexico, and
    Arizona, USA." *Copeia* 2002.3 (2002): 687-705.
Balderas, Salvador & Lozano-Vilano, Lourdes. (1996). Extinction of most Sandia
    and Potosí valleys (Nuevo León, Mexico) endemic pupfishes, crayfishes and
    snails. Ichthyol. *Explor. Freshwaters.* 7.
Echelle, Anthony A., et al. "Historical biogeography of the new-world pupfish
    genus Cyprinodon (Teleostei: Cyprinodontidae)." *Copeia* 2005.2 (2005):
    320-339.
Miller, R. R., J. D. Williams, and J. E. Williams. 1989. Extinctions of North American
    fishes during the past century. *Fisheries* 14(6):22-38.
Valdes Gonzales, A. 2019. *Megupsilon aporus. The IUCN Red List of Threatened
    Species* 2019: e.T13013A511283. https://dx.doi.org/10.2305/
    IUCN.UK.2019-2.RLTS.T13013A511283.en. Accessed on 04 April 2022.

Whitefishes
Freyhof, J., and C. Schöter. "The houting Coregonus oxyrinchus (L.)
    (Salmoniformes: Coregonidae), a globally extinct species from the North Sea
    basin." *Journal of Fish Biology* 67.3 (2005): 713-729.
Büttiker, Bernard. (2005). Evolution of fish and crayfish, and of fishery in Lake
    Geneva. *Archives des Sciences.* 58. 183-191.
Freyhof, J. & Kottelat, M. 2008. *Coregonus restrictus. The IUCN Red List of
    Threatened Species* 2008: e.T135570A4149314. https://dx.doi.org/10.2305/
    IUCN.UK.2008.RLTS.T135570A4149314.en. Accessed on 31 March 2022.
Miller, R. R., J. D. Williams, and J. E. Williams. 1989. Extinctions of North American
    fishes during the past century. *Fisheries* 14(6):22-38.
Great Lakes Fishery Commission. Sea Lamprey: A Great Lakes Invader. *Glfc.org*,
    accessed 31 March 2022. http://www.glfc.org/sea-lamprey.php.
Vonlanthen, Pascal, et al. "Eutrophication causes speciation reversal in whitefish
    adaptive radiations." *Nature* 482.7385 (2012): 357-362.

New Zealand Grayling
Lee, Finnbar, and George LW Perry. "Assessing the role of off-take and source–sink
    dynamics in the extinction of the amphidromous New Zealand grayling
    (Prototroctes oxyrhynchus)." *Freshwater Biology* 64.10 (2019): 1747-1754.
Radway Allen, K. 1949. The New Zealand Grayling - A Vanishing Species. *Tuatara*
    2(1): 22-27.
Fyfe, Roger & Bradshaw, Julia. (2020). A review of the role of diadromous ikawai
    (freshwater fish) in the Māori economy and culture of Te Wai Pounamu (South
    Island), *Aotearoa New Zealand.* 2020. 35-55.

Mammals
Pickrell, John. "How the earliest mammals thrived alongside dinosaurs." *Nature*
    574.7779 (2019): 468-473.

Burgin, Connor J., et al. "How many species of mammals are there?." *Journal of Mammalogy* 99.1 (2018): 1-14.

Mammal Diversity Database. (2021). *Mammal Diversity Database* (Version 1.7) [Data set]. Zenodo. http://doi.org/10.5281/zenodo.4139818 DOI

Burns, A. 2013. "*Craseonycteris thonglongyai*" (On-line), *Animal Diversity Web*. Accessed January 20, 2022 at https://animaldiversity.org/accounts/Craseonycteris_thonglongyai/

Fox, D. 2002. "*Balaenoptera musculus*" (On-line), *Animal Diversity Web*. Accessed January 20, 2022 at https://animaldiversity.org/accounts/Balaenoptera_musculus/

Ponganis,Paul J.,Gerald L. Kooyman. "How do deep-diving sea creatures withstand huge pressure changes?". *Scientific American*, 21 Aug. 2006. https://www.scientificamerican.com/article/how-do-deep-diving-sea-cr/

Schorr, Gregory S., et al. "First long-term behavioral records from Cuvier's beaked whales (Ziphius cavirostris) reveal record-breaking dives." *PloS one* 9.3 (2014): e92633.

Peter L. Tyack, Mark Johnson, Natacha Aguilar Soto, Albert Sturlese, Peter T. Madsen; Extreme diving of beaked whales. *J Exp Biol* 1 November 2006; 209 (21): 4238–4253. doi:

Moss, C.F., Schnitzler, H.U. Accuracy of target ranging in echolocating bats: acoustic information processing. *J. Comp. Physiol.* 165, 383–393 (1989). https://doi.org/10.1007/BF00619357

Moss, Cynthia F., and Annemarie Surlykke. "Probing the natural scene by echolocation in bats." *Frontiers in behavioral neuroscience* 4 (2010): 33.

Metzner, W. "Echolocation Behaviour in Bats." *Science Progress* (1933-), vol. 75, no. 3/4 (298), Temporary Publisher, 1991, pp. 453–65, http://www.jstor.org/stable/43421284.

Bogoni, Juliano A., Carlos A. Peres, and Katia MPMB Ferraz. "Extent, intensity and drivers of mammal defaunation: a continental-scale analysis across the Neotropics." *Scientific reports* 10.1 (2020): 1-16.

Rija AA, Critchlow R, Thomas CD, Beale CM (2020) Global extent and drivers of mammal population declines in protected areas under illegal hunting pressure. *PLoS ONE* 15(8): e0227163. https://doi.org/10.1371/journal.pone.0227163

Brodie, Jedediah F., Sara Williams, and Brittany Garner. "The decline of mammal functional and evolutionary diversity worldwide." *Proceedings of the National Academy of Sciences* 118.3 (2021).

Zhang, Fuhua, et al. "Reducing pangolin demand by understanding motivations for human consumption in Guangdong, China." *Frontiers in Ecology and Evolution* 8 (2020): 456.

Challender, Daniel WS, et al. "International trade and trafficking in pangolins, 1900–2019." *Pangolins*. Academic Press, 2020. 259-276.

Estoque, R.C., Ooba, M., Avitabile, V. et al. The future of Southeast Asia's forests. *Nat Commun* 10, 1829 (2019). https://doi.org/10.1038/s41467-019-09646-4

Estrada, Alejandro, et al. "Impending extinction crisis of the world's primates: Why primates matter." *Science advances* 3.1 (2017): e1600946.

Tikhonov, A. 2008. *Bos primigenius. The IUCN Red List of Threatened Species* 2008: e.T136721A4332142. https://dx.doi.org/10.2305/ IUCN.UK.2008.RLTS.T136721A4332142.en. Accessed on 28 January 2022.

MacPhee, Ross DE, and Hans-Dieter Sues, eds. *Extinctions in near time*. Vol. 2. Springer Science & Business Media, 1999.

Thylacine

Sleightholme, Stephen R., and Cameron R. Campbell. "A retrospective assessment of 20th century thylacine populations." *Australian Zoologist* 38.1 (2016): 102-129.

Carlson, Colin J., Alexander L. Bond, and Kevin R. Burgio. "Estimating the extinction date of the thylacine with mixed certainty data." *Conservation Biology* 32.2 (2018): 477-483

Miller, Webb, et al. "The mitochondrial genome sequence of the Tasmanian tiger (Thylacinus cynocephalus)." *Genome research* 19.2 (2009): 213-220.

M.R.G. Attard, U. Chamoli, T.L. Ferrara, T.L. Rogers and S. Wroe. Skull mechanics and implications for feeding behaviour in a large marsupial carnivore guild: the thylacine, Tasmanian devil and spotted-tailed quoll. *Journal of Zoology*, 31 August 2011 DOI: 10.1111/j.1469-7998.2011.00844.x

Dixon, J. M. 1989. "Thylacinidae". In: D. W. Walton and B. J. Richardson (eds.), *Fauna of Australia, Mammalia*, Vol. 1B, pp. 1-20. Canberra: Australian Govt. Printing Service, p. 4.

Bluebuck

Sclater, Philip Lutley, and Oldfield Thomas. *The book of antelopes*. Vol. 4. RH Porter, 1900.

Hempel, E., Bibi, F., Faith, J.T. et al. Identifying the true number of specimens of the extinct blue antelope (Hippotragus leucophaeus). *Sci Rep* 11, 2100 (2021). https://doi.org/10.1038/s41598-020-80142-2

Colahan, B. D. "Did the last blue antelope Hippotragus leucophaeus die in the eastern Orange Free State, South Africa?." *South African Journal of Science* 86.11 (1990): 477-478.

Tyler Faith, J., and Jessica C. Thompson. "Fossil evidence for seasonal calving and migration of extinct blue antelope (Hippotragus leucophaeus) in southern Africa." *Journal of Biogeography* 40.11 (2013): 2108-2118.

GonÇalo Espregueira Themudo, Paula F Campos, Phylogenetic position of the extinct blue antelope, Hippotragus leucophaeus (Pallas, 1766) (Bovidae: Hippotraginae), based on complete mitochondrial genomes, *Zoological Journal of the Linnean Society*, Volume 182, Issue 1, January 2018, Pages 225–235, https://doi.org/10.1093/zoolinnean/zlx034

Falkland Islands Wolf

Oshman, K. 2012. "*Dusicyon australis*" (On-line), *Animal Diversity Web*. Accessed February 03, 2022 at https://animaldiversity.org/accounts/ Dusicyon australis/

The zoology of the voyage of H.M.S. Beagle, under the command of Captain
    Fitzroy, R.N., during the years 1832 to 1836 Smith, Elder and Co, London,
    London (1838)
Slater, Graham J., et al. "Evolutionary history of the Falklands wolf." *Current
    biology* 19.20 (2009): R937-R938.
Austin, Jeremy J., et al. "The origins of the enigmatic Falkland Islands wolf."
    Nature Communications 4.1 (2013): 1-7.
Sillero-Zubiri, C. 2015. *Dusicyon australis. The IUCN Red List of Threatened Species*
    2015: e.T6923A82310440. https://dx.doi.org/10.2305/
    IUCN.UK.2015-4.RLTS.T6923A82310440.en. Accessed on 02 February 2022.

Extinct Bandicoots of Australia
Woinarski, John CZ, Andrew A. Burbidge, and Peter L. Harrison. "Ongoing
    unraveling of a continental fauna: decline and extinction of Australian
    mammals since European settlement." *Proceedings of the National Academy of
    Sciences* 112.15 (2015): 4531-4540.
Westerman, M., et al. "Phylogenetic relationships of living and recently extinct
    bandicoots based on nuclear and mitochondrial DNA sequences." *Molecular
    Phylogenetics and Evolution* 62.1 (2012): 97-108.
Abbott, Ian. "Historical perspectives of the ecology of some conspicuous
    vertebrate species in south-west Western Australia." *Conservation Science
    Western Australia* 6.3 (2008).
New South Wales Government. Pig-footed bandicoot - profile. *Office of
    Environment and Heritage*, 7 Sept. 2017.
    https://www.environment.nsw.gov.au/threatenedspeciesapp/profile.aspx?
    id=20186
Kenny J. Travouillon et al. 2019. Hidden in plain sight: reassessment of the pig-
    footed bandicoot, Chaeropus ecaudatus (Peramelemorphia, Chaeropodidae),
    with a description of a new species from central Australia, and use of the fossil
    record to trace its past distribution. *Zootaxa* 4566 (1); doi: 10.11646/
    zootaxa.4566.1.1
Singh, A. 2001. "Macrotis leucura" (On-line), *Animal Diversity Web*. Accessed
    February 08, 2022 at https://animaldiversity.org/accounts/Macrotis_leucura/
Burbidge, A.A. & Woinarski, J. 2016. *Macrotis leucura. The IUCN Red List of
    Threatened Species 2016*: e.T12651A21967376. https://dx.doi.org/10.2305/
    IUCN.UK.2016-2.RLTS.T12651A21967376.en. Accessed on 08 February 2022.
Burbidge A. A. , Johnson K. A. , Fuller P. J. Southgate R. I. (1988) Aboriginal
    knowledge of the mammals of the central deserts of Australia. *Wildlife Research*
    15, 9-39.
Abbott, Ian. "The spread of the cat, Felis catus, in Australia: re-examination of the
    current conceptual model with additional information." *Conservation Science
    Western Australia* 7.1 (2008).
Abbott, Ian. "The importation, release, establishment, spread, and early impact on
    prey animals of the red fox Vulpes vulpes in Victoria and adjoining parts of
    south-eastern Australia." *Australian Zoology* 35.3 (2011): 463-533.

Hare Wallabies

Burbidge, A.A., Johnson, K.A., Fuller, P.J. and Southgate, R.I. 1988. Aboriginal knowledge of the mammals of the central deserts of Australia. *Australian Wildlife Research* 15: 9-39.

— & Woinarski, J. 2016. *Lagorchestes leporides. The IUCN Red List of Threatened Species* 2016: e.T11163A21954274. https://dx.doi.org/10.2305/ IUCN.UK.2016-2.RLTS.T11163A21954274.en. Accessed on 09 February 2022.

— & Woinarski, J. 2016. *Lagorchestes asomatus. The IUCN Red List of Threatened Species* 2016: e.T11160A21954573. https://dx.doi.org/10.2305/ IUCN.UK.2016-2.RLTS.T11160A21954573.en. Accessed on 09 February 2022.

Krefft, G. 1866. On vertebrate animals of the Lower Murray and Darling, their habits, economy and geographical distribution. *Transactions of the Philosophical Society of New South Wales* 1862-65: 1-33.

New South Wales Government. Eastern Hare-wallaby - profile. *Office of Environment and Heritage*, 7 Sept. 2017. https://www.environment.nsw.gov.au/threatenedspeciesapp/profile.aspx?id=20195

Adkins, J. 2007. "*Lagorchestes hirsutus*" (On-line), *Animal Diversity Web*. Accessed February 09, 2022 at https://animaldiversity.org/accounts/ Lagorchestes_hirsutus/

Finlayson, Hedley Herbert. (1943). A new species of Lagorchestes (Marsupialia). *Transactions of the Royal Society of South Australia* 67: 319-321.

Caribbean Monk Seal

McClenachan, L. and Cooper, A.B. 2008. Extinction rate, historical population structure and ecological role of the Caribbean monk seal. *Proceedings of the Royal Society* B 275: 1351-1358.

Adam, Peter J. "Monachus tropicalis." *Mammalian Species* 2004.747 (2004): 1-9.

Lowry, L. 2015. *Neomonachus tropicalis. The IUCN Red List of Threatened Species* 2015: e.T13655A45228171. https://dx.doi.org/10.2305/ IUCN.UK.2015-2.RLTS.T13655A45228171.en. Accessed on 14 February 2022.

Japanese Sea Lion

Lee, Y.-J.; Cho, G.; Kim, S.; Hwang, I.; Im, S.-O.; Park, H.-M.; Kim, N.-Y.; Kim, M.-J.; Lee, D.; Kwak, S.-N.; et al. The First Population Simulation for the Zalophus japonicus (Otariidae: Sea Lions) on Dokdo, Korea. *J. Mar. Sci. Eng.* 2022, 10, 271. https://doi.org/10.3390/ jmse10020271

Kim, Eun-Bi et al. "The complete mitochondrial genome of Japanese sea lion, Zalophus japonicus (Carnivora: Otariidae) analyzed using the excavated skeletal remains from Ulleungdo, South Korea." *Mitochondrial DNA*. Part B, Resources vol. 6,11 3184-3185. 14 Oct. 2021, doi:10.1080/23802359.2021.1945503

Lowry, L. 2017. Zalophus japonicus (amended version of 2015 assessment). The IUCN Red List of Threatened Species 2017: e.T41667A113089431. https://

dx.doi.org/10.2305/IUCN.UK.2017-1.RLTS.T41667A113089431.en. Accessed on 18 February 2022.

Wolf, J.B., Tautz, D. & Trillmich, F. Galápagos and Californian sea lions are separate species: Genetic analysis of the genus Zalophus and its implications for conservation management. *Front Zool* 4, 20 (2007). https://doi.org/10.1186/1742-9994-4-20

Baji

Braulik, G. T., Reeves, R. R., Wang, D., Ellis, S., Wells, R. S., & Dudgeon, D. (2005). Report of the workshop on conservation of the baiji and Yangtze finless porpoise. Gland, Switzerland: World Conservation Union.

Turvey, Samuel T et al. "First human-caused extinction of a cetacean species?." *Biology letters* vol. 3,5 (2007): 537-40. doi:10.1098/rsbl.2007.0292

Miller, Gerrit Smith. A New River-dolphin from China:(with 13 Plates) by Gerritt S. Miller, Jr. *Smithsonian Institution*, 1918.

Hrbek T, da Silva VMF, Dutra N, Gravena W, Martin AR, Farias IP (2014) A New Species of River Dolphin from Brazil or: How Little Do We Know Our Biodiversity. *PLoS ONE* 9(1): e83623. https://doi.org/10.1371/journal.pone.0083623

Grigg, S. 2003. "*Lipotes vexillifer*" (On-line), *Animal Diversity Web*. Accessed February 28, 2022 at https://animaldiversity.org/accounts/Lipotes_vexillifer/

Smith, B.D., Wang, D., Braulik, G.T., Reeves, R., Zhou, K., Barlow, J. & Pitman, R.L. 2017. *Lipotes vexillifer. The IUCN Red List of Threatened Species* 2017: e.T12119A50362206. https://dx.doi.org/10.2305/IUCN.UK.2017-3.RLTS.T12119A50362206.en. Accessed on 28 February 2022.

Wang, Ding, et al. "Conservation of the Baiji: No Simple Solution." *Conservation Biology*, vol. 20, no. 3, 2006, pp. 623–25, http://www.jstor.org/stable/3879219.

Flying Foxes

Cheng, Tina L., et al. "The scope and severity of white-nose syndrome on hibernating bats in North America." *Conservation Biology* 35.5 (2021): 1586-1597.

Rebitzke, J. 2002. "*Pteropus tokudae*" (On-line), *Animal Diversity Web*. Accessed February 21, 2022 at https://animaldiversity.org/accounts/Pteropus_tokudae/

Wiles, G. Recovery Plan for the Mariana Fruit Bat and Little Mariana Fruit Bat. *USFWS*, 1990.

Helgen, K.M., Helgen, L.E., Wilson, D.E. 2009. Pacific Flying Foxes (Mammalia: Chiroptera): Two New Species of Pteropus from Samoa, Probably Extinct. *American Museum Novitates* 3646: 1-37.

Government of Australia. Listing Advice Pteropus brunneus. *Threatened Species Scientific Committee*, 3 March 2021. http://www.environment.gov.au/biodiversity/threatened/species/pubs/184-listing-advice-03032021.pdf

Tsang, S.M. 2020. *Pteropus brunneus. The IUCN Red List of Threatened Species*
2020: e.T18718A22078015. https://dx.doi.org/10.2305/
IUCN.UK.2020-3.RLTS.T18718A22078015.en. Accessed on 23 February 2022.

Wiles, G. J., J. Engbring, and D. Otobed. "Abundance, biology, and human
exploitation of bats in the Palau Islands." *Journal of Zoology* 241.2 (1997):
203-227.

Mickleburgh, S., Hutson, A.M., Bergmans, W. & Howell, K. 2020. *Pteropus subniger.
The IUCN Red List of Threatened Species* 2020: e.T18761A22088168. https://
dx.doi.org/10.2305/IUCN.UK.2020-3.RLTS.T18761A22088168.en. Accessed on
23 February 2022.

Christmas Island Pipistrelle

Government of Australia. Listing Advice Pipistrellus murrayi. *Threatened Species
Scientific Committee*, 3 March 2021.
http://www.environment.gov.au/biodiversity/threatened/species/pubs/
64383-listing-advice-03032021.pdf

Lumsden, L.F., Racey, P.A. & Hutson, A.M. 2017. *Pipistrellus murrayi* (errata
version published in 2021). *The IUCN Red List of Threatened Species* 2017:
e.T136769A209549918. https://dx.doi.org/10.2305/
IUCN.UK.2017-2.RLTS.T136769A209549918.en. Accessed on 24 February
2022.

Martin, Tara G., et al. "Acting fast helps avoid extinction." *Conservation Letters* 5.4
(2012): 274-280.

There is Hope

Dinerstein, Eric, et al. "A "Global Safety Net" to reverse biodiversity loss and
stabilize Earth's climate." *Science advances* 6.36 (2020): eabb2824.

Bastin, Jean-Francois, et al. "The global tree restoration potential." *Science*
365.6448 (2019): 76-79.

Yang, Yi, et al. "Soil carbon sequestration accelerated by restoration of grassland
biodiversity." *Nature communications* 10.1 (2019): 1-7.

RIntoul, Jesse. "Farming for the future: why the Netherlands is the 2nd largest
food exporter in the world", *Dutchreview*, 20 August, 2020.
https://dutchreview.com/culture/innovation/second-largest-agriculture-
exporter/

U.S. Department of Agriculture. 2012 Census Highlights: Farm Economics.
ACH12-2, May 2014. See also Environmental Working Group, Farm Subsidy
Database, https://farm.ewg.org.

Yang, Yi, et al. "Soil carbon sequestration accelerated by restoration of grassland
biodiversity." *Nature communications* 10.1 (2019): 1-7.

Joshi, S., Mittal, S., Holloway, P. et al. High resolution global spatiotemporal
assessment of rooftop solar photovoltaics potential for renewable electricity
generation. *Nat Commun* 12, 5738 (2021). https://doi.org/10.1038/
s41467-021-25720-2

Pasquali, Matteo, and Carl Mesters. Opinion: We can use carbon to decarbonize—and get hydrogen for free. *Proceedings of the National Academy of Sciences* 118.31 (2021).

Vernon, Nate, Ian Parry, and Simon Black. "Still Not Getting Energy Prices Right: A Global and Country Update of Fossil Fuel Subsidies." (2021).

Allan, James R., et al. "The minimum land area requiring conservation attention to safeguard biodiversity." *Science* 376.6597 (2022): 1094-1101.

Deryabina, T. G., et al. "Long-term census data reveal abundant wildlife populations at Chernobyl." *Current Biology* 25.19 (2015): R824-R826.

Greenwald, Noah, et al. "Extinction and the US endangered species act." *PeerJ* 7 (2019): e6803.

Stalmans, Marc E., et al. "War-induced collapse and asymmetric recovery of large-mammal populations in Gorongosa National Park, Mozambique." *PloS ONE* 14.3 (2019): e0212864.

Bouley P, Paulo A, Angela M, Du Plessis C, Marneweck DG (2021) The successful reintroduction of African wild dogs (Lycaon pictus) to Gorongosa National Park, Mozambique. *PLoS ONE* 16(4): e0249860. https://doi.org/10.1371/journal.pone.0249860

Aburto-Oropeza O, Erisman B, Galland GR, Mascareñas-Osorio I, Sala E, Ezcurra E (2011) Large Recovery of Fish Biomass in a No-Take Marine Reserve. *PLoS ONE* 6(8): e23601. https://doi.org/10.1371/journal.pone.0023601

Kurle, C.M., Zilliacus, K.M., Sparks, J. et al. Indirect effects of invasive rat removal result in recovery of island rocky intertidal community structure. *Sci Rep* 11, 5395 (2021). https://doi.org/10.1038/s41598-021-84342-2

Kopf, R. Keller, et al. "Confronting the risks of large-scale invasive species control." *Nature Ecology & Evolution* 1.6 (2017): 1-4.

MMSD. Milwaukee deep tunnels. *Milwaukee Metropolitan Sewerage District*, accessed 5 May 2022. https://www.mmsd.com/what-we-do/wastewater-treatment/deep-tunnel

Weiss, Gabrielle. Are lawns a waste of space and resources. The Bard CEP Eco Reader, *Bard Center of Environmental Policy*, 3 May 2016. https://www.bard.edu/cep/blog/?p=8238

Sharma, Lyonpo Loknath; Adhikari, Ratnakar. What Bhutan got right about happiness - and what other countries can learn. *World Economic Forum*, 25 Oct 2021. https://www.weforum.org/agenda/2021/10/lessons-from-bhutan-economic-development/

Milesi, Cristina, et al. "A strategy for mapping and modeling the ecological effects of US lawns." *J. Turfgrass   Manage 1.1* (2005): 83-97.

Ellsmoor, James. New Zealand ditches GDP for happiness and wellbeing. *Forbes*, 11 July 2019. https://www.forbes.com/sites/jamesellsmoor/2019/07/11/new-zealand-ditches-gdp-for-happiness-and-wellbeing/?sh=56c85bf71942

Mair, L., Bennun, L.A., Brooks, T.M. et al. A metric for spatially explicit
    contributions to science-based species   targets. *Nat Ecol Evol 5*, 836–844
    (2021). https://doi.org/10.1038/s41559-021-01432J. Mason Heberling,
Joseph T. Miller, Daniel Noesgaard, Scott B. Weingart, Dmitry Schigel, Data
    integration enables global biodiversity synthesis. *Proceedings of the National
    Academy of Sciences* Feb 2021, 118 (6) e2018093118; DOI: 10.1073/
    pnas.2018093118

Made in the USA
Las Vegas, NV
26 February 2024

86358377R00203